THE VIKING PORTABLE
Niccolò Machiavelli

Niccolò Machiavelli was born in Florence in 1469 of an old citizen family. Little is known about his life until 1498, when he was appointed secretary and Second Chancellor to the Florentine Republic. During his time of office his journeys included missions to Louis XII and to the Emperor Maximilian; he was with Cesare Borgia in the Romagna; and after watching the Papal election of 1503 he accompanied Julius II on his first campaign of conquest. In 1507, as chancellor of the newly appointed Nove di Milizia, he organized an infantry force which fought at the capture of Pisa in 1509. Three years later it was defeated by the Holy League at Prato, the Medici returned to Florence, and Machiavelli was excluded from public life. After suffering imprisonment and torture, he retired to his farm near San Casciano, where he lived with his wife and six children and gave his time to study and writing. His works included *The Prince*; the *Discourses on the First Decade of Livy*; *The Art of War*; and the comedy, *Mandragola*, a satire on seduction. In 1520, Cardinal Giulio de' Medici secured him a commission to write a history of Florence, which he finished in 1525. After a brief return to public life, he died in 1527.

Peter Bondanella is Director of the Center for Italian Studies at Indiana University. He is the author of *Machiavelli and the Art of Renaissance History*.

Mark Musa is Professor at the Center for Italian Studies at Indiana University. A former Fulbright and Guggenheim Fellow, he has translated Dante's *Vita Nuova* and *Inferno*.

Each volume in The Viking Portable Library either presents a representative selection from the works of a single outstanding writer or offers a comprehensive anthology on a special subject. Averaging 700 pages in length and designed for compactness and readability, these books fill a need not met by other compilations. All are edited by distinguished authorities, who have written introductory essays and included much other helpful material.

The Portable

Machiavelli

*Newly translated and edited,
and with a Critical Introduction, by*

PETER BONDANELLA
AND MARK MUSA

PENGUIN BOOKS

PENGUIN BOOKS
Published by the Penguin Group
Penguin Books USA Inc.,
375 Hudson Street, New York, New York 10014, U.S.A.
Penguin Books Ltd, 27 Wrights Lane, London W8 5TZ, England
Penguin Books Australia Ltd, Ringwood, Victoria, Australia
Penguin Books Canada Ltd, 10 Alcorn Avenue, Su
Toronto, Ontario, Canada M4V 3B2
Penguin Books (N.Z.) Ltd, 182–190 Wairau Road,
Auckland 10, New Zealand

Penguin Books Ltd, Registered Offices:
Harmondsworth, Middlesex, England

First published in the United States of America
in simultaneous hardcover and paperback editions by
Viking Penguin Inc. 1979

21 23 25 24 22 20

LIBRARY OF CONGRESS CATALOGING IN PUBLICATION DATA
Machiavelli, Niccolò, 1469–1527.
The portable Machiavelli.
A Penguin Book.
Bibliography: p. 41.
1. Machiavelli, Niccolò, 1469–1527. 2. Political
science—Early works to 1700. I. Bondanella,
Peter E., 1943-   II. Musa, Mark.   III. Title.
JC143.M1463 1979   320.1′092′4   78-13961
ISBN 0 14 015.092 7

Printed in the United States of America
Set in CRT Times Roman

CONTENTS

INTRODUCTION
An Essay on Machiavelli

MACHIAVELLI'S LIFE AND TIMES

When Niccolò di Bernardo Machiavelli entered the world on May 3, 1469, his prospects were modest at best. The Machiavelli were an established middle-class family from the Oltrarno district of Florence, and its members had held an impressive number of offices in the city's government, including twelve terms as gonfaloniere, or standard-bearer, and fifty-four terms as prior. Niccolò's father, Bernardo, however, was not one of the more prosperous members of the clan, and Machiavelli could never hope to rival the wealth or influence of the greater patrician families of Florence, such as the Ridolfi, the Rucellai, the Strozzi, or the Guicciardini. But if Bernardo's means were insufficient to guarantee his son instant access to economic and political power, his great interest in books, particularly the Latin classics, was perhaps a more valuable legacy. We know that he possessed a copy of Flavio Biondo's *Decades,* that he borrowed a copy of Justin's history, and that he obtained a prized copy of Livy's history of republican Rome in return for laboriously compiling for the printer an index of Livy's place-names.

Relatively little is known of Machiavelli's activities until he entered the Florentine chancery, in 1498, only a few days after the execution of Girolamo Savonarola in the Piazza della Signoria. On June 19, 1498, his election as chancellor of the Second Chancery was confirmed by the Grand Council. Earlier in February of the same year,

Machiavelli had been considered for a post in the government but was defeated. This earlier election was the last in which the supporters of Savonarola retained a majority; indeed, Machiavelli's lack of sympathy for Savonarola, the man he would later remember in *The Prince* as the prototype of the "unarmed prophet" doomed to failure, is already evident in an early letter he composed in 1498 which describes one of the friar's sermons. When Machiavelli was finally elected to the chancery, he benefited from a period of anti-Savonarolan feeling; he filled a vacancy caused by the expulsion of a Savonarola supporter.

The secretary's duties in the Second Chancery often overlapped with those of the more important and prestigious First Chancery. Both dealt with Florentine domestic and foreign affairs, including war and defense; both helped provide the Florentine republic with the governmental continuity and stability that might have otherwise been lacking in the republic's rapid succession of officeholders on its deliberative bodies. Machiavelli was confirmed on January 27, 1500, and reelected annually until 1512. On July 14, 1498, he received the post of secretary to the Ten of War without, however, any additional staff or salary. Later he was also assigned to serve the newly created Nine of the Militia, a body designed to organize a militia from the Florentine countryside to avoid reliance on mercenary troops. He had supported a citizens' militia after watching professional troops in the local wars against Pisa, and his faith in citizen soldiers never wavered throughout his life. His views on this topic, as well as on many others, were thus formed not only by the example of the ancient Romans, whom he always admired and cited, but also by his practical, formative years in the Florentine government.

Machiavelli's service in the chancery also let him observe firsthand the major European political figures of the period—although his post would never permit him to wield the reins of political power on anything but a very limited scale. Even before his mentor Piero Soderini was named gonfaloniere for life on September 22, 1502, Machiavelli had become his trusted assistant. In 1500 he was sent abroad on his first diplomatic mission to the court of Louis XII, king of France. Arriving there with Caesar's *Commentaries on the Gallic Wars* in his saddlebags, Machiavelli met the king (for whom he had little respect) and his powerful minister, Georges d'Amboise, cardinal of Rouen. Not one to be overly impressed by rank or title, Machiavelli eventually had a sharp exchange of views with d'Amboise over the political talents of the French and his own countrymen, one which he would later repeat in *The Prince* (III): "When the Cardinal of Rouen told me that Italians understood little about war, I replied to him that the French understood little about politics." He would return to France on three other occasions: in 1503, 1510, and 1511.

Machiavelli's three encounters with Cesare Borgia, the warrior son of Pope Alexander VI, were even more important for the formation of his ideas. These meetings took place in Urbino, Imola, and Rome between 1502 and 1503. Many of the dispatches sent to the republic by their envoys during these missions (some of which Machiavelli either wrote personally or helped others to compose) are still extant, and we may compare Machiavelli's early assessment of this condottiere in his diplomatic letters to later treatments in several minor works and in the memorable seventh chapter of *The Prince*. When Machiavelli first met him at Urbino, after he had captured the city without a struggle, Borgia delivered an ultimatum to Florence which gave the young Machiavelli a lesson in power politics he would never forget: "This government in Florence does not please me, and you must guarantee the observance of what you have promised me; otherwise, you will understand in a very brief time that I do not wish to live in this manner; and if you do not desire me as a friend, you will find me an enemy." While the territorial ambitions of Cesare Borgia represented a serious threat to

Florentine hegemony in central Italy, Machiavelli could not help admiring the man's boldness, resolution, and cunning. In one of his dispatches describing the duke's character, we find one of the first instances in his works where ability or ingenuity (*virtù*) and good fortune (*fortuna*) are joined together in the person of a single historical figure. This is a theme that will occupy much of Machiavelli's attention in *The Prince*, where, once again, Borgia's role will be of crucial importance.

While in Imola at Borgia's court, Machiavelli wrote his friend Biagio Buonaccorsi for a copy of Plutarch's *Parallel Lives.* Here at court Machiavelli had before him the flesh-and-blood prototype of the modern ruler in *The Prince* while at the same time examining equally heroic figures from Plutarch's biography. His use of examples from past or present history as a guide for his revolutionary political theory was a completely natural procedure for him, far removed from any purely scholarly, pedantic intent. For Machiavelli, Livy's Romans were no less real than the warrior standing before him at Imola. But contemporary political leaders such as Louis XII or Borgia could also provide useful information for the discerning observer. Modern political theory did not depend exclusively upon the "golden words," as he often called them, of classical theorists or historians. In other words, the weight of classical authority is always present in his works but tempered by direct observation. An earlier generation of scholars was fond of describing Machiavelli as the first "scientist" of politics, since he was thought to have based his social theories upon empirical judgments in a manner similar to that employed by Galileo in the natural sciences; in a certain limited sense, these men were not mistaken.

While Machiavelli was to include many of his diplomatic experiences in his later historical and political works, he was not always consistent about the importance of the events he had witnessed. A case in point is his assessment of Cesare Borgia in dispatches written from

Rome in 1503 after Pope Alexander VI had suddenly died. At Urbino and Imola, Borgia is pictured as a formidable figure and is recognizable to the reader as the man who will play a major role in *The Prince.* But in the Roman dispatches his hero is seen as defeated by an equally wily opponent, Pope Julius II. The figure whose earlier resolution and cunning he had praised he now sarcastically sets aside as a loser, and names his mistakes in ironic terms: "Now we see that the duke's sins have little by little brought him to penitence." As Borgia has broken the unwritten but immutable rules of politics by placing more trust in the words of Julius than in his own strength, his "penitence" for this completely secular "sin" is the oblivion of political defeat. When, years later, Machiavelli returned to Borgia in *The Prince,* his judgment would be less harsh, perhaps because his own personal failures had taught him to be more tolerant of men who dared much but achieved less than they dared.

Other diplomatic missions of consequence required Machiavelli to visit Pope Julius II (1506) and the Emperor Maximilian (1507–1508). The first mission eventually produced one of the most memorable passages in *The Discourses*—the discussion of damaging middle ways of behavior and the fact that men rarely know how to be completely good or completely evil (I, xxvii). The specific occasion for these observations was the removal by Pope Julius of Giovampagolo Baglioni from the tyranny of the city of Perugia in order to return it to the control of the Church. Since Julius entered the town with no escort, Baglioni had an opportunity to murder the Pope but chose not to do so. In *The Discourses* Machiavelli has modified his earlier description contained in the original dispatches. In the latter, Baglioni was pictured as a perfect gentleman whose human qualities and prudence caused him to reject a drastic means of resolving a political dilemma; now he becomes a rather despicable petty tyrant capable only of crimes and unworthy of great (if infamous) actions. On the other hand, Julius II—an impetu-

ous man who always seemed to succeed in his rash
undertakings when wiser men counseled moderation—is
here and elsewhere pictured by Machiavelli as a man
whose success is due to a propitious coincidence of personal attributes and the tenor of the times, and Machiavelli cites as his classical examples Scipio Africanus,
Hannibal, Fabius Maximus, and others to parallel
Julius.

Machiavelli's experiences at Maximilian's court led to
his close friendship with Francesco Vettori. Soderini had
wanted to send Machiavelli as the head of the delegation
since he trusted him completely, but the patricians opposed to Soderini's increasing power wanted to send
someone of their own class, and Vettori was finally chosen; Soderini was eventually able to send Machiavelli to
join Vettori with further instructions. During his stay at
the emperor's court, Machiavelli was able to observe the
peoples he had previously known only through the classical histories of Tacitus. When Machiavelli refers to the
German people in his works, he means not the northern
sections of modern Germany but parts of Switzerland, the
Tyrol, and the southern section of the country. His views
on these peoples were always colored by the contrasts he
found in Tacitus between the then corrupted Romans of
the imperial period and the strong, independent Ger-
manic peoples whose simplicity and lack of corrupting
luxuries helped to protect their liberty. Rightly or
wrongly, Machiavelli seemed to detect these same qualities in the Germans of his day, and his fervent hope was
that his native Florence might discover some means to return her defective government to the pure origins of a former time when her population, too, was similar to these
northerners.

Machiavelli's diplomatic experiences thus had a direct
influence upon the development of his political theory.
They provided him with a ready source of examples to
compare against those in his favorite classical authors and
supplied him with an experimental laboratory in which
he could measure his emerging theories against the yard-

stick of observable political behavior. His post also gave him practical experience in systematizing his thoughts and polishing his magnificent prose style, both of which are apparent even in his early diplomatic correspondence.

A number of minor works, including brief essays or sketches, were also produced during the years Machiavelli served the chancery. These, too, reflect the experiences of his diplomatic missions and, like his letters, reappear in his major political and historical writings composed after 1513. *A Description of the Method Used by Duke Valentino in Killing Vitellozzo Vitelli, Oliverotto da Fermo, and Others* (1503) presents Cesare Borgia and his treacherous deeds at Sinigaglia, later to be treated in *The Prince*. *Remarks on the Raising of Money* (1503) employs both classical and contemporary historical examples, underlining the didactic value of historical study. *On the Method of Dealing with the Rebellious Peoples of the Valdichiana* (1503) opens with a direct contrast between Livy's description of how the Romans dealt correctly with a rebellion and the mistakes of Machiavelli's own Florentines in a similar situation; Borgia is again held up as a model to be imitated. In addition to these works treating essentially Italian protagonists or situations, Machiavelli composed a number of brief sketches or portraits of foreign nations and rulers, all of which are based upon his experiences abroad: *On the French National Character* (1503); *Report on Germany* (1508); *Discourse on Germany and the Emperor* (1509); *Description of German Affairs* (after 1512); and *Description of French Affairs* (1512–1513).

Because of Machiavelli's close relationship to Piero Soderini, it was not surprising that he was purged from office on November 7, 1512, when the Medici returned to power and ousted Soderini. On February 12, 1513, Machiavelli was arrested and tortured because his name was found on a list of possible anti-Medici conspirators that had been drawn up by two young Florentines. As far as we can determine, Machiavelli's name had been placed on the list without his knowledge; this unfortunate fact,

combined with his reputation as a strong supporter of Soderini, would have been sufficient to prohibit the Medici
from ever employing him in a position of trust. When
Giovanni de' Medici was elected to St. Peter's throne as
Leo X on March 11, 1513, it became clear to all but the
most embittered enemies of the Medici faction in
Florence that any hope for future employment in the
city's government would rest in their hands. Forced into
retirement, Machiavelli returned to his nearby country
villa and began writing *The Prince,* which he was to dedicate to two successive Medici princes. The explanation he
gives to his friend Francesco Vettori about the circumstances of the work's composition is contained in a letter
(reprinted in this edition) dated December 10, 1513,
wherein Machiavelli's almost religious veneration for the
lessons he learned from the classical historians is
revealed.

Although the fall of Soderini's government was a personal misfortune for Machiavelli, his enforced retirement
seems to have acted as a catalyst for his political imagination. After 1513 he composed not only the brief treatise
on which his fame predominantly rests, but all of his
major literary, historical, and political works as well, including *The Art of War, The Discourses, The History of
Florence, The Mandrake Root, Belfagor, The Life of Castruccio Castracani, Clizia, A Dialogue on Language,* and
The Golden Ass. Moreover, he began to frequent the Oricellari Gardens, where a circle of Florentine intellectuals,
including many of the friends to whom some of his later
works are dedicated, met to discuss important political
and literary matters. The Oricellari Gardens, owned by
Cosimo Rucellai, are used by Machiavelli as the back-
ground for the discussions recounted in *The Art of War,*
the highly stylized dialogue in that work on warfare must
reflect the tone of the friendly sessions there.

After 1513 Machiavelli also became a close friend of
Francesco Guicciardini, the greatest of Renaissance historians and a member of an old patrician family in Florence

closely associated with both Leo X and Clement VII, the two Medici popes of the period. The exchange of letters between Machiavelli and Guicciardini is one of the most remarkable correspondences of the century. This friendship led Guicciardini to compose his *Considerations on the Discourses of Machiavelli*, the first coherent critique of Machiavelli's political theory. When Machiavelli eventually received a commission from the Medici family, it was to complete a history of Florence rather than to occupy a position of power commensurate with his own estimation of his talents and merits. But he lived long enough to see a republic reestablished in Florence in 1527 as an indirect result of the sack of Rome in that year. This momentous event stirred all of European Christendom and has been vividly described in Guicciardini's *History of Italy* and Benvenuto Cellini's *Autobiography*. This attack upon the Eternal City forced Pope Clement VII to seek safety in the Castel Sant'Angelo, thus granting anti-Medici forces in Florence the opportunity to drive the Medici out once again and to reestablish a republic there.

Machiavelli died in 1527 and was consequently unable to observe the heroic defense of the Florentine republic, in 1530, against a far superior imperial army sent to Florence to return the Medici to power. But Machiavelli's unwavering faith in the potential power of a united people ruled by a republican form of government and defended by its own citizen-soldiers would have been sustained by the sight.

THE HISTORICAL CONTEXT OF *THE PRINCE*

Machiavelli's reputation rests primarily on a single treatise, *The Prince*. It is a remarkable book, one which fascinated or horrified generations of readers and became, along with Castiglione's *Book of the Courtier*, the intellectual property of every well-read European during the sixteenth century. Much of its subsequent fame was due to its unsavory reputation as an immoral or amoral work, a handbook for tyrants advocating the pernicious doctrine that "the ends justify the means" and presenting the infamous Cesare Borgia (murderer, incestuous lover of his own sister, Lucrezia, and tyrant) as a model for the new prince.

Any understanding of the real significance of this book and its author must therefore begin with the complex and always controversial issue of Machiavelli's intentions. With this treatise Machiavelli addresses a new kind of political figure—the "new" prince whose power lacked a basis in tradition, history, and custom. In the course of his discussion, Machiavelli examines a number of important philosophical and political issues: the nature of man and the question of free will; the importance of individual *virtù*; the role of *fortuna* in human affairs; the moral attributes of the new prince; and the proper goal toward which this revolutionary new figure should strive.

Although the impact of this work was immediate and unprecedented, its author seems to have intended *The Prince* for a specific, historically defined situation, one which would be superseded within a decade after its composition. This occasional nature sets the work apart from *The Discourses*—a study Machiavelli considered more important, more comprehensive, and closer to his own republican sympathies—which he apparently interrupted to compose *The Prince* in a matter of months. In 1513 the Medici family was offered a singular opportunity: the son of Lorenzo il Magnifico had just been elected to the throne of St. Peter as Leo X; and in Florence, Giuliano de' Medici, the Pope's brother, seemed destined to become its arbiter now that the republic served by Machiavelli and headed by Soderini had been abolished. The Medici family fortunes remained unshaken after the sudden and unexpected death of Giuliano in 1516, for his replacement by Lorenzo de' Medici, Duke of Urbino, as the heir apparent of Medici interests actually modified very little the circumstances surrounding the composition of *The Prince* The death did. of course, force Machiavelli to change his opening dedication from Giuliano to Lorenzo. But for a space of a few years, and at a critical moment in Italian history marked by foreign invasions and internal dissension, there coexisted in the peninsula a Medici pope controlling church revenues as well as the important papal states in Central Italy, and a Medici ruler in Florence and Tuscany. The combination of these two spheres of influence might constitute the basis for a strong, central Italian state around which Italian resistance to foreign invasions could coalesce.

To use the terms Machiavelli consistently employs in *The Prince,* this rare historical opportunity (*occasione*) was a challenge to the new prince's ingenuity, ability, or skill (*virtù*), and was a gift from a benevolent Fortune (*fortuna*), the classical female goddess who now replaced Christian Providence. Only once in recent memory had the same *occasione* presented itself to a man of *virtù* favored by *fortuna*. This occurred during the papacy of Rodrigo Borgia, Pope Alexander VI (1492–1503), whose son Cesare seemed destined to conquer much of the Romagna until the untimely death of his father cut short his plans. Most of Machiavelli's contemporaries were convinced that Alexander and his son intended to establish a Borgia dynasty by combining the son's conquests with the lands controlled by the Pope. Alexander's sudden death, however, and the fact that Cesare allowed his father's bitterest enemy, Giuliano della Rovere, to be elected as Pope Julius II, destroyed any hope of bringing such a scheme to completion.

Thus, a specific historical opportunity links the Medici family to the infamous Borgias, just as the fateful year of 1503, which witnessed the height of Cesare Borgia's power, seems related to that of 1513, the year of the composition of *The Prince.* This similarity in the opportunities presented to two influential families does not yet answer the charges of immorality often leveled at Machiavelli because of his admiration for Cesare Borgia and the latter's appearance in *The Prince* as a positive model to be imitated. Machiavelli could not have been aware, in 1513, that the unfavorable rumors surrounding the Borgias during their lifetime would later be exploited by a number of anti-Catholic and anti-Italian apologists, mostly Protestant reformers in the North. The gossip about the incestuous relationships of Alexander, Cesare, and Lucrezia Borgia, as well as their legendary homicides with doses of poison treacherously administered, had yet to enjoy wide European circulation when Machiavelli composed his treatise. With the publication, in 1561, of Francesco Guicciardini's *History of Italy,* however, these stories, although founded primarily on rumor and flimsy evidence, would spread over the entire continent and would be cited as proof that Italy was a land of atheism, treachery, "Machiavellian" politics, and perversion.

The charge that Machiavelli wrote an immoral guidebook for authoritarian tyrants has often been made. Furthermore, the fact that his two major works (*The Prince* and *The Discourses*) focus, respectively, upon a principality and a republic presents the reader with an apparent dilemma: how can the author of *The Prince* also have written *The Discourses*? If the same man writes two such books, each of which advocates an entirely different form of government, must he not be confused, guilty of hypocrisy and intellectual dishonesty, or both? This need not bother a reader firmly convinced of Machiavelli's immorality since an immoral man would not hesitate to write contradictory books. But any reader with an open mind will probably raise this legitimate and baffling question about Machiavelli's intentions. Thus we are forced again to return to the problem of Machiavelli's purpose, his views on morality in politics, and the apparent conflict in the content of his two major political works.

POLITICS AND MORALITY IN MACHIAVELLI

No brief treatment of Machiavelli's views on the relationship of politics and ethics will resolve an issue which has guaranteed Machiavelli avid readers. A variety of conflicting interpretations has been placed upon key sections of his works—particularly chapters VII–VIII and XV–XVIII of *The Prince*—and a number of influential critics and philosophers have argued that Machiavelli did separate morality and politics and did, at least, discuss the mechanics of evildoing, even if he did not actually advocate the habitual commission of it. In this regard, the reader is best advised to read Machiavelli's own words with care before he accepts the interpretations of others, but he should beware of the simplistic formula intended to summarize Machiavelli's political theory, namely, "the ends justify the means." This statement is actually a gross mistranslation of a key passage from *The Prince* (XVIII) which, in this popular and vulgarized form, has erected an almost insurmountable barrier to a clear understanding of Machiavelli's views on the relationship of politics and ethics. The mere mention of the phrase conjures up a vision of power-mad rulers who have justified any political means in a single-minded quest for immoral political ends. But Machiavelli says nothing about *justifying* political means in this passage; he merely states that "in the actions of all men, and especially of princes, where there is no impartial arbiter, one must consider the final result." *Si guarda al fine*—to consider or examine political goals is a far cry from justifying any political action so long as it purports to lead to a desired goal. Moreover, it would be difficult to imagine any political theory that could overlook an attention to the goals proposed by the theorist.

Machiavelli never justified all political means by reference to any political ends, and he never completely separated politics from morality, as so many scholars have claimed. This is evident from an important but infrequently cited remark Machiavelli makes in reference to Agathocles, the tyrant of Syracuse, in *The Prince* (VIII): "Still, it cannot be called skill [*virtù*] to kill one's fellow citizens, to betray friends, to be without faith, without mercy, without religion; by these means one can acquire power but not glory." Machiavelli analyzes both successful rulers and unsuccessful ones; each group may contain praiseworthy men of *virtù*, depending upon the nature of the goals toward which they strive. A man such as Agathocles, whose personality seems to conform perfectly to the list of scandalous moral attributes Machiavelli discusses in chapters XV–XVIII of *The Prince,* is, paradoxically, condemned by Machiavelli. Power does not, therefore, automatically confer glory or *virtù*, nor is might synonymous with right for Machiavelli. A successful prince may often act outside the boundaries of traditional ethical or religious codes. Machiavelli recognizes this fact and accepts it—although the fact that he does so perturbs many of his more squeamish readers—but he separates the merely powerful rulers from the praiseworthy men of *virtù* by reference to the ends or goals toward which these rulers strive. Clearly, a careful analysis of *The Prince* and *The Discourses* reveals that Machiavelli does not argue that *all* means are justified in the pursuit of *any* ends, and does not completely separate moral standards from political actions. Dealing with this issue in *The Discourses* (I, ix) in an assessment of the murder of Remus by his brother Romulus, the founder of Rome, Machiavelli says: "It is, indeed, fitting that while the action accuses him, the result excuses him; and when this result is good, as it was with Romulus, it will always excuse him; for one should reproach a man who is violent in order to destroy, not one who is violent in order to mend things." Although Machiavelli accepts the necessity of violence in politics, he is not justifying any end here. On the contrary, he is praising a most specific goal, namely, the establishment of the most durable and powerful republican government in human history by an admittedly violent (but unavoidable) action performed in the public interest rather than for private advantage. In such a narrowly circumscribed situation, where the violence is clearly in the public interest, Machiavelli does accept actions that would be condemned by the traditional ethical and religious standards of his day. He would claim, however, that those who condemn such violent acts openly performed and honestly admitted are themselves often guilty of paying only lip service to such principles.

Thus, in 1513 the Medici family had a unique opportunity: *fortuna* made it possible for them to free Italy from her barbarian invaders and to establish a strong government around which other Italians could rally. Note that Machiavelli concentrates his attention upon *virtù,* a human quality without which there is no hope of success. This individualistic perspective marks his thought as reflective of the preconceptions of the age. Unlike such later Reformation thinkers as Calvin or Luther, Machiavelli accepts the optimistic premises of such Italian humanists as Pico della Mirandola and Leon Battista Alberti and argues for at least limited free will—man controls roughly half of his actions while *fortuna* rules the other half. Human *virtù* must contend with *fortuna,* the personification of all the contingent forces in the world. The fortuitous conjunction of a man of *virtù* and a favorable *fortuna*—who, like a woman, is always more likely to smile upon an energetic and courageous young man—may allow a new prince, like the two Medici, to take advantage of any historical opportunity or *occasione.* Success in this sublunary world, however, is never completely guaranteed, as the case of Cesare Borgia demonstrates.

Given a serious emergency, such as Italy's invasion by foreign powers, and a unique opportunity to resolve this crisis by creating a strong, central principality from the combination of Florentine resources and those of the papacy, Machiavelli, the republican secretary, may accept a single ruler or prince, even one whose actions (like those of Romulus) are not in agreement with traditional Christian moral principles. His reliance upon a single heroic individual whose actions will establish a body politic is not limited to *The Prince* or its specific historical context, for Machiavelli also believes that great actions by single individuals are required to found republics, create religions, and reform corrupt military, political, or religious institutions. This individualism is one of the strongest connections between *The Prince* and *The Discourses,* and Machiavelli's emphasis in the first work upon a single individual, a "new" prince—whether he be Cesare Borgia, a Medici figure, Moses, Romulus, Theseus, or Cyrus—is, therefore, no valid evidence that he advocated an authoritarian form of government. For Machiavelli, the state's internal stability and external independence are of primary concern. He will always prefer a republican form of self-government, but a principality with stability and freedom to act in foreign affairs is always preferable to a weak republic torn apart by internal conflict and endangered by foreign armies. In this sense, there is no real ideological separation between *The Prince* and *The Discourses* (or the other political works). The first treatise was written in a few feverish months for a specific crisis at a time when a particular solution was feasible; the second commentary was the product of calmer, more deliberate study and reflected the author's republican bias and the fact that the proposed solution in *The Prince* was dictated by a specific historical opportunity that would soon pass. To consider Machiavelli's political theory with reference only to *The Prince* would reduce this complex and original thinker's significance and virtually ignore many of his important statements on the nature of politics, social conflict, human nature, civic corruption, the didactic value of history, and the relationship of civilian and military life—many of which are better expressed or more fully treated in sections of *The Discourses, The Art of War, The Life of Castruccio Castracani,* or *The History of Florence.* Each of these works is represented in this volume, preceded by a brief editorial comment on the text.

MACHIAVELLI AND HUMAN NATURE

Machiavelli's political theory operates within a clear definition of human nature. Although Machiavelli discusses the role of historical opportunities (*occasione*) and the influence of *fortuna,* as a practical man he devotes much attention to outlining his views on human nature, since he emphasizes the political protagonist in his works rather than broader social or economic forces of a more abstract nature. In many ways, his opinions on this subject are traditional ones and can be found in earlier Christian writers or later Reformation theologians. The conclusions he draws, however, are strikingly different from earlier or subsequent ones.

Machiavelli defines man as a selfish animal ruled by the insatiable desire for material gain and driven by the principle of self-interest. A man is not to be trusted (unless his trust is based upon fear rather than love), and he is easily fooled and deceived by appearances. As he notes in *The Prince* (XVII): "One can generally say this about men: that they are ungrateful, fickle, simulators and deceivers, avoiders of danger, greedy for gain . . . men are less hesitant about harming someone who makes himself loved than one who makes himself feared because love is held together by a chain of obligation which, since men are a sorry lot, is broken on every occasion in which their own self-interest is concerned; but fear is held together by a dread of punishment which will never abandon you." Furthermore, man's nature is such that it never changes or evolves with the passage of time but always remains constant and immutable. But this extremely pessimistic and negative assessment of human nature leads, paradoxically, to a positive and optimistic evaluation of human possibilities through the study of history. For if the actions of men are grounded upon their evil nature, these actions are as unchanging and as repetitive as the nature they reflect; and as they recur in time, they are capable of being organized, collected, studied, and used as the basis for future prediction and present understanding.

This static quality of man's character led Machiavelli toward an empirical science of politics, even though his primitive conception of it was far different from any such modern understanding. His emphasis upon a constant human nature yielded two important conclusions. First, it led him to a conception of the past generally held in the Renaissance, a view of human history as a vast reservoir of models and guides. Second, and perhaps more important, it led him to an identification of politics with conflict and to a most original belief that social conflict of a certain kind was a positive force within a political organization. This insight moved him to examine in some detail and from a fresh perspective the related but subordinate problems of political corruption, factions, and conspiracies.

HISTORY AND THE DOCTRINE OF IMITATION IN MACHIAVELLI

Every major work by Machiavelli and many of his minor writings underscore his faith in the didactic potential of exemplary models from ancient or contemporary history. In *The Prince* (VII) he compares men to prudent archers who aim at targets beyond their reach in order to strike those within their range. In the introduction to the first book of *The Discourses* he indignantly describes how Italians of his day valued a broken piece of sculpture from the past as a model for their own works of art but ignored the more practical benefits of imitating the ancients in their political institutions. Unlike post-Enlightenment political theorists, whose works often reflect at least an implicit belief in progress, Machiavelli believes that history progresses not in a forward or unilinear direction but in a circle or a cycle. Since he locates the standard of excellence in the past and asserts that the present must attempt to conform to the past rather than striving to surpass it, the only positive direction for political change is back to beginnings—rebirth, regeneration, renewal; in short, a renaissance of past virtues. Thus, the most revolutionary social thinker of the sixteenth century was, paradoxically, obsessed with returning present practice to an ancient norm.

By turning to the past, Renaissance men could learn from it and might avoid common errors, thereby profiting from the positive examples provided by ancient historians or contemporary observation. Machiavelli's hope, best expressed in *The Art of War* (VII), is that the artistic and cultural Renaissance, which he believed was directly linked to a rebirth of classical forms, themes, and values in the plastic arts and literature, might be extended to the more practical realm of political affairs: "I would not have you be afraid or dismayed for this province of Italy, for it seems it was born to revive dead things, as we have seen in its poetry, painting, and sculpture."

From our own perspective, locating perfection in a distant past seems to present the political leader with a pessimistic, hopeless situation. We are so accustomed to the belief in progress implicit in a number of widely held social theories prevalent in our era that we view any denial of this hope with some suspicion and as a constraint upon practical action. But the educated reader of Machiavelli's day, still dazzled by the majesty of a classical civilization yet only dimly understood, and intimidated by what he considered to be the obvious superiority of the ancients in various fields—notably political theory, law, history, and philosophy—viewed Machiavelli's nostalgia for the classical past with hope and a sense of liberation rather than despair. Although the Romans were almost impossible to surpass, nevertheless they too were men and their nature was similar to that of contemporary man. Modern Italians could thus create a government modeled after the ancients; they likewise enjoyed a measure of free will and were to some extent the masters of their destinies. No longer was it necessary for a divine Providence or a blind Fortune to control human history. The state, in Burckhardt's classic formulation, could finally become a work of art, the product of conscious human planning, reason-

ing, and action on a purely secular level. All of these no-
tions were implicit in Machiavelli's view of history and
imitation, and his contemporaries immediately grasped
the implications of these liberating ideas. In fact, Machiavelli's metaphor for the ruler in several important passages of *The Prince* is that of the architect, the physician,
or the artist. The state is variously compared to a building
with solid foundations designed by a master builder; a
patient whose illness must be diagnosed properly by a
skilled and prudent physician; or a work of art which
must be given aesthetic form by a sensitive artist in order
to transform it from an amorphous material state into a
pleasing structure. First and foremost, therefore, in his
emphasis upon human nature and his interest in the didactic value of human history, Machiavelli uses his revolutionary political theory to return politics to the realm of
the possible and the state to the hand of man.

POLITICS AS CONFLICT

Machiavelli's belief in a constant, immutable human
nature led him to develop an original view of social conflict as the essence of political behavior. In all his works,
political activity is more often characterized by motion,
conflict, and dynamic or violent change than by stasis, cooperation, and a rigid social structure. Several important
assumptions underlie this belief. First, his view of human
nature as naturally acquisitive and insatiable in its desires
is followed by a second, less explicit, premise about economic life. While human desires are defined as insatiable,
fortuna prohibits men from possessing sufficient *virtù* or
ability to obtain all of what they desire. In effect, there is a
universal principle of economic scarcity in operation in
the world, and man's hopes simply outrun the potential of
this world's goods. There is not enough material wealth to
satisfy the boundless human desire to acquire more
wealth. When such an acquisitive, aggressive human nature is combined with severely restricted resources, politi-

cal conflict is the inevitable result. Such conflict is not seen as an abnormal state of affairs, nor is the goal of political theory defined as the search for a body politic which has abolished social struggle. Conspiracies, invasions, wars, and all manner of internal or external violence are natural phenomena in Machiavelli's political universe and are not defined as aberrations from a stable norm.

But the mere recognition of the existence of conflict in society is insufficient grounds for establishing the originality of Machiavelli's views. The truly original conception, in this regard, was Machiavelli's belief that such conflict might, in fact, produce beneficial results in a properly organized government controlled by stable political institutions. Renaissance thinkers seemed to agree that the burden of classical authority had demonstrated the inherent instability of a republican form of government and often used this tradition to criticize the concept of self-government, thereby praising the rule of princes or kings as a more stable system. Rather than avoiding this issue by offering his reader a utopian vision of a republic (such as More's *Utopia*), the kind of states "that have never been seen nor known to exist in reality," as he puts it in *The Prince* (XV), Machiavelli moved to refute the traditional claim that republican government was inherently undesirable because of its instability. In *The Discourses* he presented a view of the cycle of governments—the three good forms of states: principality, aristocracy, and democracy; and their three corrupt counterparts: tyranny, oligarchy, and anarchy—which he found in the writings of a number of earlier classical theorists. For him, however, "all the forms of government listed are defective: the three good ones because of the brevity of their lives, and the three bad ones because of their inherent harmfulness" (*Discourses*, I, ii). As a result, he aligns himself with classical theorists advocating a mixed form of government as the most stable.

But political stability, in Machiavelli's view, is not

achieved by the absence of conflict or by a static social structure where no change or movement is permitted. On the contrary, a healthy body politic is one characterized by social friction and conflict. In the Roman republic, the best historical example of a self-governing republic founded upon the principle of mixed government, it was precisely the social friction between the plebeians and the aristocrats of the senate that contributed to the city's greatness and its liberty. Machiavelli's interpretation of these conflicts moved him to propose a model for political stability based upon a dynamic equilibrium between political forces rather than upon their suppression in order to create a false stability. This led him to a closer examination, in *The Discourses,* of the problem of civic stability, political corruption, and the creation of institutions to regulate such social conflict, and resulted in a related analysis of a typical modern republic in *The History of Florence.*

While a modern reader may be able to assimilate Machiavelli's conception of social conflict to contemporary political theory with little difficulty, a corollary of his views on internal conflicts may not be quite as acceptable. For Machiavelli also affirms that there exist two types of republics: static states ruled by the nobles (Venice, ancient Sparta) and others in which the protection of liberty has been placed in the hands of the plebeians. Moreover, he believes that the republics of Venice or Sparta were satisfied with relatively limited external expansion, while the Roman republic became an imperial power precisely because the internal struggles between the plebeians and the nobles created a powerful populace which was required to further Roman foreign policy but which could not be docilely managed when peacetime returned. Machiavelli is clearly not a pacifist, and just as he accepts what to many readers is an intolerable level of violence within the state's borders (particularly in the form of conspiracies against institutions or individuals holding power), he also assumes the inevitability of war between sovereign states and, indeed, praises those republics, such as Rome, which are well adapted to this natural condition. In Machiavelli's view of both domestic and foreign affairs, as well as in his conception of the political hero, armed conflict will often determine the ablest, most versatile government or ruler, and he has little sympathy for the governments which do not defend themselves with resolution and foresight or rulers who prefer a policy of temporizing to one of decisive action. The place of military affairs in his political theory is, therefore, fundamental.

POLITICS AND WARFARE

In all Machiavelli's works, military strength is a decisive criterion in the evaluation of a state's independence. In *The Prince* (X), for example, the strength of a principality is primarily measured by the ruler's military self-sufficiency and his ability to field an army against any of his potential enemies. In both a principality and a republic, moreover, good laws and good armies provide the "principal foundations," but it seems clear that Machiavelli gives priority to arms over laws "since there cannot exist good laws where there are no good armies, and where there are good armies there must be good laws" (*The Prince,* XII). In general, as we already know, Machiavelli blames the ruinous condition of Italian political affairs upon the institution of mercenary troops, and he always admired those governments (ancient Rome or Sparta, the Swiss of his own day) which defended their freedom with armies of free citizens. His interest in military matters was primarily a practical one, for he could see no reason to establish civilian institutions without first guaranteeing their protection from internal or external enemies: "Good institutions without military backing undergo the same sort of disorder as the rooms of a splendid and regal palace which, adorned with gems and gold but without a roof, have nothing to protect them from the rain" (*The Art of War,* preface).

Machiavelli also posited a necessary link between the existence of a free, republican form of government and a citizens' militia. He believed that an army composed of the prince's subjects or the republic's citizens had political as well as military advantages. In both kinds of governments, such an army could serve as an educational force by instilling the values of the citizenry in its young men, and its victories would naturally become a source of legitimate civic pride. But most important, such a military force in a republic might act as a bulwark against the growth and implementation of tyrannical power. Since Machiavelli viewed military power as the foundation of civil society, military adventures abroad might also encourage the growth of useful civic virtues in the state's citizens and might test the strength of the state's political institutions. His belief in a necessary link between a militia of citizen-soldiers and a republican form of government is one of the most influential of Machiavelli's ideas. It was to be repeated in many republican works written in subsequent periods to justify the revolutions during the seventeenth and eighteenth centuries in England, France, and America; the antipathy to standing professional armies and the preference for a militia of citizen-soldiers found in early America may be seen as one of Machiavelli's most enduring legacies to the practice and theory of republicanism.

It is also a mark of Machiavelli's belief in the importance of this military role that, of the many individual political models he analyzes in his collected works, a large number of them are soldiers—Castruccio Castracani, Cesare Borgia, Cyrus, Romulus, Theseus, Fabius Maximus, Scipio Africanus. Even Moses and Pope Julius II, both normally considered to be religious figures, are esteemed by Machiavelli for their secular skills as leaders of men in predominantly military situations (the exodus from

Egypt, the wars organized by Julius to expel foreigners from Italy and to consolidate the church's temporal power in central Italy).

CORRUPTION AND CIVIC STABILITY

Once the state's independence (regardless of its particular republican or monarchical form) is guaranteed by military power, Machiavelli turns his attention to more complex matters. First among these concerns in *The Discourses,* his most comprehensive work, is an analysis of the manner in which a republican form of government might counteract the ubiquitous cycle which would inevitably corrupt its foundations and its first principles. Since *The Prince*'s purpose, as we have seen, was a limited one, it gave relatively little attention to governmental institutions, except for the army and the ruler's closest advisers. Its individualistic bias, with its concentration upon a single protagonist, the "new" prince, is not abandoned in *The Discourses* but incorporated into the search for stable institutions. *Virtù,* the key term of *The Prince,* is now supplanted in the commentary on Livy by the word *ordini,* meaning institutions, constitutions, and, in general, organization of various aspects of the state. The man of *virtù* is still necessary, for only a single man's actions can found a new republic or principality or reform completely its corrupted *ordini* (*Discourses,* I, ix). In *The Discourses,* Machiavelli's problem becomes how to move from individual *virtù* to social *ordini,* how to institutionalize the ability of a government's creator or founder so that it can defend itself from civic corruption and inevitable destruction.

The sources of corruption are many. One can be found in the lack of a sense of religion. Machiavelli views pagan religions as secular institutions providing the state with a defense by guaranteeing the observance of oaths and by instilling courage in the citizenry. In ancient Rome religion was an *instrumentum regni,* a means of political control. But the Christian faith, according to Machiavelli, has glorified humility rather than courage or bold actions; furthermore, the Roman church's moral corruption and quest for secular power has rendered it unfit to act as the moral arbiter of Italy's citizens.

Another obvious cause of corruption is the concentration of excessive wealth, excessive power, or both in the hands of a few individuals. It is his opinion that governments are more secure when the commonwealth is rich while its members remain relatively poor. In this regard, Machiavelli considers civilization itself a corrupting influence. He believes that relatively backward nations of his own times (such as Germany and Switzerland) can provide a more fertile ground for the growth of republican virtue than can the jaded citizenry of the many inordinately cultivated Italian city-states. As he puts it in *The Discourses* (I, xi): "Anyone wishing to establish a republic in our present day would find it easier to do so among mountaineers where there is no culture than among men who are accustomed to living in cities where culture is corrupt; in like manner, a sculptor can more easily carve a beautiful statue out of a rough piece of marble than he can from one poorly blocked out by someone else." Machiavelli's picture of Italy is thus not a pretty one. Almost everywhere he looks, when the governments in the Italian peninsula are compared to that of republican Rome, he perceives political corruption in a variety of forms. The only optimistic note he sounds more than once is his assertion that Italy's rulers are the ultimate source of this state of affairs. Italy's peoples, if properly governed, still possess a potential for civic renewal.

Machiavelli's works focus upon two republics separated by centuries and by vastly different institutions: the relatively uncorrupted republic of Rome (the primary subject of *The Discourses*) and the corrupt republic of Florence (analyzed at length in *The History of Florence*). In chapter 1, book III of this history Machiavelli explicitly compares the two cities. The key distinction between their governments is not between stability and political conflict (for we have already seen that Machiavelli regarded the class struggles in republican Rome as a healthy, beneficial phenomenon); it is rather Florence's *type* of internal struggles as compared to those of Rome. In the ideal republican era Machiavelli praises in Rome (the three-hundred-year period from the Tarquins to the Gracchi), Rome's conflicts were between the plebeians and the aristocrats and were carried on without factions, sects, or partisans. Factions or sects arise when a private citizen acquires excessive power, influence, or wealth through private means and employs it for private ends. The people he rallies to his support become partisans rather than citizens working toward the common good and for public ends. Political factions favor the interest of restricted groups of individuals and destroy the very bedrock of the polis, the sense of a shared community of values and goals accepted by all citizens. Factions promote the concentration of power and wealth, two major sources of political corruption, and rarely contribute to the general welfare of the state.

Rome was fortunate enough to be able to channel her conflicts among different classes in a useful direction by virtue of the institutions she had evolved over a number of years. In Florence the conflicts were primarily between members of the same class. Unchecked by vigorous institutions, they usually involved private quarrels over wealth and prestige rather than general public issues. Foremost among the means by which the Romans protected themselves from the rise of such factions, according to Machiavelli, were the offices which represented the interests of the parties to the conflicts—the senate, the consuls, the tribunes of the plebeians. Their existence enabled these diverse groups to express their legitimate interests without the need to form factions. Moreover, the right to bring public charges against citizens suspected of working for private interests through such factions helped to curb this potential source of corruption (although false accusations could have an equally adverse effect). The absence of such an institution in Florence was detrimental.

Because civic corruption occupied so much of Machiavelli's attention, it was only logical that he should deal
with the problem of political renewal. Again, his belief in
the creative role of the heroic individual is central to his
treatment of political reform: "If a prince truly seeks
worldly glory, he should hope to possess a corrupt city—
not in order to ruin it completely as Caesar did but to reorganize it as Romulus did. And the heavens cannot truly
bestow upon men a greater opportunity for obtaining
glory than this, nor can men desire a greater one" (*Discourses,* I, x). As we have already seen in our analysis of
Machiavelli's views on history, reform involves the return
of a political, religious, or military institution to its original principles or beginnings, usually following a model
supplied by classical practice. This can be accomplished
either through farsighted constitutional provisions contained in the structure of the institution itself or through
some event external to this structure. Self-regeneration in
a political institution is, however, quite rare, and Machiavelli believes that political reform is most likely to take
place as a result of some external event. The traumatic
shock of the taking of the city of Rome by the Gauls in
390 B.C. is a case in point, for its ultimate effect was a re-
vival of the original principles in the republic (*Discourses,*
III, i). Similarly beneficial effects can arise from internal
changes which, like external shocks, act as a catalyst for
social reform. These result most commonly from some
new law, such as the creation of the tribunes of the plebeians, or of the censors, or from the example of a virtuous
man's heroic deeds. Here Machiavelli cites a number of
men, including not only political and military leaders but
also St. Francis of Assisi and St. Dominic, the two principal religious reformers of the Middle Ages.

While Machiavelli is most concerned with the means of
avoiding civic corruption and, consequently, of prolong-
ing the life span of the body politic, several political phenomena also hold his attention—the institution of the

dictatorship in republican Rome and the genesis and mechanism of a political conspiracy or a coup d'état. Machiavelli, the republican enthusiast, sees no necessary conflict between a republican form of government and a dictatorship (*Discourses,* I, xxxiv). He regards this institution as a threat to republican institutions and liberty only if the dictator has unlimited powers to modify the *ordini* of the state itself and is subject to no time limitation on his powers. But republican Rome employed the institution of the dictatorship only for fixed periods of time and for specified emergencies, and in no way was the dictator allowed to alter the actual structure of the state's *ordini.* Instead, he was created during those situations when the slow-moving republican institutions were unsuited to dealing with rapidly developing problems (such as a foreign invasion). The dictatorship was, in reality, merely a safety valve employed to safeguard the republican institutions.

Machiavelli's discussion of political conspiracies is equally original. Chapter vi, book III of *The Discourses* (the longest chapter in the work) is entirely devoted to this subject, and much of *The History of Florence* examines historical intrigues in some detail. It represents the most intricate and comprehensive treatment of conspiracies that had yet been attempted. The picture of the practical difficulties involved offers little comfort to those who might wish to employ his analysis as a technical guidebook. This is rather curious, for such a means to power is one which he commonly ascribes to many of the political figures he has examined, including Castruccio Castracani and a host of classical examples.

MACHIAVELLI TODAY

In the four and one-half centuries since Machiavelli's death, no single and unanimously accepted interpretation of his ideas has succeeded in imposing itself upon the lively debate over the meaning of his works. Yet there has never been any doubt about the fundamental importance of Machiavelli's contribution to Western political theory. Critical disagreement has always centered upon how best to evaluate his influence and to characterize his originality. The most popular and widely held opinion of Machiavelli has concerned itself with his views on politics and morality. This critical perspective, spread beyond the Alps by such diverse writers as Reginald Cardinal Pole, Innocent Gentillet, Frederick the Great, and a number of Elizabethan dramatists—including Marlowe and Shakespeare—has given the English language the derogatory terms "Machiavellian" and "Machiavellianism," both of which connote political behavior characterized by immorality, deceit, expediency, and lack of scruples. Such an interpretation of Machiavelli's works dominated critical debate until the eighteenth century, when a number of writers began to see him in a different light, either as a forerunner in the heroic struggle for Italian independence or as a lover of freedom who revealed to the people, under the guise of a book on tyrants, the true nature of tyranny. The focus of the polemical debate shifted from moral questions to a new concern for the author and his intentions.

In recent years Machiavelli has once again become the subject of much critical debate, and this has produced a number of novel approaches to his life and works. New archival discoveries, better editions of many of his works, and fresh critical perspectives have all contributed to this recent upsurge in interest. A number of influential thinkers in this century have pursued the traditionally accepted view of Machiavelli as a teacher of evil. He has been proclaimed as the political thinker who first established the theoretical autonomy of politics, separating it from ethics or theology. Others hailed Machiavelli as the first empirical political scientist, comparing his method to that of Galileo in the physical sciences. Some view him as the first political realist, or as the founder of elitist theory traceable in our own time to the works of Michels, Mosca, and Pareto. While he has received the praise of many un-popular political figures, including that of the Fascist dictator Benito Mussolini, for his astute counsel to states-men, he nevertheless continues to elicit the attention of thinkers with diametrically opposed ideologies. Thus, An-tonio Gramsci, Italy's most original Marxist thinker (and certainly no epigone of Mussolini), defined Machiavelli's "new" prince as the perfect example of a political myth and maintained that the modern political party should fulfill the functions of that heroic figure in the contempo-rary world.

While the weight of traditional critical opinion seems to favor the view that Machiavelli is the supreme realist, there is another current in recent criticism which stresses his literary and imaginative qualities: the impact of his prose style upon his ideas; his creation of quasimythical characters from the raw materials of ancient or contempo-rary history; and the meaning of his particular political vocabulary. Current interest in Machiavelli's works may be characterized by all of the following: increased atten-tion to his early career in the Florentine Chancery; re-newed study of his relationships with important historical figures (Savonarola, Borgia, Soderini, Guicciardini, Vet-tori); a more precise definition of his political terminol-ogy; and greater attention to questions of style and literary history. A general tendency of recent scholarship, one reflected by the variety of materials selected for in-clusion in this volume, is to examine all of Machiavelli's works. No longer is Machiavelli treated as the author of a single, albeit very important, treatise on principalities. In remedying the traditional overemphasis upon *The Prince,* recent criticism has also shifted attention to Machiavelli's role as a republican theorist and to his many original contributions in his analysis of the dynamics of political behavior in a self-governing body politic. Furthermore, Machiavelli's ideas have had an unexpected impact upon new disciplines. They have, for instance, inspired a recent best-seller by Antony Jay on business management and corporate politics. They have also served as the basis for an empirical psychological test measuring "Machiavellianism" and its relationship to interpersonal relations. Subjects scoring high on a "Mach" scale (derived from a list of ideologically loaded statements, many of which are taken from Machiavelli's works) have displayed a remarkable degree of success in manipulating their lower-scoring competitors in interpersonal situations. Contemporary management theory and psychological testing have thus provided us with additional proof (whether desirable or not) of Machiavelli's relevance to our own times.

Like the shape of the mythical figure Proteus, Machiavelli's critical profile seems capable of an infinite number of variations. In the debate that has raged over his works ever since their first appearance in the sixteenth century, the views that have been expressed often reveal as much about the preconceptions of an age as they do about the meaning of Machiavelli's ideas. Benedetto Croce once remarked that Machiavelli raises a critical question which may never be resolved. But if the true test of a classic lies in its ability to serve as a mirror to successive generations rather than in providing specific answers to particular questions which invariably become obsolete with the passage of time, then Machiavelli's works will continue to fascinate today's readers, who, like those of the past 450 years, will discover themselves in his writings.

Peter Bondanella
Mark Musa

*Center for Italian Studies
Indiana University*
September 1978

MACHIAVELLI:
A Selective Bibliography of
Translations, Editions, and Criticism

I. TRANSLATIONS

COLLECTED WORKS

Christian E. Detmold, ed. and trans., *The Historical, Political, and Diplomatic Works of Niccolò Machiavelli*, 4 vols. (Boston: James R. Osgood, 1882); Allan Gilbert, ed. and trans., *Machiavelli: The Chief Works and Others*, 3 vols. (Durham: Duke University Press, 1965).

INDIVIDUAL WORKS OR GROUPS OF WORKS

James B. Atkinson, ed. and trans., *The Prince* (Indianapolis: Bobbs-Merrill, 1976); Thomas G. Bergin, ed., *The Prince* (Northbrook, Ill.: AHM Publishing Corporation, 1947); Bernard Crick, ed., *The Discourses* (Baltimore: Penguin, 1970—Walker translation revised by Brian Richardson); Oliver Evans, ed. and trans., *Clizia* (Great Neck, N.Y.: Barron's, 1962); Allan Gilbert, ed. and trans., *The Letters of Machiavelli* (New York: Capricorn, 1961); Felix Gilbert, ed., *The History of Florence and the Affairs of Italy* (New York: Harper, 1960); J. R. Hale, ed. and trans., *The Literary Works of Machiavelli* (London: Oxford University Press, 1961); Max Lerner, ed., *The Prince and The Discourses* (New York: Random House, 1950—translation of *The Prince* by Luigi Ricci and of *The Discourses* by Christian Detmold); Mark Musa, ed. and trans., *Machiavelli's* The Prince: *A Bilin-*

gual Edition (New York: St. Martin's Press, 1964); Anne and Henry Paolucci, eds. and trans., *Mandragola* (Indianapolis: Bobbs-Merrill, 1957); Joseph Tusiani, ed. and trans., *Lust and Liberty: The Poems of Machiavelli* (New York: Obolensky, 1963); Leslie J. Walker, ed. and trans., *The Discourses of Niccolò Machiavelli,* 2 vols. (New Haven: Yale University Press, 1950); Neal Wood, ed., *The Art of War* (Indianapolis: Bobbs-Merrill, 1965—revised version of 1775 Farnsworth translation).

II. ITALIAN EDITIONS

Sergio Bertelli, ed., *Arte della guerra e scritti politici minori* (Milan: Feltrinelli, 1961), *Legazioni e commissarie,* 3 vols. (Milan: Feltrinelli, 1964), and *Il Principe e Discorsi sopra la prima deca di Tito Livio* (Milan: Feltrinelli, 1960); L. Arthur Burd, ed., *Il Principe* (Oxford: The Clarendon Press, 1891); Fredi Chiappelli, ed., *Legazioni, commissarie, scritti di governo* (Bari: Laterza, 1971–); Franco Gaeta, ed., *Istorie fiorentine* (Milan: Feltrinelli, 1962), *Lettere* (Milan: Feltrinelli, 1961), and *Il Teatro e tutti gli scritti letterari* (Milan: Feltrinelli, 1965); Mario Martelli, ed., *Tutte le opere* (Florence: Sansoni, 1972); Guido Mazzoni and Mario Casella, eds., *Tutte le opere storiche e letterarie* (Florence: G. Barbera, 1929).

III. SECONDARY MATERIALS GROUPED BY TOPIC

THE PRIVATE LETTERS

Giorgio Bàrberi Squarotti, *La forma tragica del Principe e altri saggi sul Machiavelli* (Florence: Olschki, 1966); Peter E. Bondanella, *Machiavelli and the Art of Renaissance History* (Detroit: Wayne State University Press, 1974); Robert J. Clements and Lorna Levant, eds., *Renaissance Letters: Revelations of a World Reborn* (New

York: New York University Press, 1976); Franco Fido, "Appunti sulla memoria letteraria di Machiavelli," *MLN* 89 (1974), 1–13; Allan Gilbert, ed., *The Letters of Machiavelli*; Mario Martelli, "Ancora sui 'Ghiribizzi' a Giovan Battista Soderini," *Rinascimento* 10 (1970), 3–27, and "I 'Ghiribizzi' a Giovan Battista Soderini," *Rinascimento* 9 (1969), 147–180; Franco Masciandaro, "I 'castellucci' e i 'ghiribizzi' del Machiavelli epistolografo," *Italica* 46 (1969), 135–148; K. R. Minogue, "Theatricality and Politics: Machiavelli's Concept of *Fantasia*," in B. Parekh and R. N. Berki, eds., *The Morality of Politics* (New York: Crane and Russak, 1972); Roberto Ridolfi and Paolo Ghiglieri, "I 'Ghiribizzi' al Soderini," *La Bibliofilia* 72 (1970), 53–74; Gennaro Sasso, "Qualche osservazione sui *Ghiribizzi* di Machiavelli al Soderini," in Walter Binni *et al.*, *Letteratura e critica: studi in onore di Natalino Sapegno*, vol. 3 (Rome: Bulzoni, 1976); Giuseppe Velli, "Machiavelli's Letters," *Italian Quarterly* 6 (1962), 99–111.

THE PRINCE

Sydney Anglo, *Machiavelli: A Dissection* (New York: Harcourt Brace Jovanovich, 1969); Alfredo Bonadeo, *Corruption, Conflict, and Power in the Works and Times of Niccolò Machiavelli* (Berkeley: University of California Press, 1973); Peter E. Bondanella, *Machiavelli and the Art of Renaissance History*; Federico Chabod, *Machiavelli and the Renaissance* (New York: Harper, 1965) and *Scritti su Machiavelli* (Turin: Einaudi, 1964); Fredi Chiappelli, *Studi sul linguaggio del Machiavelli* (Florence: Il Saggiatore, 1952); Martin Fleischer, ed., *Machiavelli and the Nature of Political Thought* (New York: Atheneum, 1972); Allan Gilbert, *Machiavelli's* Prince *and Its Forerunners: The Prince as a Typical Book* De Regimine Principum (Durham: Duke University Press, 1938); Myron P. Gilmore, ed., *Studies on Machiavelli* (Florence: Sansoni, 1972); J. H. Hexter, *The Vision of Politics on the Eve of the*

Reformation: More, Machiavelli, and Seyssel (New York: Basic Books, 1972); De Lamar Jensen, *Machiavelli: Cynic, Patriot, or Political Scientist?* (Boston: D. C. Heath, 1960); Joseph A. Mazzeo, *Renaissance and Revolution: Backgrounds to Seventeenth-Century English Literature* (New York: Random House, 1967); Anthony Parel, ed., *The Political Calculus: Essays on Machiavelli's Philosophy* (Toronto: University of Toronto Press, 1972); J. G. A. Pocock, *The Machiavellian Moment: Florentine Political Thought and the Atlantic Republican Tradition* (Princeton: Princeton University Press, 1975); Russell Prince, "The Senses of *Virtù* in Machiavelli," *European Studies Review* 3 (1975), 315–345; Roberto Ridolfi, *The Life of Niccolò Machiavelli* (Chicago: University of Chicago Press, 1963); Gennaro Sasso, *Machiavelli e Cesare Borgia: storia di un giudizio* (Rome: Ateneo, 1966); Leo Strauss, *Thoughts on Machiavelli* (Seattle: University of Washington Press, 1969); J. H. Whitfield, *Discourses on Machiavelli* (Cambridge, England: W. Heffer, 1969) and *Machiavelli* (Oxford: Blackwells, 1947); Neal Wood, "Machiavelli's Concept of *Virtù* Reconsidered," *Political Studies* 15 (1967), 160–172.

THE DISCOURSES

Sydney Anglo, *Machiavelli: A Dissection*; Hans Baron, "The *Principe* and the Puzzle of the Date of the *Discorsi*," *Bibliothèque d'Humanisme et de Renaissance* 18 (1956), 405–428; Alfredo Bonadeo, *Corruption, Conflict, and Power*; Peter E. Bondanella, *Francesco Guicciardini* (Boston: Twayne, 1976) and *Machiavelli and the Art of Renaissance History*; Martin Fleischer, ed., *Machiavelli and the Nature of Political Thought*; Felix Gilbert, "The Composition and Structure of Machiavelli's *Discorsi*," *Journal of the History of Ideas* 14 (1953), 136–156; Myron P. Gilmore, ed., *Studies on Machiavelli*; I. Hannaford, "Machiavelli's Concept of *Virtù* in *The Prince* and *The Discourses* Reconsidered," *Political Studies* 20 (1972),

185–189; Anthony Parel, ed., *The Political Calculus*; J. G. A. Pocock, *The Machiavellian Moment*; Brian Richardson, "The Structure of Machiavelli's *Discorsi*," *Italica* 49 (1972), 46–71; Leo Strauss, *Thoughts on Machiavelli*; Giuseppe Toffanin, *Machiavelli e il Tacitismo* (Naples: Guida, 1972; rpt. of 1921 edn.); J. H. Whitfield, *Discourses on Machiavelli, Machiavelli,* and "Machiavelli's Use of Livy," in T. A. Dorey, ed., *Livy* (London: Routledge & Kegan Paul, 1971).

BELFAGOR

Giorgio Bàrberi Squarotti, *La forma tragica del Principe*; Peter E. Bondanella, *Machiavelli and the Art of Renaissance History*; Robert J. Clements, "Anatomy of the Novella," *Comparative Literature Studies* 9 (1972), 3–16, rpt. in Giovanni Boccaccio, *The Decameron: A Norton Critical Edition,* ed. Mark Musa and Peter E. Bondanella (New York: Norton, 1977); Joseph Gibaldi, "The Renaissance Theory of the Novella," *Canadian Review of Comparative Literature* 2 (1975), 201–227, and "Towards a Definition of the Novella," *Studies in Short Fiction* 12 (1975), 91–98; Luigi Russo, *Machiavelli* (Bari: Laterza, 1969).

THE MANDRAKE ROOT

Giovanni Aquilecchia, "La favola *Mandragola* si chiama," in Giovanni Aquilecchia *et al.,* eds., *Collected Essays on Italian Language and Literature Presented to Kathleen Speight* (Manchester: Manchester University Press, 1971); Sergio Bertelli, "When Did Machiavelli Write *Mandragola*?" *Renaissance Quarterly* 24 (1971), 317–326; Franco Fido, "Machiavelli 1469–1969: Politica e teatro nel badalucco di Messer Nicia," *Italica* 69 (1969), 359 375; Martin Fleischer, "Trust and Deceit in Machiavelli's Comedies," *Journal of the History of Ideas* 26 (1966), 365–380; Douglas Radcliff-Umstead, *The Birth of*

Modern Comedy in Renaissance Italy (Chicago: University of Chicago Press, 1969); Ezio Raimondi, *Politica e commedia* (Bologna: Il mulino, 1972); Roberto Ridolfi, *Studi sulle commedie del Machiavelli* (Pisa: Nistri-Lischi, 1968); Luigi Russo, *Machiavelli.*

THE ART OF WAR

Sydney Anglo, *Machiavelli: A Dissection*; Giorgio Bàrberi Squarotti, *"L'arte della guerra o l'azione impossibile,"* *Lettere italiane* 20 (1968), 281–306; Charles C. Bayley, *War and Society in Renaissance Florence* (Toronto: University of Toronto Press, 1961); Felix Gilbert, "Bernardo Rucellai and the Orti Oricellari: A Study in the Origins of Modern Political Thought," *Journal of the Warburg and Courtauld Institutes* 12 (1949), 101–131, and "Machiavelli: The Renaissance of the Art of War," in E. M. Earle, ed., *Makers of Modern Strategy* (Princeton: Princeton University Press, 1944); Michael Mallett, *Mercenaries and Their Masters: Warfare in Renaissance Italy* (Totowa, N.J.: Rowman and Littlefield, 1974); J. G. A. Pocock, *The Machiavellian Moment*; F. L. Taylor, *The Art of War in Italy, 1494–1529* (Cambridge, England: Cambridge University Press, 1921); Neal Wood, "Introduction" to Niccolò Machiavelli, *The Art of War.*

THE LIFE OF CASTRUCCIO CASTRACANI OF LUCCA

Giorgio Bàrberi Squarotti, *"La vita di Castruccio o la storia come invenzione,"* *L'Approdo letterario* 59–60 (1972), 89–113; Peter E. Bondanella, "Castruccio Castracani: Machiavelli's Archetypal Prince," *Italica* 49 (1972), 302–314, rpt. in *Machiavelli and the Art of Renaissance History*; *Castruccio Castracani degli Anteminelli: miscellanea di studi storici e letterari* (Florence: Tipocalcografia Classica, 1936); Guido Guarino, "Two Views of a Renaissance Tyrant," *Symposium* 19 (1956), 285–290; Alessandro Montevecchi, *"La vita di Castruccio Castracani e lo* stile storico di Machiavelli," *Letterature moderne* 12 (1962), 513–521; Bernard Shea, "Machiavelli and Fielding's *Jonathan Wild,*" *PMLA* 72 (1957), 55–73; J. H. Whitfield, "Machiavelli and Castruccio," *Italian Studies* 8 (1953), 1–28, rpt. in *Discourses on Machiavelli.*

THE HISTORY OF FLORENCE

Sydney Anglo, *Machiavelli: A Dissection*; Alfredo Bonadeo, *Corruption, Conflict, and Power*; Peter E. Bondanella, *Machiavelli and the Art of Renaissance History*; Peter Burke, *The Renaissance Sense of the Past* (New York: St. Martin's Press, 1969); Felix Gilbert, *Machiavelli and Guicciardini: Politics and History in Sixteenth-Century Florence* (Princeton: Princeton University Press, 1965) and "Machiavelli's *Istorie fiorentine:* An Essay in Interpretation," in Myron P. Gilmore, ed., *Studies on Machiavelli*; Marina Marietti, "Machiavel historiographe des Médicis," in André Rochon, ed., *Les Écrivains et le pouvoir en Italie à l'époque de la Renaissance* (Paris: Université de la Sorbonne Nouvelle, 1974); Rudolf von Albertini, *Firenze dalla repubblica al principato* (Turin: Einaudi, 1970); Donald J. Wilcox, *The Development of Florentine Humanist Historiography in the Fifteenth Century* (Cambridge, Mass.: Harvard University Press, 1969).

MACHIAVELLI'S INFLUENCE

N. W. Bawcutt, "Machiavelli and Marlowe's *The Jew of Malta,*" *Renaissance Drama* 3 (1970), 3–49; Donald W. Bleznick, "Spanish Reaction to Machiavelli in the Sixteenth and Seventeenth Centuries," *Journal of the History of Ideas* 19 (1958), 542–550; Willis H. Bowen, "Sixteenth-Century French Translations of Machiavelli," *Italica* 27 (1950), 313–320; James Burnham, *The Machiavellians: Defenders of Freedom* (New York: John Day, 1943); C. Cardascia, "Machiavel et Bodin," *Bibliothèque d'Humanisme et de Renaissance* 3 (1943), 29–167; Richard Christie and Florence L. Geis, *Studies in Machiavellianism* (New York: Academic Press, 1970); Antonio D'Andrea, "Machiavelli, Satan, and the Gospel," *Yearbook of Italian Studies* 1 (1971), 156–177, "The Political and Ideological Content of Innocent Gentillet's *Anti-Machiavel*," *Renaissance Quarterly* 23 (1970), 397–411, and "Studies on Machiavelli and His Reputation in the Sixteenth Century," *Medieval and Renaissance Studies* 5 (1961), 214–248; Armand De Gaetano, "The Influence of Machiavelli on the Neapolitan Intellectual Leaders of the Risorgimento," *Italian Quarterly* 5 (1961), 45–60; Dante Della Terza, "The Most Recent Image of Machiavelli: The Contribution of the Linguist and the Historian," *Italian Quarterly* 14 (1970), 91–113; Peter S. Donaldson, ed. and trans., *A Machiavellian Treatise by Stephen Gardiner* (Cambridge, England: Cambridge University Press, 1975); K. Dreyer, "Commynes and Machiavelli: A Study in Parallelism," *Symposium* 6 (1951), 38–61; Felix Gilbert, "Machiavelli in Modern Historical Scholarship," *Italian Quarterly* 14 (1970), 9–26, and *Niccolò Machiavelli e la vita culturale del suo tempo* (Bologna: Il mulino, 1964); Antonio Gramsci, *The Modern Prince and Other Writings* (New York: International Publishers, 1957); E. Harris Harbison, "The Intellectual as Social Reformer: Machiavelli and Thomas More," *Rice Institute Pamphlet* 44 (1957), 1–45; Norman Holland, *"Measure for Measure*: The Duke and the Prince," *Comparative Literature* 11 (1959), 16–20; Antony Jay, *Management and Machiavelli: An Inquiry into the Politics of Corporate Life* (New York: Holt, Rinehart & Winston, 1968); Vincenzo Luciani, "Bacon and Machiavelli," *Italica* 24 (1947), 26–40, "Raleigh's *Discourse of War* and Machiavelli's *Discorsi*," *Modern Philology* 46 (1948), 122–131, and "Raleigh's *Discourses on the Savoyan Matches* and Machiavelli's *Istorie Fiorentine*," *Italica* 29 (1952), 103–107; Friedrich Meinecke, *Machiavellism: The Doctrine of* Raison d'Etat *and Its Place in Modern History* (London: Routledge and Kegan Paul, 1957); Napoleone Orsini, *Bacone e Machiavelli* (Genoa: degli

Orfini, 1936); J. G. A. Pocock, *The Machiavellian Moment*; Mario Praz, *The Flaming Heart* (New York: Norton, 1973); Giuliano Procacci, *Studi sulla fortuna del Machiavelli* (Rome: Istituto storico italiano per l'età moderna e contemporanea, 1965); Felix Raab, *The English Face of Machiavelli: A Changing Interpretation 1500–1700* (Toronto: University of Toronto Press, 1964); Irving Ribner, "Bolingbroke: A True Machiavellian," *Modern Language Quarterly* 9 (1948), 177–184, "Machiavelli and Sidney: The *Arcadia* of 1590," *Studies in Philology* 47 (1950), 152–172, "Marlowe and Machiavelli," *Comparative Literature* 6 (1954), 349–356, and "Sidney's *Arcadia* and the Machiavelli Legend," *Italica* 27 (1950), 225–235; Robert Shackleton, "Montesquieu and Machiavelli: A Reappraisal," *Comparative Literature Studies* 1 (1964), 1–14; Robert I. Williams, "Machiavelli's *Mandragola*, Touchwood Senior, and the Comedy of Middleton's *A Chaste Maid in Cheapside*," *Studies in English Literature* 10 (1970), 385–396.

A number of significant publications should be added to the bibliography of major interpretations of Niccolò Machiavelli's thought that appeared in the original printing of this edition.

Several important studies in Italy should be noted: Jean-Jacques Marchand, *Niccolò Machiavelli: i primi scritti (1499—1512)* (Padua: Editrice Antenore, 1975); Gian Mario Anselmi, *Ricerche sul Machiavelli storico* (Pisa: Pacini Editore, 1979); Gennaro Sasso, *Niccolò Machiavelli: storia del suo pensiero politico* (Bologna: Il Mulino, 1980); Ugo Dotti, *Niccolò Machiavelli: la fenomenologia del potere* (Milan: Feltrinelli, 1979); and Carlo Dionisotti, *Machiavellerie: storia e fortuna di Machiavelli* (Turin: Einaudi, 1980).

In English, a number of works covering the entire range of Machiavelli's writings have appeared, testifying to the ever increasing interest in the Florentine's works: Quentin Skinner's *The Foundations of Modern Political Thought*, 2 vols. (Cambridge: Cambridge University Press, 1978), or his briefer *Machiavelli* (Oxford: Oxford University Press, 1981); Silvia Russo Fiore, *Niccolò Machiavelli* (Boston: Twayne, 1982); and Hanna Fenichel Pitkin, *Fortune is a Woman: Gender and Politics in The Thought of Niccolò Machiavelli* (Berkeley: University of California Press, 1984). Most recently, Sebastian de Grazia has completed an interesting intellectual biography of Machiavelli entitled *Machiavelli in Hell* (Princeton: Princeton University Press, 1989); and Wayne A. Rebhorn's *Foxes and Lions: Machiavelli's Confidence Men* (Ithaca: Cornell University Press, 1988) provides an original analysis of how literary traditions inform Machiavelli's works.

While all aspects of Machiavelli's life and writings have attracted critical attention, the emphasis in the literature during the last decade has been upon Machiavelli's republicanism and the political tradition represented by his *Discourses*. For this aspect of Machiavelli, see: Harvey Mansfield, Jr., *Machiavelli's New Modes and Orders* (Ithaca: Cornell University Press, 1979), or the new and complete translation of Machiavelli's *Florentine Histories*, trans. Laura F. Banfield and Harvey C. Mansfield, Jr. (Princeton: Princeton University Press, 1988); Mark Hulliung, *Citizen Machiavelli* (Princeton: Princeton University Press, 1983); William R. Everdell, *The End of Kings: A History of Republics and Republicans* (New York: Free Press, 1983); and Peter Bondanella, *The Eternal City: Roman Images in the Modern World* (Chapel Hill: University of North Carolina Press, 1987).

—Peter Bondanella
Indiana University

The Portable
MACHIAVELLI

THE PRIVATE LETTERS

EDITORS' NOTE

One of the most characteristic literary forms during the European Renaissance was the private letter, a vogue begun in the fourteenth century by the indefatigable father of humanism, Petrarch (Francesco Petrarca), and continued by his humanist successors for the next two centuries. Within the context of Italian Renaissance literature, the collections of letters by Petrarch, Michelangelo, Pietro Aretino, and Machiavelli—to mention only the most important and best known—not only constitute a rich source of valuable information about the lives and times of these men, but also contain some of the period's best prose. While other literary genres had more confining boundaries, the private letter allowed a Renaissance writer the freedom to express his personal feelings to a friend in a relaxed tone, much as he might have done in an informal conversation. But while these familiar letters were usually addressed to close friends, they were almost always intended for a wider audience and, eventually, for posterity.

Machiavelli's correspondence is notable for its striking mixture of styles and for the engaging self-portrait it contains of a man whose warmth and good humor belie the evil legends that have sprung up around his name. In a letter dated January 31, 1515, and addressed to Francesco Vet-

tori, Machiavelli himself notes that his tone may surprise some readers in the future:

Anyone who might see our letters, my dear friend, and might note their diversity would be very amazed, for at one point he would think that we were very serious men, involved in weighty matters, and that we never entertained a thought which was not lofty and honest. But then, turning the page, he would discover that these same serious men were frivolous, inconstant, lustful, and occupied with trifles. This manner of ours, although to some it may be disgraceful, seems worthy of praise to me, because we imitate Nature, which herself is various, and anyone who imitates Nature cannot be criticized.

The following selection presents only seven of the nearly two hundred and fifty private letters which have been preserved from Machiavelli's hand. And this large number does not include the even more numerous edited and still unedited letters and chancery documents which he wrote or had written in his capacity as an employee of the Florentine republic. The first and earliest letter is addressed to the Florentine envoy at the papal court in Rome, Ricciardo Becchi. It describes Machiavelli's reaction to one of Savonarola's sermons and should be read together with Machiavelli's remarks in The Prince *about "unarmed prophets" (VI) and the views he expresses on religion in* The Discourses. *As far as contemporary scholars can determine, Machiavelli probably received his post in the government because of his lack of sympathy for the friar's views, or "lies," as he terms them here.*

I
TO RICCIARDO BECCHI

In order to give you, as you requested, a complete report of things here concerning the friar, I would have you know that after delivering the two sermons, of which you have already received a copy, he preached on the Sunday of the carnival, and after saying many things, he invited all his devotees to share communion with him on carnival day at San Marco. And he said that he wanted to pray to God that He give some clear sign if the things that he had predicted did not come from Him; and he did this, as some say, in order to unify his following and to make it stronger in his defense, fearing that the newly elected (but not announced) Signoria might be opposed to him. When the Signoria was announced on Monday, an event of which you must be already fully aware, he judged it more than two thirds hostile to him, and since the Pope had sent a directive which summoned him, under pain of interdiction, and since he was worried that the Signoria might want him to obey immediately, he decided, whether by his own choice or whether so advised by others, to renounce the preaching in Santa Reparata and to go to San Marco. And so, on Thursday morning, when the Signoria assumed its authority, he announced in Santa Reparata that in order to avoid any scandal and to serve the honor of God, he wished to withdraw from his position and that the men should come to listen to him in San Marco while the women should go to San Lorenzo to hear Brother Domenico. When our friar found himself in his own home, you can well imagine with what audacity he began his sermons and with what audacity he continued them; since he was afraid for himself, he believed that the new Signoria would not hesitate to harm him, and since he had decided that a good many citizens would accompany him in his downfall, he began his talk by frightening everybody; he used arguments that were very convincing to those who did not examine them carefully, showing how his followers were the most excellent of men and his enemies the most wicked, using every rhetorical device that existed to weaken his opponents and to strengthen his own faction. Since I was present, let me tell you briefly about a few of these devices.

The source of his first sermon in San Marco was this passage from Exodus: "But the more they tortured them, the more they multiplied and grew" [1: 12]; and before he came to the explanation of these words, he showed why he had withdrawn and said: "Prudence is right thinking in practical affairs."[1] Then he said that all men have had and still do have a purpose, but that they are different ones: "For Christians, their goal is Christ; for other men, either present or past, it has been and still is something different, according to their religion. Since we who are Christians are directed to that end which is Christ, we should, with the utmost prudence and following the customs of the times, preserve His honor; and when it is time for a man to hide himself, he should hide, as we read of Christ and of Saint Paul"; and thus, he added, "It is our duty to do this and we have done it, for when it was time to resist danger, we did it, as was the case on Ascension Day, for to do so was demanded by the honor of God and the times. Now the honor of God requires that we yield to anger, and we have yielded." And having given this brief speech, he described two groups of people—one that fought for God, this was himself and his devotees, and the other commanded by the Devil, which was his opponents. And having discussed this in great detail, he entered into an exposition of the words he had cited from Exodus, and he said that through tribulations good men increased in two ways, in spirit and in number; in spirit, since men join themselves more closely with God when adversity confronts them and they become stronger, as their source is nearer, just as hot water set near a fire becomes hotter, since it is nearer its source. Men grow also in number. There are three types of men: the good man, and these are those who follow him; the perverse and obstinate, and these are his enemies; and another kind of man who is careless, devoted to pleasures, neither obstinate in evildoing nor dedicated to good deeds, since he cannot discern the one from the other; but when between the good and the bad there arises some factual difference (since opposites placed together are more clearly contrasted), he recognizes the evil of the wicked and the simplicity of the

[1] A reference to St. Thomas Aquinas, *Summa Theologica* (II, 2).

good, and he flees from the former and draws nearer to
the latter, since all men avoid evil and willingly, by nature, they seek out the good; and so it is this way that in
times of adversity the good increase and the evil become
fewer. I recount this to you briefly, since the space of a
letter does not permit a long explanation. Next, di-
gressing, as is his habit, in order to weaken his enemies as
well as to introduce his next sermon, he said that our internal strife could enable a tyrant to rise up who would
destroy our homes and lay waste our lands; and this was
not contrary to that which he had already preached, that
is, that Florence was going to be prosperous and would
rule all of Italy, since it would be only a short time before
the tyrant would be driven out; and on this note he completed his sermon.

The next morning, still preaching on Exodus and coming to that section where the Bible says that Moses killed
an Egyptian, the friar declared that the Egyptian symbol-
ized evil men and that Moses represented the prophet
who killed them by uncovering their evil ways, and he
said: "O Egyptian, I shall give you a thrust of my sword!";
and here he began to flip through your books, O you
priests, and treated you in such a manner that not even a
dog would come near you. Then he added, and this is
what he was trying to get at all along, that he wanted to
give the Egyptian another and greater wound, and he said
that God had told him that there was one in Florence who
sought to make himself a tyrant and who was scheming to
achieve this goal: and that to attempt to drive out the
friar, to excommunicate the friar, and to persecute the
friar, meant simply that he wanted to be a tyrant; and he
added that the laws should be observed. And he said so
much about it that men later in the day publicly specu-
lated about the man to whom the friar referred, a man
who is about as close to becoming tyrant of Florence as
you are to heaven! But since the Signoria later on wrote in
his favor to the Pope, and since he saw that he need no
longer fear his enemies in Florence, where before he
wanted only to unite his own faction by attacking his en-

emies and to frighten them with the name of the tyrant, now, when he no longer need do so, he has changed his disguise: now he tries to turn all of them against the Holy Father, still encouraging them to join in the alliance already formed without mentioning either the name of the tyrants or their evilness, and toward the Supreme Pontiff he turns his churlish yappings and says of him what one would say of only the most evil of men; and thus, according to my view, he keeps changing with the times and makes his lies more believable.

Now, whatever the common herd is saying and what men are hoping or fearing, I shall leave to your judgment, since you are prudent and can evaluate that better than I; you understand our internal quarrels and the temper of the times and, since you are in Rome, you are also very aware of the Pope's feelings. I beg of you only one thing: that if you have not found reading these letters of mine tiring, may you also not find it burdensome to write me, giving me your judgment of the nature of these times and telling me what you make of our affairs. Farewell. In Florence, March 8, 1498.

Your Niccolò Machiavelli
Son of Bernardo

The second letter, dated 1509, is addressed to Luigi Guicciardini (a member of the family of the more famous Francesco) and contains an unusual portrait of a grotesque prostitute, a figure no doubt born of an authentic experience and Machiavelli's vivid imagination.

II
TO LUIGI GUICCIARDINI IN MANTUA

To Signor Luigi Guicciardini
as his dearest brother, in Mantua

Damn it all, Luigi! You see how fortune can bring about in men different results in similar matters. You,

when you have screwed her once, you still get the urge to
screw her again—you still want another go at her. But I,
having been here several days, going blind crazy without
my wife, came across an old woman who washed my
shirts; she lives in a house that is practically underground,
and the only light that comes in is from the door. I was
passing by there one day, and she recognized me and
made a big fuss over me; she said that if I wished, she
would show me some beautiful shirts that I might want to
buy. I believed her—innocent prick that I am! And when
I was inside I dimly saw a woman hiding in a corner, pretending to be bashful with a towel over her head and face.
The old hag took me by the hand and led me to the
woman, saying: "This is the shirt that I want to sell, but I
want you to try it on first and pay later." Timid as I am, I
was now completely terrified; nevertheless, since I was
alone with her and in the dark (the old lady left the house
immediately and shut the door), I gave her a good hump.
Even though I found her thighs flabby and her cunt wa-
tery and her breath stinking a bit, my lust was so desperate that I went ahead and gave it to her anyway! And once
I had her, I had the urge to see my merchandise and I
took a brand from the fireplace near me and lit a lamp
that was above it; and hardly was it lit when the light almost dropped from my hand. My God! The woman was
so ugly that I almost dropped dead. The first thing I noticed was a tuft of hair, half white and half black, and although the top of her head was bald, which allowed you
to observe a number of lice taking a stroll, nevertheless a
few hairs mingled with the whiskers that grew around her
face; and on top of her small, wrinkled head there was a
scar-burn which made her look as if she had been
branded at the market; her eyebrows were full of nits; one
eye looked down, the other up, and one was larger than
the other. Her tear ducts were full of mucus and her eye-
lashes plucked; her nose was twisted into a funny shape,
the nostrils were full of snot, and one of them was half cut
off; her mouth looked like Lorenzo de' Medici's, but it

was twisted on one side and drooled a bit since she had no teeth to keep the saliva in her mouth; her upper lip was covered with a thin but rather long moustache; her chin was long and sharp, pointed up, and from it hung a bit of skin that dangled to her Adam's apple. As I stood there, amazed at this monster, she noticed my surprise and tried to say: "What is the trouble, sir?"; but she could not, since she was a stutterer; and as she opened her mouth there came from it such a stinking breath that my eyes and my nose, the two gateways of the two most outraged senses, found themselves offended by this pestilence; this was such a shock to my stomach that, not being able to bear it, it heaved so much that I vomited all over her. And so, having paid her in the way she deserved, I left. And I swear to God, I don't believe that my lust will return as long as I am in Lombardy. So you can praise God in the hope of enjoying your pleasures again, while I shall be thankful because I have lost the fear of ever again having such an unfortunate experience.

I think that I will have some money left from this trip, and I would like to put it into some small investment when I am back in Florence. I thought about setting up a poultry yard; I need some employee to run it for me. I hear that Piero di Martino is interested; I would like to hear from him if he is able and to have you reply to me. Because if he doesn't want to, I have to find someone else.

Giovanni will give you the news from here. Give Jacopo my regards and remember me to him and don't forget Marco. In Verona on December 9, 1509.

Niccolò Machiavelli

[P.S.] I am awaiting the reply of Gualtieri about my poem.

The third letter presents some difficulties. Although scholars have traditionally believed it to be addressed to Piero Soderini around 1512–1513, recent evidence suggests that the letter was actually composed in 1506. Furthermore, some scholars contend that it was addressed not to Piero Soderini

(1452–1522), Machiavelli's patron and superior in the Florentine chancery (he was elected gonfaloniere for life in 1502, only to lose his position with the return of the Medici and the downfall of the republic), but to his nephew, Giovan Battista Soderini. Since the ideas discussed in the letter are closely related to important sections of both The Prince *and* The Discourses, *the earlier composition would indicate that some of Machiavelli's fundamental concepts were formulated considerably earlier than many scholarly accounts of their development might indicate.*

III

TO GIOVAN BATTISTA SODERINI
OR PIERO SODERINI
IN PERUGIA

A disguised letter of yours reached me—but I knew it was yours after reading ten words. I can imagine how many people came to meet you at Piombino, and I am sure of your annoyances and those of Filippo, since I know how one of you is offended by too much light and the other by too little. January does not bother me, as long as I can be sure that February improves. I am sorry about Filippo's suspicion and await the result anxiously. [The man who does not know how to fence confuses one who does.]¹ Your letter was brief, but I manage to make it longer by rereading it. I appreciated it, since it gave me the opportunity to do something I was afraid to do and which you warn me not to do; and only this part of the letter have I ignored. I would be surprised by this, if my fate had not shown me so many and so great a variety of things that I am forced to be seldom astonished or to admit having learned little while reading about and participating in the actions of men and the methods of their deeds.

---

¹ Material in brackets represents marginal notes from the original manuscript of the letter.

I know you and the compass by which you steer, and even if it were to be faulty, which it cannot be, I would not condemn it, seeing to what ports it has guided you, [the ranks with which it has honored you] and with what hope it nourishes you. Therefore I see, not with your mirror, where nothing is seen without prudence, but with that of the multitude, that one is obliged to look to the results of an action, to see how it was accomplished, and not to the means by which it was achieved. [Each man governs himself according to his fantasy.] And I see how different courses of action bring about the same result, as different roads lead to the same destination, and how many who use different means achieve the same goal—the actions of this Pope and the results they have achieved were all that was needed to prove this opinion. [Do not give advice to anyone nor accept any, except for general opinions; each man should do what his spirit tells him, and with boldness.] Hannibal and Scipio were both excellent military leaders: the first, by means of cruelty, treachery, and disdain for religion, kept his armies united in Italy and made himself admired by the peoples, who, in order to follow him, rebelled against Rome; the second, by means of piety, faith, and respect for religion in Spain, had the same following from those peoples; and both the one and the other won victory after victory. But since it is not fashionable to cite the Romans, Lorenzo de' Medici disarmed the people in order to hold Florence, while Giovanni Bentivoglio armed them to hold Bologna; the Vitelli at Castello and the present Duke of Urbino in his state destroyed fortresses in order to hold those states, while Count Francesco and many others built them within their states to hold them. [Trust Fortune, the friend of young men, and adapt yourself to the situation. But you cannot both have fortresses and not have them, be both cruel and pious.] The Emperor Titus thought he would lose his empire the day he failed to do a favor for someone; some other ruler might fear to lose his state the day he pleased someone. Many men succeed in their plans by weighing and measuring everything. [When Fortune becomes weary, disaster ensues. The family, the city, each man has its fortune founded on its method of proceeding, and each of these becomes weary, and when Fortune is run down, one must revive it with another method. Compare this to a horse led for too long a time around the same fortress.] This Pope Julius, who has neither a scale nor a measure, achieves by chance while disarmed what with proper preparation and arms he could attain only with difficulty. We have seen and still see the above examples and countless others of like fashion which could be cited concerning the acquisition of kingdoms and dominions or the loss of them, according to circumstances; and when a method led to success it was praised; when it led to failure, it was condemned; and sometimes after a lengthy prosperity, loss is blamed not on oneself but on heaven and the disposition of the Fates. But why it happens that the same actions are sometimes equally effective and equally damaging I do not know, but I should like very much to find out; thus, in order to hear your opinion, I will be presumptuous enough to tell you mine.

I believe that as Nature has given every man a different face, so she also has given each a different character and imagination. From this it follows that each man governs himself according to his particular character and imagination. And because, on the other hand, times change and the order of things always shifts, the fortunate man, the one whose wishes are completely fulfilled, is he who fits his plan of action to the times; to the contrary, the unhappy man is he who fails to match his actions to the times and to the order of things. Thus, it can easily occur that two men, acting in different ways, can achieve the same result, since each of them can fit themselves to the circumstances, for patterns of events are as many as the number of provinces or states. But because the times and affairs are often transformed, both in general and in particulars, and men do not change their imaginations nor their methods, it happens that one man has in one instance good fortune and in another bad. And, truly, anyone so wise as to understand the times and the order of things and be able to accommodate himself to them would always have good fortune, or at least he would avoid the bad, and then the truth would emerge: that the wise man can command the stars and the Fates. But since such men cannot be found, men being only shortsighted and unable to discipline their characters, it follows that Fortune changes and commands men and keeps them under her yoke. And to verify this opinion, the examples above are sufficient; I founded my view on them, and they should support it. Cruelty, perfidy, and contempt for religion help to increase the reputation of a new ruler in a province where humanity, faith, and religion have long been abandoned; in like manner, humanity, faith, and religion are efficacious where cruelty, perfidy, and contempt for religion have reigned for a time; for just as bitter things disturb the taste and sweet things glut it, so men grow tired of the good and complain of the bad. These, among other causes, opened Italy to Hannibal and Spain to Scipio, and thus each corresponded, according to his manner of proceeding, to the times and the order of things. At that same time, a man like Scipio would not have been so fortunate in Italy, nor one like Hannibal so successful in Spain, as both the one and the other were in their respective areas.

Niccolò Machiavelli

The next three letters are addressed to Francesco Vettori (1474–1539), the Florentine ambassador to Rome from 1513 to 1515, who had become Machiavelli's friend during an earlier diplomatic mission which took them both to Germany. All three letters were written after Machiavelli's enforced retirement from political life and reveal his moods during the important period in which The Prince *was composed. The letter describing the work's composition is per-*

haps the most famous letter in Italian Renaissance literature
and is a moving testament to Machiavelli's love for the classics which inspired his treatise.

IV
TO FRANCESCO VETTORI IN ROME

Magnifice domine orator,

> And I, aware of his changed color, said:
> "But how can I go on if you are frightened?
> You are my constant strength when I lose heart."[1]

This letter of yours has scared me more than the rack,
and I am sorry about any idea you may have that I am
angry, not for my own sake, because I am used to no
longer desiring anything passionately, but for yours, and I
beg you to imitate others who make a place for themselves with astuteness and insistence, rather than with talent and prudence; and as for that story about Totto, it
displeases me if it displeases you. Furthermore, I do not
think about it, and if I cannot be enrolled, I'll roll on;[2] and
I ask you once and for all not to worry about the requests
I make of you, since I will not be upset if I do not obtain
them.

If you are tired of discussing affairs, since many times
you see them end up in a way contrary to the concepts
and arguments that you form about them, you are correct,
because the same thing has happened to me. Yet, if I
could speak to you, I would do nothing more than fill
your head with imaginary plans, since Fortune has decided that I must talk about the state—not knowing how
to discuss either the silk trade or the wool business, either
profits or losses. I have to vow either to remain silent or to

[1] Dante, *Inferno,* IV, 16–18.
[2] A play on words: *rotolare* ("to enroll") refers to being placed
on the pope's list of dependents (*rotulo*).

speak of this. If I could leave Florentine territory, I too would certainly go to see if the Pope were at home; but in spite of so many favors dispensed, I was ignored by him because of my negligent absence. I shall wait for September.

I understand that Cardinal Soderini has many dealings with the Pope. I should like you to advise me if you think it would be fitting for me to write him a letter asking that he commend me to His Holiness; or if it might be best that you speak privately on my behalf with the cardinal; or if neither should be done—in which case you might send me a short reply.

As for the horse, you make me laugh by reminding me of it. Only when I remember it will you have to pay, and not otherwise.

Our archbishop must be dead by this hour; may God receive his soul and those of his family. *Valete.* In Florence, April 9, 1513.

Niccolò Machiavelli
formerly Secretary

V

TO FRANCESCO VETTORI IN ROME

Magnificent Ambassador. Divine favors were never late.[1] I say this because it appears that I have not lost but have rather misplaced your favor, since you have not written to me for quite a long time, and I was in doubt as to the cause. And I paid little attention to all the reasons that came to mind, except for one: I feared that you had stopped writing to me because you heard that I was not a good guardian for your letters; and I knew that outside of Filippo [Casavecchia] and Paolo [Vettori], no one else, as far as I know, has seen them. But now I have found your favor once again in your last letter of the twenty-third of

[1] A reference to Petrarch's *Triumphs* ("Triumph of Eternity," l.13).

the past month. I am very happy to see how regularly and calmly you carry on your public office, and urge you to continue in this way, since anyone who loses his own interests for those of others sacrifices his own and receives no thanks from the others. And since it is Fortune that does everything, it is she who wishes us to leave her alone, to be quiet and not to give her trouble, and to wait until she allows us to act again; then you will do well to strive harder, to observe things more closely, and it will be time for me to leave my country home and say: "Here I am!" In the meantime, I can only tell you in this letter of mine what my life is like, wishing to match favor with favor, and if you think you would like to exchange yours for mine, I would be very happy to do so.

I live in the country, and since my recent misadventures in Florence I have not spent, in total, twenty days there. Until recently, I have been snaring thrushes with my own hands. Rising before daybreak, I prepare the birdlime and go out with such a bundle of bird cages on my back that I look like Geta when he returned from port with the books of Amphitryon;[2] I usually catch at least two, at the most six thrushes. I spent all of September doing this. Then this pastime, vile and foreign to my nature as it is, came to an end, to my displeasure; let me tell you what my life is like now: I rise in the morning with the sun and go into a wood that I am having cut, where I remain two hours in order to check the work done the day before and to pass the time with the woodcutters, who always have some argument at hand among themselves or with their neighbors. And concerning this wood, I could tell you a thousand entertaining things that have happened to me in my affairs with Frosino da Panzano and with others who wanted part of it. And Frosino, especially—he sent for several cords of wood without even saying anything, and on payment he wanted to hold back ten lire which he says

[2]An allusion to a popular novella of the fifteenth century, *Geta and Birria*.

he should have had from me four years ago when he beat me at cards at Antonio Guicciardini's. I began to raise the devil and was going to accuse the carter who had come to steal the wood, but Giovanni Machiavelli entered the matter and made peace. Batista Guicciardini, Filippo Ginori, Tommaso del Bene, and some other citizens each bought a cord from me when that north wind was blowing.[3] I made promises to them all and sent one cord to Tommaso, which, by the time it reached Florence, turned out to be half a cord because he and his wife, his children, and the help piled it, so that it looked like Gabburra[4] and his boys butchering an ox on a Thursday. So, when I saw who was making a profit on this, I told the others that I had no more wood left, and they all made a big thing of it, especially Batista, who adds this to his other misfortunes of Prato.

Leaving the wood, I go to a spring, and from there to my bird-snare. I have a book with me, either Dante or Petrarca or one of the lesser poets like Tibullus, Ovid, and the like: I read about their amorous passions and about their loves, I remember my own, and I revel for a moment in this thought. I then move on up the road to the inn, I speak with those who pass, and I ask them for news of their area; I learn many things and note the different and diverse tastes and ways of thinking of men. Lunchtime comes, when my family and I eat that food which this poor farm and my meager patrimony permit. After eating, I return to the inn: there I usually find the innkeeper, a butcher, a miller, and two bakers. With these men I waste my time playing cards all day and from these games a thousand disagreements and countless offensive words arise, and most of the time our arguments are over a few cents; nevertheless, we can be heard yelling from San Ca-

[3]An allusion either to Machiavelli's difficulties with the Medici after the collapse of the Florentine republic in 1512 or to the sack of Prato in 1512, which was administered at the time by Batista Guicciardini.
[4]Gabburra was probably a well-known butcher.

sciano. Caught this way among these lice I wipe the mold from my brain and release my feeling of being ill-treated by Fate; I am happy to be driven along this road by her, as I wait to see if she will be ashamed of doing so.

When evening comes, I return to my home, and I go into my study; and on the threshold, I take off my everyday clothes, which are covered with mud and mire, and I put on regal and curial robes; and dressed in a more appropriate manner I enter into the ancient courts of ancient men and am welcomed by them kindly, and there I taste the food that alone is mine, and for which I was born; and there I am not ashamed to speak to them, to ask them the reasons for their actions; and they, in their humanity, answer me; and for four hours I feel no boredom, I dismiss every affliction, I no longer fear poverty nor do I tremble at the thought of death: I become completely part of them. And as Dante says that knowledge does not exist without the retention of it by memory,[5] I have noted down what I have learned from their conversation, and I composed a little work, *De principatibus,* where I delve as deeply as I can into thoughts on this subject, discussing what a principality is, what kinds there are, how they are acquired, how they are maintained, why they are lost. And if any of my fantasies has ever pleased you, this should not displease you; and to a prince, and especially to a new prince, it should be welcomed; therefore, I am dedicating it to his Magnificence, Giuliano.[6] Filippo Casavecchia has seen it; he can give you some idea both of the work itself and of the discussion we have had concerning it, although I am still enlarging it and polishing it up.

You would like me, Magnificent Ambassador, to leave this life here and to come to enjoy yours with you. I shall do it, come what may, but what keeps me back at present

[5] *Paradiso,* V, 41–42.
[6] Initially *The Prince* was dedicated to Giuliano de' Medici, but after his death in 1516 the work was addressed to his successor, Lorenzo de' Medici, Duke of Urbino.

are certain affairs of mine which I shall settle within six weeks. What makes me hesitate is that the Soderini[7] are there, and I would be obliged, coming there, to visit them and speak to them. I would not be surprised if on my return I might have to stay at the Bargello prison rather than at home, since although this state has very strong foundations and great security, it is also new and, because of this, suspicious, and there are plenty of sly men who, to appear like Pagolo Bertini,[8] would put others in debt and leave the worries to me. I beg you to relieve me of this fear, and then, whatever happens, I shall come within the time established to find you.

I talked with Filippo about this little book of mine: whether or not I should present it to him [Giuliano], and whether, giving it to him, I should bring it myself or have it delivered to you. Giving it makes me afraid that Giuliano won't read it and that Ardinghelli[9] will take the credit for this, my latest labor. I am urged to give it by the necessity that drives me: I am wearing myself away, and I cannot remain in this state for long without being despised for my poverty, not to mention my desire that these Medici lords begin to make use of me, even if they start me off by rolling stones. If I could not win their favor with this work, then I should have myself to blame; and in this work, if it were read, they would see that I have been at the study of statecraft for fifteen years and have not slept nor played about; and each one of them should be happy to obtain the services of one who is full of experience at another man's expense. And they should not doubt my

---

[7]Machiavelli here refers to his former superior, Piero Soderini, and his brother, Cardinal Francesco Soderini, both of whom had received permission from the Medici Pope, Leo X, to reside in Rome. Machiavelli's visit might have aroused Medici suspicion that he was in league with a Soderini-led republican plot.

[8]One of the ardent Medici supporters and, therefore, a potential enemy of Machiavelli.

[9]Pietro Ardinghelli, a papal secretary at Leo X's court.

loyalty, for always having kept my word, I have not now learned to break it; and anyone who has been faithful and honest for forty-three years, as I have been, cannot change his character; and my poverty is witness to my honesty and goodness.

I should like you, therefore, to write me what you think about this matter, and I commend myself to you. *Sis felix.* December 10, 1513.

Niccolò Machiavelli in Florence

VI

TO FRANCESCO VETTORI IN ROME

Magnificent Ambassador Francesco Vettori,
My friend, you have kept me in good spirits with these accounts of your Roman love affair, and you have lifted from my mind countless problems as I read and think about your pleasures and your fits of anger—one could not be without the other. And truly Fortune has brought me to a place where I can return the favor to you: living in the country, I met a creature so gentle, so delicate, so noble, both in her nature and in her temperament, that I could neither praise her nor love her so much that she would not deserve more. I should, as you did with me, tell about the beginnings of this love, with what snares it took me, where Love set them, of what quality they were: they were nets of gold, spread among flowers, embroidered by Venus, so soft and pleasing that although a crude heart could have broken them, nonetheless, I did not wish to, and for a spell I enjoyed myself in them, so much that the tender threads became hardened and fastened with knots impossible to loosen. And do not think that Love used ordinary measures to capture me, for knowing that they would not suffice, he employed extraordinary means, of which I knew nothing nor did I turn to avoid them. You must realize that as I near fifty years of age, neither does the harsh sun bother me, nor the rough roads tire me, nor

the darkness of the night frighten me. Everything seems simple to me, and to her every whim I adapt myself, no matter how strange and contrary to my nature. And although I seem to have gotten into great difficulty, I feel, nevertheless, such sweetness in it—both because of what that sweet and rare face does to me and also because it has let me put aside the recollection of all my problems—that I do not want to free myself from it for anything in the world, even if I could. I have, therefore, abandoned thoughts of great and serious affairs; neither reading about ancient times nor discussing the present delights me further; everything has changed into sweet conversations, for which I thank Venus and all her Cyprian island. So if it occurs to you to write something about your lady, write it, and as far as other matters are concerned, you can discuss them with those who value them more and understand them better, since I have never had anything but loss from them, whereas in matters of love I have always found pleasure and good. *Valete. Ex Florentia, die* III *Augusti* 1514.

> *Your Niccolò Machiavelli*

The final letter, dated 1521, is addressed to Francesco Guicciardini (1483–1540), Renaissance Italy's foremost historian and Machiavelli's first important critic and interpreter. Since Guicciardini was a key administrator in the papal states and the confidant of the Medici Pope Clement VII, Machiavelli obviously hoped that his friendship might also assist him in regaining the favor of his former adversaries. Although Guicciardini was usually not a man to accept Machiavelli's belief in historical repetition, he noted a poignant parallel between Machiavelli's ill fortune and that of another great man in a letter written in reply to the one reprinted here:

My dear Machiavelli. When I read your titles of orator of the republic to the Minor Friars and I consider with how many kings, dukes, and princes you have negotiated in other times, I recall

Lysander to whom, after so many victories and triumphs, was given the task of passing out rations to those same soldiers he had formerly commanded gloriously. And I say: see how the same events repeat themselves, the faces of the protagonists and the superficial appearances only having changed.

The situation described in Machiavelli's letter shows that even in the midst of adversity he never failed to retain his sense of humor. His scheme to impress the gullible friars with Guicciardini's cooperation while he searched for a Lenten preacher more to his liking was successful and resulted in an immediate improvement in his standing among the churchmen there, as well as a rise in the quality of his bed and board.

VII

TO FRANCESCO GUICCIARDINI IN MODENA

Magnifice vir, maior observandissime:

When your letter arrived, I was sitting on the toilet thinking about the vanities of this world, and I was completely absorbed in constructing a preacher after my own tastes for Florence, one that would suit me perfectly, for in this I want to be as stubborn as in my ideas on other matters. And because I have never failed in my duty to the Republic by not helping her whenever I could—if not with works, at least with words, if not with words, then at least with gestures—I do not intend to fail her in this. It is true that I differ with my fellow citizens in this as well as in other matters, for they want a preacher to show them the way to Paradise, and I want to find one that will show them how to go to the devil; they want a man who is serious and prudent, and I want one who is crazier than Pozzo, smarter than Brother Girolamo, and more hypocritical than Brother Alberto. This would be nice,

¹ Many commentators believe this Brother Alberto to be the unworthy priest of Boccaccio's *Decameron* (IV, 2). But since

something worthy of our time: to see what we have experienced in many priests all in one man—I believe that the true way of going to Paradise is to learn the way to Hell in order to avoid it. Besides this, seeing how much credit is given to a poor wretch who hides himself under the cloak of religion, one can easily imagine how much credit a good man would receive who actually, and not in disguise, trudged the muddy paths of St. Francis. As this train of thought pleases me, I intend to pick Rovaio, and I think that if he is like his brothers and sisters, he will be just the choice. I would appreciate your opinion about it if you write again.

I remain idle here because I cannot carry out my mission until the general and the assessors are elected, and I keep wondering how to cause so much trouble among these friars that they might, here or in other places, beat each other up with their sandals; and if I do not lose my wits I believe that I shall succeed; and I think that your Excellency's advice and help will be of great use to me. And if you were to come here on the pretext of taking a pleasure trip, that would be fine, or, at least, if you could give me in writing a few master strokes—in fact, if you would keep in touch with me on this account by sending me a messenger once a day, as you have done today, you would help me even more: in the first place, you would clarify things and advise me on the scheme; in the second place, you would increase my prestige here, when the friars see the dispatches pouring in. Let me tell you that when your crossbowman arrived with your letter, bowing

---

the other two priests referred to in the passage are identifiable historical figures (Brother Girolamo being Girolamo Savonarola and Pozzo being one of his adversaries), it is also possible that the Brother Alberto here referred to is Alberto da Orvieto, the priest sent to Florence by Pope Alexander VI in 1495. This man had advised the Borgia Pope, Savonarola's most dangerous enemy, to summon Savonarola to Rome under some pretext in order to imprison him when he arrived. Both Boccaccio's literary character and the historical figure would have reflected a perfect example of hypocrisy in a churchman.

to the ground, saying that he was sent especially and in haste, every one of those priests bristled with so much respect and with such an uproar that everything was turned topsy-turvy, and many of them asked me what the news was; and I, to enhance my importance, said that the Emperor was waiting at Trent and that the Swiss had called new diets, and that the King of France wished to parlay personally with that ruler, but that his counselors were advising him against it; and so, all of them stood there with their mouths wide open with hat in hand; and even now while I am writing this to you there is a circle of them around me, watching me write and for so long a time they are amazed and they look at me as if I were possessed; and to amaze them even more, I pause over my pen from time to time and sigh, and they stand there with their mouths wide open—if they knew what I was writing to you, they would really be astonished! Your Lordship knows that when a person, according to these friars, is confirmed in a state of grace, the Devil no longer has the power to tempt him—well, I am not afraid that these friars will turn me into a hypocrite, since I think I am well confirmed.

As for the lies of the people of Carpi, I can match them all, since for a long time now I have been educating myself in that art so that I don't need Francesco Martelli's help; it has been a long time since I have said what I think or have believed what I said, and if I do speak the truth sometimes, I hide it among so many lies that it is difficult to find it again.

I have not spoken to the Governor because, having found lodgings, I felt that speaking to him was useless. This morning in church I stared at him a bit while he was looking at some paintings. I think that he is perfectly made: since the part corresponds to the whole, we can believe that he is what he appears to be—that his deformity does not lie. If I had had your letter with me, I might have drawn a bucketful from it. But nothing has come of it, and I wait for tomorrow to come with advice from you about my affairs. I hope you will send one of those cross-bowmen of yours: make him gallop and arrive here all sweaty so that the people will be astonished; by doing this you will do me honor and will also give your crossbowmen a bit of exercise, which is also very good for horses at this time of the year. I would write you more if I wished to tax my fantasy, but I want to keep it as fresh as I can for tomorrow. I send my regards to Your Lordship, *quae semper ut vult valeat.* In Carpi, May 17, 1521.

Your Niccolo Machiavelli,
Ambassador to the Minor Friars

THE PRINCE

EDITORS' NOTE

This, the most famous and controversial of Machiavelli's works, was first printed in 1532, some seven years after the death of its author, although manuscript copies of the work circulated earlier. There is general agreement among scholars that the origins of The Prince *and* The Discourses *are closely interrelated. It seems, as has been explained in the Introduction, that Machiavelli interrupted the composition of* The Discourses *to turn to this shorter treatise of a more occasional nature between July and December of 1513. Giuliano de' Medici's sudden death on March 17, 1516, led Machiavelli to change his intended dedication from Giuliano to Lorenzo, Duke of Urbino (1492–1519) and grandson of the more illustrious Lorenzo il Magnifico (1449–1492). Some scholars are inclined to view chapter XXV on Fortune as the logical conclusion to the treatise and to interpret chapter XXVI, with its exhortation to free Italy from the barbarians, as a means of linking the conclusion of the work to the second dedication.*

Niccolò Machiavelli to
Lorenzo de' Medici, the Magnificent

In most instances, it is customary for those who desire to win the favor of a Prince to present themselves to him

77

with those things they value most or which they feel will most please him; thus, we often see Princes given horses, arms, vestments of gold cloth, precious stones, and similar ornaments suited to their greatness. Wishing, therefore, to offer myself to Your Magnificence with some evidence of my devotion to you, I have not found among my belongings anything that I might value more or prize so much as the knowledge of the deeds of great men, which I learned from a long experience in modern affairs and a continuous study of antiquity; having with great care and for a long time thought about and examined these deeds, and now having set them down in a little book, I am sending them to Your Magnificence.

And although I consider this work unworthy of your station, I am sure, nevertheless, that your humanity will move you to accept it, for there could not be a greater gift from me than to give you the means to be able, in a very brief time, to understand all that I, in many years and with many hardships and dangers, came to understand and to appreciate. I have neither decorated nor filled this work with fancy sentences, with rich and magnificent words, or with any other form of rhetorical or unnecessary ornamentation which many writers normally use in describing and enriching their subject matter; for I wished that nothing should set my work apart or make it pleasing except the variety of its material and the seriousness of its contents. Neither do I wish that it be thought presumptuous if a man of low and inferior station dares to debate and to regulate the rule of princes; for, just as those who paint landscapes place themselves in a low position on the plain in order to consider the nature of the mountains and the high places and place themselves high atop mountains in order to study the plains, in like manner, to know well the nature of the people one must be a prince, and to know well the nature of princes one must be of the people.

Accept, therefore, Your Magnificence, this little gift in the spirit that I send it; if you read and consider it carefully, you will discover in it my most heartfelt desire that you may attain that greatness which Fortune and all your own capacities promise you. And if Your Magnificence will turn your eyes at some time from the summit of your high position toward these lowlands, you will realize to what degree I unjustly suffer a great and continuous malevolence of Fortune.

CHAPTER I. HOW MANY KINDS OF PRINCIPALITIES THERE ARE AND THE WAY THEY ARE ACQUIRED

All states and all dominions that have had and continue to have power over men were and still are either republics or principalities. And principalities are either hereditary, in which instance the family of the prince has ruled for generations, or they are new. And the new ones are either completely new, as was Milan for Francesco Sforza, or they are like members added to the hereditary state of the prince who acquires them, as is the Kingdom of Naples for the King of Spain. Dominions taken in this way are either used to living under a prince or are accustomed to being free; and they are gained either by the arms of others or by one's own, either through Fortune or through cleverness.

CHAPTER II. ON HEREDITARY PRINCIPALITIES

I shall set aside any discussion of republics, because I treated them elsewhere at length. I shall consider solely the principality, developing as I go the topics mentioned above; and I shall discuss how these principalities can be governed and maintained.

I say, then, that in hereditary states accustomed to the rule of their prince's family there are far fewer difficulties in maintaining them than in new states; for it suffices simply not to break ancient customs, and then to suit one's actions to unexpected events; in this manner, if such a prince is of ordinary ability, he will always maintain his state, unless some extraordinary and inordinate force deprive him of it; and although it may be taken away from him, he will regain it with the slightest mistake of the usurper.

As an example, we have in Italy the Duke of Ferrara, who withstood the assaults of the Venetians in 1484 and those of Pope Julius in 1510 for no other reason than the tradition of his rule in that dominion. Because a prince by birth has fewer reasons and less need to offend his subjects, it is natural that he should be more loved; and if no unusual vices make him hated, it is reasonable that he be naturally well liked by them. And in the course and continuity of his rule, memories and the causes for innovations die out, because one change always leaves space for the construction of another.

CHAPTER III.   ON MIXED PRINCIPALITIES

But it is the new principality that causes difficulties. In the first place, if it is not completely new but is instead an acquisition (so that the two parts together may be called mixed), its difficulties derive from one natural problem inherent in all new principalities: men gladly change their masters, thinking to better themselves; and this belief causes them to take arms against their ruler; but they fool themselves in this, since with experience they see that things have become worse. This stems from another natural and ordinary necessity, which is that a new prince must always offend his new subjects with both his soldiers and other countless injuries that accompany his new conquest; thus, you have made enemies of all those you injured in occupying the principality and you are unable to maintain as friends those who helped you to rise to power, since you cannot satisfy them in the way that they had supposed, nor can you use strong measures against them, for you are in their debt; because, although one may have the most powerful of armies, he always needs the support of the inhabitants to seize a province. For these reasons, Louis XII, King of France, quickly occupied Milan and just as quickly lost it; and the first time, the troops of Ludovico alone were needed to retake it from him, because those citizens who had opened the gates of the city to the king, finding themselves deceived in their opinions and in that future improvement they had anticipated, could not support the offenses of the new prince.

It is indeed true that when lands which have rebelled once are taken a second time, it is more difficult to lose them; for the lord, taking advantage of the revolt, is less reticent about punishing offenders, ferreting out suspects, and shoring up weak positions. So that, if only a Duke Ludovico threatening the borders was sufficient for France to lose Milan the first time, the whole world had to oppose her and destroy her armies or chase them from Italy to cause her to lose it the second time; and this happened for the reasons mentioned above. Nevertheless, it was taken from her both the first and the second time.

The general explanations for the first loss have been discussed; now there remains to specify those for the second, and to see what remedies the King of France had, and those that one in the same situation might have, so that he might be able to maintain a stronger grip on his conquest than did France. Therefore, I say that those dominions which, upon being conquered, are added to the long-established state of him who acquires them are either of the same province and language or they are not. When they are, it is easier to hold them, especially when they are unaccustomed to freedom; and to possess them securely, it is only necessary to have extinguished the family line of the prince who ruled them, because insofar as other things are concerned, men live peacefully as long as their old way of life is maintained and there is no change in customs: thus, we have seen what happened in the case of Burgundy, Brittany, Gascony, and Normandy, which have been part of France for such a long time; and although there is a slight difference in the language, nevertheless the customs are similar and they have been able to get along together easily. And anyone who acquires

these lands and wishes to maintain them must bear two
things in mind: first, that the family line of the old prince
must be extinguished; second, that neither their laws nor
their taxes be altered; as a result they will become in a
very brief time one body with the old principality.

But when dominions are acquired in a province that is
not similar in language, customs, and laws, it is here that
difficulties arise; and it is here that one needs much good
fortune and much diligence to hold on to them. And one
of the best and most efficacious remedies would be for the
person who has taken possession of them to go and live
there. This would make that possession more secure and
durable, as the Turks did with Greece; for with all the
other precautions they took to retain that dominion, if
they had not gone there to live, it would have been impossible for them to hold on to it. Because, by being on
the spot, one sees trouble at its birth and one can quickly
remedy it; not being there, one hears about it after it has
grown and there is no longer any remedy. Moreover, the
province would not be plundered by one's own officers;
the subjects would be pleased in having direct recourse to
their prince; thus, wishing to be good subjects, they have
more reason to love him and, wanting to be otherwise,
more reason to fear him. Anyone who might wish to invade that dominion from abroad would be more hesitant;
so that, living right there, the prince can only with the
greatest of difficulties lose it.

The other and better solution is to send colonies into
one or two places that will act as supports for your own
state; for it is necessary that either the prince do this or
maintain a large number of infantry and cavalry. Colonies do not cost much, and with little or no expense a
prince can send and maintain them; and in so doing he
offends only those whose fields and houses have been
taken and given to the new inhabitants, who are only a
small part of that state; and those that he offends, being
dispersed and poor, cannot ever threaten him, and all the
others remain on the one hand unharmed (and because of

this, they should remain silent), and on the other afraid of making a mistake, for fear that what happened to those who were dispossessed might happen to them. I conclude that these colonies are not expensive, they are more faithful, and they create fewer difficulties; and those who are hurt cannot pose a threat, since they are poor and scattered, as I have already said. Concerning this, it should be noted that one must either pamper or do away with men, because they will avenge themselves for minor offenses while for more serious ones they cannot; so that any harm done to a man must be the kind that removes any fear of revenge. But by maintaining soldiers there instead of colonies, one spends much more, being obliged to consume all the revenues of the state in guarding its borders, so that the profit becomes a loss; and far greater offense is committed, since the entire state is harmed by the army changing quarters from one place to another; everybody resents this inconvenience, and everyone becomes an enemy; and these are enemies that can be harmful, since they remain, although conquered, in their own homes. And so, in every respect, this kind of defense is as useless as the other kind, colonization, is useful.

Moreover, anyone who is in a province that is unlike his own in the ways mentioned above should make himself the leader and defender of the less powerful neighbors and do all he can to weaken those who are more powerful, and he should be careful that, for whatever reason, no foreigner equal to himself in strength enter there. And it will always happen that the outsider will be brought in by those who are dissatisfied, either because of too much ambition or because of fear, as was once seen when the Aetolians brought the Romans into Greece; and in every other province that the Romans entered, they were brought in by the inhabitants. What occurs is that as soon as a powerful foreigner enters a province, all who are less powerful cling to him, moved by the envy they have for the one who has ruled over them; so that, concerning these weaker powers, he has no trouble whatsoever in winning them over, since all of them will immediately and willingly become part of the state that he has acquired. He has only to be on his guard that they do not seize too much power and authority; and he can, very easily, with his force and their support, put down those who are powerful in order to remain, in everything, arbiter of that province. And anyone who does not follow this procedure will quickly lose what he has taken, and while he holds it, he will find it full of infinite difficulties and worries.

In the provinces that they seized, the Romans observed these procedures very carefully; they sent colonies, kept the less powerful at bay without increasing their strength, put down the powerful, and did not allow powerful foreigners to gain prestige there. And I shall cite only the province of Greece as an example: the Romans kept the Achaeans and the Aetolians in check; the Macedonian kingdom was put down; Antiochus was driven out; nor were they ever persuaded by the merits of the Achaeans or the Aetolians to allow them any gain of territory; nor did the persuasion of Philip of Macedonia ever convince them to make him their friend without first humbling him; nor could the power of Antiochus force their consent to his having any authority whatsoever in that province. For the Romans did in these instances what all wise princes should do: these princes have not only to watch out for present problems but also for those in the future, and try diligently to avoid them; for once problems are recognized ahead of time, they can be easily cured; but if you wait for them to present themselves, the medicine will be too late, for the disease will have become incurable. And what physicians say about disease is applicable here: that at the beginning a disease is easy to cure but difficult to diagnose; but as time passes, not having been recognized or treated at the outset, it becomes easy to diagnose but difficult to cure. The same thing occurs in affairs of state; for by recognizing from afar the diseases that are spreading in the state (which is a gift given only to the prudent ruler), they can be cured quickly; but when, not having been recognized, they are left to grow to the extent that everyone recognizes them, there is no longer any cure.

Thus, seeing from afar any difficulties, the Romans always found a remedy; and they never let them develop in order to avoid a war, because they knew that war cannot be avoided but can only be put off to the advantage of others; therefore, they wanted to go to war with Philip and Antiochus in Greece in order not to have to combat them in Italy; and they could have, at the time, avoided the one and the other, but they did not want to. Nor did they ever like what is always on the tongues of our wise men today, to enjoy the benefits of time, but they enjoyed instead the benefits of their strength and prudence; for time brings with it all things, and it can bring with it the good as well as the bad and the bad as well as the good.

But let us return to France and determine if she did any of the things we have just mentioned; and I shall speak of Louis and not of Charles, and therefore about the one whose progress has been observed better because he held territory in Italy for a longer period; and you will see that he did the contrary of those things that must be done in order to hold one's rule in a foreign province.

King Louis was installed in Italy because of the ambition of the Venetians, who wanted by his coming to gain for themselves half of Lombardy. I will not criticize the enterprise the King undertook; for, wishing to establish a first foothold in Italy and not having any friends in this land and, furthermore, having all the gates closed to him because of the actions of King Charles, he was forced to strike up whatever friendships he could; and this worthy undertaking would have succeeded if he had not erred in his other moves. After having taken Lombardy, then, the King immediately regained the prestige that Charles had lost him: Genoa surrendered; the Florentines became his allies; the Marquis of Mantua, the Duke of Ferrara, the Bentivogli, the Countess of Forlì, the lords of Faenza,

Pesaro, Rimini, Camerino, and Piombino, and the people of Lucca, Pisa, and Siena all rushed to gain his friendship. And at that point the Venetians could see the recklessness of the enterprise they had undertaken; in order to acquire a bit of Lombardy, they had made the King the master of a third of Italy.

Consider, now, with what little trouble the King might have maintained his reputation in Italy if he had followed the rules listed above and kept secure and defended all those friends of his who, there being a goodly number of them, both weak and fearful, some of the Church, others of the Venetians, were always forced to be his allies; and through them he could have easily secured himself against the remaining great powers. But no sooner was he in Milan than he did the contrary, giving assistance to Pope Alexander so that he could seize Romagna. Nor did he realize that with this decision he had made himself weaker, abandoning his allies and those who had thrown themselves into his lap, and made the Church stronger by adding to it so much temporal power in addition to the spiritual power from which it derives so much authority. And having made one first mistake, he was obliged to make others; so that in order to put an end to the ambition of Alexander and to keep him from becoming lord of Tuscany, he was forced to come to Italy. He was not satisfied to have made the Church powerful and to have lost his allies, for, coveting the Kingdom of Naples, he divided it with the King of Spain; and where he first had been the arbiter of Italy, he brought in a partner so that the ambitious and the malcontents of that province had someone else to turn to; and where he could have left a figurehead king to rule that kingdom, he replaced him, establishing one there who could, in turn, drive Louis out.

The desire to acquire is truly a very natural and normal thing; and when men who can do so, they will always be praised and not condemned; but when they cannot and wish to do so at any cost, herein lies the error and the blame. If France, therefore, could have assaulted Naples with her own troops, she should have done so; if she could not, she should not have shared it. And if the division of Lombardy with the Venetians deserves to be overlooked, since it allowed Louis to gain a foothold in Italy, the other division deserves to be criticized, since it cannot be excused by necessity.

Thus, Louis had made these five mistakes: he had destroyed the weaker powers; he increased the power of another force in Italy; he had brought into that province a powerful foreigner; he did not come there to live; and he did not send colonies there. In spite of this, these mistakes, had he lived, might not have damaged him if he had not made a sixth: that of reducing the Venetians' power; for if he had not made the Church stronger, nor brought Spain into Italy, it would have been most reasonable and necessary to put them down; but, having taken those first initiatives, he should never have agreed to their ruin; for as long as they were powerful they would have always kept the others from trying to seize Lombardy, partly because the Venetians would not have allowed this unless they themselves became the rulers of Lombardy, and partly because the others would not have wanted to take it away from France to give it to the Venetians; and they would not have had the nerve to provoke both of them. And if someone were to say: King Louis relinquished Romagna to Alexander and the Kingdom of Naples to Spain in order to avoid a war, I would reply with the arguments given above: that one should never allow chaos to develop in order to avoid going to war, because one does not avoid a war but instead puts it off to his disadvantage. And if some others were to note the promise that the King had made the Pope to undertake that enterprise in return for the annulment of his marriage and for the Cardinal's hat of Rouen, I should answer with what I shall say further on about the promises of princes and how they should be observed.

King Louis lost Lombardy, therefore, by not following any of the principles observed by others who had taken provinces and who wished to retain them. Nor is this in any sense a miracle, but very ordinary and reasonable. And I spoke about this at Nantes with the Cardinal of Rouen when Valentino (for this was what Cesare Borgia, son of Pope Alexander, was commonly called) occupied Romagna; for when the Cardinal of Rouen told me that Italians understood little about war, I replied to him that the French understood little about politics; for if they did understand, they would not permit the Church to gain so much power. And we have learned through experience that the power of the Church and of Spain in Italy has been caused by France, and that her downfall has been brought about by them. From this one can derive a general rule which rarely, if ever, fails: that anyone who is the cause of another's becoming powerful comes to ruin himself, because that power is the result either of diligence or of force, and both of these two qualities are suspect to the one who has become powerful.

CHAPTER IV. WHY THE KINGDOM OF DARIUS, OCCUPIED BY ALEXANDER, DID NOT REBEL AGAINST HIS SUCCESSORS AFTER THE DEATH OF ALEXANDER

Considering the difficulties one has in maintaining a newly acquired state, one might wonder how it happened that when Alexander the Great, having become lord of Asia in a few years and having hardly occupied it, died—wherefore it would have seemed reasonable for the whole state to revolt—Alexander's successors nevertheless managed to hold on to it; and they had, in keeping it, no other difficulty than that which was born among themselves from their own ambition. Let me reply that all principalities known to us are governed in one of two different ways: either by one prince with the others as his servants, who, as ministers, through his grace and permission, assist in governing that kingdom; or by a prince and barons who hold that position not because of any grace of their master but because of the nobility of their birth. Such barons as these have their own dominions and subjects who recognize them as masters and are naturally fond of them. Those dominions governed by a prince and his ministers hold their prince in greater authority, for in all his province there is no one that may be recognized as superior to him; and if they do obey any other, they do so as his minister and officer, and they do not harbor any special affection for him.

Examples of these two different kinds of governments in our own times are the Turkish Emperor and the King of France. The entire kingdom of the Turk is ruled by one master; the others are his servants; and dividing his kingdom into parts, he sends various administrators there, and he moves them and changes them as he pleases. But the King of France is placed among a group of established nobles who are recognized in that state by their subjects and who are loved by them; they have their hereditary rights; the King cannot remove them without danger to himself. Anyone, therefore, who considers these two states will find that the difficulty lies in taking possession of the Turkish state, but once it has been conquered, it is very simple to retain it. And therefore, on the contrary, you will find that in some ways it is easier to seize the French state, but it is extremely difficult to hold on to it.

The reasons for the difficulty in being able to occupy the Turkish kingdom are that it is not possible to be summoned there by the prince of that kingdom, nor to hope to make your enterprise easier with the rebellion of those the ruler has around him. This is because of the reasons mentioned above: since they are all slaves and dependent on the ruler, it is more difficult to corrupt them; and even if they were corrupted, you cannot hope that they will be very useful, not being able to attract followers for the reasons already discussed. Therefore, anyone who attacks the Turks must consider that he will find them completely united, and it is best that he rely more on his own strength than on their lack of unity. But once beaten and broken in battle so that they cannot regroup their troops, there is nothing else to be feared but the family of the prince; once it is extinguished, there remains no one else to be feared, for the others have no credit with the people; and just as the victor before the victory could not place hope in them, so he need not fear them afterward.

The opposite occurs in kingdoms governed like that of France, because you can enter them with ease once you have won to your side some baron of the kingdom; for you always find malcontents and those who desire changes; these people, for the reasons already given, can open the way to that state and facilitate your victory. Then, wishing to hold on to it is accompanied by endless problems, problems with those that have aided you and with those you have suppressed; nor does it suffice to do away with the family of the prince, because the lords who make themselves heads of new factions still remain; and you lose that state at the first occasion, for you are neither able to make them happy nor are you able to do away with them.

Now, if you will consider the type of government Darius established, you will find it similar to the kingdom of the Turks; and therefore Alexander first had to overwhelm it totally and defeat it in battle; after this victory, Darius being dead, that state remained securely in Alexander's hands for the reasons discussed above. And his successors would have enjoyed it without effort had they been united; for in that kingdom no disorders arose other than those they themselves had caused. But in states organized like that of France, it is impossible to hold them with such ease. Because of this, there arose the frequent revolts of Spain, France, and Greece against the Romans, all because of the numerous principalities that were in those states; as long as the memory of them lasted, the Romans were always unsure of their power; but once that memory had been extinguished, they became completely theirs. Afterward, when the Romans fought among themselves, each one was able to draw a following from those provinces, according to the authority he enjoyed there;

and since the families of their former rulers had been extinguished, they recognized only the Romans. Taking all these things into account, therefore, no one at all should marvel at the ease with which Alexander retained the state of Asia, or at the problems that others suffered in preserving their acquisition, such as Pyrrhus and others. This is not caused by the greater or lesser skill of the victor but rather by the difference of the situations.

CHAPTER V.   HOW CITIES OR PRINCIPALITIES SHOULD BE
GOVERNED THAT LIVED BY THEIR OWN LAWS BEFORE THEY
WERE OCCUPIED

As I have said, when those states that are acquired are used to living by their own laws and in freedom, there are three methods of holding on to them: the first is to destroy them; the second is to go there in person to live; the third is to allow them to live with their own laws, forcing them to pay a tribute and creating therein a government made up of a few people who will keep the state friendly toward you. For such a government, having been created by that prince, knows that it cannot last without his friendship and his power, and it must do everything possible to maintain them; and a city used to living in freedom is more easily maintained through the means of its own citizens than in any other way, if you decide to preserve it.

As examples, there are the Spartans and the Romans. The Spartans held Athens and Thebes by building therein a government consisting of a few people; eventually they lost them both. The Romans, in order to hold Capua, Carthage, and Numantia, destroyed them and did not lose them; they wished to hold Greece by almost the same manner as the Spartans held it, making it free and leaving it under its own laws, and they did not succeed; thus, they were obliged to destroy many of the cities in that province in order to retain it. For, in truth, there is no secure means of holding on to them except by destroying them. And anyone who becomes lord of a city used to living in liberty and does not destroy it may expect to be destroyed by it; because such a city always has as a refuge, in any rebellion, the name of liberty and its ancient institutions, neither of which are ever forgotten either because of the passing of time or because of the bestowal of benefits. And it matters little what one does or foresees, since if one does not separate or scatter the inhabitants, they will not forget that name or those institutions; and immediately, in every case, they will return to them just as Pisa did after one hundred years of being held in servitude by the Florentines. But when cities or provinces are accustomed to living under a prince and the family of that prince has been extinguished, they, being on the one hand used to obedience and, on the other, not having their old prince and not being able to agree on choosing another from amongst themselves, yet not knowing how to live as free men, are as a result hesitant in taking up arms, and a prince can win them over and assure himself of their support with greater ease. But in republics there is greater vitality, greater hatred, greater desire for revenge; the memory of ancient liberty does not and cannot allow them to rest, so that the most secure way is either to destroy them or to go there to live.

CHAPTER VI.   ON NEW PRINCIPALITIES ACQUIRED BY ONE'S OWN ARMS AND BY SKILL

No one should marvel if, in speaking of principalities that are totally new as to their prince and organization, I use the most illustrious examples; since men almost always tread the paths made by others and proceed in their affairs by imitation, although they are not completely able to stay on the path of others nor reach the skill of those they imitate, a prudent man should always enter those paths taken by great men and imitate those who have been most excellent, so that if one's own skill does not match theirs, at least it will have the smell of it; and he should proceed like those prudent archers who, aware of the strength of their bow when the target they are aiming at seems too distant, set their sights, much higher than the designated target, not in order to reach to such a height with their arrow but rather to be able, with the aid of such a high aim, to strike their target.

I say, therefore, that in completely new principalities, where there is a new prince, one finds in maintaining them more or less difficulty according to the greater or lesser skill of the one who acquires them. And because this act of transition from private citizen to prince presupposes either ingenuity or Fortune, it appears that either the one or the other of these two things should, in part, mitigate many of the problems; nevertheless, he who has relied upon Fortune less has maintained his position best. Things are also facilitated when the prince, having no other dominions to govern, is constrained to come to live there in person. But to come to those who, by means of their own skill and not because of Fortune, have become princes, I say that the most admirable are Moses, Cyrus, Romulus, Theseus, and the like. And although we should not discuss Moses, since he was a mere executor of things ordered by God, nevertheless he must be admired, if for nothing but that grace which made him worthy of talking with God. But let us consider Cyrus and the others who have acquired or founded kingdoms; you will find them all admirable; and if their deeds and their particular institutions are considered, they will not appear different from those of Moses, who had so great a guide. And examining their deeds and their lives, one can see that they received nothing but the opportunity from Fortune, which then gave them the material they could mold into whatever form they desired; and without that opportunity the strength of their spirit would have been extinguished, and without that strength the opportunity would have come in vain.

It was therefore necessary for Moses to find the people of Israel slaves in Egypt and oppressed by the Egyptians in order that they might be disposed to follow him to escape this servitude. It was necessary for Romulus not to stay in Alba and to be exposed at birth so that he might become King of Rome and founder of that nation. It was necessary for Cyrus to find the Persians discontented with the empire of the Medes and the Medes soft and effeminate after a lengthy peace. Theseus could not have shown his skill if he had not found the Athenians scattered. These opportunities, therefore, made these men successful, and their outstanding ingenuity made that opportunity known to them, whereby their nations were ennobled and became prosperous.

Like these men, those who become princes through their skill acquire the principality with difficulty, but they hold on to it easily; and the difficulties they encounter in acquiring the principality grow, in part, out of the new institutions and methods they are obliged to introduce in order to found their state and their security. And one should bear in mind that there is nothing more difficult to execute, nor more dubious of success, nor more dangerous to administer than to introduce a new system of things: for he who introduces it has all those who profit from the old system as his enemies, and he has only lukewarm allies in all those who might profit from the new system. This lukewarmness partly stems from fear of their adversaries, who have the law on their side, and partly from the skepticism of men who do not truly believe in new things unless they have actually had personal experience of them. Therefore, it happens that whenever those who are enemies have the chance to attack, they do so in a partisan manner, and those others defend hesitantly, so that they, together with the prince, are in danger.

It is necessary, however, if we desire to examine this subject thoroughly, to note whether these innovators act on their own or are dependent on others: that is, if they are forced to beg or are able to use power in conducting their affairs. In the first case, they always end up badly and never accomplish anything; but when they lean on their own resources and can use power, then only seldom do they find themselves in peril. From this comes the fact that all armed prophets were victorious and the unarmed came to ruin. Besides what has been said, people are fickle by nature; and it is simple to convince them of something but difficult to hold them in that conviction; and, therefore, affairs should be managed in such a way that when they no longer believe, they can be made to believe by force. Moses, Cyrus, Theseus, and Romulus could not have made their institutions long respected if they had been unarmed; as in our times it befell Brother Girolamo Savonarola, who was ruined by his new institutions when the populace began no longer to believe in them; and he had no way of holding steady those who had believed nor of making the disbelievers believe. Therefore, such men have great problems in getting ahead, and they meet all their dangers as they proceed, and they must overcome them with their skill; but once they have overcome them and have begun to be respected, having removed those who were envious of their merits, they remain powerful, secure, honored, and happy.

To such noble examples I should like to add a minor one; but it will have some relation to the others, and I should like it to suffice for all similar cases: and this is Hiero of Syracuse. From a private citizen, this man became the prince of Syracuse; he did not receive anything from Fortune except the opportunity, for since the citizens of Syracuse were oppressed, they elected him as their leader; and from that he earned the right to be their prince. And he was so skillful that while still a private citizen someone who wrote about him said "that he lacked nothing save a kingdom to reign." He abolished the old militia and established a new one; he left behind old friendships and made new ones; and since he had allies and soldiers that depended on him, he was able to construct whatever building he wished on such a foundation; so that this required of him great effort to acquire but little to maintain.

CHAPTER VII.   ON NEW PRINCIPALITIES ACQUIRED WITH
THE ARMS AND FORTUNES OF OTHERS

Those private citizens who become princes through
Fortune alone do so with little effort, but they maintain
their position only with a great deal; they meet no obstacles along their way since they fly to success, but all their
problems arise when they have arrived. And these are the
men who are granted a state either because they have
money or because they enjoy the favor of him who grants
it: this occurred to many in Greece in the cities of Ionia
and the Hellespont, where Darius created princes in order
that he might hold these cities for his security and glory;
in like manner were set up those emperors who from private citizens came to power by bribing the soldiers. Such
men depend solely upon two very uncertain and unstable
things: the will and the fortune of him who granted them
the state; they do not know how and are not able to maintain their position. They do not know how, since if men
are not of great intelligence and ingenuity, it is not reasonable that they know how to rule, having always lived
as private citizens; they are not able to, since they do not
have forces that are friendly and faithful. Besides, states
that rise quickly, just as all the other things of nature that
are born and grow rapidly, cannot have roots and ramifi-
cations; the first bad weather kills them, unless these men
who have suddenly become princes, as I have noted, are
of such ability that they know how to prepare themselves
quickly and to preserve what Fortune has put in their
laps, and to construct afterward those foundations that
others have built before becoming princes.

Regarding the two methods just listed for becoming a
prince, by skill or by Fortune, I should like to offer two
examples from our own day: these are Francesco Sforza
and Cesare Borgia. Francesco, through the required
means and with a great deal of ingenuity, became Duke
of Milan from his station as a private citizen, and that
which he had acquired with a thousand efforts he main-

tained with little trouble. On the other hand, Cesare Borgia (commonly called Duke Valentino) acquired the state because of his father's fortune and lost it in the same manner, and this despite the fact that he did everything and used every means that a prudent and skillful man ought to use in order to root himself securely in those states that the arms and fortune of others had granted him. Because, as stated above, anyone who does not lay his foundations beforehand could do so later only with great skill, although this would be done with inconvenience to the architect and danger to the building. If, therefore, we consider all the steps taken by the Duke, we shall see that he laid sturdy foundations for his future power; and I do not judge it useless to discuss them, for I would not know of any better precepts to give to a new prince than the example of his deeds; and if he did not succeed in his plans, it was not his fault but was instead the result of an extraordinary and extreme instance of ill fortune.

Alexander VI, in his attempts to advance his son, the Duke, had many problems, both present and future. First, he saw no means of making him master of any state that did not already belong to the Church; and if he attempted to seize anything belonging to the Church, he knew that the Venetians and the Duke of Milan would not agree to it because Faenza and Rimini were already under the protection of the Venetians. Moreover, he saw that the troops of Italy, and especially those he would have to use, were in the hands of those who had reason to fear the Pope's power; and he could not count on them, since they were all Orsini, Colonnesi, and their allies. Therefore, he had to disturb the order of things and cause turmoil among these states in order securely to make himself master of a part of them. This was easy for him to do, for he found that the Venetians, moved by other motives, had decided to bring the French back into Italy; not only did he not oppose this, but he rendered it easier by annulling King Louis' first marriage. The King, therefore, entered

Italy with the aid of the Venetians and the consent of
Alexander; and no sooner was he in Milan than the Pope
procured troops from him for the Romagna campaign;
these were granted to him because of the reputation of the
King.

Having seized, then, Romagna and having beaten the
Colonna, the Duke, wishing to maintain his gain and to
advance further, was held back by two things: first, his
troops' lack of loyalty; second, the will of France; that is,
the troops of the Orsini, which he had been using, might
let him down and not only keep him from acquiring more
territory but even take away what he had already conquered; and the King, as well, might do the same. He had
one experience like this with the Orsini soldiers, when,
after the seizure of Faenza, he attacked Bologna and saw
them go reluctantly into battle; as for the King, he learned
his purpose when he invaded Tuscany after the capture of
the Duchy of Urbino; the King forced him to abandon
that campaign. As a consequence, the Duke decided to
depend no longer upon the arms and fortune of others.
And his first step was to weaken the Orsini and Colonna
factions in Rome; he won over all their followers who
were noblemen, making them his own noblemen and giving them huge subsidies; and he honored them, according
to their rank, with military commands and civil appointments; as a result, in a few months their affection for the
factions died out in their hearts and all of it was turned toward the Duke. After this, he waited for the opportunity
to do away with the Orsini leaders, having already scattered those of the Colonna family; and good opportunity
arose and the use he put it to was even better; for when
the Orsini later realized that the greatness of the Duke
and of the Church meant their ruin, they called together a
meeting at Magione, in Perugian territory. From this resulted the rebellion of Urbino and the uprisings in Romagna, and endless dangers for the Duke, all of which he
overcame with the aid of the French. And when his reputation had been regained, placing no trust either in

France or other outside forces, in order not to have to test
them, he turned to deceptive methods. And he knew how
to falsify his intentions so well that the Orsini themselves,
through Lord Paulo, made peace with him; the Duke did
not fail to use all kinds of gracious acts to reassure Paulo,
giving him money, clothing, and horses, so that the stupidity of the Orsini brought them to Sinigaglia and into
his hands. Having removed these leaders and having
changed their allies into his friends, the Duke had laid
very good foundations for his power, having all of Romagna along with the Duchy of Urbino, and, more important, it appeared that he had befriended Romagna and
had won the support of all of its populace once the people
began to taste the beneficial results of his rule.

And because this matter is notable and worthy of imitation by others, I shall not pass it over. After the Duke
had taken Romagna and had found it governed by powerless lords who had been more anxious to plunder their
subjects than to govern them and had given them reason
for disunity rather than unity, so that the entire province
was full of thefts, fights, and of every other kind of insolence, he decided that if he wanted to make it peaceful
and obedient to the ruler's law it would be necessary to
give it good government. Therefore, he put Messer Remirro de Orco, a cruel and able man, in command there
and gave him complete authority. This man, in little time,
made the province peaceful and united, and in doing this
he made for himself a great reputation. Afterward, the
Duke decided that such excessive authority was no longer
required, for he was afraid that it might become despised;
and he set up in the middle of the province a civil court
with a very distinguished president, wherein each city had
its own counselor. And because he realized that the rigor-
ous measures of the past had generated a certain amount
of hatred, he wanted to show, in order to purge men's
minds and to win them to his side completely, that if any
form of cruelty had arisen, it did not originate from him
but from the harsh nature of his minister. And having

come upon the opportunity to do this, one morning at Cesena he had Messer Remirro placed on the piazza in two pieces with a block of wood and a bloody sword beside him. The ferocity of such a spectacle left those people satisfied and amazed at the same time.

But let us return to where we digressed. I say that the Duke, finding himself very powerful and partially secured from present dangers, having armed himself the way he wanted to, and having in large measure destroyed those nearby forces that might have harmed him, still had to take into account the King of France if he wished to continue his conquests, for he realized that the King, who had become aware of his error too late, would not support further conquest. And because of this, he began to seek out new allies and to temporize with France during the campaign the French undertook in the Kingdom of Naples against the Spaniards who were besieging Gaeta. His intent was to make himself secure against them; and he would have quickly succeeded in this if Alexander had lived.

And these were his methods concerning present things. But as for future events, he had first to fear that a new successor in control of the Church might not be his friend and might try to take away from him what Alexander had given him. Against this possibility he thought to secure himself in four ways: first, by putting to death all the relatives of those lords that he had dispossessed in order to prevent the Pope from employing that opportunity; second, by gaining the friendship of all the noblemen of Rome, as already mentioned, in order to hold the Pope in check by means of them; third, by making the College of Cardinals as much his own as he could; fourth, by acquiring such a large territory before the Pope died that he would be able to resist an initial attack without need of allies. Of these four things, he had achieved three by the time of Alexander's death; the fourth he had almost achieved, for he killed as many of the dispossessed noblemen as he could seize, and very few saved themselves; and he had won over the Roman noblemen; and he had a great following in the College of Cardinals; and as for the acquisition of new territory, he had planned to become lord of Tuscany and was already in possession of Perugia and Piombino and had taken Pisa under his protection. And as soon as he no longer needed to respect the wishes of France (for he no longer had to, since the French had already been deprived of the kingdom by the Spaniards, so that it was necessary for both of them to purchase his friendship), he would attack Pisa. After this, Lucca and Siena would have immediately surrendered, partly to spite the Florentines and partly out of fear, and the Florentines would have had no means of preventing it. If he had carried out these designs (and he would have brought them to fruition during the same year that Alexander died), he would have gathered together so many forces and such a reputation that he would have been able to stand alone and would no longer have had to rely upon the fortune and forces of others, but rather on his own power and ingenuity. But Alexander died five years after he had drawn his sword. He left his son, gravely ill, with only the state of Romagna secured and with all the others up in the air, between two very powerful enemy armies. And there was in the Duke so much ferocity and so much ability, and so well did he understand how men can be won or lost, and so firm were the foundations that he had laid in such a short time, that if he had not had those armies upon him or if he had been healthy, he would have overcome every difficulty. And that his foundations were good is witnessed by the fact that Romagna waited more than a month for him; in Rome, still half alive, he was safe; and although the Baglioni, the Vitelli, and the Orsini came to Rome, they found none of their allies opposed to him; if he could not set up a Pope he wanted, at least he could act to ensure that it would not be a man he did not want. But if he had been healthy at the time of Alexander's demise, everything would have been simple. And he himself said to me, on the day when Julius II was

crowned Pope, that he had thought of what might happen
on his father's death, and he had found a remedy for
everything, except he never dreamed that at the time of
his father's death he too would be at death's door.

. Now, having summarized all of the Duke's actions, I
would not know how to censure him; on the contrary, I
believe I am correct in proposing that he be imitated by
all those who have risen to power through Fortune and
with the arms of others. Because he, possessing great
courage and noble intentions, could not have conducted
himself in any other manner; and his plans were frus-
trated solely by the brevity of Alexander's life and by his
own illness. Anyone, therefore, who determines it necessary in his newly acquired principality to protect himself
from his enemies, to win friends, to conquer either by
force or by fraud, to make himself loved and feared by the
people, to be followed and respected by his soldiers, to
put to death those who can or should do him harm, to replace ancient institutions with new ones, to be severe and
gracious, magnanimous and generous, to do away with
unfaithful soldiers and to select new ones, to maintain the
friendship of kings and of princes in such a way that they
must assist you gladly or offend you with caution—that
person cannot find more recent examples than this man's
deeds. One can only censure him for making Julius Pope;
in this he made a bad choice, since, as I said before, not
being able to elect a Pope of his own, he could have kept
anyone he wished from the papacy; and he should have
never agreed to raising to the papacy any cardinal he
might have offended or who, upon becoming Pope, might
have cause to fear him. For men do harm either out of
fear or hatred. Those he had injured were, among others,
San Pietro ad Vincula, Colonna, San Giorgio, Ascanio;
any of the others, upon becoming Pope, would have to
fear him, except for Rouen and the Spaniards: the latter
because they were related to him and were in his debt, the
former because of his power, since he was joined to the
kingdom of France. Therefore, the Duke, above all else,

should have made a Spaniard Pope; failing in that, he should have agreed to the election of Rouen and not to that of San Pietro ad Vincula. And anyone who believes that new benefits make men of high station forget old injuries is deceiving himself. The Duke, then, erred in this election, and it was the cause of his ultimate downfall.

CHAPTER VIII. ON THOSE WHO HAVE BECOME PRINCES THROUGH WICKEDNESS

But because there are yet two more ways one can from an ordinary citizen become prince, which cannot completely be attributed to either Fortune or skill, I believe they should not be left unmentioned, although one of them will be discussed at greater length in a treatise on republics. These two are: when one becomes prince through some wicked and nefarious means or when a private citizen becomes prince of his native city through the favor of his fellow citizens. And in discussing the first way, I shall cite two examples, one from classical times and the other from recent days, without otherwise entering into the merits of this method, since I consider them sufficient for anyone forced to imitate them.

Agathocles the Sicilian, not only from being an ordinary citizen but from being of low and abject status, became King of Syracuse. This man, a potter's son, lived a wicked life at every stage of his career; yet he joined to his wickedness such strength of mind and of body that, when he entered upon a military career, he rose through the ranks to become commander of Syracuse. Once placed in such a position, having considered becoming prince and holding with violence and without any obligations to others what had been granted to him by universal consent, and having made an agreement with Hamilcar the Carthaginian, who was waging war with his armies in Sicily, he called together one morning the people and the senate of Syracuse as if he were going to discuss things concerning the state; and with a prearranged signal, he had his troops kill all the senators and the richest members of the populace; and when they were dead, he seized and held the rule of the city without any opposition from the citizenry. And although he was twice defeated by the Carthaginians and eventually besieged, not only was he able to defend his city but, leaving part of his troops for the defense of the siege, with his other men he attacked Africa, and in a short time he freed Syracuse from the siege and forced the Carthaginians into dire straits: they were obliged to make peace with him and to be content with possession of Africa and to leave Sicily to Agathocles.

Anyone, therefore, who examines the deeds and the life of this man will observe nothing or very little that can be attributed to Fortune; since, as was said earlier, not with the aid of others but by rising through the ranks, which involved a thousand hardships and dangers, did he come to rule the principality which he then maintained by many brave and dangerous efforts. Still, it cannot be called skill to kill one's fellow citizens, to betray friends, to be without faith, without mercy, without religion; by these means one can acquire power but not glory. For if one were to consider Agathocles's ability in getting into and out of dangers, and his greatness of spirit in supporting and in overcoming adversities, one can see no reason why he should be judged inferior to any most excellent commander; nevertheless, his vicious cruelty and inhumanity, along with numerous wicked deeds, do not permit us to honor him among the most excellent of men. One cannot, therefore, attribute to either Fortune or skill what he accomplished without either the one or the other.

In our own days, during the reign of Alexander VI, Oliverotto of Fermo, who many years before had been left as a child without a father, was brought up by his maternal uncle, Giovanni Fogliani. In the early days of his youth he was sent to serve as a soldier under Paulo Vitelli so that, once he was versed in that skill, he might attain some outstanding military position. Then, after Paulo died, he served under his brother, Vitellozzo; and in a very brief time, because of his intelligence and his vigorous body and mind, he became the commander of his troops. But since he felt it was servile to work for others, he decided to seize Fermo with the aid of some citizens of Fermo who preferred servitude to the liberty of their native city, and with the assistance of the followers of Vitellozzo; and he wrote to Giovanni Fogliani about how, having been away many years from home, he wished to come to see him and his city and to inspect his inheritance; and since he had exerted himself for no other reason than to acquire glory, he wanted to arrive in honorable fashion, accompanied by an escort of a hundred horsemen from among his friends and servants so that his fellow citizens might see that he had not spent his time in vain; and he begged his uncle to arrange for an honorable reception from the people of Fermo, one which might bring honor not only to Giovanni but also to himself, being his pupil. Giovanni, therefore, in no way failed in his duty toward his nephew: he had him received in honorable fashion by the people of Fermo, and he gave him rooms in his own house. Oliverotto, after a few days had passed and he had secretly made the preparations necessary for his forthcoming wickedness, gave a magnificent banquet to which he invited Giovanni Fogliani and all of the first citizens of Fermo. And when the meal and all the other entertainment customary at such banquets were completed, Oliverotto, according to plan, began to discuss serious matters, speaking of the greatness of Pope Alexander and his son, Cesare, and of their undertakings. After Giovanni and the others had replied to his comments, he suddenly rose up, announcing that these were matters to be discussed in a more secluded place; and he retired into another room, followed by Giovanni and all the other citizens. No sooner were they seated than from secret places in the room out came soldiers who killed Giovanni and all the others. After this murder, Oliverotto mounted his horse, paraded through the town, and besieged the chief officials in the government palace; so that out of fear they were forced to obey him and to constitute a government of which he made himself prince. And when all those were killed who, if they had been discontent, might have threatened him, he strengthened himself by instituting new civil and military laws; so that, in the space of the year that he held the principality, not only was he secure in the city of Fermo, but he had become feared by all its neighbors. His expulsion would have been as difficult as that of Agathocles if he had not permitted himself to be tricked by Cesare Borgia, when at Sinigaglia, as was noted above, the Duke captured the Orsini and the Vitelli; there he, too, was captured, a year after he committed the parricide, and together with Vitellozzo, who had been his teacher in ingenuity and wickedness, he was strangled.

One might wonder how Agathocles and others like him, after so many betrayals and cruelties, could live for such a long time secure in their cities and defend themselves from outside enemies without being plotted against by their own citizens; many others, using cruel means, were unable even in peaceful times to hold on to their state, not to speak of the uncertain times of war. I believe that this depends on whether cruelty be well or badly used. Well used are those cruelties (if it is permitted to speak well of evil) that are carried out in a single stroke, done out of necessity to protect oneself, and are not continued but are instead converted into the greatest possible benefits for the subjects. Badly used are those cruelties which, although being few at the outset, grow with the passing of time instead of disappearing. Those who follow the first method can remedy their condition with God and with men as Agathocles did; the others cannot possibly survive.

Wherefore it is to be noted that in taking a state its conqueror should weigh all the harmful things he must do and do them all at once so as not to have to repeat them every day, and in not repeating them to be able to make men feel secure and to win them over with the benefits he bestows upon them. Anyone who does otherwise, either out of timidity or because of poor advice, is always obliged to keep his knife in his hand; nor can he ever count upon his subjects, who, because of their fresh and continual injuries, cannot feel secure with him. Injuries, therefore, should be inflicted all at the same time, for the less they are tasted, the less they offend; and benefits should be distributed a bit at a time in order that they may be savored fully. And a prince should, above all, live with his subjects in such a way that no unforeseen event, either good or bad, may make him alter his course; for when emergencies arise in adverse conditions, you are not in time to resort to cruelty, and that good you do will help you little, since it will be judged a forced measure and you will earn from it no thanks whatsoever.

CHAPTER IX. ON THE CIVIL PRINCIPALITY

But coming to the second instance, when a private citizen, not through wickedness or any other intolerable violence, but with the favor of his fellow citizens, becomes prince of his native city (this can be called a civil principality, the acquisition of which neither depends completely upon skill nor upon Fortune, but instead upon a mixture of shrewdness and luck), I maintain that one reaches this princedom either with the favor of the common people or with that of the nobility. For these two different humors are found in every body politic; and they arise from the fact that the people do not wish to be commanded or oppressed by the nobles, and the nobles desire to command and to oppress the people; and from these two opposed appetites there arises one of three effects: either a principality or liberty or anarchy.

A principality is brought about either by the common people or by the nobility, depending on which one of the two parties has the opportunity. For when the nobles see that they cannot resist the populace, they begin to support one among them and make him prince in order to be able, under his shadow, to satisfy their appetites. The common people as well, seeing that they cannot resist the nobility, give their support to one man and make him prince in order to have the protection of his authority. He who attains the principality with the aid of the nobility maintains it with more difficulty than he who becomes prince with the assistance of the common people, for he finds himself a prince amidst many who feel themselves to be his equals, and because of this he can neither govern nor manage them as he might wish. But he who attains the principality because of popular favor finds himself alone and has around him either no one or very few who are not ready to obey him. Moreover, one cannot honestly satisfy the nobles without harming others, but the common people can surely be satisfied: their desire is more honest than that of the nobles—the former wishing not to be oppressed and the latter wishing to oppress. Moreover, a prince can never make himself secure when the people are his enemy because they are so many; he can make himself secure against the nobles because they are so few. The worst that a prince can expect from a hostile people is to be abandoned by them; but with a hostile nobility not only does he have to fear being abandoned but also that they will unite against him; for, being more perceptive and shrewder, they always have time to save themselves, to seek the favors of the side they believe will win. Furthermore, a prince must always live with the same common people; but he can easily do without the same nobles, having the power to create them and to destroy them from day to day and to take away and give back their reputation as he sees fit.

And in order to clarify this point better, I say that the nobles should be considered chiefly in two ways: either they govern themselves in such a way that they commit themselves completely to your fortunes or they do not. Those who commit themselves and are not greedy should be honored and loved; those who do not are to be examined in two ways. They act in this manner out of fear and a natural lack of courage, and then you make use of them, especially those who are wise advisers, since in prosperous times they will gain you honor and in adverse times you need not fear them. But when, deliberately and influenced by ambition, they refrain from committing themselves to you, this is a sign that they think more of themselves than of you; and the prince should be wary of such men and fear them as if they were open enemies, because they will always, in adverse times, help to ruin him.

However, one who becomes prince with the support of the common people must keep them as his friends; this is easy for him, since the only thing they ask of him is that they not be oppressed. But one who, against the will of the common people, becomes prince with the assistance of the nobility must, before all else, seek to win the people's support, which should be easy if he takes them under his protection. And because men, when they are well treated by those from whom they expected harm, are more obliged to their benefactor, the common people quickly become better disposed toward him than if he had become prince with their support. And a prince can gain their favor in various ways, but because they vary according to the situation no fixed rules can be given for them, and therefore I shall not talk about them. I shall conclude by saying only that a prince must have the friendship of the common people; otherwise he will have no support in times of adversity.

Nabis, prince of the Spartans, withstood the attacks of all of Greece and of one of Rome's most victorious armies, and he defended his city and his state against them; and when danger was near he needed only to protect himself from a few of his subjects; but if he had had the common people against him, this would not have been sufficient. And let no one dispute my opinion by citing that trite proverb: "He who builds upon the people builds upon the mud" because that is true when a private citizen lays his foundations and allows himself to believe that the common people will free him if he is oppressed by enemies or by the public officials (in this case a man might often find himself fooled, like the Gracchi of Rome or like Messer Giorgio Scali of Florence); but when the prince who builds his foundations on the people is one who is able to command and is a man of spirit, not confused by adversities, and does not lack other necessities, and through his courage and his institutions keeps up the spirits of the populace, he will never find himself deceived by the common people, and he will discover that he has laid sound foundations.

Principalities of this type usually are endangered when they are about to change from a republic to an absolute form of government. For these princes either rule by themselves or by means of public officials; in the latter case their position is weaker and more dangerous since they depend entirely upon the will of those citizens who are appointed to hold the offices; these men, especially in adverse times, can very easily seize the state either by open opposition or by disobedience. And in such times of danger the prince has no time for taking absolute control, for the citizens and subjects who are used to receiving their orders from public officials are, in these crises, not willing to obey his orders; and in doubtful times he will always find a scarcity of men he can trust. Such a prince cannot rely upon what he sees during periods of calm, when the citizens need his rule, because then everyone comes running, makes promises, and each one is willing to die for him—since death is unlikely; but in times of adversity, when the state needs its citizens, then few are to be found. And this experiment is so much the more dangerous in that it cannot be made but once. And, therefore, a wise prince should think of a method by which his citizens, at all times and in every circumstance, will need the assistance of the state and of himself; and then they will always be loyal to him.

CHAPTER X.　HOW THE STRENGTH OF ALL PRINCIPALITIES
SHOULD BE MEASURED

In analyzing the qualities of these principalities, another consideration must be discussed; that is, whether the
prince has so much power that he can, if necessary, stand
on his own, or whether he always needs the protection of
others. And in order to clarify this section, I say that I
judge those princes self-sufficient who, either through
abundance of troops or of money, are able to gather together a suitable army and fight a good battle against
whoever should attack them; and I consider those who always need the protection of others to be those who cannot
meet their enemy in the field, but must seek refuge behind
their city walls and defend them. The first case has already been treated, and later on I shall say whatever else
is necessary on the subject. Nothing more can be added to
the second instance than to encourage such princes to
fortify and provision their cities and not to concern themselves with the surrounding countryside. And anyone who
has well fortified his city and has well managed his affairs
with his subjects in the manner I detailed above (and discuss below) will be besieged only with great caution; for
men are always enemies of undertakings that reveal their
difficulties, and it cannot seem easy to attack someone
whose city is well fortified and who is not despised by his
people.

The cities of Germany are completely free, they have
little surrounding territory, they obey the emperor when
they wish, and they fear neither him nor any other nearby
power, as they are fortified in such a manner that everyone thinks their capture would be a tedious and difficult
affair. For they all have sufficient moats and walls; they
have adequate artillery; they always store in their public
warehouses enough to drink and to eat and to burn for a
year; and besides all this, in order to be able to keep the
lower classes fed without exhausting public funds, they
always have in reserve a year's supply of raw materials

sufficient to give these people work at those trades which are the nerves and the lifeblood of that city and of the industries from which the people earn their living. Moreover, they hold the military arts in high regard, and they have many regulations for maintaining them.

Therefore, a prince who has a strong city and who does not make himself hated cannot be attacked; and even if he were to be attacked, the enemy would have to depart in shame, for human affairs are so changeable that it is almost impossible that one maintain a siege for a year with his troops idle. And to anyone who might answer me: if the people have their possessions outside the city and see them destroyed, they will lose patience, and the long siege and self-interest will cause them to forget their prince, I reply that a powerful and spirited prince will always overcome all such difficulties, inspiring his subjects now with the hope that the evil will not last long, now with the fear of the enemy's cruelty, now by protecting himself with clever maneuvers against those who seem too outspoken. Besides this, the enemy will naturally burn and waste the surrounding country on arrival, just when the spirits of the defenders are still ardent and determined on the city's defense; and thus the prince needs to fear so much the less, because after a few days, when their spirits have cooled down a bit, the damage has already been inflicted and the evils suffered, and there is no means of correcting the matter; and now the people will rally around their prince even more, for it would appear that he is bound to them by obligations, since their homes were burned and their possessions wasted in his defense. And the nature of men is such that they find themselves obligated as much for the benefits they confer as for those they receive. Thus, if everything is taken into consideration, it will not be difficult for a prudent prince to keep high the spirits of his citizens from the beginning to the conclusion of the siege, so long as he does not lack enough food and the means for his defense.

CHAPTER XI. ON ECCLESIASTICAL PRINCIPALITIES

There remain now only the ecclesiastical principalities to be discussed: concerning these, all the problems occur before they are acquired; for they are acquired either through ability or through Fortune and are maintained without either; they are sustained by the ancient institutions of religion, which are so powerful and of such a kind that they keep their princes in power in whatever manner they act and live their lives. These princes alone have states and do not defend them, subjects and do not rule them; and the states, remaining undefended, are never taken away from them; and the subjects, being ungoverned, never sense any concern, and they do not think about, nor are they able to sever, their ties with them. These principalities, then, are the only secure and happy ones. But since they are protected by higher causes that the human mind is unable to reach, I shall not discuss them; for, being exalted and maintained by God, it would be the act of a presumptuous and foolhardy man to discuss them. Nevertheless, someone might ask me why it is that the Church, in temporal matters, has arrived at such power when, until the time of Alexander, the Italian powers—not just those who were the established rulers, but every baron and lord, no matter how weak—considered her temporal power as insignificant, and now a King of France trembles before it and it has been able to throw him out of Italy and to ruin the Venetians; although this situation may already be known, it does not seem superfluous to me to recall it to memory in some detail.

Before Charles, King of France, came into Italy, this country was under the rule of the Pope, the Venetians, the King of Naples, the Duke of Milan, and the Florentines. These rulers had to keep two major problems in mind: first, that a foreigner could enter Italy with his armies; second, that no one of them increase his territory. Those whom they needed to watch most closely were the Pope and the Venetians. And to restrain the Venetians the alliance of all the rest was necessary, as was the case in the defense of Ferrara; and to keep the Pope in check they made use of the Roman barons, who, divided into two factions, the Orsini and the Colonna, always had a reason for squabbling amongst themselves; they kept the papacy weak and unstable, standing with their weapons in hand right under the Pope's eyes. And although from time to time there arose a courageous Pope like Pope Sixtus, neither Fortune nor wisdom could ever free him from these inconveniences. And the brevity of the reigns of the popes was the cause; for in ten years, the average life expectancy of a papacy, he might with difficulty put down one of the factions; and if, for example, one Pope had almost extinguished the Colonna, a new Pope who was the enemy of the Orsini would emerge, enabling the Colonna to grow powerful again, and yet he would not have time enough to destroy the Orsini.

As a consequence, the temporal powers of the Pope were little respected in Italy. Then Alexander VI came to power, and he, more than any of the popes who ever reigned, showed how well a Pope, with money and troops, could succeed; and he achieved, with Duke Valentino as his instrument and the French invasion as his opportunity, all those things that I discussed earlier in describing the actions of the Duke. And although his intention was not to make the Church great but rather the Duke, nevertheless what he did resulted in the increase of the power of the Church, which, after his death and once the Duke was destroyed, became the heir of his labors. Then came Pope Julius, and he found the Church strong, possessing all of Romagna, having destroyed the Roman barons, and, by Alexander's blows, having snuffed out their factions; and he also found the way open for the accumulation of wealth by a method never before used by Alexander or his predecessors. These practices Julius not only continued but intensified; and he was determined to take Bologna, to crush the Venetians, and to drive the

French from Italy, and he succeeded in all these under-takings; and he is worthy of even more praise, since he did everything for the increased power of the Church and not for any special individual. He also managed to keep the Orsini and the Colonna factions in the same condition in which he found them; and although there were some leaders among them who wanted to make changes, there were two things which held them back: one, the power of the Church, which frightened them; and, two, not having any of their own family as cardinals, who were the source of the conflicts among them. For these factions will never be at peace as long as they have cardinals, since such men foster factions, both in Rome and outside it, and those barons are compelled to defend them; and thus, from the ambitions of the priests are born the discords and the tumults among the barons. Therefore, His Holiness Pope Leo has found the papacy very powerful indeed; and it is to be hoped that if his predecessors made it great by feats of arms, he, through his kindness and countless other virtues, will make it even greater and respected.

CHAPTER XII.   ON THE VARIOUS KINDS OF TROOPS AND MERCENARY SOLDIERS

Having treated in detail all the characteristics of those principalities which I proposed to discuss at the beginning, and having considered, to some extent, the reasons for their success or shortcomings, and having demonstrated the ways by which many have tried to acquire them and to maintain them, it remains for me now to speak in general terms of the kinds of offense and defense that can be adopted by each of the previously mentioned principalities. We have said above that a prince must have laid firm foundations; otherwise he will of necessity come to grief. And the principal foundations of all states, the new as well as the old or mixed, are good laws and good armies. And since there cannot exist good laws where there are no good armies, and where there are good armies there must be good laws, I shall leave aside the treatment of laws and discuss the armed forces.

Let me say, therefore, that the armies with which a prince defends his state are made up of either his own people or of mercenaries, either auxiliary or mixed troops. The mercenaries and the auxiliaries are useless and dangerous. And if a prince holds on to his state by means of mercenary armies, he will never be stable or secure; for they are disunited, ambitious, without discipline, disloyal; they are brave among friends; among enemies they are cowards; they have no fear of God and no faith in men; and your downfall is deferred only so long as the attack is deferred; and in peace you are plundered by them, in war by your enemies. The reason for this is that they have no other love nor other motive to keep them in the field than a meager wage, which is not enough to make them want to die for you. They love being your soldiers when you are not making war, but when war comes they either desert or depart. This would require little effort to demonstrate, since the present ruin of Italy is caused by nothing other than her dependence for a long period of time on mercenary forces. These forces did, at times, help some get ahead, and they appeared courageous in combat with other mercenaries; but when the invasion of the foreigner came they showed themselves for what they were; and thus, Charles, King of France, was permitted to take Italy with a piece of chalk.[1] And the man who said that our sins were the cause of this disaster spoke the truth; but they were not at all those that he thought, but rather these that I have described; and because they were the sins of princes, the princes in turn have suffered the penalty for them.

I wish to demonstrate more fully the sorry nature of

[1]This expression refers to the practice Charles followed in marking the houses that were to be used to quarter his troops during the invasion of Italy in 1494–1495. Machiavelli implies by this that Italian resistance to Charles' invasion was nonexistent.

such armies. Mercenary captains are either excellent soldiers or they are not; if they are, you cannot trust them, since they will always aspire to their own greatness either by oppressing you, who are their master, or by oppressing others against your intent; but if the captain is without skill, he usually ruins you. And if someone were to reply that anyone who bears arms will act in this manner, mercenary or not, I would answer that armies have to be commanded either by a prince or by a republic: the prince must go in person and perform the duties of a captain himself; the republic must send its own citizens; and when they send one who does not turn out to be an able man, they must replace him; and if he is capable, they ought to restrain him with laws so that he does not go beyond his authority. And we see from experience that only princes and armed republics make very great advances, and that mercenaries do nothing but harm; and a republic armed with its own citizens is less likely to come under the rule of one of its citizens than a city armed with foreign soldiers.

Rome and Sparta for many centuries stood armed and free. The Swiss are extremely well armed and are completely free. An example from antiquity of the use of mercenary troops is the Carthaginians; they were almost overcome by their own mercenary soldiers after the first war with the Romans, even though the Carthaginians had their own citizens as officers. Philip of Macedonia was made captain of their army by the Thebans after the death of Epaminondas; and after the victory he took their liberty from them. The Milanese, after the death of Duke Philip, employed Francesco Sforza to war against the Venetians; having defeated the enemy at Caravaggio, he joined with them to oppress the Milanese, his employers. Sforza, his father, being in the employ of Queen Giovanna of Naples, all at once left her without defenses; hence, in order not to lose her kingdom, she was forced to throw herself into the lap of the King of Aragon. And if the Venetians and the Florentines have in the past increased their possessions with such soldiers, and their captains have not yet made themselves princes but have instead defended them, I answer that the Florentines have been favored in this matter by luck; for among their able captains whom they could have had reason to fear, some were defeated, others met with opposition, and others turned their ambition elsewhere. The one who did not win was John Hawkwood, whose loyalty, since he did not succeed, will never be known; but anyone will admit that had he succeeded, the Florentines would have been at his mercy. Sforza always had the Bracceschi as enemies so that each checked the other. Francesco turned his ambition to Lombardy; Braccio against the Church and the Kingdom of Naples.

But let us come to what has occurred just recently. The Florentines made Paulo Vitelli their captain, a very prudent man and one who rose from private life to achieve great fame. If this man had taken Pisa, no one would deny that the Florentines would have had to become his ally; for, if he had become employed by their enemies, they would have had no defense, and if they had kept him on, they would have been obliged to obey him. As for the Venetians, if we examine the course they followed, we see that they operated securely and gloriously as long as they fought with their own troops (this was before they started fighting on land); with their nobles and their common people armed, they fought courageously. But when they began to fight on land, they abandoned this successful strategy and followed the usual practices of waging war in Italy. As they first began to expand their territory on the mainland, since they did not have much territory there and enjoyed a high reputation, they had little to fear from their captains; but when these men grew in power, as they did under Carmagnola, the Venetians had a taste of this mistake; for, having found him very able, since under his command they had defeated the Duke of Milan, and knowing, on the other hand, that he had lost some of his fighting spirit, they judged that they could no longer conquer under him, for he had no wish to do so; yet they could not dismiss him for fear of losing what they had acquired; so in order to secure themselves against him, they were forced to execute him. Then they had as their captains Bartolomeo da Bergamo, Roberto da San Severino, the Count of Pitigliano, and the like; with such as these they had to fear their losses, not their acquisitions, as occurred later at Vailà, where, in a single day, they lost what had cost them eight hundred years of exhausting effort to acquire. From these soldiers, therefore, come only slow, tardy, and weak conquests and sudden and astonishing losses. And because with these examples I have begun to treat of Italy, which has for many years been ruled by mercenary soldiers, I should like to discuss the matter more thoroughly, in order that when their origins and developments are evident they can be more easily corrected.

You must, then, understand how in recent times, when the Empire began to be driven out of Italy and the Pope began to win more prestige in temporal affairs, Italy was divided into more states; for many of the large cities took up arms against their nobles, who, at first backed by the Emperor, had kept them under their control; and the Church supported these cities to increase its temporal power; in many other cities citizens became princes. Hence, Italy having come almost entirely into the hands of the Church and of several republics, those priests and those other citizens who were not accustomed to bearing arms began to hire foreigners. The first to give prestige to such troops was Alberigo of Conio, a Romagnol. From this man's school emerged, among others, Braccio and Sforza, who in their day were the arbiters of Italy. After them came all the others who, until the present day, have commanded these soldiers. And the result of their ability has been that Italy has been overrun by Charles, plundered by Louis, violated by Ferdinand, and insulted by the Swiss. Their method was first to increase the reputation of their own forces by taking away the prestige of the infantry. They did so because they were men without a state of their own who lived by their profession; a small number of foot soldiers could not give them prestige, and they could not afford to hire a large number of them; and so they relied completely upon cavalry, since for having only a reasonable number of horsemen they were provided for and honored. And they reduced things to such a state that in an army of twenty thousand troops, one could hardly find two thousand foot soldiers. Besides this, they had used every means to spare themselves and their soldiers hardship and fear, not killing each other in their battles but rather taking each other prisoner without demanding ransom; they would not attack cities at night; and those in the cities would not attack the tents of the besiegers; they built neither stockades nor trenches around their camps; they did not campaign in the winter. And all these things were permitted by their military institutions and gave them a means of escaping, as was stated, hardships and dangers: so that these condottieri have led Italy into slavery and humiliation.

CHAPTER XIII. ON AUXILIARY, MIXED, AND CITIZEN SOLDIERS

Auxiliary troops, the other kind of worthless armies, are those that arrive when you call a powerful man to bring his forces to your aid and defense, as was done in recent days by Pope Julius, who, having witnessed in the campaign of Ferrara the sorry test of his mercenary soldiers, turned to auxiliary soldiers and made an agreement with Ferdinand, King of Spain, that he assist him with his troops and his armies. These soldiers can be useful and good in themselves, but for the man who summons them they are almost always harmful; for, if they lose you remain defeated; if they win you remain their prisoner. And although ancient histories are full of such instances, nevertheless I am unwilling to leave unexamined this recent example of Pope Julius II, whose policy could not have been more poorly considered, for, in wanting to take Ferrara, he threw himself completely into the hands of a foreigner. But his good fortune brought about a third development so that he did not gather the fruit of his poor decision: for after his auxiliaries were routed at Ravenna, the Swiss rose up and, to the consternation of Pope Julius as well as everyone else, chased out the victors. Thus, he was neither taken prisoner by his enemies, since they had fled, nor by his auxiliaries, since he triumphed with arms other than theirs. And the Florentines, completely unarmed, hired ten thousand French soldiers to take Pisa; such a plan endangered them more than any of their previous predicaments. The emperor of Constantinople, in order to oppose his neighbors, brought ten thousand Turkish troops into Greece, who, when the war was over, did not want to leave; this was the beginning of Greek servitude under the infidel.

Anyone, therefore, who does not wish to conquer should make use of these soldiers, for they are much more dangerous than mercenary troops. Because with them defeat is certain: they are completely united and all under the command of others; but the mercenaries need more time and a greater opportunity if they are to harm you after they have been victorious, for they are not a united body and are hired and salaried by you; a third party whom you may make their leader cannot immediately seize enough authority to harm you. And so, with mercenaries the greatest danger is their cowardice, with auxiliaries their courage.

A wise prince has always rejected these soldiers and has relied upon his own men; and he has chosen to lose with his own troops rather than to conquer with those of others, judging no true victory one gained by means of foreign armies. I shall never hesitate to cite Cesare Borgia and his deeds as an example. This duke entered Romagna with auxiliary forces, leading an army composed entirely of Frenchmen; and with them he captured Imola and Forlì. But not thinking such troops reliable, he turned to mercenary forces, judging them to be less dangerous, and he hired the Orsini and Vitelli. When he found out that they were doubtful, unfaithful, and treacherous, he destroyed them and turned to his own men. And it is easy to see the difference between these two sorts of troops if we examine the difference between the Duke's reputation when he had only French troops and when he had the Orsini and Vitelli, as opposed to when he was left with his own troops and himself to depend on: we find that his reputation always increased; never was he esteemed so highly than when everyone saw that he was complete master of his own army.

I did not wish to depart from citing recent Italian examples; yet I do not want to omit Hiero of Syracuse, one of those I mentioned above. This man, as I said previously, having been named by the Syracusans captain of their armies, immediately realized that mercenary forces were useless, composed, as they were, of men resembling our own Italian condottieri; and it seemed to him that he could neither keep them on nor dismiss them, so he had them all cut into little pieces: and afterward he made war with his own troops and not with those of foreigners. I would also like to recall to memory an example from the Old Testament that fits this argument. David offered himself to Saul to battle against Goliath, the Philistine challenger; Saul, in order to give him courage, armed him with his own armor, which David, when he had put it on, cast off, declaring that with it he could not test his true worth; he therefore wished to meet the enemy with his own sling and his own sword.

In short, the arms of another man either slide off your back, weigh you down, or tie you up. Charles VII, father of Louis XI, having freed France of the English by means of his good fortune and his ability, recognized the necessity of arming himself with his own men, and he set up in his kingdom an ordinance to procure cavalry and infantry. Later, his son, King Louis, abolished the ordinance of the infantry and began to hire Swiss troops; this mistake, followed by others as we can now witness, is the cause of the many threats to that kingdom. By giving prestige to the Swiss, he discredited his own troops; for he completely abolished his foot soldiers and obliged his cavalry to depend upon the soldiers of others; being accustomed to fighting with the Swiss, the French horsemen felt that they could not conquer without them. From this it came about that the French were not strong enough to match the Swiss, and without the Swiss they did not dare to meet others. The armies of France have, therefore, been mixed, partly mercenaries and partly citizen troops; armies combined together in such a fashion are much better than a purely auxiliary force or a purely mercenary army, and are greatly inferior to one's own troops. And the example just cited should suffice, for the kingdom of France would be invincible if Charles' policy had been developed or retained. But the shortsightedness in human nature will begin a policy that seems good at the outset but does not notice the poison that is underneath, as I said earlier in connection with consumptive fevers.

And thus anyone who does not diagnose the ills when they arise in a principality is not really wise; and this skill is given to few men. And if the primary cause of the downfall of the Roman Empire is examined, one will find it to be only when the Goths began to be hired as mercenaries; because from that beginning the strength of the Roman Empire began to be weakened, and all that strength was drained from it and was given to the Goths.

I conclude, therefore, that without having one's own soldiers, no principality is safe; on the contrary, it is completely subject to Fortune, not having the power and the loyalty to defend it in times of adversity. And it was always the opinion and belief of wise men that "nothing is so unhealthy or unstable as the reputation for power that is not based upon one's own power." And one's own troops are those which are composed either of subjects or of citizens or your own dependents; all others are either mercenaries or auxiliaries. And the means to organize a citizen army are easily discovered if the methods followed

by those four men I have cited above are examined, and if
one observes how Philip, father of Alexander the Great,
and many republics and princes have armed and organized themselves: in such methods I have full confidence.

CHAPTER XIV.   A PRINCE'S DUTY CONCERNING MILITARY
MATTERS

A prince, therefore, must not have any other object nor
any other thought, nor must he take anything as his profession but war, its institutions, and its discipline; because
that is the only profession which befits one who commands; and it is of such importance that not only does it
maintain those who were born princes, but many times it
enables men of private station to rise to that position; and,
on the other hand, it is evident that when princes have
given more thought to personal luxuries than to arms,
they have lost their state. And the first way to lose it is to
neglect this art; and the way to acquire it is to be well
versed in this art.

Francesco Sforza became Duke of Milan from being a
private citizen because he was armed; his sons, since they
avoided the inconveniences of arms, became private citizens after having been dukes. For, among the other bad
effects it causes, being disarmed makes you despised; this
is one of those infamies a prince should guard himself
against, as will be treated below: for between an armed
and an unarmed man there is no comparison whatsoever,
and it is not reasonable for an armed man to obey an unarmed man willingly, nor that an unarmed man should be
safe among armed servants; since, when the former is suspicious and the latter are contemptuous, it is impossible
for them to work well together. And therefore, a prince
who does not understand military matters, besides the
other misfortunes already noted, cannot be esteemed by
his own soldiers, nor can he trust them.

He must, therefore, never raise his thought from this
exercise of war, and in peacetime he must train himself

more than in time of war; this can be done in two ways: one by action, the other by the mind. And as far as actions are concerned, besides keeping his soldiers well disciplined and trained, he must always be out hunting, and must accustom his body to hardships in this manner; and he must also learn the nature of the terrain, and know how mountains slope, how valleys open, how plains lie, and understand the nature of rivers and swamps; and he should devote much attention to such activities. Such knowledge is useful in two ways: first, one learns to know one's own country and can better understand how to defend it; second, with the knowledge and experience of the terrain, one can easily comprehend the characteristics of any other terrain that it is necessary to explore for the first time; for the hills, valleys, plains, rivers, and swamps of Tuscany, for instance, have certain similarities to those of other provinces; so that by knowing the lay of the land in one province one can easily understand it in others. And a prince who lacks this ability lacks the most important quality in a leader; because this skill teaches you to find the enemy, choose a campsite, lead troops, organize them for battle, and besiege towns to your own advantage.

Philopoemen, Prince of the Achaeans, among the other praises given to him by writers, is praised because in peacetime he thought of nothing except the means of waging war; and when he was out in the country with his friends, he often stopped and reasoned with them: "If the enemy were on that hilltop and we were here with our army, which of the two of us would have the advantage? How could we attack them without breaking formation? If we wanted to retreat, how could we do this? If they were to retreat, how could we pursue them?" And he proposed to them, as they rode along, all the contingencies that can occur in an army; he heard their opinions, expressed his own, and backed it up with arguments; so that, because of these continuous deliberations, when leading his troops no unforeseen incident could arise for which he did not have the remedy.

But as for the exercise of the mind, the prince must read histories and in them study the deeds of great men; he must see how they conducted themselves in wars; he must examine the reasons for their victories and for their defeats in order to avoid the latter and to imitate the former; and above all else he must do as some distinguished man before him has done, who elected to imitate someone who had been praised and honored before him, and always keep in mind his deeds and actions; just as it is reported that Alexander the Great imitated Achilles; Caesar, Alexander; Scipio, Cyrus. And anyone who reads the life of Cyrus written by Xenophon then realizes how important in the life of Scipio that imitation was to his glory and how much, in purity, goodness, humanity, and generosity, Scipio conformed to those characteristics of Cyrus that Xenophon had written about.

Such methods as these a wise prince must follow, and never in peaceful times must he be idle; but he must turn them diligently to his advantage in order to be able to profit from them in times of adversity, so that, when Fortune changes, she will find him prepared to withstand such times.

CHAPTER XV.   ON THOSE THINGS FOR WHICH MEN, AND PARTICULARLY PRINCES, ARE PRAISED OR BLAMED

Now there remains to be examined what should be the methods and procedures of a prince in dealing with his subjects and friends. And because I know that many have written about this, I am afraid that by writing about it again I shall be thought of as presumptuous, since in discussing this material I depart radically from the procedures of others. But since my intention is to write something useful for anyone who understands it, it seemed more suitable to me to search after the effectual truth of the matter rather than its imagined one. And many writers have imagined for themselves republics and principalities that have never been seen nor known to exist in reality; for there is such a gap between how one lives and how one ought to live that anyone who abandons what is done for what ought to be done learns his ruin rather than his preservation: for a man who wishes to make a vocation of being good at all times will come to ruin among so many who are not good. Hence it is necessary for a prince who wishes to maintain his position to learn how not to be good, and to use this knowledge or not to use it according to necessity.

Leaving aside, therefore, the imagined things concerning a prince, and taking into account those that are true, I say that all men, when they are spoken of, and particularly princes, since they are placed on a higher level, are judged by some of these qualities which bring them either blame or praise. And this is why one is considered generous, another miserly (to use a Tuscan word, since "avaricious" in our language is still used to mean one who wishes to acquire by means of theft; we call "miserly" one who excessively avoids using what he has); one is considered a giver, the other rapacious; one cruel, another merciful; one treacherous, another faithful; one effeminate and cowardly, another bold and courageous; one humane, another haughty; one lascivious, another chaste; one trustworthy, another cunning; one harsh, another lenient; one serious, another frivolous; one religious, another unbelieving; and the like. And I know that everyone will admit that it would be a very praiseworthy thing to find in a prince, of the qualities mentioned above, those that are held to be good; but since it is neither possible to have them nor to observe them all completely, because human nature does not permit it, a prince must be prudent enough to know how to escape the bad reputation of those vices that would lose the state for him, and must protect himself from those that will not lose it for him, if this is possible; but if he cannot, he need not concern himself unduly if he ignores these less serious vices. And, moreover, he need not worry about incurring the bad reputation of those vices without which it would be difficult to hold his state; since, carefully taking everything into account, one will discover that something which appears to be a virtue, if pursued, will end in his destruction; while some other thing which seems to be a vice, if pursued, will result in his safety and his well-being.

CHAPTER XVI.   ON GENEROSITY AND MISERLINESS

Beginning, therefore, with the first of the above-mentioned qualities, I say that it would be good to be considered generous; nevertheless, generosity used in such a manner as to give you a reputation for it will harm you; because if it is employed virtuously and as one should employ it, it will not be recognized and you will not avoid the reproach of its opposite. And so, if a prince wants to maintain his reputation for generosity among men, it is necessary for him not to neglect any possible means of lavish display; in so doing such a prince will always use up all his resources and he will be obliged, eventually, if he wishes to maintain his reputation for generosity, to burden the people with excessive taxes and to do everything possible to raise funds. This will begin to make him hateful to his subjects, and, becoming impoverished, he will not be much esteemed by anyone; so that, as a consequence of his generosity, having offended many and rewarded few, he will feel the effects of any slight unrest and will be ruined at the first sign of danger; recognizing this and wishing to alter his policies, he immediately runs the risk of being reproached as a miser.

A prince, therefore, unable to use this virtue of generosity in a manner which will not harm himself if he is known for it, should, if he is wise, not worry about being called a miser; for with time he will come to be considered more generous once it is evident that, as a result of his parsimony, his income is sufficient, he can defend himself from anyone who makes war against him, and he can undertake enterprises without overburdening his people, so that he comes to be generous with all those from whom he takes nothing, who are countless, and miserly with all those to whom he gives nothing, who are few. In our times we have not seen great deeds accomplished except by those who were considered miserly; all others were done away with. Pope Julius II, although he made use of his reputation for generosity in order to gain the papacy, then decided not to maintain it in order to be able to wage war; the present King of France has waged many wars without imposing extra taxes on his subjects, only because his habitual parsimony has provided for the additional expenditures; the present King of Spain, if he had been considered generous, would not have engaged in nor won so many campaigns.

Therefore, in order not to have to rob his subjects, to be able to defend himself, not to become poor and contemptible, and not to be forced to become rapacious, a prince must consider it of little importance if he incurs the name of miser, for this is one of those vices that permits him to rule. And if someone were to say: Caesar with his generosity came to rule the empire, and many others, because they were generous and known to be so, achieved very high positions; I reply: you are either already a prince or you are on the way to becoming one; in the first instance such generosity is damaging; in the second it is very necessary to be thought generous. And Caesar was one of those who wanted to gain the principality of Rome; but if, after obtaining this, he had lived and had not moderated his expenditures, he would have destroyed that empire. And if someone were to reply: there have existed many princes who have accomplished great deeds with their armies who have been reputed to be generous; I answer you: a prince either spends his own money and that of his subjects or that of others; in the first case he must be economical; in the second he must not restrain any part of his generosity. And for that prince who goes out with his soldiers and lives by looting, sacking, and ransoms, who controls the property of others, such generosity is necessary; otherwise he would not be followed by his troops.

And with what does not belong to you or to your subjects you can be a more liberal giver, as were Cyrus, Caesar, and Alexander; for spending the wealth of others does not lessen your reputation but adds to it; only the spending of your own is what harms you. And there is nothing that uses itself up faster than generosity, for as you employ it you lose the means of employing it, and you become either poor or despised or, in order to escape poverty, rapacious and hated. And above all other things a prince must guard himself against being despised and hated; and generosity leads you to both one and the other. So it is wiser to live with the reputation of a miser, which produces reproach without hatred, than to be forced to incur the reputation of rapacity, which produces reproach along with hatred, because you want to be considered as generous.

CHAPTER XVII.   ON CRUELTY AND MERCY AND WHETHER IT IS BETTER TO BE LOVED THAN TO BE FEARED OR THE CONTRARY

Proceeding to the other qualities mentioned above, I say that every prince must desire to be considered merciful and not cruel; nevertheless, he must take care not to misuse this mercy. Cesare Borgia was considered cruel; nonetheless, his cruelty had brought order to Romagna, united it, restored it to peace and obedience. If we examine this carefully, we shall see that he was more merciful than the Florentine people, who, in order to avoid being considered cruel, allowed the destruction of Pistoia. Therefore, a prince must not worry about the reproach of cruelty when it is a matter of keeping his subjects united and loyal; for with a very few examples of cruelty he will be more compassionate than those who, out of excessive mercy, permit disorders to continue, from which arise murders and plundering; for these usually harm the community at large, while the executions that come from the prince harm one individual in particular. And the new prince, above all other princes, cannot escape the reputation of being called cruel, since new states are full of dangers. And Virgil, through Dido, states: "My difficult condition and the newness of my rule make me act in such a manner, and to set guards over my land on all sides."[1]

Nevertheless, a prince must be cautious in believing and in acting, nor should he be afraid of his own shadow; and he should proceed in such a manner, tempered by prudence and humanity, so that too much trust may not render him imprudent nor too much distrust render him intolerable.

From this arises an argument: whether it is better to be loved than to be feared, or the contrary. I reply that one should like to be both one and the other; but since it is difficult to join them together, it is much safer to be feared than to be loved when one of the two must be lacking. For one can generally say this about men: that they are ungrateful, fickle, simulators and deceivers, avoiders of danger, greedy for gain; and while you work for their good they are completely yours, offering you their blood, their property, their lives, and their sons, as I said earlier, when danger is far away; but when it comes nearer to you they turn away. And that prince who bases his power entirely on their words, finding himself stripped of other preparations, comes to ruin; for friendships that are acquired by a price and not by greatness and nobility of character are purchased but are not owned, and at the proper moment they cannot be spent. And men are less hesitant about harming someone who makes himself loved than one who makes himself feared because love is held together by a chain of obligation which, since men are a sorry lot, is broken on every occasion in which their own self-interest is concerned; but fear is held together by a dread of punishment which will never abandon you.

A prince must nevertheless make himself feared in such

[1] *Aeneid*, II, 563–564.

a manner that he will avoid hatred, even if he does not acquire love; since to be feared and not to be hated can very well be combined; and this will always be so when he keeps his hands off the property and the women of his citizens and his subjects. And if he must take someone's life, he should do so when there is proper justification and manifest cause; but, above all, he should avoid the property of others; for men forget more quickly the death of their father than the loss of their patrimony. Moreover, the reasons for seizing their property are never lacking; and he who begins to live by stealing always finds a reason for taking what belongs to others; on the contrary, reasons for taking a life are rarer and disappear sooner.

But when the prince is with his armies and has under his command a multitude of troops, then it is absolutely necessary that he not worry about being considered cruel; for without that reputation he will never keep an army united or prepared for any combat. Among the praiseworthy deeds of Hannibal is counted this: that, having a very large army, made up of all kinds of men, which he commanded in foreign lands, there never arose the slightest dissention, neither among themselves nor against their prince, both during his good and his bad fortune. This could not have arisen from anything other than his inhuman cruelty, which, along with his many other abilities, made him always respected and terrifying in the eyes of his soldiers; and without that, to attain the same effect, his other abilities would not have sufficed. And the writers of history, having considered this matter very little, on the one hand admire these deeds of his and on the other condemn the main cause of them.

And that it be true that his other abilities would not have been sufficient can be seen from the example of Scipio, a most extraordinary man not only in his time but in all recorded history, whose armies in Spain rebelled against him; this came about from nothing other than his excessive compassion, which gave to his soldiers more liberty than military discipline allowed. For this he was censured in the senate by Fabius Maximus, who called him the corruptor of the Roman militia. The Locrians, having been ruined by one of Scipio's officers, were not avenged by him, nor was the arrogance of that officer corrected, all because of his tolerant nature; so that someone in the senate who tried to apologize for him said that there were many men who knew how not to err better than they knew how to correct errors. Such a nature would have, in time, damaged Scipio's fame and glory if he had maintained it during the empire; but, living under the control of the senate, this harmful characteristic of his not only concealed itself but brought him fame.

I conclude, therefore, returning to the problem of being feared and loved, that since men love at their own pleasure and fear at the pleasure of the prince, a wise prince should build his foundation upon that which belongs to him, not upon that which belongs to others: he must strive only to avoid hatred, as has been said.

CHAPTER XVIII.   HOW A PRINCE SHOULD KEEP HIS WORD

How praiseworthy it is for a prince to keep his word and to live by integrity and not by deceit everyone knows; nevertheless, one sees from the experience of our times that the princes who have accomplished great deeds are those who have cared little for keeping their promises and who have known how to manipulate the minds of men by shrewdness; and in the end they have surpassed those who laid their foundations upon honesty.

You must, therefore, know that there are two means of fighting: one according to the laws, the other with force; the first way is proper to man, the second to beasts; but because the first, in many cases, is not sufficient, it becomes necessary to have recourse to the second. Therefore, a prince must know how to use wisely the natures of the beast and the man. This policy was taught to princes allegorically by the ancient writers, who described how Achilles and many other ancient princes were given to

Chiron the Centaur to be raised and taught under his discipline. This can only mean that, having a half-beast and half-man as a teacher, a prince must know how to employ the nature of the one and the other; and the one without the other cannot endure.

Since, then, a prince must know how to make good use of the nature of the beast, he should choose from among the beasts the fox and the lion; for the lion cannot defend itself from traps and the fox cannot protect itself from wolves. It is therefore necessary to be a fox in order to recognize the traps and a lion in order to frighten the wolves. Those who play only the part of the lion do not understand matters. A wise ruler, therefore, cannot and should not keep his word when such an observance of faith would be to his disadvantage and when the reasons which made him promise are removed. And if men were all good, this rule would not be good; but since men are a sorry lot and will not keep their promises to you, you likewise need not keep yours to them. A prince never lacks legitimate reasons to break his promises. Of this one could cite an endless number of modern examples to show how many pacts, how many promises have been made null and void because of the infidelity of princes; and he who has known best how to use the fox has come to a better end. But it is necessary to know how to disguise this nature well and to be a great hypocrite and a liar: and men are so simpleminded and so controlled by their present necessities that one who deceives will always find another who will allow himself to be deceived.

I do not wish to remain silent about one of these recent instances. Alexander VI did nothing else, he thought about nothing else, except to deceive men, and he always found the occasion to do this. And there never was a man who had more forcefulness in his oaths, who affirmed a thing with more promises, and who honored his word less; nevertheless, his tricks always succeeded perfectly since he was well acquainted with this aspect of the world.

Therefore, it is not necessary for a prince to have all of

the above-mentioned qualities, but it is very necessary for him to appear to have them. Furthermore, I shall be so bold as to assert this: that having them and practicing them at all times is harmful; and appearing to have them is useful; for instance, to seem merciful, faithful, humane, forthright, religious, and to be so; but his mind should be disposed in such a way that should it become necessary not to be so, he will be able and know how to change to the contrary. And it is essential to understand this: that a prince, and especially a new prince, cannot observe all those things by which men are considered good, for in order to maintain the state he is often obliged to act against his promise, against charity, against humanity, and against religion. And therefore, it is necessary that he have a mind ready to turn itself according to the way the winds of Fortune and the changeability of affairs require him; and, as I said above, as long as it is possible, he should not stray from the good, but he should know how to enter into evil when necessity commands.

A prince, therefore, must be very careful never to let anything slip from his lips which is not full of the five qualities mentioned above: he should appear, upon seeing and hearing him, to be all mercy, all faithfulness, all integrity, all kindness, all religion. And there is nothing more necessary than to seem to possess this last quality. And men in general judge more by their eyes than their hands; for everyone can see but few can feel. Everyone sees what you seem to be, few perceive what you are, and those few do not dare to contradict the opinion of the many who have the majesty of the state to defend them; and in the actions of all men, and especially of princes, where there is no impartial arbiter, one must consider the final result.[1] Let a prince therefore act to seize and to

[1] The Italian original, *si guarda al fine*, has often been mistranslated as "the ends justify the means," something Machiavelli never wrote. For another important statement concerning ends and means, see Machiavelli's remarks about Romulus in *Discourses*, I, ix.

maintain the state; his methods will always be judged honorable and will be praised by all; for ordinary people are always deceived by appearances and by the outcome of a thing; and in the world there is nothing but ordinary people; and there is no room for the few, while the many have a place to lean on. A certain prince of the present day, whom I shall refrain from naming, preaches nothing but peace and faith, and to both one and the other he is entirely opposed; and both, if he had put them into practice, would have cost him many times over either his reputation or his state.

CHAPTER XIX.   ON AVOIDING BEING DESPISED AND HATED

But since, concerning the qualities mentioned above, I have spoken about the most important, I should like to discuss the others briefly in this general manner: that the prince, as was noted above, should think about avoiding those things which make him hated and despised; and when he has avoided this, he will have carried out his duties and will find no danger whatsoever in other vices. As I have said, what makes him hated above all else is being rapacious and a usurper of the property and the women of his subjects; he must refrain from this; and in most cases, so long as you do not deprive them of either their property or their honor, the majority of men live happily; and you have only to deal with the ambition of a few, who can be restrained without difficulty and by many means. What makes him despised is being considered changeable, frivolous, effeminate, cowardly, irresolute; from these qualities a prince must guard himself as if from a reef, and he must strive to make everyone recognize in his actions greatness, spirit, dignity, and strength; and concerning the private affairs of his subjects, he must insist that his decision be irrevocable; and he should maintain himself in such a way that no man could imagine that he can deceive or cheat him.

That prince who projects such an opinion of himself is

greatly esteemed; and it is difficult to conspire against a man with such a reputation and difficult to attack him, provided that he is understood to be of great merit and revered by his subjects. For a prince must have two fears: one, internal, concerning his subjects; the other, external, concerning foreign powers. From the latter he can defend himself by his good troops and friends; and he will always have good friends if he has good troops; and internal affairs will always be stable when external affairs are stable, provided that they are not already disturbed by a conspiracy; and even if external conditions change, if he is properly organized and lives as I have said and does not lose control of himself, he will always be able to withstand every attack, just as I said that Nabis the Spartan did. But concerning his subjects, when external affairs do not change, he has to fear that they may conspire secretly: the prince secures himself from this by avoiding being hated or despised and by keeping the people satisfied with him; this is a necessary matter, as was treated above at length. And one of the most powerful remedies a prince has against conspiracies is not to be hated by the masses; for a man who plans a conspiracy always believes that he will satisfy the people by killing the prince; but when he thinks he might anger them, he cannot work up the courage to undertake such a deed; for the problems on the side of the conspirators are countless. And experience demonstrates that conspiracies have been many but few have been concluded successfully; for anyone who conspires cannot be alone, nor can he find companions except from amongst those whom he believes to be dissatisfied; and as soon as you have uncovered your intent to one dissatisfied man, you give him the means to make himself happy, since he can have everything he desires by uncovering the plot; so much is this so that, seeing a sure gain on the one hand and one doubtful and full of danger on the other, if he is to maintain faith with you he has to be either an unusually good friend or a completely determined enemy of the prince. And to treat the matter briefly, I say that on the part of the conspirator there is nothing but fear, jealousy, and the thought of punishment that terrifies him; but on the part of the prince there is the majesty of the principality, the laws, the defenses of friends and the state to protect him; so that, with the good will of the people added to all these things, it is impossible for anyone to be so rash as to plot against him. For, where usually a conspirator has to be afraid before he executes his evil deed, in this case he must be afraid, having the people as an enemy, even after the crime is performed, nor can he hope to find any refuge because of this.

One could cite countless examples on this subject; but I want to satisfy myself with only one which occurred during the time of our fathers. Messer Annibale Bentivogli, prince of Bologna and grandfather of the present Messer Annibale, was murdered by the Canneschi family, who conspired against him; he left behind no heir except Messer Giovanni, then only a baby. As soon as this murder occurred, the people rose up and killed all the Canneschi. This came about because of the good will that the house of the Bentivogli enjoyed in those days; this good will was so great that with Annibale dead, and there being no one of that family left in the city who could rule Bologna, the Bolognese people, having heard that in Florence there was one of the Bentivogli blood who was believed until that time to be the son of a blacksmith, went to Florence to find him, and they gave him the control of that city; it was ruled by him until Messer Giovanni became of age to rule.

I conclude, therefore, that a prince must be little concerned with conspiracies when the people are well disposed toward him; but when the populace is hostile and regards him with hatred, he must fear everything and everyone. And well-organized states and wise princes have, with great diligence, taken care not to anger the nobles and to satisfy the common people and keep them contented; for this is one of the most important concerns that a prince has.

Among the kingdoms in our times that are well organized and well governed is that of France: in it one finds countless good institutions upon which depend the liberty and the security of the king; of these the foremost is the parliament and its authority. For he who organized that kingdom, recognizing the ambition of the nobles and their insolence, and being aware of the necessity of keeping a bit in their mouths to hold them back, on the one hand, while, on the other, knowing the hatred, based upon fear, of the populace for the nobles, and wanting to reassure them, did not wish this to be the particular obligation of the king. In order to relieve himself of the burden he might incur from the nobles if he supported the common people, and from the common people if he supported the nobles, he established a third judicial body that might restrain the nobles and favor the masses without burdening the king. This institution could neither be better nor more prudent, nor could there be a better reason for the safety of the king and the kingdom. From this one can extract another notable observation: that princes must delegate distasteful tasks to others; pleasant ones they should keep for themselves. Again I conclude that a prince must respect the nobles but not make himself hated by the common people.

It could possibly seem to many who have studied the lives and deaths of some Roman emperors that they represent examples contrary to my point of view; for we shall find that some of them have always lived nobly and have demonstrated great strength of character yet have nevertheless lost their empire or have been killed by their own subjects who have plotted against them. Wishing, therefore, to reply to these objections, I shall discuss the traits of several emperors, showing the reasons for their ruin, which are not different from those which I myself have already deduced; and I shall bring forward for consideration those things which are worthy of note for anyone who reads about the history of those times. And I shall let it suffice to choose all those emperors who succeeded to the throne from Marcus the philosopher to Maximinus: these were Marcus, his son Commodus, Pertinax, Julian, Severus, Antoninus Caracalla his son, Macrinus, Heliogabalus, Alexander, and Maximinus. And it is first to be noted that where in other principalities one has only to contend with the ambition of the nobles and the arrogance of the people, the Roman emperors had a third problem: they had to endure the cruelty and the avarice of the soldiers. This was such a difficult thing that it was the cause of the downfall of many of them, since it was hard to satisfy both the soldiers and the populace; for the people loved peace and quiet and because of this loved modest princes, while the soldiers loved the prince who had a military character and who was arrogant, cruel, and rapacious; they wanted him to practice such qualities on the people so that they might double their salary and unleash their avarice and cruelty. As a result of this situation, those emperors always came to ruin who by nature or by guile did not have so great a reputation that they could keep both the people and the soldiers in check; and most of them, especially those who came to power as new princes, recognizing the difficulty resulting from these two opposing factions, turned to appeasing the soldiers, caring little about injuring the people. Such a decision was necessary; since princes cannot avoid being hated by somebody, they must first seek not to be hated by the bulk of the populace; and when they cannot achieve this, they must try with every effort to avoid the hatred of the most powerful group. And therefore, those emperors who had need of extraordinary support because of their newness in power allied themselves with the soldiers instead of the people; nevertheless, this proved to their advantage or not, according to whether the prince knew how to maintain his reputation with the soldiers.

For the reasons listed above, it came about that, of Marcus, Pertinax, and Alexander, all of whom lived modest lives, were lovers of justice, enemies of cruelty, humane, and kindly, all except Marcus came to an unhappy end. Marcus alone lived and died with the greatest of honor, for he succeeded to the empire by birthright, and he did not have to recognize any obligation for it either to the soldiers or to the people; then, being endowed with many characteristics which made him revered, he always held, while he was living, both the one party and the other within their limits, and he was never either hated or despised. But Pertinax was made emperor against the will of the soldiers, who, being used to living licentiously under Commodus, could not tolerate the righteous manner of life to which Pertinax wished to return them; whereupon, having made himself hated, and since to this hatred was added contempt for his old age, he came to ruin at the initial stage of his rule.

And here one must note that hatred is acquired just as much by means of good actions as by bad ones; and so, as I said above, if a prince wishes to maintain the state, he is often obliged not to be good; because whenever that group which you believe you need to support you is corrupted, whether it be the common people, the soldiers, or the nobles, it is to your advantage to follow their inclinations in order to satisfy them; and then good actions are your enemy. But let us come to Alexander. He was of such goodness that among the other laudable deeds attributed to him is this: in the fourteen years that he ruled the empire he never put anyone to death without a trial; nevertheless, since he was considered effeminate and a man who let himself be ruled by his mother, because of this he was despised, and the army plotted against him and murdered him.

Considering now, in contrast, the characteristics of Commodus, Severus, Antoninus Caracalla, and Maximinus, you will find them extremely cruel and greedy; in order to satisfy their troops, they did not hesitate to inflict all kinds of injuries upon the people; and all except Severus came to a sorry end. For in Severus there was so much ability that, keeping the soldiers as his friends even though the people were oppressed by him, he was always able to rule happily; for those qualities of his made him so esteemed in the eyes of both the soldiers and the common people that the former were awestruck and stupefied and the latter were respectful and satisfied.

And since the actions of this man were great and noteworthy for a new prince, I wish to demonstrate briefly how well he knew how to use the masks of the fox and the lion, whose natures, as I say above, a prince must imitate. As soon as Severus learned of the indecisiveness of the emperor Julian, he convinced the army of which he was in command in Slavonia that it would be a good idea to march to Rome to avenge the death of Pertinax, who had been murdered by the Praetorian Guards. And under this pretext, without showing his desire to rule the empire, he moved his army to Rome, and he was in Italy before his departure was known. When he arrived in Rome, the senate, out of fear, elected him emperor, and Julian was killed. After this beginning, there remained two obstacles for Severus if he wanted to make himself master of the whole state: the first in Asia, where Pescennius Niger, commander of the Asiatic armies, had himself named emperor; and the other in the West, where Albinus was, who also aspired to the empire. And since he judged it dangerous to reveal himself as an enemy to both of them, he decided to attack Niger and to deceive Albinus. He wrote to the latter that, having been elected emperor by the senate, he wanted to share that honor with him; and he sent him the title of Caesar and, by decree of the senate, he made him his coequal: these things were accepted by Albinus as the truth. But after Severus had conquered and executed Niger and had pacified affairs in the East, upon returning to Rome, he complained to the senate that Albinus, ungrateful for the benefits received from him, had treacherously sought to kill him, and for this he was obliged to go and punish his ingratitude. Then he went to find him in France and took both his state and his life.

Anyone, therefore, who will carefully examine the actions of this man will find him a very ferocious lion and a very shrewd fox; and he will see him feared and respected by everyone and not hated by his armies; and one should not be amazed that he, a new man, was able to hold so great an empire; for his outstanding reputation always defended him from that hatred which the common people could have produced on account of his plundering. But Antoninus, his son, was also a man who had excellent abilities which made him greatly admired in the eyes of the people and pleasing to the soldiers, for he was a military man, most able to support any kind of hardship, a despiser of all delicate foods and soft living; this made him loved by all the armies; nevertheless, his ferocity and cruelty were so great and so unusual—since he had, after countless individual killings, put to death a large part of the populace of Rome and all that of Alexandria—that he became most despised all over the world. And he aroused the fears even of those whom he had around him; so that he was murdered by a centurion in the midst of his army. From this it is to be noted that such deaths as these, which result from the deliberation of a determined individual, are unavoidable for princes, since anyone who does not fear death can harm them; but the prince must not be too afraid of such men, for they are very rare. He must only guard against inflicting serious injury on anyone who serves him and anyone he has about him in the administration of the principality: Antoninus had done this, for he had shamefully put to death a brother of that centurion, and he threatened the man every day; yet he kept him as a bodyguard. This was a dangerous decision and one that would ruin him, just as it did.

But let us come to Commodus, who held the empire with great ease, having inherited it by birth, being the son of Marcus; and it would have been enough for him to follow in the footsteps of his father in order to satisfy the soldiers and the common people. But being a cruel and bestial person by nature, in order to practice his greed upon the common people, he turned to pleasing the armies and to making them undisciplined; on the other hand, by not maintaining his dignity, frequently descending into the arenas to fight with the gladiators and doing other degrading things unworthy of the imperial majesty, he became contemptible in the sight of the soldiers. And being hated, on the one hand, and despised, on the other, he was plotted against and murdered.

The qualities of Maximinus remain to be described. He was a very warlike man; and because the armies were angered by Alexander's softness, which I explained above, after Alexander's death they elected him to the empire. He did not retain it very long, for two things made him hated and despised: the first was his base origin, having herded sheep once in Thrace (this fact was well known everywhere and it caused him to lose considerable dignity in everyone's eyes); the second was that at the beginning of his reign he deferred going to Rome to take possession of the imperial throne, and he had given himself the reputation of being very cruel, having through his prefects, in Rome and in all other parts of the empire, committed many cruelties. As a result, the entire world was moved by disgust for his ignoble birth and by the hatred brought about by fear of his cruelty; first Africa revolted, then the senate with the entire populace of Rome, and finally all of Italy conspired against him. To this was added even his own army; for, while besieging Aquileia and finding the capture difficult, angered by his cruelty and fearing him less, seeing that he had many enemies, they murdered him.

I do not wish to discuss Heliogabalus or Macrinus or Julian, who, since they were universally despised, were immediately disposed of; but I shall come to the conclusion of this discourse. And I say that the princes of our times suffer less from this problem of satisfying their soldiers by extraordinary means in their affairs; for, although they have to observe some consideration toward them, yet they resolve the question quickly, for none of these princes has standing armies which have evolved along with the government and the administration of the provinces as did the armies of the Roman empire. And therefore, if it was then necessary to satisfy the soldiers more than the common people, it was because the soldiers could do more than the common people; now it is more necessary for all princes, except the Turk and the Sultan, to satisfy the common people more than the soldiers, since the people can do more than the soldiers. I make an exception of the Turk, for he always maintains near him twelve thousand infantrymen and fifteen thousand cavalrymen, upon whom depend the safety and the strength of his kingdom, and it is necessary that, setting aside all other concerns, that ruler maintain them as his friends. Likewise, the kingdom of the Sultan being entirely in the hands of the soldiers, it is fitting that he, too, should maintain them as his friends without respect to the people. And you must note that this state of the Sultan is unlike all the other principalities, since it is similar to a Christian pontificate, which cannot be called either a hereditary principality or a new principality; for it is not the sons of the old prince that are the heirs and that remain as lords, but instead the one who is elected to that rank by those who have the authority to do so. And because this system is an ancient one, it cannot be called a new principality, for in it are none of these difficulties that are to be found in new ones; since, although the prince is new, the institutions of that state are old and are organized to receive him as if he were their hereditary ruler.

But let us return to our subject. Let me say that anyone who will consider the discourse written above will see how either hatred or contempt has been the cause of the ruin of these previously mentioned emperors; and he will also recognize how it comes to pass that, although some acted in one way and others in a contrary manner, in each of these groups one man had a happy end and the others an unhappy one. Because for Pertinax and Alexander, being new princes, it was useless and damaging to wish to imitate Marcus, who was installed in the principality by hereditary right; and likewise for Caracalla, Commodus, and Maximinus, it was disastrous to imitate Severus, since they did not have enough ability to follow in his footsteps. Therefore, a new prince in a new principality cannot imitate the deeds of Marcus, nor yet does he need to follow those of Severus; instead, he should take from Severus those attributes which are necessary to found his state and from Marcus those which are suitable and glorious in order to conserve a state which is already established and stable.

CHAPTER XX. ON WHETHER FORTRESSES AND MANY THINGS THAT PRINCES EMPLOY EVERY DAY ARE USEFUL OR HARMFUL

Some princes have disarmed their subjects in order to hold the state securely; others have kept their conquered lands divided; some have encouraged hostilities against themselves; others have turned to winning the support of those who were suspect at the beginning of their rule; some have built fortresses; others have torn them down and destroyed them. And although one cannot give a definite rule concerning these matters without knowing the particular details of those states wherein one had to take some similar decision, nevertheless I shall speak in as general a manner as the subject matter will allow.

There has never been, therefore, a time when a new prince disarmed his subjects; on the contrary, when he has found them unarmed he has always armed them, because when armed those arms become yours; those whom you suspect become faithful, and those who were faithful remain so, and they become your partisans rather than your subjects. And since all of your subjects cannot be armed, when those you arm are favored you can deal more securely with the others; and that distinction in treatment which they recognize toward themselves makes them obliged to you; the others excuse you, judging it necessary that those who are in more danger and who hold more responsibility should have more reward. But when you disarm them you begin to offend them; you demonstrate that you have no trust in them, either out of cowardice or from little confidence in them; and the one and the other of these opinions breed hatred against you. And since you cannot be unarmed, you will have to turn to mercenary soldiers who have the characteristics explained above; and even if they were good, they could not be strong enough to defend you from powerful enemies and from unfaithful subjects. Therefore, as I have said, a new prince in a new principality has always instituted an army; and histories are full of such examples.

But when a prince acquires a new state that, like a member, is joined to his old one, then it is necessary to disarm that state, except for those who have been your partisans in its acquisition; and they as well, with time and the appropriate opportunity, must be rendered weak and effeminate; and things must be organized in such a fashion that the armed strength of your entire state will be concentrated in your own troops who live near to you in your older state.

Our ancestors, and those who were considered wise, used to say that it was necessary to hold Pistoia by factions and Pisa by fortresses; and because of this they would encourage factional strife in some of their subject towns in order to control them more easily. This advice, during those times when Italy had, to a certain extent, a balance of power, may have been a good policy; but I do not believe that today it can be given as a rule, since I do not think that factions ever did any good. On the contrary, when the enemy approaches, divided cities are, of necessity, always lost; for the weaker factions will always join the external forces and the others will not be able to resist.

The Venetians, moved by the reasons stated above, as I believe, encouraged the Guelf and Ghibelline factions in their subject cities; and although they never permitted matters to come to bloodshed, they still fostered these quarrels between them so that those citizens, busy with their own disputes, would not unite against them. This, as we have seen, did not result in their gain; for, having been defeated at Vailà, one faction of these cities immediately took courage and seized the entire territory from them. Methods such as these, however, imply weakness in a prince; for in a strong principality such divisions will never be allowed, since they are profitable only in peacetime, allowing the subjects to be more easily controlled by their means; but when war comes such a policy shows its defects.

Without a doubt, princes become great when they overcome difficulties and obstacles that are imposed on them; and therefore Fortune, especially when she wishes to increase the reputation of a new prince, who has a greater need to acquire prestige than a hereditary prince does, creates enemies for him and has them take action against him so that he will have the chance to overcome them and to climb higher up the ladder his enemies have brought him. Therefore many judge that a wise prince must, whenever he has the occasion, foster with cunning some hostility so that in stamping it out his greatness will increase as a result.

Princes, and especially those who are new, have discovered more loyalty and more utility in those men who, at the beginning of their rule, were considered suspect than in those who were at first trusted. Pandolfo Petrucci, prince of Siena, ruled his state more with the assistance of men who had been held in suspicion than by others. But on this issue one cannot speak in generalities, for it varies according to the case. I shall only say this: that the prince will always easily win the support of those men who had been enemies at the start of a principality, the kind who must have support in order to maintain themselves; and they are even more obliged to serve him faithfully inasmuch as they recognize the need, through their actions, to cancel the suspicious opinion that the prince had of them. And thus, the prince will always derive more profit from them than from those who, serving him with too much security, neglect his affairs.

And since the subject requires it, I do not wish to fail to remind princes who have conquered a state recently by means of assistance from its inhabitants to consider carefully what cause may have moved those who have helped him to do so; and if it is not natural affection for him, but simply because they were not happy with the preceding state, he will be able to keep them as his allies only with hard work and the greatest of difficulty, since it will be impossible for him to satisfy them. And considering carefully the reason for this, with the examples taken from antiquity and from modern times, he will see that he can more easily win friends for himself from among those men who were content with the preceding state, and therefore were his enemies, than from those who, since they were not satisfied with it, became his allies and helped him to occupy it.

In order to hold their states more securely, princes have been accustomed to build fortresses that may serve as the bridle and bit for those who might plot an attack against them, and to have a secure shelter from a sudden rebellion. I praise this method, since it was used in ancient times; nevertheless, Messer Niccolò Vitelli, in our own times, was seen to demolish two fortresses in Città di Castello in order to hold that state; Guido Ubaldo, Duke of Urbino, on returning to the rule from which Cesare Borgia had driven him, completely destroyed all the fortresses of that province, and he decided that without them it would be more difficult to recapture that state; the Bentivogli, having returned to power in Bologna, took similar measures. Fortresses, then, are either useful or not, according to the circumstances: if they benefit you in one way they injure you in another. This matter may be dealt with as follows: that prince who is more afraid of his own people than of foreigners should build fortresses; but one who is more afraid of foreigners than of his people should not consider constructing them. The castle of Milan, which Francesco Sforza built there, has caused and will cause more wars against the Sforza family than any other disorder in that state. However, the best fortress that exists is not to be hated by the people; because, although you may have fortresses, they will not save you if the people hate you; for once the people have taken up arms, they never lack for foreigners who will aid them. In our times we have not seen that they have benefited any prince except the Countess of Forlì after her husband, Count Girolamo, was killed; for because of her castle she was able to escape the popular uprising and to wait until help arrived from Milan in order to regain her state. And the times were such at that moment that no foreigner could give assistance to her people. But then fortresses were of little use to her when Cesare Borgia attacked her and when her hostile populace joined with the foreigner. Therefore, then and earlier, it would have been safer for her not to have been despised by her people than to have had the fortresses.

Considering all these matters, therefore, I shall praise both those princes who build fortresses and those who do not; and I shall criticize any prince who, trusting in fortresses, considers the hatred of the people to be of little importance.

CHAPTER XXI.   HOW A PRINCE SHOULD ACT TO ACQUIRE ESTEEM

Nothing makes a prince more esteemed than great undertakings and examples of his unusual talents. In our own times we have Ferdinand of Aragon, the present King of Spain. This man can be called almost a new prince, since from being a weak ruler he became, through fame and glory, the first king of Christendom; and if you will consider his accomplishments, you will find them all very grand and some even extraordinary. In the beginning of his reign he attacked Granada, and that enterprise was the basis of his state. First, he acted while things were peaceful and when he had no fear of opposition: he kept the minds of the barons of Castile busy with this, and they, concentrating on that war, did not consider reforms at home. And he acquired, through that means, reputation and power over them without their noticing it; he was able to maintain armies with money from the Church and the people, and with that long war he laid a basis for his own army, which has since brought him honor. Besides this, in order to be able to undertake greater enterprises, always using religion for his own purposes, he turned to a pious cruelty, hunting down and clearing out the Moors from his kingdom: no example could be more pathetic or more unusual than this He attacked Africa, under the same cloak of religion; he undertook the invasion of Italy; he finally attacked France. And in such a manner, he has always done and planned great deeds which have always kept the minds of his subjects in suspense and amazed and occupied with their outcome. And these actions of his are born from each other in such a way that between one and another he would never give men enough time to be able to work calmly against him.

It also helps a prince a great deal to display rare examples of his skills in dealing with internal affairs, such as those which are reported about Messer Bernabò Visconti of Milan. When the occasion arises that a person in public life performs some extraordinary act, be it good or evil, he should find a way of rewarding or punishing him that will provoke a great deal of discussion. And above all, a prince should strive in all of his deeds to give the impression of a great man of superior intelligence.

A prince is also respected when he is a true friend and a true enemy; that is, when he declares himself on the side of one prince against another without any reservation. Such a policy will always be more useful than that of neutrality; for if two powerful neighbors of yours come to blows, they will be of the type that, when one has emerged victorious, you will either have cause to fear the victor or you will not have. In either of these two cases, it will always be more useful for you to declare yourself and to fight an open war; for, in the first case, if you do not declare your intentions, you will always be the prey of the victor to the delight and satisfaction of the vanquished, and you will have no reason why anyone would come to your assistance; because whoever wins does not want reluctant allies who would not assist him in times of adversity; and whoever loses will not give you refuge since you were unwilling to run the risk of coming to his aid.

Antiochus came into Greece, sent there by the Aetolians to drive out the Romans. Antiochus sent envoys to the Achaeans, who were friends of the Romans, to encourage them to adopt a neutral policy; and, on the other hand, the Romans were urging them to take up arms on their behalf. This matter came up for debate in the council of the Achaeans, where the legate of Antiochus persuaded them to remain neutral; to this the Roman legate replied: "The counsel these men give you about not entering the war is indeed contrary to your interests; without respect, without dignity, you will be the prey of the victors."

And it will always happen that he who is not your friend will request your neutrality and he who is your friend will ask you to declare yourself by taking up your arms. And irresolute princes, in order to avoid present dangers, follow the neutral road most of the time, and most of the time they are ruined. But when the prince declares himself vigorously in favor of one side, if the one with whom you have joined wins, although he may be powerful and you may be left to his discretion, he has an obligation to you and there does exist a bond of friendship; and men are never so dishonest that they will crush you with such a show of ingratitude; and then, victories are never so sure that the victor need be completely free of caution, especially when justice is concerned. But if the one with whom you join loses, you will be taken in by him; and while he is able, he will help you, and you will become the comrade of a fortune which can rise up again.

In the second case, when those who fight together are of such a kind that you need not fear the one who wins, it is even more prudent to join his side, since you go to the downfall of a prince with the aid of another prince who should have saved him if he had been wise; and in winning he is at your discretion, and it is impossible for him not to win with your aid.

And here it is to be noted that a prince should avoid ever joining forces with one more powerful than himself against others unless necessity compels it, as was said above; for you remain his prisoner if you win, and princes should avoid, as much as possible, being left at the mercy of others. The Venetians allied themselves with France against the Duke of Milan; and they could have avoided that alliance, which resulted in their ruin. But when such an alliance cannot be avoided (as happened to the Florentines when the Pope and Spain led their armies to attack Lombardy), then a prince should join in, for the reasons given above. Nor should any state ever believe that it can always choose safe courses of action; on the contrary, it should think that they will all be doubtful; for we find this to be in the order of things: that we never try to avoid one disadvantage without running into another; but prudence consists in knowing how to recognize the nature of disadvantages and how to choose the least bad as good.

A prince also should demonstrate that he is a lover of talent by giving recognition to men of ability and by honoring those who excel in a particular field. Furthermore, he should encourage his subjects to be free to pursue their trades in tranquillity, whether in commerce, agriculture, or in any other trade a man may have. And he should act in such a way that a man is not afraid to increase his goods for fear that they will be taken away from him, while another will not be afraid to engage in commerce for fear of taxes; instead, he must set up rewards for those who wish to do these things, and for anyone who seeks in any way to aggrandize his city or state. He should, besides this, at the appropriate times of the year, keep the populace occupied with festivals and spectacles. And because each city is divided into guilds or clans, he should take account of these groups, meet with them on occasion, offer himself as an example of humanity and munificence, always, nevertheless, maintaining firmly the dignity of his position, for this should never be lacking in any way.

CHAPTER XXII.   ON THE PRINCE'S PRIVATE ADVISERS

The choice of advisers is of no little import to a prince; and they may be good or not, according to the wisdom of the prince. The first thing one does to evaluate the wisdom of a ruler is to examine the men that he has around him; and when they are capable and faithful one can always consider him wise, for he has known how to recognize their ability and to keep them loyal; but when they are otherwise one can always form a low impression of him; for the first error he makes is made in this choice of advisers.

There was no one who knew Messer Antonio da Venafro, adviser of Pandolfo Petrucci, Prince of Siena, who did not judge Pandolfo to be a very worthy man for having him as his minister. For there are three types of intelligence: one understands on its own, the second discerns what others understand, the third neither understands by itself nor through the intelligence of others; that first kind is most excellent, the second excellent, the third useless; therefore, it was necessary that if Pandolfo's intelligence were not of the first sort it must have been of the second: for, whenever a man has the intelligence to recognize the good or the evil that a man does or says, although he may not have original ideas of his own, he recognizes the sorry deeds and the good ones of the adviser, and he is able to praise the latter and to correct the others; and the adviser cannot hope to deceive him and thus he maintains his good behavior.

But as to how a prince may know the adviser, there is this way which never fails. When you see that the adviser thinks more about himself than about you, and that in all his deeds he seeks his own self-interest, such a man as this will never be a good adviser and you will never be able to trust him; for a man who has the state of another in his hand must never think about himself but always about his prince, and he must never be concerned with anything that does not concern his prince. And on the other hand, the prince should think of the adviser in order to keep him good—honoring him, making him wealthy, putting him in his debt, giving him a share of the honors and the responsibilities—so that the adviser sees that he cannot exist without the prince and so his abundant wealth will not make him desire more riches, or his many duties make him fear innovations. When, therefore, advisers and princes are of such a nature in their dealings with each other, they can have faith in each other; and when they are otherwise, the outcome will always be harmful either to the one or to the other.

CHAPTER XXIII. ON HOW TO AVOID FLATTERERS

I do not wish to omit an important matter and an error from which princes protect themselves with difficulty if they are not very clever or if they do not have good judgment. And these are the flatterers which fill the courts; for men delight so much in their own concerns, deceiving themselves in this manner, that they protect themselves from this plague with difficulty; and wishing to defend oneself from them brings with it the danger of becoming despised. For there is no other way to guard yourself against flattery than by making men understand that telling you the truth will not offend you; but when each man is able to tell you the truth you lose their respect. Therefore, a wise prince should take a third course, choosing wise men for his state and giving only those free rein to speak the truth to him, and only on those matters as he inquires about and not on others. But he should ask them about everything and should hear their opinions, and afterward he should deliberate by himself in his own way;

and with these counsels and with each of his advisers he should conduct himself in such a manner that all will realize that the more freely they speak the more they will be acceptable to nim; besides these things, he should not want to hear any others, he should follow through on the policy decided upon, and he should be firm in his decisions. Anyone who does otherwise is either prey for flatterers or changes his mind often with the variance of opinions: because of this he is not respected.

I wish, in this regard, to cite a modern example. Father Luca, the representative of the present Emperor Maximilian, explained, speaking about His Majesty, how the emperor never sought advice from anyone, nor did he ever do anything in his own way; this came about because of the emperor's secretive nature, a policy contrary to the one discussed above. He communicates his plans to no one, he accepts no advice about them; but as they begin to be recognized and discovered as they are put into effect, they begin to be criticized by those around him; and he, being easily influenced, is drawn away from his plans. From this results the fact that those things he achieves in one day he destroys during the next, and no one ever understands what he wishes or plans to do, and one cannot rely upon his decisions.

A prince, therefore, should always seek counsel, but when he wishes and not when others wish it; on the contrary, he should discourage anyone from giving him counsel unless it is requested. But he should be a great inquisitor and then, concerning the matters inquired about, a patient listener to the truth; furthermore, if he learns that anyone, for any reason, does not tell him the truth, he should become angry. And although many feel that any prince who is considered clever is so reputed not because of his own character but because of the good advisers he has around him, without a doubt they are deceived. For this is a general rule which never fails: that a prince who is not wise in his own right cannot be well advised, unless by chance he has submitted himself to a single person who governed him in everything and who was a very prudent individual. In this case he could well receive good advice, but it would not last long because that adviser would in a brief time take the state away from him. But if he seeks advice from more than one, a prince who is not wise will never have consistent advice, nor will he know how to make it consistent on his own; each of his advisers will think about his own interests; he will not know either how to correct or to understand them. And one cannot find advisers who are otherwise, for men always turn out badly for you unless some necessity makes them good. Therefore, it is to be concluded that good advice, from whomever it may come, must arise from the prudence of the prince and not the prince's prudence from the good advice.

CHAPTER XXIV. WHY ITALIAN PRINCES HAVE LOST THEIR STATES

The things written above, if followed prudently, make a new prince seem well established and render him immediately safer and more established in his state than if he had been in it for some time. For a new prince is far more closely observed in his activities than is a hereditary prince; and when his deeds are recognized as skillful they attract men much more and bind them to him more strongly than does ancient blood. For men are much more taken by present concerns than by those of the past; and when they find the present good they enjoy it and seek nothing more; in fact, they will seize every measure to defend the new prince as long as he is not lacking in his other responsibilities. And thus he will have a double glory: that of having given birth to a new principality and of having decorated it and strengthened it with good laws, good arms, and good examples; as that one will have double shame who, having been born a prince, loses his principality on account of his lack of prudence.

And if one will consider those rulers in Italy that have

lost their states in our times, such as the King of Naples, the Duke of Milan, and others, one will discover in them, first, a common defect insofar as arms are concerned, for the reasons that were discussed at length earlier; and then, one will see that some of them either will have had the people as their enemy or, if they have had the people as their friend, they will not have known how to secure themselves against the nobles; for without these defects states are not lost which have enough nerve to take an army into battle. Philip of Macedonia—not the father of Alexander but the one who was defeated by Titus Quintius—did not have much of a state compared to the greatness of the Romans and of Greece that attacked him; nonetheless, because he was a good soldier and knew how to hold the people and to secure himself from the nobility, he carried on war against them for many years; and if at the end he lost the control of several cities, he was nevertheless left with the kingdom.

Therefore, these princes of ours who have been in their principalities for many years, and who have then lost them, must not blame Fortune but instead their own idleness: for, never having thought in peaceful times that things might change (which is a common defect in men, not to consider in good weather the possibility of a tempest), when adverse times finally arrived they thought about running away and not about defending themselves; and they hoped that the people, after having been angered by the insolence of the victors, would recall them. This policy, when others are lacking, is good; but it is indeed bad to have disregarded all other solutions for this one; for you should never wish to fall, believing that you will find someone else to pick you up; because whether this occurs or not, it does not increase your security, that method being a cowardly defense and one not dependent upon your own resources. And only those defenses are good, certain, and lasting that depend on yourself and on your own ability.

CHAPTER XXV.   ON FORTUNE'S ROLE IN HUMAN AFFAIRS
AND HOW SHE CAN BE DEALT WITH

It is not unknown to me that many have held, and still
hold, the opinion that the things of this world are, in a
manner, controlled by Fortune and by God, that men
with their wisdom cannot control them, and, on the contrary, that men can have no remedy whatsoever for them;
and for this reason they might judge that they need not
sweat much over such matters but let them be governed
by fate. This opinion has been more strongly held in our
own times because of the great variation of affairs that has
been observed and that is being observed every day which
is beyond human conjecture. Sometimes, as I think about
these things, I am inclined to their opinion to a certain
extent. Nevertheless, in order that our free will not be extinguished, I judge it to be true that Fortune is the arbiter
of one half of our actions, but that she still leaves the control of the other half, or almost that, to us. And I compare
her to one of those ruinous rivers that, when they become
enraged, flood the plains, tear down the trees and buildings, taking up earth from one spot and placing it upon
another; everyone flees from them, everyone yields to
their onslaught, unable to oppose them in any way. And
although they are of such a nature, it does not follow that
when the weather is calm we cannot take precautions with
embankments and dikes, so that when they rise up again
either the waters will be channeled off or their impetus
will not be either so disastrous or so damaging. The same
things happen where Fortune is concerned: she shows her
force where there is no organized strength to resist her;
and she directs her impact there where she knows that
dikes and embankments are not constructed to hold her.
And if you will consider Italy, the seat of these changes
and the nation which has set them in motion, you will see
a country without embankments and without a single
bastion: for if she were defended by the necessary forces,

like Germany, Spain, and France, either this flood would not have produced the great changes that it has or it would not have come upon us at all. And this I consider enough to say about Fortune in general terms.

But, limiting myself more to particulars, I say that one sees a prince prosper today and come to ruin tomorrow without having seen him change his character or any of his traits. I believe that this comes about, first, because of the reasons that have been discussed at length earlier; that is, that a prince who relies completely upon Fortune will come to ruin as soon as she changes; I also believe that the man who adapts his course of action to the nature of the times will succeed and, likewise, that the man who sets his course of action out of tune with the times will come to grief. For one can observe that men, in the affairs which lead them to the end that they seek—that is, glory and wealth—proceed there in different ways; one by caution, another with impetuousness; one through violence, another with guile; one with patience, another with its opposite; and each one by these various means can attain his goals. And we also see, in the case of two cautious men, that one reaches his goal while the other does not; and, likewise, two men equally succeed using two different means, one being cautious and the other impetuous: this arises from nothing else than the nature of the times that either suit or do not suit their course of action. From this results that which I have said, that two men, working in opposite ways, can produce the same outcome; and of two men working in the same fashion one achieves his goal and the other does not. On this also depends the variation of what is good; for, if a man governs himself with caution and patience, and the times and conditions are turning in such a way that his policy is a good one, he will prosper; but if the times and conditions change, he will be ruined because he does not change his method of procedure. Nor is there to be found a man so prudent that he knows how to adapt himself to this, both because he cannot deviate from that to which he is by nature inclined and also because he cannot be persuaded to depart from a path, having always prospered by following it. And therefore the cautious man, when it is time to act impetuously, does not know how to do so, and he is ruined; but if he had changed his conduct with the times, Fortune would not have changed.

Pope Julius II acted impetuously in all his affairs; and he found the times and conditions so apt to this course of action that he always achieved successful results. Consider the first campaign he waged against Bologna while Messer Giovanni Bentivogli was still alive. The Venetians were unhappy about it; so was the King of Spain; Julius still had negotiations going on about it with France; and nevertheless, he started personally on this expedition with his usual ferocity and lack of caution. Such a move kept Spain and the Venetians at bay, the latter out of fear and the former out of a desire to regain the entire Kingdom of Naples; and at the same time it drew the King of France into the affair, for when the king saw that the Pope had already made this move, he judged that he could not deny him the use of his troops without obviously harming him, since he wanted his friendship in order to defeat the Venetians. And therefore Julius achieved with his impetuous action what no other pontiff would ever have achieved with the greatest of human wisdom; for, if he had waited to leave Rome with agreements settled and things in order, as any other pontiff might have done, he would never have succeeded, because the King of France would have found a thousand excuses and the others would have aroused in him a thousand fears. I wish to leave unmentioned his other deeds, which were all similar and which were all successful. And the brevity of his life did not let him experience the opposite, since if times which necessitated caution had come his ruin would have followed from it: for never would he have deviated from those methods to which his nature inclined him.

I conclude, therefore, that since Fortune changes and men remain set in their ways, men will succeed when the two are in harmony and fail when they are not in accord. I am certainly convinced of this: that it is better to be impetuous than cautious, because Fortune is a woman, and it is necessary, in order to keep her down, to beat her and to struggle with her. And it is seen that she more often allows herself to be taken over by men who are impetuous than by those who make cold advances; and then, being a woman, she is always the friend of young men, for they are less cautious, more aggressive, and they command her with more audacity.

CHAPTER XXVI.   AN EXHORTATION TO LIBERATE ITALY FROM THE BARBARIANS

Considering, therefore, all of the things mentioned above, and thinking to myself about whether the times are suitable, at present, to honor a new prince in Italy, and if there is the material that might give a skillful and prudent prince the opportunity to form his own creation that would bring him honor and good to the people of Italy, it seems to me that so many circumstances are favorable to such a new prince that I know of no other time more appropriate. And if, as I said, it was necessary that the people of Israel be slaves in Egypt in order to recognize Moses' ability, and it was necessary that the Persians be oppressed by the Medes to recognize the greatness of spirit in Cyrus, and it was necessary that the Athenians be dispersed to realize the excellence of Theseus, then, likewise, at the present time, in order to recognize the ability of an Italian spirit, it was necessary that Italy be reduced to her present condition and that she be more enslaved than the Hebrews, more servile than the Persians, more scattered than the Athenians; without a leader, without organization, beaten, despoiled, ripped apart, overrun, and prey to every sort of catastrophe.

And even though before now some glimmer of light may have shown itself in a single individual, so that it was possible to believe that God had ordained him for Italy's redemption, nevertheless it was witnessed afterward how at the height of his career he was rejected by Fortune. So now Italy remains without life and awaits the man who can heal her wounds and put an end to the plundering of Lombardy, the ransoms in the Kingdom of Naples and in Tuscany, and who can cure her of those sores which have been festering for so long. Look how she now prays to God to send someone to redeem her from these barbaric cruelties and insolence; see her still ready and willing to follow a banner, provided that there be someone to raise it up. Nor is there anyone in sight, at present, in whom she can have more hope than in your illustrious house, which, with its fortune and ability, favored by God and by the Church, of which it is now prince, could make itself the head of this redemption. This will not be very difficult if you keep before you the deeds and the lives of those named above. And although those men were out of the ordinary and marvelous, they were nevertheless men; and each of them had less opportunity than the present one; for their enterprises were no more just, nor easier, nor was God more a friend to them than to you. Here justice is great: "Only those wars that are necessary are just, and arms are sacred when there is no hope except through arms."[1] Here there is a great willingness; and where there is a great willingness there cannot be great difficulty, if only you will use the institutions of those men I have proposed as your target. Besides this, we now see extraordinary, unprecedented signs brought about by God: the sea has opened up; a cloud has shown you the path; the rock pours forth water; it has rained manna here; everything has converged for your greatness. The rest you must do yourself. God does not wish to do everything, in order not to take from us our free will and that part of the glory which is ours.

And it is no surprise if some of the Italians mentioned previously were not capable of doing what it is hoped

[1] Livy, IX, i.

may be done by your illustrious house, and if, during the many revolutions in Italy and the many campaigns of war, it always seems that her military ability is spent. This results from the fact that her ancient institutions were not good and that there was no one who knew how to discover new ones; and no other thing brings a new man on the rise such honor as the new laws and the new institutions discovered by him. These things, when they are well founded and have in themselves a certain greatness, make him revered and admirable. And in Italy there is no lack of material to be given a form: here there is great ability in her members, were it not for the lack of it in her leaders. Consider how in duels and skirmishes involving just a few men the Italians are superior in strength, dexterity, and cunning; but when it comes to armies they do not match others. And all this comes from the weakness of her leaders; for those who know are not followed; and with each one seeming to know, there has not been to the present day anyone who has known how to set himself above the others, either because of ingenuity or fortune, so that others might yield to him. As a consequence, during so much time and many wars fought over the past twenty years, whenever there has been an army made up completely of Italians it has always made a poor showing. As proof of this, there is first Taro, then Alexandria, Capua, Genoa, Vailà, Bologna, and Mestri.[2]

Therefore, if your illustrious house desires to follow these excellent men who redeemed their lands, it is necessary before all else, as a true basis for every undertaking, to provide yourself with your own native troops, for one cannot have either more faithful, more loyal, or better troops. And although each one separately may be brave, all of them united will become even braver when they find themselves commanded, honored, and well treated by their own prince. It is necessary, therefore, to prepare

---

[2] Here Machiavelli refers to the battle of Fornovo (1495) and the taking of Alexandria (1499), Capua (1501), Genoa (1507), Vailà (1509), Bologna (1511), and Mestri (1513).

yourself with such troops as these, so that with Italian strength you will be able to defend yourself from foreigners. And although Swiss and Spanish infantry may be reputed terrifying, nevertheless both have defects, so that a third army could not only oppose them but be confident of defeating them. For the Spanish cannot withstand cavalry and the Swiss have a fear of foot soldiers they meet in combat who are as brave as they are. Therefore, it has been witnessed and experience will demonstrate that the Spanish cannot withstand French cavalry and the Swiss are ruined by Spanish infantrymen. And although this last point has not been completely confirmed by experience, there was nevertheless a hint of it at the battle of Ravenna,[3] when the Spanish infantry met the German battalions, who follow the same order as the Swiss; and the Spanish, with their agile bodies, aided by their spiked shields, entered between and underneath the Germans' long pikes and were safe, without the Germans having any recourse against them; and had it not been for the cavalry charge that broke them, the Spaniards would have slaughtered them all. Therefore, as the defects of both these kinds of troops are recognized, a new type can be instituted which can stand up to cavalry and will have no fear of foot soldiers: this will come about by creating new armies and changing battle formations. And these are among those matters that, when newly organized, give reputation and greatness to a new prince.

This opportunity, therefore, must not be permitted to pass by so that Italy, after so long a time, may behold its redeemer. Nor can I express with what love he will be received in all those provinces that have suffered through these foreign floods; with what thirst for revenge, with what obstinate loyalty, with what compassion, with what tears! What doors will be closed to him? Which people will deny him obedience? What jealousy could oppose

[3] On April 11, 1512, the French were victorious under the leadership of Gaston de Foix.

him? What Italian would deny him homage? This barbarian dominion stinks to everyone! Therefore, may your illustrious house take up this mission with that spirit and with that hope in which just undertakings are begun; so that under your banner this country may be ennobled and, under your guidance, those words of Petrarch may come true:

> Discipline over rage
> Will take up arms; and the battle will be short.
> For ancient valor
> In Italian hearts is not yet dead.[4]

---

[4] From Petrarch's famous *canzone,* "Italia mia" (ll. 93–96).

THE DISCOURSES

EDITORS' NOTE

First published in 1531, The Discourses *apparently grew out of marginal notes Machiavelli assembled from a reading of Livy's account of the history of Rome. After setting this longer work aside, in 1513, to complete* The Prince, *Machiavelli returned to it in 1515 and worked on it from time to time until 1517. The prefaces and the dedication were added to the commentary last, it seems, but the entire work was probably never put into a finished form by its author. Although* The Discourses *are less well known than* The Prince, *they nevertheless contain many of Machiavelli's most original ideas and reflect the author's republican stance, a position which would subsequently puzzle many later critics and scholars intent upon branding Machiavelli as an authoritarian thinker and an enemy of republican liberty. This abridged translation of* The Discourses *contains, in their entirety, all the prefaces and dedication plus sixty-four chapters of its three books; the remaining seventy-six chapters are abridged (within brackets) so that the reader may follow Machiavelli's arguments with no loss of continuity.*

DISCOURSES ON THE
FIRST TEN BOOKS OF TITUS LIVIUS
Niccolò Machiavelli to
Zanobi Buondelmonti and Cosimo Rucellai, Greetings

I am sending you a gift which, even though it may not match the obligations I have to you, is, without a doubt, the best that Niccolò Machiavelli can send to you; in it I have expressed all I know and all that I have learned from long experience and continuous study of worldly affairs. And since it is not possible for you or anyone else to ask more of me, you cannot complain if I have not given you more. You may very well complain about the poverty of my wit when my arguments are weak, and about the fallacious quality of my judgment if, in the course of my reasonings, I often manage to deceive myself. This being the case, I do not know which of us should be less obliged to the other: whether I should be so to you, who have encouraged me to write what I never would have written by myself, or you to me, since I may have written without satisfying you. Take this, then, as you would accept something from a friend: there one considers the intention of the sender more than the quality of the thing which is sent. And rest assured that in this venture I have one consolation, for I believe that although I may have deceived myself in many of its particulars, in one matter I know that I have not made an error; that is, to have chosen you above all others to whom I should dedicate these *Discourses* of mine, both because in so doing I believe that I have shown my gratitude for the benefits I have received and because I felt that I had departed from the common practice of those who write and always address their works to some prince and, blinded by ambition and by avarice, praise him for all his virtuous qualities when they ought to be blaming him for all his bad qualities. So, to avoid this mistake, I have chosen not those who are princes but those who, because of their numerous good qualities, deserve to be princes; not those who might shower me with offices, honors, and wealth, but those who, although unable, would like to do so. If men wish to judge correctly, they must esteem those who are generous, not those who are potentially generous; and, in like manner, they must esteem those who know how to rule a kingdom, not those who, without knowing how, have the power to do so. Thus, historians praise Hiero the Syracusan more when he was a private citizen than they do Perseus of Macedonia when he was king: for Hiero lacked nothing to be prince save a kingdom, while the other had no attribute of a king except his kingdom. Therefore, enjoy this good or bad work which you yourselves have requested; and if you persist in erroneously finding pleasure in my opinions, I shall not fail to follow this with the rest of the history, as I promised you in the beginning. Farewell.

BOOK I

INTRODUCTION

Because of the envious nature of men, it has always been no less dangerous to discover new methods and institutions than to explore unknown oceans and lands, since men are quicker to criticize than to praise the deeds of others. Nevertheless, driven by that natural desire I have always felt to work on whatever might prove beneficial to everyone, I have determined to enter a path which has not yet been taken by anyone; although it may bring me worry and difficulty, yet I may find my reward among those who study kindly the goal of these labors of mine. And if my feeble intelligence, my limited experience of current events, and my weak knowledge of ancient ones should make this attempt of mine defective and of little use, it may, at least, show the way to someone with more ability, more eloquence, and more judgment who will be able to fulfill my intention; so that if I do not earn praise, I should not receive blame.

When we consider, then, how much honor is attributed to antiquity, and how many times (leaving aside numerous other examples) a fragment of an ancient statue has been bought at a great price so that the buyer may have it near him to decorate his house or to have it imitated by those who take pleasure in that art; and when we see, on the other hand, the powerful examples which history shows us that have been accomplished by ancient kingdoms and republics, by kings, captains, citizens, and legislators who have exhausted themselves for their fatherland, examples that have been more often admired than imitated (or so much ignored that not the slightest trace of this ancient ability remains), I cannot but be at the same time both amazed and sorry. And I am even more amazed when I see that in civil disputes which arise among citizens, or in sicknesses that break out, men always have recourse to those judgments or remedies which were pronounced or prescribed by the ancients. For civil law is nothing other than the judgments given by ancient jurists which, organized into a system, instruct our jurists today. Nor is medicine anything other than the experiments carried out by ancient doctors on which the doctors of today base their diagnoses. Nevertheless, in instituting republics, maintaining states, governing kingdoms, organizing the army and administering a war, dispensing justice to subjects, and increasing an empire one cannot find a prince or a republic that has recourse to the examples of the ancients.

This, in my opinion, arises not so much from the weakness into which the present religion has brought the world or from the harm done to many Christian provinces and cities by an idle ambition as from not possessing a proper knowledge of histories, for in reading them we do not draw out of them that sense or taste that flavor which they have in themselves. Hence it happens that an infinite number of people read them and take pleasure in hearing about the variety of incidents which are contained in them without thinking to imitate them, for they consider imitation not only difficult but impossible; as if the heavens, the sun, the elements, and men had varied in their motion, their order, and their power from what they were in ancient times. Wishing, therefore, to free men of this erroneous way of thinking, I deemed it necessary to write about all those books by Livy which the malignity of time has not taken from us; I wish to write what I, according to my knowledge of ancient and modern affairs, judge necessary for a better understanding of them, so that those who read these statements of mine may more easily draw from them that practical knowledge one should seek from an acquaintance with history books. And although this undertaking is difficult, nevertheless, aided by those who have encouraged me to shoulder this burden, I believe I can carry it in such a manner that only a short distance will remain for another to bring it to the destined goal.

CHAPTER I.   WHAT THE BEGINNINGS OF ALL CITIES HAVE BEEN AND WHAT, IN PARTICULAR, WAS THE BEGINNING OF ROME

Those who read of the origin of the city of Rome, its lawgivers, and how it was organized will not be surprised that so much ability was preserved in that city for so many centuries, and that afterward there developed from it the empire which that republic achieved. And wishing first to discuss its origin, let me say that all cities are built either by men native to a region or by foreigners. The first situation occurs when inhabitants, dispersed in many small groups, feel they cannot live securely, since each single group, because of its location or its small number, cannot resist the assault of anyone who may attack it, and if the enemy arrives, they are not in time to unite for their defense; if there is time, they have to abandon many of their strong fortifications, and thus they remain at the mercy of their enemies. Hence, to escape these dangers, moved either by their own decision or by someone among them of greater authority, they join together to live as a group in a place chosen by them that is more convenient to live in and easier to defend.

This was what happened to Athens and Venice, among many others. The first of these cities, under the authority of Theseus, was built for such reasons by the inhabitants, who were a scattered people. As to the other city, many sought refuge on various small islands which were at the edge of the Adriatic Sea in order to escape the wars that arose each day as a result of the arrival of new barbarians after the decline of the Roman empire. The second city was built by its people without a particular prince to establish law and order, and they began on their own to live under those laws which appeared to them to be most suitable for their maintenance. This turned out well for them because of the lengthy peace which their location afforded them, for that sea had no harbor and the peoples who were molesting Italy had no ships with which to invade them; thus, this meager beginning was such that they were able to arrive at their present greatness.

The second instance occurs when a city is built by foreigners and originates either from free men or from those who depend on others, such as the colonies sent either by a republic or by a prince to relieve their lands of the inhabitants, or for the defense of a land which, newly acquired, they wish to maintain securely and without expenditure. The Roman people built many such cities throughout their empire. They may also be built by a prince, not in order to live there but rather for his own glorification, as was the case with the city of Alexandria for Alexander. And since these cities are not by origin free, it rarely happens that they make great progress and can be numbered among the chief capitals of kingdoms. The building of Florence was similar to that of such cities, for (either built by the soldiers of Sulla or perhaps by the inhabitants of the mountains of Fiesole, who came to live in the Arno plain because they had faith in the long peace that was born in the world under Octavian) she was built under the Roman empire, and she could not, in the beginning, experience any growth except that which the goodwill of her prince allowed her.

The builders of cities are free men when any people, either under the rule of a prince or on their own, are forced to abandon their native land and to find themselves a new home, either because of pestilence, famine, or war. Such men either inhabit the cities that they find in the lands which they conquer, as Moses did, or they build new ones, as Aeneas did. In this case we are able to see the ability of the builder in the fortune of what he builds, for the city is more or less remarkable according to whether he who has been its cause is more or less able. The ability of the man is recognized in two ways: the first is in his selection of a site, the second in the organization of the laws. And since men act either out of necessity or by choice, and since we know that there is more ability where free choice has less authority, it must be considered whether it might be best to select barren places for the building of cities so that men, forced to become industrious and less idle, will live more united, having less cause for discord because of the poverty of the site—as happened in Ragusa and in many other cities built in similar spots. Such a selection would, without a doubt, be most wise and useful if men were content to live on what they had and did not wish to try to govern others. Nevertheless, since men cannot make themselves secure without power, it is necessary for them to avoid the barren places in the country and to establish themselves in very fertile places where, the fruitfulness of the site permitting expansion of the city, men can both defend themselves from anyone who attacks them and overcome anyone who opposes their greatness. And as for that idleness which the site invites, one should organize the laws in such a way that they force upon the city those necessities which the location does not impose; and one should imitate the wise men who have lived in the most beautiful and fertile of lands, lands more apt to produce idle men unfit for any vigorous activity; in order to avoid the harm which the pleasant nature of the land might have caused because of idleness, they constrained their soldiers to undergo such training and exercise that better soldiers are produced there than in lands which are naturally harsh and barren. Among kingdoms like these was the kingdom of the Egyptians, where, notwithstanding the fact that the land was very pleasant, the necessity imposed by the laws was so powerful that it produced very excellent men; and if their names had not been destroyed by time, we would see that they merit more praise than Alexander the Great and many others still fresh in our memory. And if one considers the Kingdom of the Sultan, or the organization of the Mamelukes and that of their army before they were destroyed by Selim the Great Turk, one will see that there were many kinds of training exercises that the troops underwent, and one would also see how much they feared that idleness which the beneficence of the land might have brought upon them if they had not prevented it with the strictest of laws.

I say, therefore, that it is more prudent to select a fertile site when that fertility's influence is kept within certain bounds by the laws. When Alexander the Great wanted to construct a city to his glory, the architect Dinocrates came to him and showed him how he could build a city on top of Mount Athos, a place which, besides being strong, could be shaped in such a way that a human form would be given to that city, a most marvelous and rare thing and one worthy of his greatness. And when Alexander asked him how its inhabitants would live, he answered that he had not thought about that; at this Alexander laughed and put that mountain site aside and built Alexandria, where the inhabitants were happy to live because of the fertility of the land and the convenience of the sea and the Nile. Anyone who examines, then, the building of Rome, taking Aeneas as her first founder, will count her as one of those cities built by foreigners: if Romulus is taken as her first founder, he will consider her as one of those cities constructed by men native to the site; and in any case, he will see her as having had a free beginning, with no dependence upon anyone; and furthermore, he will see how many necessities were imposed upon her by the laws instituted by Romulus, Numa, and others so that the fertility of the location, the convenience of the sea, the frequent victories, and the grandeur of her empire were not able to corrupt her for many centuries; these laws kept her very rich in ability, richer than any other city or republic that was as well adorned.

And because the deeds she accomplished (of which Livy preserves the memory) were done either by public decree or private initiative, either inside or outside the city, I shall begin by discussing those internal affairs which happened as a result of public decree, which I judge to be most worthy of attention, adding to them everything that depended upon them; to these *Discourses* this first book, or rather this first part, will be limited.

CHAPTER II.   OF HOW MANY KINDS OF REPUBLICS THERE
ARE AND OF WHAT KIND THE ROMAN REPUBLIC WAS

I wish to put aside a discussion of those cities which, at their beginnings, were subject to others; and I shall speak about those which have had their beginnings far from any foreign servitude and have been governed from the beginning by their own judgment, either as republics or as principalities, and which have had different laws and institutions just as they have had different origins. Some of them, either at their start or after very little time, were given laws by a single man and at one time, as Lycurgus did with the Spartans; others acquired their laws by chance, at different times and according to circumstances, as occurred in Rome. A republic can, indeed, be called fortunate if it produces a man so prudent that he gives it laws organized in such a manner that it can live securely under them without needing to revise them. And it seems that Sparta observed its laws more than eight hundred years without corrupting them or without any dangerous upheaval. Unfortunate, on the contrary, is the city which is forced to reorganize itself, not having chanced to encounter a prudent organizer. And of these cities, the one which is the furthest from order is the most unfortunate; and that one is furthest from it which in its institutions is completely off the straight path which could lead it to its perfect and true goal, because for those who find themselves in this state it is almost impossible that by any happening they can be set on the right path again. Those other cities that have had a good beginning and are capable of becoming better, even if they have not had a perfect constitution, can, by means of an unexpected course of events, become perfect. But it is very true that institutions are never established without danger; for most men never agree to a new law that concerns a new order in the city unless a necessity demonstrates to them that it is required; and since this necessity cannot arise without danger, the republic may easily be destroyed before it is brought to a perfection of organization. The Republic of Florence testifies to this: reorganized after what occurred at Arezzo in 1502, it was disorganized by what occurred at Prato in 1512.[1]

Since I wish to discuss what the institutions of the city of Rome were and the circumstances which led to their perfection, let me say that those who have written about republics declare that there are in them three kinds of governments, which they call principality, aristocracy, and democracy; and that those who organize a city most often turn to one of these, depending upon whichever seems more appropriate to them. Others—and wiser men, according to the judgment of many—are of the opinion that there are six types of government: three of these are

[1] Machiavelli here refers both to the constitutional changes in Florence after the suppression of a rebellion at Arezzo and to the return of the Medici and the fall of Soderini's republic after the sack of Prato.

very bad; three others are good in themselves but are so easily corruptible that they, too, can become pernicious. Those which are good are the three mentioned above; those which are bad are three others which depend upon the first three, and each of them is, in a way, similar to its good counterpart, so that they easily jump from one form to another. For the principality easily becomes tyrannical; aristocrats can very easily produce an oligarchy; democracy is converted into anarchy with no difficulty. So that if a founder of a republic organizes one of these three governments in a city, he organizes it there for a brief period of time only, since no precaution can prevent it from slipping into its contrary on account of the similarity, in such a case, of the virtue and the vice.

These variations of government are born among men by chance: for in the beginning of the world, when its inhabitants were few, they lived at one time dispersed and like wild beasts; then, when their numbers multiplied, they gathered together and, in order to defend themselves better, they began to search among themselves for one who was stronger and braver, and they made him their leader and obeyed him. From this sprang the knowledge of what things are good and honorable, as distinct from the pernicious and the evil: for if someone were to harm his benefactor, this aroused hatred and compassion among men, since they cursed the ungrateful and honored those who showed gratitude; and thinking that the same injuries could also be committed against themselves, they made laws to avoid similar evils and instituted punishments for transgressors. Thus, the recognition of justice came about. The result was that, later on, when they had to elect a prince, they did not select the bravest man but rather the one who was most prudent and most just. But when they began to choose the prince by hereditary succession rather than by election, the heirs immediately began to degenerate from the level of their ancestors and, putting aside acts of valor, they thought that princes had nothing to do but to surpass other princes in luxury, lasciviousness, and in every other form of pleasure. So, as the prince came to be hated he became afraid of this hatred and quickly passed from fear to violent deeds, and the immediate result was tyranny.

From this there came next the destructions, the conspiracies, and the plots against princes, carried out not by those who were either timid or weak but by those who surpassed others in generosity, greatness of spirit, wealth, and nobility: these men could not stand the disreputable life of such a prince. The masses, therefore, following the authority of these powerful men, took up arms against the prince, and after he had been eliminated they obeyed those men as their liberators. And since those men hated the very idea of a single ruler, they constituted for themselves a government, and in the beginning, since they remembered the past tyranny, they governed according to the laws instituted by themselves, subordinating their own interests to the common good, and they managed and maintained both their private and public affairs with the greatest of care. When this administration later passed to their sons, who did not understand the changeability of Fortune, had never experienced bad times, and could not be satisfied with equality among citizens, they turned to avarice, ambition, and the violation of other men's women, and they caused a government of the aristocrats to become a government of the few, with no regard to any civil rights; so that in a short time they experienced the same fate as the tyrant, for as the masses were sick of their rule, they assisted, in any way they could, anyone who might plan to attack these rulers, and thus there soon arose someone who, with the aid of the masses, destroyed them. And since the memory of the prince and of the injuries received from him was still fresh, they turned to a democratic form of government, having destroyed the government ruled by a few men and not wishing to return to that ruled by a prince; and they organized it in such a way that neither the few powerful men nor a prince might have any authority whatsoever in it. And because all governments are, at the outset, respected, this democratic government was maintained awhile, but not for a long time, particularly after the generation that organized it passed away; it immediately turned to anarchy, where neither the individual citizen nor the public official is feared; each individual lived according to his own wishes, so that every day a thousand wrongs were done; and so, constrained by necessity, either because of the suggestion of some good man or in order to flee such anarchy, it returned again to the principality; and from that, step by step, the government moved again in the direction of anarchy, in the manner and for the reasons just given.

And this is the cycle through which all states that have governed themselves or that now govern themselves pass; but rarely do they return to the same forms of government, for virtually no state can possess so much vitality that it can sustain so many changes and remain on its feet. But it may well happen that while a state lacking counsel and strength is in difficulty, it becomes subject to a neighboring state which is better organized; but if this were not the case, then a state might be liable to pass endlessly through the cycle of these governments.

Let me say, therefore, that all the forms of government listed are defective: the three good ones because of the brevity of their lives, the three bad ones because of their inherent harmfulness. Thus, those who were prudent in establishing laws recognized this fact and, avoiding each of these forms in themselves, chose one that combined them all, judging such a government to be steadier and more stable, for when there is in the same city-state a principality, an aristocracy, and a democracy, one form keeps watch over the other.

Among those who have deserved great praise for having established such constitutions is Lycurgus, who organized his laws in Sparta in such a manner that, assigning to the king, the aristocrats, and the people their

respective roles, he created a state which lasted more than
eight hundred years, to his everlasting credit, and resulted
in the tranquillity of that city. The contrary happened to
Solon, who organized the laws in Athens: for in organizing only a democratic state there he made it of such a
brief existence that before he died he saw arise the tyranny of Pisistratus; and although forty years later the latter's heirs were driven away and Athens returned to its
freedom, having reestablished the democratic state according to the institutions of Solon, it did not last more
than a hundred years. In spite of the fact that many laws
which were not foreseen by Solon were established in
Athens in order to restrain the insolence of the upper class
and the anarchy of the populace, nevertheless Athens
lived a very brief time in comparison to Sparta because
Solon did not mix democracy with the power of the principality and with that of the aristocrats.

But let us come to Rome. In spite of the fact that she
never had a Lycurgus to organize her at the beginning so
that she might exist free for a long time, nevertheless, because of the friction between the plebeians and the senate,
so many circumstances attended her birth that chance
brought about what a lawgiver had not accomplished. If
Rome did not receive Fortune's first gift, she received the
second: for her early institutions, although defective, nevertheless did not deviate from the right path that could
lead them to perfection. Romulus and all the other kings
passed many good laws in accordance with a free government; but since their goal was to found a kingdom and
not a republic, when that city became free she lacked
many institutions which were necessary to organize her
under freedom, institutions which had not been set up by
those kings. And when it happened that her kings lost
their power for the reasons and in the ways described earlier, nonetheless those who drove them out, having immediately established two consuls in place of the king,

drove out only the title of king and not royal power; so that, as there were in that republic the consuls and the senate, it came to be formed by only two of the three above-mentioned elements, that is, the principality and the aristocrats. There remained only to make a place for the democratic part of the government. When the Roman nobility became insolent, for the reasons that will be listed below, the people rose up against them; in order not to lose everything, the nobility was forced to concede to the people their own share; and on the other hand, the senate and the consuls retained enough authority so that they could maintain their rank in that republic. And thus there came about the creation of the tribunes of the plebeians, after which the government of the republic became more stable, since each of the three elements of government had its share. And Fortune was so favorable to Rome that even though she passed from a government by kings and aristocrats to one by the people, through those same steps and because of those same reasons which were discussed above, nevertheless the kingly authority was never entirely abolished to give authority to the aristocrats, nor was the authority of the aristocrats diminished completely to give it to the people; but since these elements remained mixed, Rome was a perfect state; and this perfection was produced through the friction between the plebeians and the senate, as the two following chapters will demonstrate at greater length.

CHAPTER III. WHICH EVENTS CAUSED THE CREATION OF THE TRIBUNES OF THE PLEBEIANS IN ROME, MAKING THE REPUBLIC MORE PERFECT

As is demonstrated by all those who discuss civic life (and as history is full of such examples), it is necessary for anyone who organizes a republic and institutes laws to take for granted that all men are evil and that they will always express the wickedness of their spirit whenever they have the opportunity; and when such wickedness remains hidden for a time, this is due to a hidden cause that is not recognized by those without experience of its contrary; but then time, which is said to be the father of every truth, will uncover it.

It seemed that there was the greatest of harmony in Rome between the plebeians and the senate after the Tarquins had been expelled, and that the nobles had set aside their pride and had become more like the people in spirit and were tolerated by all, even the lowest of citizens. This misunderstanding remained concealed, nor was the reason for it evident as long as the Tarquins were alive; for the nobility feared them and were afraid that if they mistreated the plebeians the latter would ally themselves with the Tarquins, and so they treated that class humanely. But when the Tarquins were dead and the fears of the nobility had been lessened, they began to vent upon the plebeians all that poison which they had held within their breasts, and they insulted them in every way they could. Such a thing testifies to what I said above, that men never do good except out of necessity; but when they have the freedom to choose and can do as they please, everything immediately becomes confused and disorderly. Hence it is said that hunger and poverty make men industrious and laws make them good. And where, without laws, something works well by itself, then laws are not necessary; but when this good custom is lacking, laws are immediately necessary. Therefore, when the Tarquins were gone and the fear of them no longer held the nobility in check, it was necessary to consider a new institution which might produce the same effect that the Tarquins produced while they were alive. So, after much uproar and confusion, and when the danger of scandal had been caused by the conflicts between the plebeians and the nobility, the creation of the tribunes came about for the security of the plebeians: and these tribunes were granted such prerogatives and such respect that they could, henceforth, always act as mediators between the plebeians and the senate and could check the insolence of the nobles.

CHAPTER IV.   HOW THE CONFLICT BETWEEN THE PLEBE-
IANS AND THE ROMAN SENATE MADE THAT REPUBLIC FREE
AND POWERFUL

I would not wish to fail to discuss those disturbances which erupted in Rome from the time of the death of the Tarquins to the creation of the tribunes; then I shall bring up other things to argue against the opinion of many who say that Rome was a turbulent republic, full of so much confusion that if good fortune and military ability had not made up for her defects she would have been inferior to any other republic. I cannot deny that Fortune and military organization were reasons for Roman power; but it seems clear to me that these thinkers fail to realize that where there is a good military organization there must also be good institutions, and only rarely does it occur that there is not good fortune as well. But let us go on to other details about this city.

It seems to me that those who criticize the conflicts between the nobles and the plebeians condemn those very things which were the primary cause of Roman liberty, and that they pay more attention to the noises and cries raised by such quarrels than to the good effects that they brought forth; nor do they consider that in every republic there are two different inclinations: that of the people and that of the upper class, and that all the laws which are made in favor of liberty are born of the conflict between the two, as one can easily see from what happened in Rome. From the time of the Tarquins to that of the Grac-chi, a period of more than three hundred years, the quar-rels of Rome rarely led to exile and very rarely to bloodshed. Thus, one cannot judge these dissensions harmful or such a republic as divided, for in so much time its conflicts sent no more than eight or ten citizens into exile, executed very few of them, and condemned not many more to pay monetary fines. Nor can one reasonably in any way call a republic disordered where such outstanding examples of ability appear, since good examples are born from good education, good education from good laws, and good laws from those quarrels which many condemn without due consideration; for anyone studying carefully the goal of these laws will find that they did not result in any exile or violence out of harmony with the common good, but rather that they gave rise to laws and institutions which benefited public liberty. And if anyone should say that the means were unlawful and almost savage, for the people were crying out against the senate, and the senate against the people; the population was running wildly through the streets, closing their shops, and leaving the city in droves—events which frighten even those who read about them—I reply that every city must have a means by which the people can express their ambition, and especially those cities that wish to make use of the people in important affairs: the city of Rome was among those possessing such means, for when the people wished to obtain a law they either did some of the things mentioned above or they refused to enlist for the wars, so that in order to placate them it was necessary to satisfy them in some measure. And the desires of free peoples are very rarely pernicious to liberty, for they arise from being oppressed or from the suspicion of future oppression. And should these opinions prove to be mistaken, there is the remedy of public meetings, in which some good man of influence may rise up and make a speech showing them that they are mistaken. And, as Cicero says,[1] although the populace may be ignorant, it is capable of understanding the truth and yields at once when it is told the truth by a man worthy of its trust.

Therefore, one should be more moderate in criticizing

---

[1] *De Amicitia*, xxv–xxvi.

the Roman government and should consider that all the many good effects which came from that republic were produced only from the best causes. And if the quarrels were the reason for the creation of the tribunes, these quarrels merit the highest praise; for besides giving to the people its share of control in the administration, the tribunes were set up as the caretakers of Roman liberty, as will be shown in the following chapter.

CHAPTER V.   WHETHER THE PROTECTION OF LIBERTY MAY BE MORE SECURELY PLACED IN THE PEOPLE OR IN THE UPPER CLASSES; AND WHICH HAS THE STRONGEST CAUSE FOR CREATING UPRISINGS, THOSE WHO WISH TO ACQUIRE OR THOSE WHO WISH TO MAINTAIN

Those who have prudently constituted a republic have considered, among the most necessary things to organize, the protection of liberty, and according to whether this is well done or not, that self-governing state will last for a longer or a shorter time. And because in every republic there are powerful men and men of the people, the question has been debated: into whose hands this protection may best be placed. It was placed in the hands of the nobles by the Spartans and, in our own time, by the Venetians; but it was placed in the hands of the plebeians by the Romans.

Therefore, it is necessary to examine which of these republics made the best choice. And if we look to the causes, there is something to be said for both sides; but if we consider the results, one might choose the side of the nobles since the liberty of Sparta and of Venice lasted longer than that of Rome. And coming to the causes, let me say, taking the side of the Romans first, that those should be put in charge of a thing who have the least desire to usurp it. And without a doubt, if we consider the goal of the nobles and the commoners, we shall see that in the former there is a great desire to dominate and in the latter only a desire not to be dominated, and, as a result, a greater will to live in liberty since they have less hope of acquiring it than the powerful: so, if the common people are set up as the caretakers of liberty, it is reasonable that they will have a greater concern for it, and since they cannot seize it themselves, they will not permit others to do so. On the other hand, those who defend the Spartan and the Venetian constitutions say that those who make powerful men the caretakers of liberty accomplish two good things: first, they more fully satisfy their ambition, and since they have a greater role in the republic, holding the reins of power in their hands, they have more reason to be content; second, they prohibit the restless minds of the plebeians from acquiring a sense of authority, a cause of infinite conflicts and scandals in a republic likely to drive the nobility to some kind of desperate act that will produce bad effects in the course of time. And those who hold this view cite as an example the same Roman republic, for while the tribunes of the people held this authority in their hands, one plebeian consul was not enough for them and they wanted to have them both. After this, they wanted the censorship, the praetorship, and all the other ranks of power in the city; nor did this suffice, for, driven by this same madness, they then began, in the course of time, to worship those men whom they saw ready to beat down the nobility. From this was born the power of Marius and the ruin of Rome. And truly, anyone who would argue well the case for one opinion and the other might remain in doubt as to which of the two ought to be chosen as the caretaker of such liberty, not knowing which type of man was more harmful to a republic: either the one who desires to maintain an honor already acquired or the one who desires to acquire what he does not possess.

And anyone who examines everything carefully will finally come to this conclusion: you either discuss a republic which desires to create an empire, like Rome, or one which is satisfied to maintain itself intact. In the first case it is necessary to do everything that Rome did; in the second instance one can imitate Venice or Sparta for the reasons that will be explained in the following chapter.

But to return to the discussion of the kinds of men that are more harmful in a republic: those who wish to acquire or those who fear losing what they have acquired. Let me say that when Marcus Menenius was made dictator and Marcus Fulvius commander of the cavalry, both of whom were plebeians, in order that they might investigate certain conspiracies which were being plotted at Capua against Rome, they were also granted the authority by the people to search for anyone in Rome who, through ambition or by irregular means, was trying to obtain the consulship and the other offices of the city. And since the nobles felt that such authority was granted to the dictator against them, they spread the rumor throughout Rome that it was not they who sought the offices out of ambition and by irregular means but the commoners, who, not trusting in their birth and their own ability, sought those ranks through unusual channels; and in particular they accused the dictator. And this accusation was so influential that after Menenius had given a speech in assembly and had complained of the false accusations lodged against him by the nobles, he renounced the dictatorship and submitted himself and his actions to the judgment of the people; and after his case had been discussed he was absolved. And there followed a great dispute about who was more ambitious, one who wished to maintain or one who wished to acquire; for one or the other passion can easily be the cause of very great disturbances. At any rate, in most cases these disturbances are caused by those who possess, for the fear of losing generates in them the same desires that those who desire to acquire possess; for men do not feel that they truly possess what they have if they do not acquire something more from others. And furthermore, those who possess much can with greater force and speed effect changes. And what is more serious, their unchecked and ambitious behavior kindles the desire for possession in the minds of those who do not possess, either in order to get revenge on the rich by taking their property away or in order to be able themselves to acquire the riches and offices which they see used so badly by others.

CHAPTER VI. WHETHER IN ROME IT WAS POSSIBLE TO INSTITUTE A GOVERNMENT THAT COULD DO AWAY WITH THE ENMITIES BETWEEN THE PEOPLE AND THE SENATE

We have discussed above the results of the controversies between the people and the senate. Now, since these continued until the time of the Gracchi, when they caused the downfall of free government, one might wish that Rome could have achieved the grand results that she did without the existence of such enmities within her. Therefore, it seems to me a matter worthy of consideration to see if in Rome one might have been able to institute a government capable of avoiding these controversies. And if we wish to study this problem, it is necessary to have recourse to those republics which, without such enmities and disturbances, have been free for a long time and to see what type of government they had and whether or not it could have been introduced in Rome. An example among ancient governments is that of Sparta; among modern governments, that of Venice, as I have already mentioned. Sparta established a king with a small senate to govern her. Venice did not distinguish by name between the parts of its government, but all those who had a place in the administration of the government were called gentlemen. This system was given to them more by chance than by the prudence of whoever instituted their laws; for, as they had taken shelter, for the reasons given earlier, on those islands where today their city now stands, many inhabitants, after they had increased to such a number that laws became necessary for them to live together, instituted one form of government; and as they often met together in their counsels to discuss the affairs of the city, when they felt that they were numerous enough to form a political organization they closed access to participation in their government to all those who might come there to live in the future; and in time, when they found that they had enough inhabitants outside the government to give reputation to those who governed, they called the latter gentlemen and the others commoners. This system could arise and maintain itself without disturbance, for when it was born anyone then residing in Venice was part of the government, so that no one was able to complain: those who came there to live afterward, finding the government closed and completed, did not have any reason or opportunity to cause a disturbance. There was no reason, since nothing of theirs had been taken from them; there was no opportunity, since anyone who ruled kept them in check and did not employ them in any manner which might allow them to acquire authority. Besides this, those who later came to live in Venice were not so numerous as to create an imbalance between those who governed and those who were governed, for the number of gentlemen was either equal to or superior to them; so that for these reasons Venice could institute that government and remain unified.

Sparta, as I have said, was governed by one king and a restricted senate. It was able to maintain itself for a long time because there were few inhabitants in Sparta and access to power had been denied to anyone who came there to live; furthermore, since the laws of Lycurgus had been adopted to the city's advantage (the observance of which prevented any cause for disturbances), the Spartans were able to live united for a long time. For Lycurgus, with his laws, established greater equality of property and less equality of rank in Sparta, so that there was an equality of poverty there, and the plebeians were less ambitious because the offices of the city were open to only a few citizens and were closed to the plebeians, nor did the nobles ever instill a desire in them to obtain these offices by mistreating the plebeians. This was the effect of the Spartan kings, who, placed in that princedom, in the midst of that nobility, had no alternative, in order to keep a firm hold on their office, but to defend the plebeians from any harm. The plebeians, as a result, had no fear or desire for power; and neither having power nor fearing it, the competition they might have had with the nobility and the cause of disturbances were removed, and they could live united for a long time. But two main things caused this union: first, the fact that Sparta had few inhabitants; second, the fact that since they did not take foreigners into their republic, the Spartans did not have the chance either to become corrupted or to grow so much that the city became impossible to manage for the few men who governed it.

When, therefore, all these matters are considered, one can see how the legislators of Rome had to do one of two things if they wished Rome to remain as peaceful as the two republics mentioned above: either follow the Venetians and not employ the plebeians in warfare or imitate the Spartans and not open their government to foreigners. But they did both one and the other. And this gave the plebeians strength, increasing their numbers, and provided them with infinite opportunities for riots. But had the Roman government been more peaceful, this disadvantage would have followed: it would have been weaker, for this would have cut short its means of coming to that greatness which it acquired; so that if Rome had wished to remove the reasons for her disturbances, she would have also removed the reasons for her expansion. And in all human affairs, he who studies them carefully will notice that one can never remove one inconvenience without causing another to arise. Therefore, if you try to make a people so numerous and so well armed that it can create a great empire, you are endowing it with qualities that will not allow you, afterward, easily to manage it as you wish; and if you keep it small or unarmed in order to be able to manage it, as you acquire dominions you will not hold on to them, or your state will become so weak that you will

be at the mercy of anyone who attacks you. And so, in all
our thinking, we must consider where the fewer inconveniences are and choose that path as the best one, because a choice which is completely clear and without
uncertainty can never be found. Rome could, therefore,
have done as Sparta did and create a ruler for life and a
small senate; but it could not, like Sparta, limit the number of its citizens since it wished to create an empire; thus,
a king for life and a small senate would have been of little
benefit in effecting her unity.

If, therefore, anyone wishes to organize a new republic,
he must first decide whether he wants it to increase in dominion and in power, as Rome did, or to be confined to
narrow limits. In the first case it is necessary to organize it
like Rome and to make room for disturbances and widespread dissension among the inhabitants as best one can,
for without a great number of well-armed men no republic will ever be able to grow or maintain itself if it does
grow. In the second case you can organize it like Sparta or
Venice; but since expansion is the poison of such republics, anyone who organizes it must, in all possible ways,
prohibit expansion, for such acquisitions founded upon a
weak republic are completely ruinous. This happened to
Sparta and to Venice: the former, after it had subjugated
almost all of Greece, demonstrated its weak foundation
with a minor incident: when Pelopidas incited the rebellion of Thebes, the other cities revolted and that republic
was completely ruined. In like manner, after Venice had
occupied a large part of Italy (most of it by financial
power and shrewdness), she lost it all in one day[1] when
she had to prove her strength. I firmly believe, therefore,
that in order to create a republic that is to endure for a
long time, the way to organize it internally would be to
follow Sparta or Venice: place the city on a site that is by

A reference to the disastrous battle of Agnadello (1509),
where the Venetians were defeated by the French. By 1517,
however, the Serenissima (Most Serene Republic) had regained much of her losses, a fact Machiavelli fails to note.

nature strong, and provide it with such strength that no one might think of overcoming it suddenly; on the other hand, the city should not be so large that it appears too formidable to its neighbors; and thus it could enjoy its independence for a long time. For war is waged upon a republic for two reasons: first, in order to subjugate it; and second, out of fear that it will subjugate you. These two reasons are almost completely eliminated by the above means of organization: for if a republic is difficult to take by force, as I suppose it to be, since it will be well organized for defense, rarely or never will conditions be such that one will plan to capture it. If it remains within its boundaries (and experience shows that there is no ambition within it), it will never happen that anyone will make war on it out of fear; and this fear will be even less likely if there is a constitution or law which prohibits it from expanding. And I believe, without a doubt, that if one is able to keep affairs balanced in this fashion, the result will be a true body politic and true tranquillity in the city. But since human affairs are constantly changing and never remain fixed, it is necessary that they either rise or fall, and many things that you are not impelled to do by reason you are impelled to do by necessity; so that, having organized a republic fit for maintaining itself without expansion, if necessity leads it to expand the process will remove its foundations and cause it to go to ruin very quickly.

Thus, on the other hand, if Heaven be so benevolent that it never has to wage war, the idleness would result in making it either effeminate or divided; these two things together, or each one in itself, would be the cause of its ruin. Therefore, not being able, as I believe, to balance matters or to maintain exactly this middle way, it is necessary in the organization of a republic to consider the most honorable choice and to organize it in such a way that should necessity impel it to expand, it may do so and conserve its acquisitions. And to return to my first argument, I believe that it is necessary to follow the organization of Rome and not that of other republics, because I do not believe that one can discover a middle way between one alternative and the other; and those enmities that arose between the people and the senate should be tolerated, considering them as an inconvenience necessary to arrive at Roman greatness. For other than the reasons cited, wherein I showed the authority of the tribunes to be necessary for the preservation of liberty, I easily observe the benefit republics derive from the right to make public charges, which was among the powers granted to the tribunes, as will be discussed in the following chapter.

CHAPTER VII. HOW THE RIGHT TO BRING PUBLIC CHARGES IS NECESSARY FOR A REPUBLIC TO PRESERVE ITS LIBERTY

No more useful and necessary authority can be granted to those who are appointed to preserve a city's liberty than the capacity to bring before the people or before some magistrate or council charges against citizens who sin in any manner against the freedom of the government. This institution produces two very useful results in a republic: first, for fear of being accused, the citizens do not attempt anything against the government, or, if they do, they are immediately suppressed without regard to their station; second, it provides an outlet for those hatreds which grow up in cities, in whatever manner, against some particular citizen: and when these hatreds do not find a legal means of expression, they have recourse to illegal means, which cause the eventual ruin of the entire republic. And so, nothing makes a republic so stable and strong as organizing it in such a way that the agitation of the hatreds which excite it has a means of expressing itself provided for by the laws. This can be demonstrated by many examples, and especially by that which Livy brings forth concerning Coriolanus, where he says that since the Roman nobility was angered at the plebeians because they felt that the plebeians had assumed too much authority as a result of the creation of the tribunes, who were to defend them, and since it happened that Rome then suffered a great scarcity of provisions and the senate had sent to Sicily for grain, Coriolanus, enemy of the popular faction, advised that the time had come to punish the plebeians by keeping them hungry and not distributing the grain, and by taking away from them the authority which they had usurped from the nobility. When this advice reached the ears of the people, they were so angry at him that he would have been murdered by the crowd as he left the senate if the tribunes had not called him to appear before them in his own defense. What was said above can be applied to this event—that is, that it is useful and necessary for republics to provide with their laws a means of expression for the wrath that the multitude feels against a single citizen, for when these legal means do not exist the people turn to illegal ones, and without a doubt the latter produce much worse effects than do the former.

For, when a citizen is legally oppressed, even if this be unjust to him, little or no disorder in the republic follows; for the execution of the act is done without private or foreign forces, which are the ones that destroy free government; but it is done with public forces and institutions which have their specific limits—nor do they transcend these limits to damage the republic. And as for corroborating this opinion with examples, that of Coriolanus from the ancients should suffice. Everyone should observe how much evil would have resulted for the Roman republic if he had been put to death by the crowd, for this would have created private grievances, which generate fear, and fear seeks defenses for which partisans are recruited, and from partisans are born the factions in cities, and from factions the ruin of the city. But since the matter was handled by those who had the authority to do so, all those evils which might have arisen by using private power were avoided.

We have witnessed in our own times what changes occurred in the Republic of Florence when the people were not able to vent their wrath legally against one of its citizens, as was the case when Francesco Valori was almost like the prince of that city. He was regarded by many as ambitious, a man who would transgress lawful government because of his audacity and hot temper; and since there was no means within the republic's existing institutions of resisting him without establishing a rival party, it came about that he set out to enlist partisans, not fearing anything but illegal methods; on the other hand, since those who opposed him had no legal way to suppress him, they turned to illegal methods and eventually resorted to arms. Given the proper legal institutions, he might have been opposed and his authority destroyed, harming only himself, but because he had to be destroyed unlawfully, this resulted in harm not only to him but also to many other noble citizens. One could also cite, in support of the above conclusion, the incident which happened in connection with Piero Soderini, which came about entirely from the absence in that republic of any means of bringing charges against the ambition of powerful citizens. For it is not enough to accuse a powerful citizen before eight judges in a republic; there must be many judges, for the few always act in favor of the few. If these methods had existed in Florence, either the citizens would have accused him if his conduct was bad—by this means, without calling in a Spanish army, they would have vented their anger—or, if his conduct was not bad, they would not have dared to act against him for fear that they themselves might be accused; and thus, in either case the appetite for conflict, which was the cause of the quarrel, would have vanished.

The following conclusion can be drawn: whenever one finds foreign forces being called in by one faction of men living in a city, it may be taken for granted that the bad ordinances of that city are the cause, for it does not have an institution that provides an outlet for the malignant humors which are born among men to express themselves without their resorting to illegal means; adequate provision for this is made by making a number of judges avail-

able before whom public indictments may be made; and
these accusations must be given proper importance. These
means were so well organized in Rome that during the
many conflicts between the plebeians and the senate neither the senate nor the plebeians nor any private citizen
ever attempted to use outside forces; for they had a remedy at home and there was no need to search for it outside. And although the above examples are more than
sufficient to prove this, I nevertheless wish to use another
taken from Livy's history: there he relates how in Chiusi,
a city which in those times was one of the most noble in
Tuscany, a certain Lucumones raped the sister of
Aruntes; unable to revenge himself because of the power
of the rapist, Aruntes went to meet with the Gauls, who at
that time ruled in the area which is now called Lombardy,
and persuaded them to come with troops to Chiusi, showing them how they would profit by avenging the injustice
he had suffered; Livy further explains how Aruntes would
not have sought barbarian troops if he had seen a way to
avenge himself through the city's institutions. But just as
public accusations are useful in a republic, so false accusations are useless and harmful, as the discussion in the
next chapter will show.

CHAPTER VIII.   FALSE ACCUSATIONS ARE AS HARMFUL TO
REPUBLICS AS THE BRINGING OF PUBLIC CHARGES IS
USEFUL

In spite of the fact that the ability of Furius Camillus,
who had freed Rome from the domination of the Gauls,
made all of the Roman citizens grant him prestige without
feeling that they had thereby lost reputation or rank—in
spite of this, Manlius Capitolinus could not stand the fact
that so much honor and glory was attributed to him, for
he felt that insofar as the salvation of Rome was concerned, he deserved as much as Camillus because he had
saved the Capitol, and that he was not inferior to him in
other praiseworthy military achievements. Therefore, so

full of envy was he because of the other's glory that he could not remain quiet, and when he found he was not able to sow discord among the senators, he turned to the plebeians, spreading among them various dangerous rumors. And among the things he said was that the treasure collected to be given to the Gauls had not been given to them but had, instead, been appropriated by private citizens, and that if it could be recovered it could be used to the public advantage, either in lightening the tax burdens of the plebeians or in resolving some private debts. These words caused a great stir among the plebeians, so much so that they began to hold meetings and cause a number of disturbances in the city; this displeased the senate, which, considering the matter momentous and dangerous, created a dictator to take charge of the case and to check the impetuosity of Manlius. Whereupon the dictator immediately cited him and had him appear in public in a direct confrontation—the dictator among the nobles and Manlius in the midst of the plebeians. Manlius was told to reveal who it was that had this treasure about which he spoke, for it was something that interested the senate as much as it did the plebeians. Manlius did not answer in detail but evaded the question by saying that it was not necessary to tell them who had it, for they already knew; so the dictator had him put in prison.

This example shows how detestable false accusations are in free cities, as well as in every other form of government, and how no institution which controls such accusations should be overlooked. Nor is there a better means of removing the possibility of false accusations than by establishing many outlets for them; for public charges benefit republics as much as false accusations harm them; and there is this difference between the one and the other: false accusations have no need either of witnesses or of any other particular corroboration to prove them, so that anyone can be slandered by anyone else, but no one can be publicly charged in this manner since such accusations require true corroboration and circumstances which demonstrate the truth of the charges. Men are publicly accused before magistrates, before the people, and before governmental councils; they are slandered in the squares and among the colonnades of the loggias. These false accusations are used more where public charges are less frequent and wherever cities are less organized to provide for them. Therefore, an organizer of a republic should arrange things in such a way that public charges can be made against any citizen without fear or hesitation; and when a charge has been made and thoroughly examined, he must severely punish false accusers, who have no right to complain of this since they had the chance to make accusations publicly and chose to make false accusations in the loggias. And wherever this function of government has not been well organized, great disorders always follow, for slander irritates but does not punish citizens, and those who are irritated will think about avenging themselves, hating rather than fearing the things that are said against them.

This function, as has been mentioned, was well organized in Rome, and it has always been poorly organized in our city of Florence. And as in Rome this institution produced much good, in Florence this lack of order created much harm. And anyone who reads the histories of this latter city will see how many slanders there were used against those of its citizens involved in its important affairs. Of one it was said that he had stolen funds from the public; of another, that he had not carried out some undertaking because he had been bribed; and of a third, that because of his ambition he had done such and such a bad action. As a result of this, hatred arose on every side, from which came divisions; from divisions came parties, and from parties ruin. And if there had been in Florence an institution for publicly bringing charges against its citizens and for punishing slanderers, the countless disturbances which ensued would not have occurred: for those citizens, both the condemned and those who were absolved, would not have been able to do harm to the city, and there would have been fewer men publicly charged than were falsely accused, for as I have said, one cannot accuse anyone publicly as easily as one can accuse him falsely.

And first among the means which a citizen has used to become great is to accuse falsely. When used against powerful citizens who are opposed to his desire for power, such means are very effective, for through them he can take the side of the people and can make them his friend by confirming their low opinion of his opponents. And although one could cite many examples of this, I shall be content with only one: the Florentine army was besieging Lucca under the command of its commissioner, Messer Giovanni Guicciardini.[1] Either because of his poor leadership or because of his bad fortune the capture of that city did not take place. At any rate, whatever the case was, Messer Giovanni was blamed for it, for it was rumored that he had been bribed by the Luccans; since this false accusation was supported by his enemies, it drove Messer Giovanni almost to complete desperation. And although he wished to be placed in the hands of the captain to clear himself, he was nonetheless never able to do so, since there was no means of doing this in that republic. This event caused much indignation among Messer Giovanni's friends, who were for the most part powerful men; among them were those who desired to make changes in Florence. Because of this affair, and for other reasons, the problem grew to such an extent that it led to the ruin of that republic.[2]

Manlius Capitolinus was, then, a slanderer and not a true accuser; and the Romans demonstrated in this instance exactly how slanderers ought to be punished. For false accusations must be turned into public accusations,

[1] This occurred between 1430 and 1433.
[2] Here Machiavelli refers to the return of Cosimo de' Medici from exile in 1434, and to his subsequent establishment of a system of government controlled by him, his family, and their partisans.

and when the accusation is legitimate, either reward it or do not punish it; but when it proves to be false, punish it as Manlius was punished.

CHAPTER IX.   HOW A MAN MUST BE ALONE IN ORDER TO FOUND A NEW REPUBLIC OR TO REFORM COMPLETELY ITS ANCIENT INSTITUTIONS

It may appear to some that I have gone too far along in Roman history without mentioning the founders of that republic or those institutions which are concerned with her religion and her militia; therefore, no longer wishing to keep the minds that wish to hear about this matter in suspense, let me say that many will perhaps judge it to be a bad example for a founder of a constitutional state, as Romulus was, to have first murdered his brother and then to have consented to the death of Titus Tatius, the Sabine, whom he had elected as his companion in his rule. Judging from this, the citizens might, out of ambition and a desire to rule, follow the example of their prince and oppress those who are opposed to their authority. This opinion might be correct, were we not to consider the goal that led Romulus to commit such a murder.

And this should be taken as a general rule: it rarely or never happens that a republic or kingdom is well organized from the beginning, or completely reformed, with no respect for its ancient institutions, unless it is done by one man alone; moreover, it is necessary that one man provide the means and be the only one from whose mind any such organization originates; therefore, a prudent founder of a republic, one whose intention it is to govern for the common good and not in his own interest, not for his heirs but for the sake of the fatherland, should try to have the authority all to himself; nor will a wise mind ever reproach anyone for some extraordinary action performed in order to found a kingdom or to institute a republic. It is, indeed, fitting that while the action accuses him, the result excuses him; and when this result is good, as it was with Romulus, it will always excuse him: for one should reproach a man who is violent in order to destroy, not one who is violent in order to mend things.[1]

The founder should be so prudent and able-minded as not to bequeath the authority he has taken to his heir; for, since men are more apt to do evil than good, his successor might use for ambitious ends what the founder had employed virtuously. Besides this, though one man alone is fit for founding a government, what he has founded will not last long if it rests upon his shoulders alone; it is lasting when it is left in the care of many and when many desire to maintain it. As the many are not fit to organize a government, for they cannot recognize the best means of doing so because of the diversity of opinion among them, just so, when they have realized that they have it they will not agree to abandon it. And that Romulus was among those who deserve to be pardoned for the death of his brother and his companion, and that what he did was for the common good and not for private ambition, is demonstrated by the fact that he immediately organized a senate with whom he would consult and whose opinions he deliberated; and anyone who would examine carefully the authority that Romulus reserved for himself will see that all he kept for himself was the power to command the army during wartime and to convoke the senate. Later, when Rome became free as a result of the expulsion of the Tarquins, we can see that the city was not given any new institutions by the Romans besides their ancient ones, except that in place of a permanent king there were two yearly consuls: this testifies to the fact that all the original institutions were more suitable to a free, self-governing state than to one which was absolutist and tyrannical.

Numerous examples could be cited in support of what I have written above, such as Moses, Lycurgus, Solon, and other founders of kingdoms and republics who were able

---

[1] Compare this statement with Machiavelli's remarks on ends and means in *The Prince* (XVIII).

to form laws for the common good because they had taken sole authority upon themselves, but I shall omit them since they are well known; instead, I shall present only one example, not so well known but worthy of examination by those who wish to be the organizers of good laws, and the example is: Agis, King of Sparta, who wished to return the Spartans to the bounds within which the laws of Lycurgus had enclosed them, for he felt that, having departed from them, his city had lost much of its former ability and, as a result, much of its strength and empire; but at the start of his efforts he was assassinated by the Spartan Ephors[2] as a man who wanted to become a tyrant. But when Cleomenes succeeded him on the throne, the same desire, after a time, arose in him as a result of reading the memoirs and writings of Agis which he had discovered, wherein he saw what his real intentions were, and he realized that he could not do this good for his country if he did not possess sole authority; for it seemed impossible, on account of man's ambition, for him to be able to help the many against the wishes of the few; so, when the right occasion arose he had all the Ephors killed and anyone else who might oppose him; then he completely restored the laws of Lycurgus. This action might have been enough to revive Sparta and to give Cleomenes the same reputation that Lycurgus had if it had not been for the power of the Macedonians and the weakness of the other Greek republics; for, after such institutions had been established, Cleomenes was attacked by the Macedonians, and when he discovered he was weaker in numbers and had nowhere to go for help, he was defeated. This plan of his, no matter how just and praiseworthy it might have been, was not carried out.

Considering all these matters, then, I conclude that it is necessary to be alone in establishing a republic; and that,

---

[2] The Ephors were five magistrates elected annually to oversee the affairs of state in Sparta.

concerning the death of Remus and Titus Tatius, Romulus deserves to be excused, not blamed.

CHAPTER X. THOSE WHO FOUND A REPUBLIC OR A KINGDOM DESERVE AS MUCH PRAISE AS THOSE WHO FOUND A TYRANNY DESERVE BLAME

Among all praiseworthy men, the most praiseworthy are those who were leaders and founders of religions; next come those who founded either republics or kingdoms; after these the most celebrated men are those who, commanding armies, have increased either their own kingdom or that of their native land; next to these may be placed men of letters, who, since they are of various types, are each praised according to their merits. To other men, whose number is infinite, some portion of praise may be attributed according to the skill they possess in their art or profession. On the other hand, men who have destroyed religions, wasted kingdoms and republics, and have been enemies of virtue, letters, and every sort of profession that brings gain and honor to the human race—such as the impious, the violent, the ignorant, the useless, the lazy, and the wicked—are considered infamous and detestable; and no one will ever be so mad or so wise, so sorry or so good that, given the choice between the two kinds of men, he will not praise those who merit praise and blame those who deserve blame.

Nevertheless, in the end nearly all men, deceived by a false appearance of good and a false sense of glory, allow themselves, either by their own choice or through their ignorance, to join the ranks of those who deserve more blame than praise; and while they have the possibility of establishing, to their perpetual honor, either a republic or a kingdom, they turn instead to tyranny, not realizing how much fame, glory, honor, security, tranquillity, and peace of mind they are losing by such a decision, and, on the other hand, how much infamy, vituperation, blame, danger, and unrest they incur.

And if they read histories and make use of the records of ancient affairs, it is impossible for those who have lived as private citizens in a republic or who have become princes either because of Fortune or ability not to wish to live, if they are private citizens, in their native land like Scipio rather than like Caesar and, if they are princes, to live like Agesilaus, Timoleon, and Dion rather than like Nabis, Phalaris, and Dionysius; for they would see how the latter are soundly condemned while the former are praised most highly; they would also see how Timoleon and the others had no less authority in their native lands than Dionysius and Phalaris had, and that they enjoyed, by far, greater security for a longer time.

Nor should anyone be deceived by Caesar's glory, so very celebrated by historians, for those who praised him were corrupted by his good fortune and amazed by the duration of the empire which, ruled in his name,[1] did not allow writers to speak freely about him. But anyone who wishes to know what free historians would say about him should examine what they say about Catiline. And Caesar is even more blameworthy, just as a man who has committed an evil deed is more to be blamed than one who has only wished to do so; moreover, let the reader see how Brutus is so highly praised, as though, unable to criticize Caesar because of his power, they praise his enemy instead.

Furthermore, let any man who has become a prince in a republic consider how much more praise those emperors deserved who lived under the laws and as good princes after Rome had become an empire than those who lived the opposite way, and he will see how Titus, Nerva, Trajan, Hadrian, Antoninus, and Marcus had no need of Praetorian guards nor a multitude of legions to defend themselves, for their customs, the goodwill of the

---

[1] Here Machiavelli alludes to the fact that the Roman emperors after Julius Caesar used his name as an honorific title, a practice that was continued until the twentieth century in the German title "kaiser" and the Russian title "czar."

people, and the love of the senate protected them; the prince will also see how the Eastern and Western armies were not sufficient for Caligula, Nero, Vitellius, and other evil emperors to save themselves from the enemies that their wicked customs and evil lives had created for them. And if the history of these men were studied carefully, it would serve as an excellent lesson to show any prince the path to glory or to censure, to his security or to his peril, for of the twenty-six emperors between Caesar and Maximinus, sixteen were murdered and ten died a natural death; and if among those who were murdered there were several good men, like Galba and Pertinax, they were killed by the corruption which their predecessors had left behind in their soldiers; and if among those who died a natural death there was a wicked man, like Severus, this was the result of his very great fortune and ability—a combination of two things which few men enjoy. A prince will also observe, through the lesson of this history, how one can organize a good kingdom: for all the emperors who assumed the imperial throne by birth, except for Titus, were bad, and those who became emperors by adoption were all good, as were the five from Nerva to Marcus; and when the empire fell into hereditary succession, it returned again to its ruin.

Therefore, let a prince examine the times from Nerva to Marcus, and let him compare them with those which came before and afterward, and then let him choose during which period he would wish to be born or in which period he would like to be made emperor. In the times when good emperors governed, he will see a ruler secure in the midst of his secure citizens, and a world of peace and justice; he will see a senate with its full authority, the magistrates with their honors, the rich citizens enjoying their wealth, the nobles and ability exalted, and he will find tranquillity and well-being in everything; and on the other hand, he will see all rancor, licentiousness, corruption, and ambition extinguished; he will see a golden age in which a man can hold and defend whatever opinion he wishes. He will, in the end, see the world rejoicing: its prince endowed with respect and glory, its peoples with love and security. If next he studies carefully the times of the other emperors, he will see them full of the atrocities of war, the conflicts of sedition, and the cruelties of both peace and war, so many princes put to death by the sword, so many civil wars, so many foreign wars, all of Italy afflicted and full of previously unknown adversities, and her cities ruined and sacked. He will see Rome burned, the Capitoline destroyed by her own citizens, her ancient temples desolate, her rituals corrupted, and the cities full of adulterous conduct; he will see the seas covered with exiles and the earth stained with blood. He will find countless cruelties in Rome and discover that nobility, wealth, past honors, and especially virtue are considered capital crimes. He will see the rewarding of those who accuse falsely, the turning of servants against their masters and freedmen against their former owners, and he will see those who, lacking enemies, are oppressed by their friends. And then he will well understand how many obligations Rome, Italy, and the world owe to Caesar!

And the prince, without a doubt, if he is a man, will be frightened away from any imitation of the bad times and will burn with an ardent desire to follow the ways of the good times. If a prince truly seeks worldly glory, he should hope to possess a corrupt city—not in order to ruin it completely as Caesar did but to reorganize it as Romulus did. And the heavens cannot truly bestow upon men a greater opportunity for obtaining glory than this, nor can men desire a greater one. And if a man who wanted to reorganize a city well had, of necessity, to renounce the principality in order to do so, he might merit some excuse if he did not reform it in order not to lose his rank; but if he were able both to retain his principality and to reform it, he would deserve no excuse whatsoever.

In conclusion, then, let those to whom the heavens grant such opportunities observe that there are two paths open to them: one allows them to live securely and makes them famous after death; the other makes them live in continuous anxiety and, after death, allows them to leave behind an eternal reputation of infamy.

CHAPTER XI.   THE RELIGION OF THE ROMANS

Even though Rome found its first institution builder in Romulus and, like a daughter, owed her birth and her education to him, nevertheless, as the heavens judged that the institutions of Romulus would not suffice for so great an empire, they inspired the Roman senate to elect Numa Pompilius as Romulus's successor so that those matters not attended to by Romulus could be seen to by Numa. Numa found the Roman people most undisciplined, and since he wanted to bring them to civil obedience by means of the arts of peace, he turned to religion as an absolutely necessary institution for the maintenance of a civic government, and he established it in such a way that for many centuries never was there more fear of God than in that republic—a fact which greatly facilitated any undertaking that the senate or those great Romans thought of doing.

And anyone who examines the many actions of the Roman people as a whole and of many individual Romans will discover how these citizens were more afraid of breaking an oath than of breaking the laws, since they respected the power of God more than that of man: this is most evident in the examples of Scipio and of Manlius Torquatus. After the rout inflicted upon the Romans by Hannibal at the battle of Cannae, many of the citizens assembled and, despairing for their native land, agreed to abandon Italy and to go to Sicily; when Scipio heard about this, he went to them, and with his bare sword in hand he forced them to swear not to abandon their fatherland. Lucius Manlius, the father of Titus Manlius (afterward called Torquatus), was accused of a crime by Marcus Pomponius, tribune of the plebeians; before the day of the trial arrived Titus went to Marcus and threatened to kill him if he did not swear to remove the indictment against his father; and when Marcus swore to do so, he withdrew the charge out of fear.

In this manner, those citizens whose love for the fatherland or its laws could not have kept them in Italy were restrained by an oath which they were forced to take; and that tribune set aside the hatred he had for the father and the injury he had suffered from the son and his own honor in order to obey the oath he had taken—all this came about from nothing other than the religion which Numa had introduced into that city.

Thus, anyone who examines Roman history closely will discover how much religion helped in commanding armies, encouraging the plebeians, keeping men good, and shaming the wicked. And so, if one were to argue about which prince Rome was more indebted to— whether Romulus or Numa—I believe that Numa would most easily be first choice: for where there is religion it is easy to introduce arms, but where there are arms without religion the latter can be introduced only with difficulty. It is evident that Romulus did not find divine authority necessary to found the senate and other civil and military institutions, but it was necessary for Numa, who pretended to have a relationship with a nymph who advised him what to say to the people; the reason was that he wanted to establish new and unfamiliar institutions in the city, and he doubted that his own authority would be sufficient to do so.

Actually, there never existed a person who could give unusual laws to his people without recourse to God, for otherwise such laws would not have been accepted: for the benefits they bring, although evident to a prudent man, are not self-explanatory enough to be evident to others. Therefore, wise men who wish to avoid this difficulty have recourse to God. Lycurgus did this, as did Solon and many others who had the same goal. Since the Roman people were amazed at the goodness and the prudence of Numa, they yielded to his every decision. It is, of course, true that those times were very religious ones and that the men with whom he had to deal were unsophisticated, thereby giving him a great deal of freedom to follow his own plans and to be able to impress upon them easily any new form he wished. And, without any doubt, anyone wishing to establish a republic in our present day would find it easier to do so among mountaineers, where there is no culture, than among men who are accustomed to living in cities where culture is corrupt; in like manner, a sculptor can more easily carve a beautiful statue out of a rough piece of marble than he can from one poorly blocked out by someone else.

Having considered everything, then, I conclude that the religion introduced by Numa was among the most important reasons for the success of that city, for it brought forth good institutions, and good institutions led to good fortune, and from good fortune came the felicitous successes of the city's undertakings. And as the observance of religious teaching is the reason for the greatness of republics, in like manner the disdain of the practice is the cause of their ruin; for where the fear of God is lacking a kingdom must either come to ruin or be sustained by the fear of a prince who makes up for the lack of religion. And since princes are short-lived, it is most likely that a kingdom will fail as quickly as the abilities of its prince fail; thus, kingdoms which depend upon the ability of a single man cannot last long, for such ability disappears with the life of the prince; and only rarely does it happen that this ability is revived by a successor, as Dante prudently declares:

> Not often in a family tree does virtue
> rise up to all its branches. This is what
> the Giver wills, that we may ask Him for it.[1]

The well-being, therefore, of a republic or a kingdom cannot rest upon a prince who governs prudently while he

[1] *Purgatorio*, VII, 121–123.

is alive, but rather upon one who organizes the government in such a way that it can be maintained in the event of his death. And, while it is true that uncultured men can be more easily persuaded to adopt a new institution or opinion, it is not, however, for this reason impossible to persuade cultured men or men who do not consider themselves uncultured to do the same. The people of Florence do not consider themselves ignorant or uncultured; nevertheless, they were persuaded by Brother Girolamo Savonarola that he spoke with God. I do not wish to judge if this were true or not, for of such a man as this one must speak with respect; but I do say that very many people believed him without ever having seen anything out of the ordinary to make them believe him, and this was the case because his life, his doctrines, and the topics about which he chose to preach from the Bible were enough to persuade them to have faith in him. No one, therefore, should despair of being able to accomplish what others have accomplished, for men—as I said in my preface—are born, live, and die always in the same way.

CHAPTER XII.   HOW MUCH IMPORTANCE MUST BE GRANTED TO RELIGION, AND HOW ITALY, WITHOUT RELIGION, THANKS TO THE ROMAN CHURCH, HAS BEEN RUINED

Princes or republics that wish to maintain themselves without corruption must, above all else, maintain free of corruption the ceremonies of their religion and must hold them constantly in veneration; for there is no greater indication of the ruin of a country than to see its religious worship not respected. This is easy to understand when one realizes upon what basis the religion of the place where a man was born is founded, because every religion has the foundation of its existence in one of its main institutions. The essence of the religion of the pagans resided in the responses of oracles and upon a sect of fortune-tellers and soothsayers: all their ceremonies, sacrifices, and rites depended upon these, for it was easy for them to believe that the god who could predict your future, good or evil, could also bring it about for you. From these arose their temples, their sacrifices, their supplications, and every other ceremony used in venerating them; from this arose the oracle of Delos, the temple of Jupiter Ammon, and other famous oracles which filled the world with admiration and devotion. Then, later, as these oracles began to speak on behalf of the powerful, their falsity was discovered by the people and men became unbelievers and were willing to upset every good institution.

Therefore, it is the duty of the rulers of a republic or of a kingdom to maintain the foundations of the religion that sustains them; and if this is done it will be easy for them to keep their republic religious and, as a consequence, good and united. And they must favor and encourage all those things which arise in favor of religion, even if they judge them to be false; the more they do this the more prudent and knowledgeable in worldly affairs they will be. And because this practice has been followed by wise men, there has arisen the belief in miracles that are celebrated even in false religions; for, no matter how they originated, men always gave them greater importance than they deserved, thus causing everyone to believe in them. There were many such miracles in Rome, among them the one that happened while the Roman soldiers were sacking the city of Veii: some of them entered the temple of Juno and, approaching the image of the goddess, asked: "Do you wish to come to Rome?" It seemed to some that she nodded her head as if to say "yes" and to others that she actually replied that she did. Since these men were deeply religious (this Livy demonstrates, for he describes them entering the temple without a sound, devout and full of reverence), perhaps it seemed to them that they heard the reply to their question which they had expected from the start; this opinion and belief was carefully encouraged and cultivated by Camillus and the other leaders of the city. If the rulers of Christian republics had maintained this sort of religion according to the system set up by its founder, Christian states and republics would be more united and happier than they are at present. Nor can there be another, better explanation of its decline than to see how those people who are closer to the Roman church, the head of our religion, are less religious. And anyone who examines the principles upon which it was based and sees how different present practice is from these principles would conclude, without a doubt, that it is drawing near either to calamity or a scourge.

And since there are many who are of the opinion that the well-being of the Italian cities comes from the Church of Rome, I wish to present some of my beliefs against such an opinion, very powerful ones which, I feel, cannot be refuted. The first is that because of the bad examples of that court of Rome this land has lost all its devotion and religion; this, in turn, brings about countless evils and countless disorders: for just as one takes for granted that all goes well where there is religion, just so, where religion is lacking one supposes the contrary. We Italians owe this first debt to the Church and to the priests—we have become irreligious and wicked; but we owe them an even greater debt still, which is the second reason for our ruin: that the Church has kept, and still keeps, this land of ours divided. And, in truth, no land is ever happy or united unless it is under the rule of one republic or one prince, as is the case with France and Spain. And the reason why Italy is not in the same condition and why she, too, has neither one republic nor one prince to govern her, lies solely with the Church: for although the Church possesses temporal power and has its seat in Italy, it has not been powerful enough nor has it possessed sufficient skill to be able to tyrannize Italy and make itself her ruler; and it has not been, on the other hand, so feeble that, when in fear of losing its control of temporal affairs, it has been unable to bring in a foreign power to defend itself from those Italian states which have become too powerful. There are many instances of this in ancient times: when, with Charlemagne's aid, the Lombards—who were in control of almost all of Italy—were driven out; and when, in our own day, the Church took power away from the Venetians with the aid of France, and then when it drove out the French with the help of the Swiss. Therefore, since the Church has not been strong enough to take possession of Italy, nor has she permitted anyone else to do so, Italy has not been able to unite under one ruler. Rather, Italy has been under many rulers and lords, and from this has come so much disunity and so much weakness that she has continued to be at the mercy not only of powerful barbarians but of anyone who might attack her. This is the debt we Italians owe the Church and no one else! And anyone who might wish to see the truth of this borne out by actual experience need only have sufficient power to send the Roman court, with the authority it possesses in Italy, to live in the lands of the Swiss, who are today the only peoples living under both religious and military institutions organized according to ancient practices; and he would see that in a short time the wicked customs of that court would create more disorder in that land than any other event occurring at any time could possibly cause there.

CHAPTER XIII.   HOW THE ROMANS USED RELIGION TO REORGANIZE THEIR CITY, TO CARRY OUT THEIR UNDERTAKINGS, AND TO QUIET DISTURBANCES

It does not seem out of order to me to present some instances in which the Romans used religion to reorganize their city and to carry out their undertakings; and though there are many of them in Livy, I wish nevertheless to limit myself to the following: after the Roman people had created the tribunes, with consular powers, all of whom, with the exception of one, were chosen from among the plebeians, and after the plague and famine of that year had been accompanied by certain portentous signs, the nobles took advantage of the opportunity caused by the new creation of the tribunes to declare that the gods were angry because Rome had badly used the majesty of her empire, and that there was no other way to placate the gods than to restore the election of the tribunes to its former system. The result was that the plebeians, terrified by this use of religion, created tribunes who were all nobles.

One can also see that in the siege of the city of Veii the leaders of the armies availed themselves of religion in order to keep their armies firm in their undertaking: that year the waters of Lake Albanus had risen a great deal, and as the soldiers were weary of the long siege and wished to return to Rome, the Romans discovered that Apollo and certain other oracles predicted that the city of Veii would be taken in the year when Lake Albanus would overflow its banks; this made the soldiers endure the hardships of the siege—motivated to capture the city, they remained content to continue the undertaking until Camillus, upon becoming dictator, took the said city after ten years of siege. And so, religion, well used, helped both in the siege of that city and in the restitution of the tribunate to the nobility: for without the said means both tasks would have been accomplished only with much difficulty.

I do not wish to omit, in this regard, another example. Many disturbances had arisen in Rome because of Terentillus the Tribune, who wanted to propose a certain law for reasons which will be explained in the proper place further on. And religion was one of the first means employed against him by the nobility, and it was used in two ways: first, they had the Sibylline books consulted and were given the answer that the city ran the risk of losing its liberty that very year because of sedition; although the tribunes discovered this ploy, it nevertheless struck so much fear into the hearts of the people that their ardent desire to follow the tribunes was cooled. The other means was as follows: one Appius Herdonius, together with a crowd of exiles and slaves numbering four thousand, occupied the Capitoline by night, causing the Romans to fear that the Aequi and the Volsci, the perpetual enemies of Rome, might come and seize the city; and as the tribunes did not cease in their obstinate course of proposing Terentillus's law, declaring that the possibility of attack was fabricated and not true, one Publius Ruberius, a serious citizen with authority, came forth from the senate and with words that were partly friendly and partly menacing showed them the city's dangers and the inopportune nature of their demands, with the result that he convinced the plebeians to swear not to swerve from the wishes of the consul; because of this, the obedient plebeians recovered the Capitoline by force. But since the consul, Publius Valerius, was killed in that battle, Titus Quintius was immediately chosen as consul; in order not to let the plebeians rest nor give them time to think about Terentillus's law, he ordered them to leave Rome and attack the Volsci, declaring that they were bound to follow him because of the oath they had sworn not to abandon the consul; but the tribunes opposed this, saying that the oath was sworn to a dead consul and not to him. Nevertheless, Livy shows how the plebeians preferred to obey the consul, out of religious fear, rather than believe the tribunes, saying the following words in favor of the ancient religion: "That lack of respect for the gods had not yet come which prevails today, nor had anyone yet interpreted the laws and oaths in his own interests."[1] Because of this, the tribunes, fearing that they might lose all their standing, agreed to obey the consul and not discuss the Terentillian law for a year, and the consuls agreed that for a year they would not lead the plebeians out of the city to war. And thus, religion helped the senate overcome those difficulties which they would never have been able to overcome without it.

[1] Livy, III, xx.

CHAPTER XIV.   THE ROMANS INTERPRETED THE AUSPICES
ACCORDING TO NECESSITY, AND THEY PRUDENTLY MADE A
SHOW OF OBSERVING RELIGION EVEN WHEN THEY WERE
FORCED NOT TO; AND IF ANYONE DARED TO DISPARAGE IT,
HE WAS PUNISHED

The auguries were not only, as was noted above, in
large measure the basis of the ancient religion of the
pagans, but also the cause of the well-being of the Roman
republic; thus, the Romans took more care of this institution than any other: they used the auspices in their consular meetings, in beginning their enterprises, in
marching forth their armies, in fighting their battles, and
in all their important actions, civil or military; never
would they have set out on an expedition without first
having persuaded their soldiers that the gods had promised them victory. And among the other auspices in their
armies they had a certain order of diviners called poultry-
diviners [*pullarii*]: every time the Romans prepared to give
battle to the enemy they required the poultry-diviners to
take the auspices; if the chickens pecked to eat their food,
they fought with a good augury; if they did not peck, they
abstained from combat. Nonetheless, when reason
showed them that they should proceed, notwithstanding
the fact that the auspices were adverse, they did so anyway; but they managed the auspices so shrewdly, with
such words and such ways, that they in no way seemed to
be doing it with disrespect to religion.

This cleverness was employed by the consul Papirius in
a most important battle which he fought with the Samnites, after which this people remained totally weak and
broken; for when Papirius was encamped opposite the
Samnites, feeling that a victory in the battle was certainly
his, he wished to attack and ordered the poultry-diviners
to take the auspices; but though the hens would not peck,
the chief of the poultry-diviners—observing the great willingness of the army to fight and the opinion of the general and all his soldiers that they would be victorious—in
order not to deprive the army of an opportunity for good

action, told the consul that the auspices were favorable. But, as Papirius was ordering the troops to draw up, certain poultry-diviners told some of the soldiers that the chickens had not pecked; they, in turn, told it to the nephew of the consul, Spurius Papirius, who then referred this news to the consul, who immediately replied that he expected him to perform his duty well and, as far as he and the army were concerned, the auspices were favorable, and if the poultry-diviners had told lies, they would turn out to their disadvantage.

And in order for the result to correspond to the prediction, he ordered his legates to put the poultry-diviners in the front lines of the battle; whereupon it happened that as they advanced against the enemy one of the Roman soldiers shot an arrow and accidentally killed the leader of the poultry-diviners; when the consul heard about this, he announced that everything was proceeding well and with the favor of the gods, for with the death of the liar the army had purged itself of any blame and from any anger which the gods might have felt against it. And thus, because he knew very well how to fit his plans to the auspices, he decided to go into battle without his army realizing that he had neglected the institutions of their religion in any way.

Appius Pulcher did just the opposite in Sicily during the First Punic War: since he wished to engage the Carthaginian forces, he had the poultry-diviners take the auspices, and when they told him that the hens did not eat, he said: "Let's see if they will drink!" and had them thrown into the sea. Whereupon after attacking the enemy he lost the battle; and he was condemned for this in Rome; but Papirius was honored: not so much because one conquered and the other was defeated, but rather because one had acted against the auspices with prudence while the other had done so with rashness. Nor did this means of taking the auspices serve any purpose other than to instill confidence in the soldiers going into battle; such confidence almost always achieved victorious results. This was practiced not only by the Romans but also by other peoples, and I think I would do well to give an example of this in the following chapter.

CHAPTER XV. THE SAMNITES TURNED TO RELIGION AS A LAST RESORT WHEN THEY WERE AFFLICTED

[After being repeatedly defeated by the Romans, the Samnites turned to religion as a last resort to encourage their soldiers, and they revived, on the advice of their high priest, Ovius Paccius, the practice of swearing an oath on pain of death. The Romans, led by Papirius, nevertheless defeated the Samnites, in spite of the courage inspired by the fear of breaking a religious oath. Regardless of this defeat, the actions of the Samnites prove how much confidence religious faith can inspire.]

CHAPTER XVI. A PEOPLE ACCUSTOMED TO LIVING UNDER A PRINCE MAINTAINS ITS FREEDOM WITH DIFFICULTY IF, BY CHANCE, IT BECOMES FREE

Countless examples in the records of ancient history demonstrate how difficult it is for a people accustomed to living under a prince to preserve its freedom afterward if, by chance, it acquires it as Rome did after the Tarquins were driven out of the city. And such a difficulty is reasonable: for these people are no different from a brutish animal which, although by nature ferocious and a dweller in the woods, has always been nourished in prison and in captivity and is then accidentally set free in a field; since it is not used to feeding itself and does not know the places where it may turn for refuge, it becomes the prey of the first person who tries to recapture it.

The same thing happens to a people accustomed to living under the rule of others: not able to think about public defense or offense, not understanding princes nor understood by them, it quickly returns under a yoke which is, in most cases, heavier than the one which, just a short time earlier, was lifted from its neck; and a people finds itself in this difficulty though its matter is not corrupt. For a people which is totally corrupt cannot live free for even a short time, as will be explained below; our discussions, therefore, will deal with those peoples in whom corruption has not spread too much and in whom there is still more goodness than corruption.

Another difficulty may be added to the one above: the state which becomes free makes enemies for itself but not friends. All those who profited from the tyrannical government, feeding upon the riches of the prince, become its enemies; since they have had their privileges taken away from them, they cannot live contented and are each forced to try to reestablish the tyranny in order to return to their former authority. Nor will such a state acquire friends, as I have said, for a free government presupposes honors and rewards based upon honest and predetermined criteria, and outside of these confers no honors or rewards; and when a person possesses those honors and advantages he believes he deserves, he does not admit an obligation to those who have rewarded him. Besides this, the common benefit that is derived from a free government is not appreciated while it is enjoyed; that is, to be able freely to enjoy one's possessions without any fear, not to fear for the honor of one's women or children, and not to fear for one's own safety—for no one will ever admit to owing an obligation to someone just because he is not harmed by the other person. And so, as I said above, a free and newly formed state comes to have enemies but not friends.

To remedy these inconveniences and the disorders which the aforementioned difficulties create, there is no more powerful remedy, nor one more efficacious, more certain, or necessary, than to murder the sons of Brutus, who, as history demonstrates, would not have been tempted to plot against their fatherland with other young Romans if it had not been for the fact that they found they could not enjoy exceptional privileges under the consuls whereas they could under the kings; in this way, it seemed that the freedom of that people had become their servitude. And anyone who undertakes to govern a body of people, either under a free system or under a principality, and does not protect himself against those who are hostile to that new order will found a state of brief duration. It is true that I consider those rulers to be unhappy who have had to employ extraordinary means to secure their state, having the multitude as their enemy: for the ruler who has the few as his enemy can protect himself from them easily and without too much trouble, but he who has the general population as an enemy can never rest secure; and the more cruelty he employs, the weaker his principality becomes. Thus, the best remedy that he has is to try to make the people friendly.

And although this argument departs from the one above, as I speak here of a prince and there of a republic, nevertheless, in order not to have to return to this subject I shall briefly speak about it here. If, then, a prince wishes to win over to his side a people that is hostile (I am speaking of those princes who have become tyrants of their fatherlands), let me say that he must first consider what the people desire, and he will find that they always desire two things: the first is to avenge themselves against those who were the cause of their being enslaved; the other is to regain their freedom. The prince can satisfy the first desire completely and the second only in part. There is an appropriate example of the first case: while Clearchus, tyrant of Heraclea, was in exile, a disagreement arose between the people and the aristocrats of Heraclea, who, realizing that they were weaker, turned to support Clearchus and, conspiring with him, set him up in power contrary to popular sentiment in Heraclea, and in so doing took freedom away from the people. When Clearchus found himself caught between the insolence of the aristocrats, whom he could neither content nor curb in any way, and the anger of the people, who could no longer endure the loss of their liberty, he decided to free himself from the annoyance of the patricians and to win over the people to his side with one blow. When the most suitable occasion arose, he cut up into pieces all the aristocrats—to the immense gratification of the people; in this manner he satisfied one of the wishes of the people, namely, to avenge themselves. But as for the other popular wish, that of having their liberty restored, since a prince cannot satisfy that, he should consider the causes that make people wish to be free: he will find that a small part of them desire to be free in order to command, but all the others, the countless majority, desire liberty in order to live in security. In all republics, no matter how they are organized, no more than forty or fifty citizens ever arrive at a position of command; since this is a small number, it is an easy matter to protect oneself from them, either by getting rid of them or by bestowing upon them so many honors that, according to their station, they will, for the most part, be content. For those others who want only to live in safety, they can easily be satisfied by establishing institutions and laws which confirm the prince's security while at the same time confirming their own. As an example of this there is the Kingdom of France, which exists securely for no other reason than the fact that its kings are limited by countless laws which also guarantee the security of all their people. And whoever established that state wanted those kings to do as they wished as far as military and financial matters are concerned, but prescribed that in any other area they should not act otherwise than in the manner established by the laws. Therefore, a prince or a republic which has not provided for its security at the outset must do so at the first opportunity, as the Romans did. Anyone who lets the occasion pass will repent too late for not having done what he should.

Since, then, the Roman people were not yet corrupt by the time they recovered their liberty, they were able to maintain it, after killing the sons of Brutus and doing away with the Tarquins, by all those ways and means discussed previously. But if that people had been corrupt, there would not have existed strong enough methods in Rome or elsewhere to maintain it, as will be shown in the following chapter.

CHAPTER XVII.   A CORRUPT PEOPLE WHICH ACQUIRES ITS FREEDOM CAN MAINTAIN ITS FREEDOM ONLY WITH THE GREATEST OF DIFFICULTY

I think that it was necessary either for the kings of Rome to be done away with or for Rome to become weak and useless in a very short period of time; for when one considers how much corruption there was in those kings, if two or three successive reigns had continued in the same way, and that corruption which was in them had spread to members of the body politic, it would no longer have been possible to reform her. But as the head was lost while the trunk was still sound, the Romans could easily bring themselves back to living an ordered and free existence. And this principle must be taken as very true: that a corrupt city which lives under a prince will never be able to regain its freedom, even if that prince and all his family are done away with; on the contrary, one prince needs to destroy the other, and without the creation of one new ruler the city will never rest unless the goodness of a single man, together with his ability, maintains her freedom; but this freedom will last only as long as the life of that man—as occurred in Syracuse with Dion and Timoleon, whose ability in different eras kept that city free while they were alive; when they died, the city returned to its former tyranny. But there is no better example of this than that of Rome; when the Tarquins were driven out, she was immediately able to seize and maintain her liberty. But after Caesar, Gaius Caligula, and Nero were dead, and the entire race of Caesar was destroyed, the city was not able to maintain her freedom or even reestablish it.

Such contrasting results in the same city arose from nothing other than the fact that the Roman people were still uncorrupt in the time of the Tarquins, while they were most corrupt in these later times; in the early days, in order to keep the people firm and disposed toward rejecting a king it was enough merely to have them swear that they would never consent to another king ruling in Rome; but in later days the authority and severity of Brutus plus all the Eastern legions were not enough to keep the people prepared to maintain their liberty, which he, like the first Brutus, had restored to them. This arose from the corruption which the faction of Marius had spread among the people; for when Caesar became the leader of this faction, he was able to blind the multitude so that they did not recognize the yoke which they themselves were placing upon their necks.

And though this example in Rome is preferable to any other, I nevertheless wish to present, on this topic, examples of other peoples known in our own times; therefore, let me say that no event—no matter how serious or violent it might be—could ever restore freedom in Milan or Naples, for their members are completely corrupt. This was evident after the death of Filippo Visconti, when Milan wished to restore her liberty but was not able to, nor did she know how to maintain it. And so it was Rome's great good fortune that her kings became corrupt early and, as a result, were driven out of the city before their corruption passed into the citizenry: this lack of total corruption was the reason why the countless disturbances which occurred in Rome never did any harm; on the contrary, they benefited the republic since the goals of the men who created them were essentially good.

It can be concluded, then, that where the material is not corrupt disturbances and other scandals can do no harm; where it is corrupt, well-organized laws do no good unless they are enforced by a man with enormous power who sees to it that they are observed in such a manner that the material becomes good. Whether this has ever happened, or might ever possibly happen, I do not know; for it is evident, as I said a little earlier, that if a city has begun to decline because of the corruption of its material, and if it ever happens to pull itself up again, this happens because of the ability of a single man living at the time and not because of the ability of the people supporting its good institutions; and as soon as that man is dead it returns to its former ways. This happened in Thebes, which, because of the ability of Epaminondas, was able to maintain a republican form of government and an empire as long as he was alive; but after he was dead it returned to its earlier disorders. The reason is that no one man can live long enough to teach good habits to a city which has for a long time known only bad ones. And if one man with an extremely long life or two strong successive reigns are not able to accomplish this, then when the reformers disappear, as was mentioned above, the city comes to ruin unless the reformers, before passing on and at the risk of many dangers and much bloodshed, have managed to bring about her rebirth. Such corruption and the inability to lead a free life arise from the inequality that exists in that city, and if one wishes to return the city to a state of equality, he will have to use drastic measures which few know how or wish to use, as will be discussed in more detail in another place.

CHAPTER XVIII. HOW A FREE GOVERNMENT CAN BE MAINTAINED IN CORRUPT CITIES IF IT EXISTS THERE ALREADY; OR, HOW TO ESTABLISH IT THERE IF IT DOES NOT ALREADY EXIST

I believe that it is not outside my subject, nor would it be contrary to the above discourse, to consider whether or not one can maintain a free government in a corrupt city if it already exists there, or whether or not one can be established there in the event that it does not already exist. Concerning this, let me say that it is very difficult to do either the one or the other; and although it is quite impossible to set up rules on the matter, for one would have to proceed according to the gradations of the corruption, nevertheless, since it is always good to discuss everything thoroughly, I shall not ignore this problem. And I shall assume that the city in question is totally corrupt, which will further increase the difficulty: for neither laws nor institutions are to be found which suffice to check a universal state of corruption. For just as good customs require laws in order to be maintained, so laws require good customs in order for them to be observed. Besides this, institutions and laws established in a republic at the time of its foundation, when men were good, are no longer acceptable later on when men have become evil; furthermore, if the laws in a city vary according to circumstances, then its institutions never or rarely ever change: because of this, new laws are not enough, for the institutions which remain intact corrupt them. And in order to make this point clearer, let me say that in Rome there was an established government, or rather an established form of the state, and then came laws which, along with the magistrates, kept the citizens in check. The state was based upon the authority of the people, the senate, the tribunes, and the consuls, and upon the means of selecting and creating the magistrates and of making the laws. These institutions changed very little or not at all, according to the course of events. The laws restraining the citizens began to change; for example, the law against adultery, the law against luxuries, the one against ambition, and many others, all of which were instituted as the citizens gradually grew more corrupt. But since the institutions of the state remained fixed and were no longer good because of corruption, the laws that were changed did not suffice to keep men good; but they would have helped very much if the institutions had been changed along with the change in the laws.

And that it is true that such institutions in a corrupt city were not good is most evident in two important instances: in the appointment of the magistrates and in the creation of the laws. The Roman people gave the consulate or the other main offices of the city only to those citizens who asked for them. This institution was good at the beginning, for only those citizens who felt themselves worthy asked to have the offices, since being refused was considered a disgrace; thus, in order to be judged worthy every citizen behaved in an honorable fashion. This system subsequently became most pernicious in the corrupt city: for those who had the most power, not those who had the most ability, sought the magistracies; and although they were capable, the powerless refrained from asking for them out of fear. Rome did not come to this situation all at once, but rather by degrees, just as she came into all her other difficulties: for after the Romans had conquered Africa and Asia and had brought almost all of Greece under their control, they became secure in their freedom and felt that they had no more enemies capable of frightening them. This security, as well as the weakness of their enemies, caused the Roman people to consider favor rather than ability in choosing their consuls, and in so doing all those who knew best how to please men were attracted to that office, instead of those who knew best how to conquer the enemy; then, from those who enjoyed the most favor they descended to giving the office to those who had more power; and so, in this way, the good citizens, because of the faults of this institution, remained completely excluded from such offices. At one time a tribune or any other citizen could propose a law to the people and everyone was able to speak either for or against it before it was finally adopted. This institution was a good one so long as the citizens were good: for it was always beneficial for a citizen to be able to propose something he felt was for the public good; it was equally beneficial for everyone to be able to express his opinion on the proposal so that the people, after hearing them all, could then select the best one. But when the citizens became wicked, such an institution became most harmful: for only the powerful were proposing laws, not in the name of common liberty but rather for their own power, and no one spoke against these men because they feared them. In such a way, the people were deceived or forced into decreeing their own ruin.

It was therefore necessary, if Rome wished to maintain her liberty amidst her corruption, that just as she had passed new laws in the course of her existence, she should have then created new institutions: for different institutions and ways of living must be instituted for a bad subject than for a good one, nor can a similar form exist in material which is completely different. But since these institutions must either be reformed all at once the moment they are recognized as being bad or reformed little by little before they are generally recognized as such, let me say that both of these two approaches are almost impossible; for it takes a prudent man who can see defects from far off and in their initial stages in order to reform them gradually, and it is not common to find a man like this in a city; and when one is found, he may never be able to persuade others to follow what he himself understands; for men are accustomed to living in one way, and they do not want to change; and this is even more true when they cannot see the evil for themselves but have to have it explained to them by abstract arguments. As for reforming these institutions all at once, when everyone realizes that they are not good, let me say that this uselessness which is easily recognized is corrected only with difficulty; for to do this it is not enough to employ lawful means, for lawful methods are now useless; it is necessary to have recourse to extraordinary measures, such as violence or arms, and to become, before all else, prince of that city in order to be able to deal with it in one's own way. But since the reforming of a city into a body politic presupposes a good man, and becoming prince of a republic through the use of violence presupposes an evil man—because of this fact we discover that it happens only very rarely that a good man wishes to become prince through evil means, even though his goal may be a good one; while, on the other hand, we discover that it is equally rare for an evil man who has become prince to act correctly, for it would never ever enter his mind to employ that authority for a good which he has acquired by evil means.

From all the above-mentioned things comes the difficulty or the impossibility of maintaining a government in a corrupt city or of establishing a new one there; if, nevertheless, one has to be set up or maintained in such a city, it must necessarily incline toward a monarchy rather than a popular government since those men who cannot be controlled by laws because of their insolence may be checked in some manner by a kind of regal power. And to try to make them become good by any other means would be either a most cruel undertaking or completely impossible, as I have said earlier when talking about Cleomenes. If he murdered the Ephors in order to rule alone, and if Romulus killed his brother and Titus Tatius, the Sabine, for the same reasons, and afterward they used this authority of theirs well, nevertheless one should remember that neither of them had a subject stained by that corruption which we have been discussing in this chapter, and therefore they had reason to hope and, in hoping, to justify their plan.

CHAPTER XIX.   A WEAK PRINCE CAN MAINTAIN HIMSELF WHEN HE SUCCEEDS AN EXCELLENT PRINCE; BUT AFTER A WEAK PRINCE ONE CANNOT MAINTAIN ANY RULE WITH ANOTHER WEAK PRINCE

[Rome was fortunate in that the first three kings of the city—Romulus, Numa, and Tullus—were all excellent rulers and thus established a tradition of strong leadership; in contrast, the virtues of David and Solomon were not enough to guarantee Rehoboam's rule of Israel since he did not possess the qualities of his father and grandfather and therefore lost much of the kingdom they had acquired. As long as Rome was governed by kings, she ran the risk of being ruined by the succession of a weak or evil king.]

CHAPTER XX. TWO CONTINUOUS SUCCESSIONS OF ABLE PRINCES PRODUCE GREAT RESULTS; AND SINCE WELL-ORGANIZED REPUBLICS HAVE, OF NECESSITY, A SUCCESSION OF ABLE RULERS, THEIR GAINS AND GROWTH ARE ALSO GREAT

[If two successive able princes were sufficient to conquer the world, as occurred with Philip of Macedonia and his son, Alexander the Great, a republic has even greater potential, for it has the same power that Rome possessed when she vested her sovereign authority in the consuls, rather than in hereditary kings, to elect an infinite number of most able rulers, one after the other.]

CHAPTER XXI. WHAT GREAT BLAME A PRINCE OR A REPUBLIC WHICH LACKS ITS OWN ARMED FORCES DESERVES

[Princes and republics of modern times should be ashamed not to have their own troops. This is the result not of a lack of suitable men but rather of their own inability to train them. The proof of this can be found in a recent example of the King of England. He dared to attack the Kingdom of France, defended by the experienced, professional soldiers from the wars in Italy, with men he had trained himself because he had not neglected the arts of war in his well-organized kingdom, even after living for over thirty years in peacetime. Similar examples may be found in Tullus of Rome or in Pelopidas and Epaminondas of Thebes.]

CHAPTER XXII. WHAT IS NOTABLE IN THE CASE OF THE THREE ROMAN HORATII AND THE THREE ALBAN CURIATII

[With the survival of one of the Horatii and the victory of Rome over Alba, the victorious Horatius returned home to see his sister weeping over her dead husband (one of the Curiatii) and killed her in anger; for this crime he was tried and eventually set free. Three things should be noted here: (1) one should never risk everything on only a portion of one's forces; (2) a man's merits should never be used to balance his faults in a well-ordered city; (3) it is unwise to make agreements whose observance is doubtful. The first two points will be covered in successive chapters.]

CHAPTER XXIII. HOW ONE SHOULD NOT JEOPARDIZE ALL OF ONE'S FORTUNE OR ALL OF ONE'S FORCES; AND, FOR THIS REASON, GUARDING PASSES IS OFTEN DANGEROUS

[Risking their kingdoms on the combat of three men, as did Tullus, King of Rome, and Mettius, King of Alba, was the height of stupidity, since they lost the years of preparations former kings had made for their defense. This procedure is, in some respects, similar to the guarding of passes, for you may, at best, only prohibit the enemy from crossing the pass. But you cannot win a clear victory without the use of all your forces, since such locations lack sufficient space for an entire army and a loss at a defended pass may frighten your remaining troops. The Romans awaited Hannibal not at the passes but in the plains. Recently, in 1515, Francis, King of France, invaded Lombardy and captured Milan by coming into Italy not by those passes guarded by Swiss troops but by a different way.]

CHAPTER XXIV. WELL-ORDERED REPUBLICS ESTABLISH REWARDS AND PUNISHMENTS FOR THEIR CITIZENS BUT NEVER BALANCE ONE WITH THE OTHER

[Although the merits of Horatius were great and served Rome well, his crime was atrocious; the Romans would have been wrong to balance his crime with his good deeds. A well-organized republic will reward good deeds and punish crimes without consideration of previous service; such a city will enjoy its liberty for a long time, but if it acts otherwise it will lose its liberty.]

CHAPTER XXV.   ONE SEEKING TO REFORM AN ESTABLISHED
STATE IN A FREE CITY SHOULD RETAIN AT LEAST A SHADOW
OF THE ANCIENT CUSTOMS

If one desires or intends to reform the government of a
city so that the reform will be acceptable and will be able
to maintain itself to everyone's satisfaction, he should retain at least the shadow of ancient customs so that it will
not seem to the people that they have changed institutions, whereas in actual fact the new institutions may be
completely different from those of the past; for the majority of men delude themselves with what seems to be rather
than with what actually is; indeed, they are more often
moved by things that seem to be rather than by things
that are. For this reason the Romans, recognizing this necessity at the foundation of their self-governing state,
when they created two consuls instead of one king decided to have no more than twelve lictors so as not to exceed the number of those who served the king. Besides
this, when an annual sacrifice was made in Rome it could
only be offered by the king in person, and since they did
not want the people to miss anything from their past customs because of the absence of the kings, the Romans
created a leader for the said sacrifice, whom they called
the King of the Sacrifice, and placed him under the command of the high priests. Thus, by this means the people
grew satisfied with this sacrifice and never had reason to
desire the return of the kings because of its absence. And
this should be observed by all those who wish to abolish
an ancient regime in a city and establish a new and free
one: for, since new things disturb the minds of men, you
should strive to see that these disturbing changes retain as
much of the ancient regime as possible; and if the number, authority, and length of office of the magistrates
change, they should at least retain their title. And, as I
have said, anyone who wishes to institute a political regime, whether it be by way of a republic or a kingdom,
should observe this; but anyone who wishes to create an

absolute rule (called a tyranny by ancient historians) ought to make everything anew, as will be explained in the next chapter.

CHAPTER XXVI.   A NEW PRINCE, IN A CITY OR PROVINCE HE HAS TAKEN, SHOULD MAKE EVERYTHING OVER ANEW

For anyone becoming a prince either of a city or a state, especially if his foundations are weak and he does not choose either a republican or a monarchical form of government, the best means he can use to hold that principality—if he is a new prince—is to begin everything in that state anew; that is, to establish new rulers with new names, new authority, and new men; to make the rich poor and the poor rich, as David did when he became king, who "hath filled the hungry with good things; and the rich he hath sent empty away."[1] Besides this, he should build new cities, destroy existing ones, move the inhabitants from one place to another; in short, leave nothing intact in that province, nor permit either rank, institution, form of government, or wealth in your city which is not recognized as coming from you; and he should choose as his example Philip of Macedonia, the father of Alexander the Great, who by such means rose from being a petty king to become the ruler of Greece. Those who write of him say that he transferred men from province to province just as shepherds move their flocks about. These methods are most cruel and are inimical to any body politic, not only to a Christian one but to any human one, and every man should avoid them and should prefer to live as a private citizen rather than as a king who does so much damage to mankind; nevertheless, anyone who does not wish to choose this first humane course of action must, if he wishes to maintain himself, enter into this evil one. But men choose certain middle

[1] Luke 1:53. The citation actually refers to God in the Magnificat. Machiavelli has confused the passage with a description of King David.

ways which are very damaging and, in so doing, are unable to be entirely good or entirely bad, as the following chapter will demonstrate by example.

CHAPTER XXVII.   MEN VERY RARELY KNOW HOW TO BE ENTIRELY GOOD OR ENTIRELY BAD

Pope Julius, upon going to Bologna in 1505 to expel from that state the Bentivogli family, which had held the city's government for one hundred years, also wanted to remove from Perugia Giovampagolo Baglioni, who was the tyrant there (for the Pope had conspired against all tyrants who held lands belonging to the Church). And having almost reached Perugia with this intention and purpose in mind, known to everyone, he did not wait but entered that city unarmed, notwithstanding the fact that Giovampagolo was inside with many of the men he had gathered around him for his defense. And thus, with the usual furor with which he governed all his affairs, Julius placed himself in the hands of his enemy with only a small bodyguard; nevertheless, he carried Giovampagolo off with him, leaving a governor in that city to act in the name of the Church. The impetuosity of Julius and the cowardice of Giovampagolo were noted by the prudent men who were with the Pope; and they could not understand why Giovampagolo had not, with a single blow, rid himself of his enemy, whereby he would have gained for himself perpetual fame and rich spoils, for the Pope was accompanied by all the cardinals and their valuable possessions. Nor could they believe that he had refrained through goodness or scruples of conscience, for in the heart of a vicious man who took his sister as his mistress and murdered his cousins and nephews in order to rule, no compassionate sentiment could be aroused; but they concluded that his behavior must be due to the fact that men do not know how to be honorably evil or perfectly good, and when an evil deed has in itself some grandeur or magnanimity, they will not know how to perform it.

Thus, Giovampagolo, who did not mind incest or public parricide, did not know how, or, to put it better, did not dare (when he had the perfect opportunity to do so) to perform an act for which everyone would have admired his courage, and which would have gained for him eternal fame as the first man to show these prelates how little esteem is merited by those who live and govern as they do; he would have done something the greatness of which would have surpassed all infamy and all danger that could have resulted from it.

CHAPTER XXVIII.   WHY THE ROMANS WERE LESS UNGRATEFUL TO THEIR CITIZENS THAN THE ATHENIANS WERE

[Rome was less ungrateful to her citizens than Athens was because she had less reason to mistrust them; from the expulsion of the kings to the times of Sulla and Marius, Rome never lost her liberty through the actions of any of her citizens. The contrary was true in Athens, and suspicion of her citizens led to the institutions of banishment and ostracism. Rome would have acted in a similar manner if, in her early days, she had, like Athens, grounds for this ingratitude.]

CHAPTER XXIX.   WHICH IS MORE UNGRATEFUL, A PEOPLE OR A PRINCE?

In connection with the matters treated above, here seems the proper place to discuss whether a people or a prince displays more striking examples of such ingratitude. And in order to argue this question better, let me say that this vice of ingratitude arises either from avarice or from suspicion. For when a people or a prince sends one of its generals abroad on an important expedition, and he acquires through his victory a good deal of glory, that prince or people is bound to reward him upon his return; but if, motivated by avarice, instead of rewarding him it dishonors or injures him—for its own greediness restrains it from giving him his due—it commits an error which has no excuse and which, moreover, brings it eternal infamy. Yet there are many princes who sin in this respect. Cornelius Tacitus gives the reason in this sentence: "It is easier to take revenge for an injustice than to repay a service, for gratitude is considered a burden and revenge a profit."[1] But when a people or a prince gives no reward or, rather, gives injury motivated not by avarice but by suspicion, then either the people or the prince deserves some excuse. We read about many such acts of ingratitude resulting from such a cause: a general who has ably conquered an empire for his lord, by overcoming his enemies and winning glory for himself and riches for his soldiers, of necessity acquires, with his soldiers, his enemies, and among the very subjects of that prince, such a reputation that his victory cannot be completely enjoyed by the lord who sent him forth. And because it is man's nature to be ambitious, suspicious, and incapable of setting limits to his own fortunes, it is impossible for this suspicion, arising immediately in the prince after the victory of his general, not to be increased by some arrogant action or display of words on the part of the general. And so, the prince is unable to think of anything other than making himself secure, and to accomplish this he considers either having the general killed or diminishing the reputation he earned with his army or among the people; and with all possible means he points out how the general's victory came about not through his ability but rather because of Fortune or through the cowardice of the enemy or because of the prudence of the other officers who were with him in battle.

While Vespasian was in Judea, he was proclaimed emperor by his army, and Antonius Primus, who found himself with another army in Illyria, took his side and came into Italy against Vitellius, who was reigning in Rome,

[1] *The Histories,* IV, iii.

and destroyed most effectively two of Vitellius's armies and occupied Rome. Mucianus, sent there by Vespasian, discovered that through Antonius's ability everything had been won and every difficulty overcome. The reward Antonius received for this was that Mucianus immediately took away his command of the army and, little by little, reduced him to a state of no authority in Rome; when Antonius went to see Vespasian, who was then in Asia, he was received by him in such a manner that, in a short time, he was reduced to no rank at all and died in despair. Our histories are full of such examples. In our own times every living soul knows how industriously and ably Gonsalvo Ferrante,[2] fighting against the French in the Kingdom of Naples for King Ferdinand of Aragon, conquered that kingdom; and that the reward he received for his victory was that, when Ferdinand left Aragon and came to Naples, he first took away Gonsalvo's command of the army, then his fortresses, and finally he took him away with him to Spain, where a short time later he died in obscurity.

This suspicion, therefore, is so natural to princes that it cannot be avoided, and it is impossible for them to show gratitude to those whose victories have effected great conquests under their flags. And since a prince cannot avoid ingratitude, it should not be surprising or noteworthy if a people too cannot avoid it. A city which lives in freedom has two goals: first, to enlarge its territories and, second, to maintain its freedom; in both one and the other of these she will most likely err through excessive love. A city's errors in enlarging her territories will be discussed in the proper place; as for the errors in maintaining freedom, there are, among others, the following: offending those citizens who should be rewarded and being suspicious of those in whom trust should be placed. Although these methods in a republic given over to corruption are the

[2] Gonzalo Fernández de Córdoba

cause of great evils and very often lead to tyranny—as occurred in Rome with Caesar, who seized by force what ingratitude had denied him—nevertheless they bring great benefits to a republic that is not corrupt and they allow her to live in freedom longer, since the fear of punishment keeps men better and less ambitious. It is true that of all peoples who ever possessed an empire, Rome was the least ungrateful for the reasons discussed above; for it can be said that there is no example of her ingratitude other than the case of Scipio, for Coriolanus and Camillus were exiled because of the harm that they both inflicted upon the plebeians. The former was never pardoned, for he always harbored a hostile spirit against the people, but the latter was not only recalled but also esteemed for the rest of his life as if he were a prince. But the ingratitude shown to Scipio was born of a suspicion which the citizens began to have of him and which they did not feel toward others—a suspicion which arose from the greatness of the enemy Scipio had defeated, the fame which the victory in such a long and dangerous war had given him, the quickness of this victory, and the favors which his youth, prudence, and other memorable virtues were gaining for him. All this was so great that even the magistrates of Rome were afraid of his authority, an affair which was displeasing to wise men, who thought it an unheard-of thing in Rome. And his way of living seemed so astonishing that Cato the Elder, considered a holy man, was the first to bring him to account for it and to say that a city could not call itself free when there was a citizen living there who was feared by the magistrates. Therefore, if in this instance the people of Rome followed the opinion of Cato, then they deserve the excuse (as I stated above) that those peoples and princes deserve who are ungrateful because of suspicion. In concluding this discourse, then, let me say that the vice of ingratitude is a result either of avarice or supicion, and it should be clear that the people never resort to it out of avarice; and they

resort to it out of suspicion much less frequently than
princes do since they have fewer reasons for suspicion, as
will be explained further on.

CHAPTER XXX.   WHAT MEANS A PRINCE OR A REPUBLIC
MAY EMPLOY TO AVOID THE VICE OF INGRATITUDE, AND
WHAT MEANS A COMMANDER OR A CITIZEN MAY EMPLOY SO
AS NOT TO BE HARMED BY IT

[To avoid feeling a sense of ingratitude toward a victorious commander, a prince should lead his forces personally; and if he wins a victory, the glory will be his alone. If
victorious, a commander should leave the army immediately after the victory so as to give the prince no reason
for suspicion; if he cannot do this, he should proceed in
precisely the opposite manner, attempting to win the
favor of his soldiers, the prince's subjects, and nearby
powers. There is no other course of action open to him,
but men rarely know how to be perfectly good or bad and
usually hesitate to follow exclusively one course or another. A republic has a more difficult problem, since it
must delegate power of command to one of its citizens.
The answer is to do as Rome did in delegating power to as
many citizens as possible, the result being the creation of
so many able men responsible for so many victories that
no one man had any reason to suspect single individuals
of excessive ambition; as a consequence, the city had no
grounds for ingratitude toward its subjects.]

CHAPTER XXXI.   ROMAN COMMANDERS WERE NEVER EX-
CESSIVELY PUNISHED FOR ERRORS THEY COMMITTED; NOR
WERE THEY EVER PUNISHED WHEN THEIR IGNORANCE OR
POOR JUDGMENT RESULTED IN HARM TO THE REPUBLIC

[The Romans acted in this manner in order to free the
minds of their commanders from concern over possible
failure and its consequences; a commander's legitimate
concern over the outcome of a battle was thus not to be
complicated by his fear of failure. The loss of a battle it-

self was felt to be sufficient punishment. Even Varro, returning from Cannae after the crushing defeat of his army by Hannibal, was not punished for his failure but was instead greeted by senators and citizens who praised him for returning to Rome and thus showing that he still had faith in the Roman cause.]

CHAPTER XXXII.   A REPUBLIC OR A PRINCE SHOULD NOT DEFER REWARDING MEN UNTIL THEY ARE IN DANGER

The Romans were fortunately generous to the people even when danger arose; for when Porsenna attacked Rome in order to restore the Tarquins, the senate, fearing at the time that the people would prefer to accept the king rather than endure a war, removed the tax on salt and other taxes in order to secure their support, declaring that the poor did enough for the public welfare by bringing up their children; and because of this benefit the people allowed themselves to undergo siege, hunger, and war. But no one, relying on this example, should put off gaining the people's support until times of danger. What the Romans succeeded in doing will never work for another, for the masses will think that they do not owe this benefit to you, but rather to your enemies, and since they will fear that once the emergency has passed you will take away from them what you have been forced to concede to them, they will feel no obligation to you. And the reason why this policy succeeded for the Romans was that their government was new and not yet stable; the people had earlier seen how laws were passed for their benefit—such as the right to appeal to the plebeians—and they could therefore persuade themselves that this benefit was not the result of the enemy's arrival but was passed because of the inclination of the senate to help them. Besides this, the memory of the kings by whom they had been despised and mistreated in many ways was still fresh in their minds. And since such circumstances only rarely occur, only rarely are such remedies of any use. Any form of government, therefore, whether it be a republic or a monarchy, should consider in advance what kinds of adverse times are likely to befall it and the people upon whom it may have to rely in times of difficulty; and it should then treat them in just the manner it thinks it would have to treat them in case an emergency should occur. A government which acts otherwise—be it a monarchy or a republic, but especially the former—a government which believes it can win men over again with benefits the moment danger arises deceives itself; for not only will it not win them over, but it will accelerate its own ruin.

CHAPTER XXXIII.   WHEN A PROBLEM HAS ARISEN EITHER WITHIN A STATE OR OUTSIDE IT, IT IS SAFER TO DELAY DEALING WITH IT THAN TO ATTACK IT

As the Roman republic grew in reputation, strength, and size, its neighbors, who at first had not considered the damage this new republic could do them, began too late to recognize their error; and in order to remedy what they had not cured earlier, forty peoples united against Rome; whereupon, from among the remedies which they usually employed during times of urgent danger, the Romans chose to create a dictator; that is, they gave to one man the power to decide on a course of action without any consultation and to execute his decision without any right of appeal. This remedy was useful at the time and was the reason why the Romans overcame imminent dangers; and it was always very useful in all those circumstances which arose at any time to hinder the growth of the republic's empire.

Concerning this matter, there is this to be said: first, when a problem arises either from within a republic or outside it, one brought about either by internal or external reasons, one that has become so great that it begins to make everyone afraid, the safest policy is to delay dealing with it rather than trying to do away with it, because those who try to do away with it almost always increase its strength and accelerate the harm which they feared might come from it. And such emergencies as these arise in a republic more often through internal than through external causes. It often happens that a citizen is allowed to acquire more power than is reasonably safe, or the administration of a law which is the nerve and life of a free government begins to be corrupted, and such an error is allowed to continue until it becomes a more dangerous policy to attempt to remedy the situation than to allow it to continue. And it is even more difficult to recognize these problems when they arise, inasmuch as it always seems more natural for men to approve the beginnings of things: such approval is most likely to be granted, above all else, to those deeds which appear to reflect in themselves some manly ability and which are carried out by young men. So if in a republic a young nobleman appears who possesses some extraordinary ability, all the citizens turn their eyes toward him and agree to honor him without reservation; thus, if in that young man there is some ambition, through a combination of the favors which Nature grants him and existing circumstances he suddenly achieves such a position that when the citizens realize their error they have few remedies to correct it; and if they attempt to make use of the remedies they have, they achieve nothing and accelerate his rise to power.

One could cite many instances of this, but I shall give only one from our own city. Cosimo de' Medici, from whom the Medici family gained the beginnings of its greatness in our city, acquired so much renown as a consequence of the favor that his prudence and the ignorance of the other citizens had won him that he began to arouse the fear of the government, to the extent that the other citizens judged it dangerous to attack him and even more dangerous to allow him to go on as he was. But in those days there lived a certain Niccolò Uzzano, a man who was considered most able in civic affairs, and while he committed the first mistake of not recognizing the dangers that could arise from Cosimo's reputation, as long as he lived he never permitted himself the second mistake, that is, to try to do away with Cosimo, for such an attempt would have meant the complete loss of control by his own faction. And this is precisely what happened after his death, for the citizens who were left did not follow his advice, banded together against Cosimo, and drove him out of Florence. The result was that Cosimo's faction, resenting this injury, later recalled him and made him prince of the republic, a rank he never would have obtained without this overt opposition.

The same thing happened to Caesar in Rome, for his ability won him the support of Pompey and the others, and yet a short time later that support turned into fear; as Cicero testified, when Pompey began to fear Caesar it was too late. This fear caused them to seek remedies, and the results then accelerated the ruin of their republic.

Let me say, therefore, that since it is difficult to recognize these evils when they arise—this difficulty being the result of how deceptive such things can be at their beginnings—it is a wiser policy to delay dealing with them until they are recognized rather than to oppose them, because, given time, either they disappear by themselves or at least the evil is deferred for a longer time. In all such cases, rulers who plan on removing these evils or impetuously opposing them by force should keep their eyes open and not magnify their problems or bring the latter upon themselves while thinking that they are diminishing them or driving them further away—as one might drown a plant by watering it too much. The strength of the disease should be well estimated, and if you see you are able to cure it, set yourself to doing so without reservation; otherwise leave it alone and attempt nothing, for what happened to Rome's neighbors (as was mentioned above) could also happen to you. Since Rome had grown so powerful, it would have been safer for them to try to placate her and hold her back by peaceful means rather than to force her to think of new methods and new defenses by means of war. For that conspiracy of theirs did nothing but make the Romans more united, braver, and intent on finding new ways to increase their power in a very short time. One of these new ways was the creation of a dictator, a new institution which not only enabled the Romans to overcome their present dangers but also helped them avoid countless evils which that republic would have incurred without this remedy.

CHAPTER XXXIV. DICTATORIAL AUTHORITY DID GOOD, NOT HARM, TO THE ROMAN REPUBLIC; AND HOW AUTHORITY THAT CITIZENS TAKE FOR THEMSELVES, NOT THAT WHICH IS GRANTED THEM BY FREE SUFFRAGE, IS HARMFUL TO CIVIC LIFE

Those Romans who found a means of creating a dictator in their city have been condemned by some writers as having created, with the passage of time, a reason for tyranny in Rome; they point out how the first tyrant in that city ruled it under the title of dictator, stating that if this office has not existed Caesar would not have been able to disguise his tyranny under some public title. Anyone, however, who holds this opinion has not considered the matter well and is accepting it without any reasonable cause; for it was neither the title nor the rank of dictator which enslaved Rome but rather the authority taken from the citizens as a result of the length of the dictator's rule; if Rome had not had the title of dictator, the dictator would have taken another title, for power easily acquires a title but titles do not acquire power. And we can observe that the dictatorship always benefited the city as long as it was created in accord with public institutions and not by the dictator's own private authority. For the creation of magistrates and the granting of power by extraordinary means harm republics, which is not the case for those which arise through normal means: it is clear that for a long period of time in Rome a dictator never did anything that did not benefit the republic.

There are obvious reasons for this. First, if a citizen is to cause harm and to seize for himself unlawful authority, he must possess many qualities which, in an uncorrupted city, he can never have: for he must be very rich and have many followers and partisans, which cannot occur where laws are observed; and even if he does have them, men like this are so dangerous that free elections never favor them. Besides this, the dictator was created for a circumscribed period of time, and only in order to deal with the problem for which he was chosen. His authority encompassed the power to decide for himself the way in which to deal with this urgent danger, to do everything without consultation, and to punish anyone without appeal; but he could do nothing which would alter the form of government, as would have been the case had he taken authority from the senate or the people, or had he abolished the city's old institutions and established new ones. And so, considering the brief time of his dictatorship, the limited authority he possessed, and the fact that the Roman people were uncorrupted, it was impossible for the dictator to overstep his limitations and do harm to the city; and experience demonstrates that the city always benefited from this institution.

Of all Roman institutions, this one truly deserves to be considered and numbered among those which were the cause of the greatness of so strong an empire: for without such an institution cities find a solution to extraordinary problems only with difficulty. Since the operation of normal institutions in republics is slow (neither a council nor any magistrate can undertake anything alone; in many cases they must consult with one another and, in harmonizing their opinions, time is spent), their remedies are very dangerous when they have to provide solutions to a problem which cannot wait. Republics, therefore, ought to have among their laws one like the following: the Venetian republic, which is among the best modern republics, has delegated authority to a small number of citizens who, in times of urgency, can deliberate among themselves and make a decision without consulting anyone else. When a republic does not have such a procedure, it must either come to ruin by following its laws or ignore the laws in order to avoid ruin; yet in a republic it is not good for something to happen which requires action outside the laws. While extraordinary measures may be beneficial at the moment, the example is nevertheless harmful, for if one forms the habit of breaking laws for a good reason, later on they can be broken for bad reasons under the same pretext of doing good. Thus, no republic will ever be perfect unless its laws make provisions for everything, and set up a remedy for every possibility and establish the means of using it. In conclusion, therefore, let me say that those republics which have not taken refuge, in times of impending danger, either in a dictatorship or in some similar authority have always come to ruin in the midst of serious difficulties. It is to be noted, in connection with this new institution, how wisely the means of choosing a dictator was provided for by the Romans. Since the choosing of a dictatorship would cast some shame upon the consuls—for they would now have to obey like all the other citizens, whereas they formerly had been the rulers of the city—and foreseeing that this would cause resentment toward them among the citizens, the Romans decided that the authority to choose the dictator should rest with the consuls, believing that they would make the selection when events occurred during which Rome required this regal authority; and since it would be they themselves who made the choice, it would pain them less, for the wounds and every other evil that a man inflicts willingly upon himself, by choice, hurt a good deal less than those which are inflicted upon you by others. In later times, moreover, instead of choosing a dictator the Romans would grant dictatorial authority to the consul with these words: "Let the consul see to it that the republic suffers no harm."

But to return to our subject, I conclude that when Rome's neighbors sought to conquer her, they forced her to pass not only laws that enabled her to defend herself but also ones which enabled her to counterattack with greater force, counsel, and authority.

CHAPTER XXXV.   THE REASON WHY THE CREATION OF THE DECEMVIRATE IN ROME WAS HARMFUL TO THE LIBERTY OF THAT REPUBLIC, NOTWITHSTANDING THE FACT THAT IT WAS CREATED BY FREE AND PUBLIC ELECTION

[The election of the decemvirate may seem to negate what was said in the previous chapter about the beneficial results of authority granted by free and public elections, for the decemvirate established a tyranny in the course of time in spite of free elections. But their authority was granted in an unrestricted manner and for a greater period of time than was advisable, and this is always harmful; furthermore, the creation of a dictator did not abolish the institutions of the consuls, the tribunes, and the senate, all of which restricted his power. On the contrary, the creation of the decemvirate suspended the consuls and the tribunes and gave the decemvirate the power to make laws; without any such restraint, they were, at the urging of Appius, able to become tyrannical. In stating that authority bestowed by a free election never harms a republic, we assume that such authority is given only under certain conditions and for a limited period of time. In the case of such well-ordered states as Sparta or Venice, both the King of Sparta and the Doge of Venice were given authority of long duration, but both were supervised so that they could not misuse this power.]

CHAPTER XXXVI.   CITIZENS WHO HAVE HELD THE HIGHEST OFFICES SHOULD NOT DISDAIN LESS IMPORTANT ONES

[Although the Romans prized glory, they never felt it beneath them to take orders from someone whom they had formerly commanded, nor to serve in an army which they had previously led. This custom has been reversed in our own day. Venice, for instance, feels that a citizen should never accept a lower office after holding a higher one. While this practice may be honorable in private life, it is of little use to the body politic, for a republic has more confidence in a citizen who descends from a high office to a lower one than a citizen who rises from a lower to a higher rank, since it cannot rely upon the latter unless he has under his command men of such ability that he can learn from their experience and counsel. Had Rome observed the custom which now prevails in modern republics and kingdoms, she would have faced countless situations threatening her liberty as a result of the inexperience and ambition of men rising up from the ranks—ambition which could have gone unchecked by the virtue of men under their command.]

CHAPTER XXXVII.   WHAT DISTURBANCES AROSE FROM THE AGRARIAN LAWS; AND HOW VERY HARMFUL IT IS FOR A REPUBLIC TO PASS A RETROACTIVE LAW WHICH IS CONTRARY TO AN ANCIENT CUSTOM OF THE CITY

[Ancient writers used to remark that men usually inflict evil upon themselves and become bored with good, and that both of these attitudes produce the same effects. "The reason is that Nature has created men in such a way that they can desire everything but are unable to obtain everything; thus, since their desire is always greater than their power of acquisition, discontent with what they possess and lack of satisfaction are the result. From this arise the variations in their fortunes, for since some desire to possess more and others fear to lose what they have acquired, enmities and war arise, and from them come the ruin of one province and the exaltation of another."[1] This discussion sheds light on the Roman experience, for the Roman

[1] The material within quotation marks is a direct translation of the original; the remainder of the material within brackets is, as usual, a paraphrase of the balance of this chapter.

plebeians were not happy after they had secured themselves against the power of the nobility through the creation of tribunes; they continued to quarrel with the nobility out of ambition, and this quarrel poisoned the body politic and led to disputes over the Agrarian Law and to the eventual destruction of the republic. The law had two provisions: first, no citizen was allowed more than a certain amount of land; second, all lands taken from an enemy would be divided equally among the people. This offended the nobility since they already possessed most of the land and would lose all land beyond the legal limit; moreover, equal division of newly acquired lands meant that they would be limited in future acquisitions. Discussion over the Agrarian Law ceased until the time of the Gracchi, when renewed conflict over the law caused the downfall of the republic. When the plebeians supported Marius by making him consul four times, the nobility backed Sulla. Civil war broke out, during which the nobility gained the upper hand. This conflict continued when Caesar became the leader of the Marian faction and Pompey led Sulla's faction. With Caesar's victory Rome acquired its first tyrant and the city never recovered its freedom. Elsewhere it was demonstrated how the conflict between the senate and the people preserved Roman liberty, and yet the effects of this Agrarian Law may seem to contradict this. Nevertheless, I shall not alter my opinion on this matter, for the ambition of the nobility is so great that it must be checked in various ways if a city is not to come to ruin. Rome would have been reduced to slavery much sooner than the three hundred years it took for the Agrarian Law to produce that effect if the plebeians had not checked the ambition of the nobility. This shows how men value their property more than positions of honor, for the Roman nobility yielded to the demands of the people in such questions, but they were more tenacious concerning property, and this tenacity caused the people to employ extraordinary measures themselves.]

CHAPTER XXXVIII.　WEAK REPUBLICS ARE INDECISIVE AND DO NOT KNOW HOW TO MAKE DECISIONS; IF THEY EVER DO ADOPT A POLICY, THEY DO SO MORE FROM NECESSITY THAN FROM CHOICE

There was a very serious plague in Rome, and this seemed to the Volsci and the Aequi the right time to crush the city; after gathering together a large army, these two peoples attacked and laid waste the lands of the Latins and the Hernici, who were forced to inform Rome of this and to beg the Romans to defend them. Since the Romans were afflicted by the plague, they replied that their allies must take measures to defend themselves with their own soldiers, for the Romans could not help them. The generosity and the prudence of the senate are revealed here, for although it always wanted, under any circumstances, to be the master of decisions that its subjects had to make, it was never ashamed to adopt a policy contrary to its usual procedure or to other decisions it had made when necessity demanded it.

I say this because at other times this very senate prohibited those same peoples from arming and defending themselves, and a less prudent senate than this one would have considered its dignity lost by conceding them the right of self-defense. But that body always judged things as they ought to be judged and always chose the policy that was less bad as the best one: it was grieved at not being able to defend its subjects and at allowing them to take up arms without its support, for the reasons mentioned as well as for many others that are understandable; nevertheless, realizing that out of necessity the subjects, with the enemy upon them, would have armed themselves in any case, it chose the honorable policy and decided that what had to be done would be better done with its permission, so that they should not, in disobeying out of necessity, become used to disobeying by choice. And although it would seem that this policy is the one that every republic should adopt, nonetheless, weak and poorly advised republics do not know enough to do so, nor do they understand how to gain honor from such conditions of necessity. Duke Valentino had taken Faenza and had forced Bologna to agree to his terms; then, wishing to return to Rome by way of Tuscany, he sent one of his men to Florence to request passage for himself and his army. A consultation took place in Florence over what to do in this matter, but no one ever counseled that he be granted this permission. In this instance the Roman procedure was not followed. Since the duke was very heavily armed and the Florentines were not sufficiently armed to prevent his passage, it would have been more honorable for them to make it appear that he passed with their permission rather than by force; if they had managed the matter differently—instead of the entire incident resulting in their complete shame—their disgrace would have appeared less severe. But the worst thing that a weak republic can do is to be indecisive, so that all the decisions it makes are made out of necessity, and if any benefit results from them, it is necessity, not the republic's prudence, that has brought it about.

I should like to give two other examples of this which occurred in our own times in the government of our city. In 1500, after King Louis XII of France had taken Milan, he was anxious to turn Pisa over to the Florentines to collect the fifty thousand ducats they had promised him after such return, and he sent his armies to Pisa under the command of Monsignor de Beaumont, who, although French, was a man in whom the Florentines had a great deal of confidence. The army and its general maneuvered between Cascina and Pisa so that they might assault the walls of the city; and as they remained there for several days to organize the expedition, Pisan envoys came to Beaumont and offered to surrender the city to the French army on condition that he promise in the king's name not to place it in the hands of the Florentines before four months' time had elapsed. This plan was refused by the Florentines, and as a result they besieged the city and departed in shame. The offer was refused solely because of their mistrust for the word of the king, into whose hands they had, at any rate, been forced to place themselves as a result of their weak planning; moreover, in not trusting him they did not see how much easier it would have been for the king to restore Pisa to them once he was inside the city, or, if he did not restore it, to reveal to them his intentions rather than to promise it to them when he did not yet have it and force them to pay for his promises. Thus, it would have been much more profitable for them to have agreed to allow Beaumont to take the city under whatever conditions, as later became evident when, in 1502, after Arezzo rebelled, Monsignor Imbault, sent by the King of France with a French army, came to the assistance of the Florentines; when he neared Arezzo, after a short time he began to discuss terms with the Aretines, who wished to surrender the city under certain conditions, like the Pisans. This offer was refused by Florence. Monsignor Imbault observed this and felt that the Florentines had understood very little of the matter; he began to hold negotiations for the surrender without the participation of the Florentine commissioners. He was successful in this maneuver and concluded an agreement on his own terms, according to which he and his soldiers entered Arezzo, giving the Florentines to understand that he considered them to be mad and without any comprehension of the ways of the world; for if they wanted Arezzo, they should let the king know about it since he could give it to them much more easily with his soldiers inside the city than outside it. There was no end in Florence to the cutting remarks and curses directed at this said Imbault; they did not stop until the Florentines finally realized that if Beaumont had acted in the same manner they would have taken Pisa as they had Arezzo.

Now, to return to our topic, indecisive republics never choose beneficial policies except through force, for when there is doubt their weakness never allows them to arrive at a decision; and if that doubt is not removed by some form of violence which drives them on, they remain forever suspended in a state of indecision.

CHAPTER XXXIX.   THE SAME EVENTS OFTEN OCCUR AMONG DIFFERENT PEOPLES

Anyone who studies present and ancient affairs will easily see how in all cities and all peoples there still exist, and have always existed, the same desires and passions. Thus, it is an easy matter for him who carefully examines past events to foresee future events in a republic and to apply the remedies employed by the ancients, or, if old remedies cannot be found, to devise new ones based upon the similarity of the events. But since these matters are neglected or not understood by those who read, or, if understood, remain unknown to those who govern, the result is that the same problems always exist in every era.

When, after 1494, the city of Florence had lost part of its empire (Pisa and other towns), it was forced to wage war against those who had possession of them; and since those who occupied them were powerful, the consequence was that a great deal of money was spent in the war with no results: a heavy taxation followed the great expenditures, and endless disputes among the people followed the heavy taxation. And because this war was administered by a magistracy of ten citizens, called the Ten of War, the masses started hating them (as if they were the cause both of the war and the war's expenses) and gradually persuaded themselves that if this magistracy were removed, the war would be ended; thus, when it was time to reappoint them, they allowed the office to come to an end by not replacing the members, and they entrusted their duties to the Signoria. This decision was so damaging that not only did it fail to end the war, as the masses had convinced themselves it would, but when those men who had governed with prudence had been removed, so much disorder followed that, in addition to losing Pisa, Florence lost Arezzo and many other towns. Hence, after the people had realized their error and saw that the cause of the disease was the fever and not the physician, they reestablished the magistracy of the Ten. This same passion was aroused in Rome against the institution of the consuls, for when that people saw one war lead to another, allowing them no rest, they should have realized that this sprang from the ambition of their neighbors, who wanted to oppress them; instead, they thought that it came about as a result of the ambition of the nobles, who wished to lead the people outside Rome under the consuls, to oppress them where they had no one at all to defend them, since inside the city of Rome the nobles were not able to punish the plebeians, who were defended there by the authority of the tribunes. And because of this, the people thought it was necessary either to abolish the consuls or regulate their power in such a way that they would have no authority over the people either inside or outside the city. The first man to propose this law was a certain Terentillus, a tribune who suggested that five men be appointed to study and limit the consuls' powers. This greatly angered the nobles, who felt that the majesty of their authority had declined to the extent that they no longer held any authority at all in the republic; nevertheless, the persistence of the tribunes was such that the title of consul was abolished, and after some other laws were passed the people were finally satisfied to appoint tribunes with consular powers rather than consuls—so much greater was the people's hatred of the consuls' titles than of their actual authority. And so, they followed this system for a long time until they finally realized their error, and just as the Florentines returned to the Ten, so the Romans reappointed their consuls.

CHAPTER XL.   ON THE CREATION OF THE DECEMVIRATE IN
ROME AND WHAT IS NOTEWORTHY ABOUT IT; WHEREIN,
AMONG MANY OTHER MATTERS, HOW THE SAME EVENT MAY
EITHER SAVE OR OPPRESS A REPUBLIC IS CONSIDERED

As I wish to discuss in detail what took place in Rome
up to the creation of the decemvirate, it does not seem superfluous to recount, first, everything which followed that
creation and, then, to discuss those things which are noteworthy in it; they are numerous and of considerable importance, both for those who desire to maintain a free
republic and for those who are planning to seize one. And
such a discussion will reveal the many errors committed
by the senate and by the plebeians to the detriment of liberty, as well as the many errors committed by Appius,
head of the decemvirate, which were detrimental to the
tyranny he had hoped to establish in Rome. After the
many disputes and struggles which took place between
the populace and the nobility over the establishment of
new laws in Rome, by means of which the liberty of that
government might be more firmly established, the two
sides agreed to send Spurius Postumius and two other citizens to Athens to obtain copies of the laws Solon gave to
that city in order that they might base the Roman laws
upon them. After these men had returned, they chose men
to examine and establish the said laws; they appointed ten
citizens for a period of one year, among whom was
Appius Claudius, a shrewd but restless man. And in order
that they might establish such laws without any restraint,
all the other magistrates, and especially the tribunes and
consuls, were done away with, as was the people's right of
appeal, so that this new magistracy came to be the absolute power in Rome. The collective authority of his other
colleagues was now assumed by Appius, since he had the
favor of the people; he had made himself so popular with
the people that it was amazing how he had so quickly acquired a new character and a new disposition, for he had
been considered a cruel persecutor of the people until that
time.

These decemvirs conducted themselves very properly, never keeping more than twelve lictors who marched in front of the leader of the Ten. And although they had absolute authority, whenever they had to punish a Roman citizen for homicide they would call him up before the people and allow them to judge him. They wrote their laws on ten tablets, and before they confirmed them they put them in view of the public for everyone to read and discuss so that if some defect were found in them it could be amended before their promulgation. Appius let it be known throughout Rome that if two tablets were to be added to the original ten they would be perfect, and this opinion gave the people the opportunity to reelect the decemvirs for another year; they agreed to do this partly because they would not have to reappoint the consuls and partly because they felt they could do without tribunes, since they themselves were acting as the judges in legal matters, as was mentioned above. When the decision was taken to reappoint them, all the nobility sought to obtain these positions, and Appius was among the foremost; he showed such kindness toward the people in requesting it that he began to arouse the suspicion of his colleagues: "For, after such arrogance, they felt that such affability could not exist without an ulterior motive."[1] Since they were hesitant to oppose him openly, they decided to do so artfully; and although he was the youngest of them all, they gave him the power of proposing the future decemvirs to the people, thinking that he would observe the limitations which others had observed by not proposing himself, for in Rome this was considered an unusual and disgraceful practice. "However, he converted the impediment into an opportunity"[2] and named himself among the first, to the amazement and displeasure of all the nobles; then he nominated nine others to suit his plans. This new selection, made for another year, showed the people and the nobility their mistake, for immediately "Appius put

[1] Livy, III, xxxv (cited by Machiavelli in Latin).
[2] Ibid.

aside his feigned character"[3] and began to reveal his innate pride; and in a few days he had tainted his colleagues with his own habits. And in order to intimidate the people and the senate, in place of the usual twelve lictors he appointed one hundred and twenty.

For several days both sides were equally afraid; but then the decemvirs began to favor the senate and to mistreat the plebeians; and if anyone who was mistreated by one of the decemvirs appealed to another, he was treated worse after his appeal than he had been in his initial sentence. And so, recognizing their mistake and griefstricken, the people began to look to the nobility "to find a breath of liberty there where they had feared servitude so strongly that they had reduced the republic to its present condition."[4] This grief of theirs was pleasing to the nobility "since, disgusted by the present state of affairs, they might wish for the return of the consuls."[5] The day that ended the year's term came to a close, and the two tablets of laws had been drawn up but not made public. From this fact the decemvirs took the opportunity of continuing their magistracy, and they began to conduct the government with violence and to make the young noblemen their dependents by giving them the goods of those whom they had condemned. "With such gifts the young men were corrupted, preferring as they did the license granted them to liberty for all."[6]

At that time it happened that the Sabines and the Volscians began to wage war against Rome, the fear of which forced the decemvirs to realize the weakness of their government, for without the senate they could not organize the war, and if they called the senate together they felt that they would lose their control of the government. Driven by necessity, they nevertheless chose the second

---

[3] Livy, III, xxxvi (cited by Machiavelli in Latin).
[4] Livy, III, xxxvii (cited by Machiavelli in Latin).
[5] Ibid.
[6] Ibid.

alternative, and when the senators gathered, many of them, Valerius and Horatius in particular, spoke against the arrogance of the decemvirs; their power would have been completely abrogated if the senate, in its hatred of the people, had not wished to demonstrate its authority, since the senators thought that if the decemvirs resigned their authority voluntarily, the tribunes of the people would be reappointed. Hence, they decided upon waging war. Two armies set forth, commanded in part by the said decemvirs; Appius remained behind to rule the city. At that time he happened to fall in love with Virginia, and since he was lusting to take her by force, her father, Virginius, killed her in order to free her. This provoked violent disturbances in Rome and in the armies: the soldiers and the people together marched to the Mons Sacer, where they remained until the decemvirs abdicated their authority and the consuls and the tribunes were reestablished, and Rome was restored to the form of her ancient liberty.

And so, one first observes from this account that in Rome the evil involved in establishing this tyranny arose from those same causes which give rise to most tyrannies in cities: that is, from too much desire on the part of the people to be free and too much desire on the part of the nobles to command. And when they do not agree in creating a law which favors liberty, but instead one of the factions throws its support in favor of one man, then tyranny is quick to arise. The people and the Roman nobles agreed to establish the decemvirs and to grant them such authority because of the desire each faction had: the people hoped to abolish the office of consul and the nobles that of the tribunate. When they were established in office, the plebeians gave their support to Appius, whom they felt had become one of them and might attack the nobility. And when a people is led to make this error—to bestow on one man the power to attack those they despise—and if that one man is shrewd, he will always turn out to be a tyrant in that city, for, with the people's support, he will wait until he has done away with the nobility, never moving to oppress the people until he has rid himself of the nobles, and by the time the people see themselves enslaved they will have no one to whom they can turn. All those who have founded tyrannies in republics have used this method; and if Appius had followed this system, that tyranny of his would have taken on more life and would not have collapsed so quickly. But he did just the opposite; he could not have conducted himself less prudently, for in order to maintain his tyranny he made himself the enemy both of those who had given it to him and who could have preserved it for him and of those who had not agreed to give it to him and who would not have been capable of maintaining it; he lost those who were his friends and sought as his friends those who could not be friends. For while nobles wish to rule as tyrants, that part of the nobility which is excluded from the tyranny is always opposed to the tyrant; nor can the tyrant ever win all their support for himself, since, owing to the great ambition and greed of the nobility, the tyrant cannot possess so much wealth or enough offices to satisfy all of them. And thus, when Appius abandoned the people to take the side of the nobles, he committed the most obvious mistake, both for the reasons explained above and because, wishing to hold something with force, the one who employs force must be more powerful than the one upon whom that greater force is being employed.

Thus, it follows that those tyrants who have the people as a friend and the nobles as enemies are most secure, since their force is maintained by greater strength than that of those tyrants who have the people as an enemy and the nobility as a friend. With this type of support internal forces are enough for survival, as they were for Nabis, tyrant of Sparta, for when all of Greece and the Roman people attacked him, having the support of just a few nobles but the friendship of all of the people, he defended himself with their aid—something he would not have been able to accomplish if they had been his enemy.

In the other case, internal forces do not suffice when the tyrant has few friends in the city, and he must seek aid from outside. This aid requires three measures: first, employing foreign attendants as your bodyguards; second, arming the countryside so that it may undertake the duty that the people should have performed; third, allying yourself with powerful neighbors who will defend you. Anyone who follows these methods and observes them well, even if he has the people as his enemy, will be able in some way to save himself. But Appius was not able to use the method of gaining the support of the country people since Rome and the countryside were not divided, and what he was able to do he did not know how to do, and so he came to ruin at the very beginning.

The senate and the people committed the gravest of errors in establishing the decemvirate, for although (as was stated above in the section treating of the dictator) those magistrates who are self-appointed, and not those whom the people create, are harmful to liberty, when the people organize the magistrates they ought nevertheless to do so in such a way that they force them to be cautious about becoming wicked. And where they should have set up a guard over magistrates to keep them good, the Romans removed it, establishing the decemvirate as the sole magistracy in Rome, annulling all others because of the excessive desire of the senate (as was explained above) to do away with the tribunes and that of the plebeians to do away with the consuls. This blinded them to the extent that they agreed to such an evil. As King Ferdinand[7] used to say: men often act like certain small birds of prey who have such a great desire to pursue their victims, as Nature prompts them to do, that they do not sense that some other larger bird is flying above them and is preparing to kill them. From this discourse, therefore, one can, as I proposed in the beginning, discover the error the Roman people committed in wishing to save their liberty as well

[7] Ferdinand III of Aragon, King of Naples.

as the errors Appius committed in wishing to maintain his tyranny.

CHAPTER XLI.   TO LEAP FROM HUMILITY TO ARROGANCE AND FROM MERCY TO CRUELTY WITHOUT APPROPRIATE STAGES IN BETWEEN IS AN IMPRUDENT AND UNPROFITABLE AFFAIR

Among the other ill-advised methods which Appius employed in order to maintain his tyranny, that of leaping too soon from one attitude to another was of no little importance. For his shrewdness in deceiving the people by pretending to be a man of the populace was well employed; also well employed were the methods he used to have the decemvirs reappointed, as was his audacity in getting himself nominated, contrary to the expectation of the nobility; well employed, too, was his appointment of colleagues suited to his purpose. Not at all well employed, however, once he had accomplished all this, was his sudden change of nature, as I said above, from being a friend of the people to showing himself as their enemy, from being humane to becoming arrogant, from being easy to reach to becoming inaccessible—and he changed so quickly and without any excuse that everybody saw the falseness of his intent. For anyone who has appeared to be good for a time and intends, for his own purposes, to become bad must do so in appropriate stages and in such a way as to be governed by circumstances, so that before your altered nature deprives you of old supporters it will have provided you with so many new ones that your authority will not be diminished; otherwise, finding yourself unmasked and without friends, you will be ruined.

CHAPTER XLII.   HOW EASILY MEN CAN BE CORRUPTED

[On the topic of the decemvirate, it is to be noted how easily men are corrupted, even when they are good and well trained—the young nobles who supported Appius in his tyranny were such men. Lawmakers should bear this in mind when they make laws to restrain human passions and to remove the possibility of evildoing with impunity.]

CHAPTER XLIII.   THOSE WHO FIGHT FOR THEIR OWN GLORY ARE GOOD AND FAITHFUL SOLDIERS

[There is a great difference between a happy army, fighting for its own glory, and one which is poorly organized, fighting to further the ambition of others. Roman armies were usually victorious under the consuls and were vanquished under the decemvirs; this example demonstrates, in part, the uselessness of mercenary soldiers who fight only for the salary you give them. Since love and devotion sufficient to resist a brave enemy are found only in your own subjects, an army must be composed of your own citizens in order to obtain good results. After the rule of the decemvirate was abolished, Roman armies fought again as free men and were again victorious, as they had formerly been.]

CHAPTER XLIV.   A MULTITUDE WITHOUT A LEADER IS INEFFECTIVE; AND HOW ONE SHOULD NOT MAKE THREATS FIRST AND THEN REQUEST AUTHORITY

Because of the incident with Virginia, the Roman people went armed to the Mons Sacer. The senate sent its ambassadors to ask by what authority they had abandoned their leaders and gone to that place. And so highly regarded was the authority of the senate that, since the people did not have their leaders among them, no man dared to reply. And Livy declares that it was not that they lacked a reason to reply but rather that they lacked only someone to make the reply. This clearly demonstrates the ineffectiveness of a multitude without a leader.

Virginius understood this confusion, and on his orders twenty military tribunes were established to act as leaders in answering and negotiating with the senate. When they asked that Valerius and Horatius be sent to them so that they could explain their demands, the two men refused to go unless the decemvirs first abandoned their magistracy. And when they arrived at the Mons Sacer, where the populace had gathered, they were asked to agree that tribunes of the people should be established, that there should be the right of appeal to the people from every magistrate, and that the decemvirs should be handed over to them, for it was their intention to burn them all alive. Valerius and Horatius praised the first of their demands but condemned the last one as impious, saying: "You who condemn cruelty now are abandoning yourselves to it";[1] and they advised them to say nothing about the decemvirs and to wait until they regained their own authority and power, for then they would not lack a means of getting satisfaction. Here one clearly sees how much stupidity and lack of prudence there is in first saying, before asking for something, "I wish to do such and such an evil with this"; for one should not reveal one's intentions but instead should try to get what he wants anyway, because it is enough to ask for a man's weapons without saying, "I wish to kill you with these." When you have the weapon in hand, then you can satisfy your desire.

CHAPTER XLV.   IT IS A BAD EXAMPLE NOT TO OBSERVE A LAW THAT HAS BEEN PASSED, ESPECIALLY ON THE PART OF ITS LEGISLATOR; AND IT IS MOST HARMFUL TO THE RULER OF A CITY TO COMMIT NEW OFFENSES EVERY DAY

When the agreement had been made and Rome had been returned to her ancient form of government, Virginius summoned Appius before the people to defend his case. The latter appeared, accompanied by many nobles, and Virginius ordered that he be put in prison. Appius began to cry out in an appeal to the people. Virginius declared that he was unworthy of that right of appeal which he had destroyed, or to have as a defender the people

[1] Livy, III, liii (cited by Machiavelli in Latin).

whom he had offended. Appius replied that the right of appeal which they had been so eager to enact should not be violated. He was, however, imprisoned, and before the day of his trial he killed himself. And although Appius's wicked life merited the greatest punishment, it was nevertheless against good governmental procedure to violate the laws, especially one that had just recently been enacted; for I believe that there is no worse example in a republic than to enact a law and then not to observe it—even more so when it is not observed by the one who created it.

After 1494, Florence reorganized her government with the aid of Brother Girolamo Savonarola, whose writings demonstrate his learning, prudence, and mental ability; and among the other provisions he had enacted to protect the citizens was a law permitting appeal to the people from the sentences of the Eight and the Signoria in cases involving the government (a law he had advocated for a long time and had obtained with the greatest difficulty); and it happened that shortly after the enactment of this law five citizens were condemned to death by the Signoria on behalf of the government, but when they wished to make an appeal they were not allowed to do so, and thus the law was not observed. This diminished much of the Brother's influence, more so than any other incident, for if the right of appeal was useful, it should have been observed, and if it was not useful, then he should not have had it approved. This event was even more notorious because the friar preached many sermons after this law had been broken yet never condemned those who broke it, nor did he try to excuse them—he did not wish to condemn something which suited his purposes, but, on the other hand, he could not excuse it either. This revealed his ambitious and partisan spirit, thus depriving him of much of his influence and causing him a great deal of difficulty.

A government also does great damage when it arouses and renews each day in the minds of its citizens ill feelings over fresh injuries done to one person or another, as occurred in Rome after the decemvirate: all of the decemvirs and other citizens were, at various times, being accused and condemned to such an extent that there arose a great fear among the nobility, who felt that such condemnations would never end, not until all the members of the nobility had been destroyed. And it would have caused great trouble in the city if the tribune Marcus Duellius had not taken measures against it: he issued an edict stating that for one year it would be unlawful for anyone to cite or accuse any other Roman citizen; this reassured the entire nobility. This demonstrates how damaging it is to a republic or to a prince to hold the spirit of subjects in fear and suspense with continuous punishments and penalties. And, without a doubt, there is nothing more injurious to a government, for when men start suspecting that they are about to suffer some evil they protect themselves from dangers at any cost and become more audacious and less cautious in planning a revolution. Therefore, it is necessary either not to injure anyone or to inflict the injuries all at once, and then to reassure men and give them a chance to calm down and settle their spirits.

CHAPTER XLVI. MEN RISE FROM ONE AMBITION TO ANOTHER; FIRST THEY SEEK TO AVOID SUFFERING INJURY THEMSELVES, THEN THEY INJURE OTHERS

When the Roman people had recovered their liberty and had returned to their former level of power—this being even greater now that many new laws had been passed confirming their strength—it seemed reasonable to expect that Rome would be quiet for a time; nevertheless, experience shows the contrary, for every day new riots and disputes arose. And since Livy very prudently explains why this happened, it does not seem beside the point to refer to his exact words where he states that the people or the nobility always acted arrogantly when one or the other group was humiliated; when the people were calm and in their place, then the young noblemen began to wrong them, and the tribunes could provide few remedies since they, too, were being attacked. The nobility, on the other hand, realizing that their younger members were too insolent, nevertheless preferred that if excesses were to be committed, their own members and not the people should commit them. Thus, in desiring to defend its liberty each side tried to become strong enough to oppress the other. And the cause of all this is that in trying to escape fear men begin to make others fearful, and the injury they themselves seek to avoid they inflict on others, as if it were absolutely necessary either to harm or to be harmed.

From this can be seen one of several ways that republics fall apart, how men rise from one ambition to another, and the truth of the remark Sallust puts in the mouth of Caesar: "All examples of evil doings arise from good beginnings."[1] As was mentioned above, the citizens of a republic who act out of ambition seek, first of all, not to be harmed, not only by private citizens but also by the magistrates; to this end, they seek out friendships, acquiring them by means which appear outwardly honest—either by assisting people with money or by defending them from the more powerful—and because this action appears to be honorable, everyone is easily deceived and so no one provides any remedy against it. The result is that such a man, persevering without obstacles, attains so much power that private citizens fear him and the magistrates show him deference. And when he has risen to such a position as this, and there has, up until now, been no opposition to his greatness, then he has attained such a position that to attack him would be most dangerous, for the reasons I stated above, where I talk about the danger that exists in attacking a problem that has already grown too serious in a city. The matter comes precisely to this: either you try to do away with the problem altogether,

[1] *The Conspiracy of Catiline,* LI.

risking the danger of an immediate disaster, or you allow
the problem to continue and so enter into a clear state of
servitude unless, of course, death or some accident frees
you. For when matters reach the stage described above
and the citizens and magistrates are afraid to harm such
an ambitious man and his friends, then not much effort is
required to make them pass judgments in his favor and at
his will. Therefore, a republic ought to have among its
laws a law which sees to it that citizens are prevented
from doing evil under the pretense of doing good and en-
sures that citizens acquire the kind of popularity which
benefits and in no way harms liberty—as will be discussed
in the appropriate section.

CHAPTER XLVII.   HOW MEN DECEIVE THEMSELVES IN GEN-
ERAL TERMS BUT NOT IN PARTICULAR DETAILS

As was stated above, when the Roman people became
annoyed with the title of consul and wanted plebeians
made eligible to become consuls—either that or curtail
consular authority—the nobility, in order not to blemish
the consular authority with either one reform or the other,
chose a middle course, agreeing to the creation of four tribunes, with consular power, to be chosen either from
among the people or the nobles. This satisfied the people,
for they felt they had abolished the consulate and were
getting their own share of this high office. A noteworthy
event arose from this: when the Roman people came to
electing these tribunes, although they could have chosen
all of them from the plebeians they chose all nobles. Livy
says, concerning this matter: "The result of these elections
demonstrated that during the struggle for liberty and
honor their spirits differed from their attitude when their
judgment was less impassioned after the struggles had
ceased."[1] And in analyzing how this might have come
about, I believe it happened because men deceive themselves greatly in general terms but not so much in particu-

[1] Livy, IV, vi (cited by Machiavelli in Latin).

lar details. The Roman people believed, in general, that they deserved the consulate, for they represented a larger portion of the city, they incurred greater risk in wartime, and they kept Rome free and made her powerful with their brawn. And since, as was said, they felt this desire of theirs was a reasonable one, they determined to get this authority at any cost. But when it came to judging individually the men of their own faction, they recognized their weakness and decided that not one of them deserved what all of them taken together seemed to merit as a group. And so, ashamed of their own, they turned to those who did merit the high office. Justifiably amazed at this decision, Livy writes: "Where today would you find in one man alone such modesty, fairness, and high-mindedness which, at that time, characterized an entire people?"[2]

In confirmation of this, one may cite another noteworthy example which occurred in Capua after Hannibal defeated the Romans at Cannae. Although all of Italy was aroused by this defeat, Capua still continued to be embroiled in her internal struggles as a result of the hatred that existed between the people and the senate. Pacuvius Calanus was the supreme magistrate at that time; realizing the danger the city risked with her quarrels, he planned to use his high office to reconcile the plebeians with the nobility; having made this decision, he convened the senate and told the senators of the hatred the people felt toward them and the dangers they faced of being murdered by the populace and of having the city surrendered to Hannibal now that the Romans were in difficulty. Then he added that if they were to leave him in charge of the problem he would act in such a way that the city's factions would be united: he would lock all the senators inside the palace and then save them by giving the people the power to punish them. The senators agreed to his idea, and, after locking the senators in the palace, he called the people together and told them that the time had come for them to tame the pride of the nobles and take

[2] Ibid.

revenge for the injustices they had received from them, since all of them had been locked up under his custody. But, he added, since he believed that they did not want their city to be left without any government, they must choose new senators if they wished to kill the old ones. In the meantime, he would put all the names of the senators in a bag and draw them out one at a time in their presence; then, in the order in which they were drawn, he would put them to death as soon as the people had found a successor. When he drew out the first name, there was a great commotion at the sound of the man's name—they called him proud, cruel, and arrogant; but when Pacuvius asked whom they would select to take his place, the entire assembly fell silent. Then, after a while, one of the plebeians was nominated, but at the sound of his name some began to whistle, others to laugh, still others to speak ill of him in one way or another: and so they passed from one name to another until, finally, all those who had been nominated were judged unworthy of the senatorial rank. At this point, seizing the opportunity, Pacuvius remarked: "Since you believe that this city cannot function without the senate and you cannot agree on replacements for the old senators, I think it would be best if you reconciled yourselves with them, for the fear which the senators have just experienced will have humbled them to such an extent that you will certainly find in them the kindness you seek elsewhere." Once they agreed to this, union with that institution followed, and the mistaken idea which had deceived them was now uncovered as soon as they were forced to deal with particulars. This example aside, the people are deceived when they judge matters and events connected with them in a general way, but when particulars about things are known error is corrected.

After 1494, when the rulers of Florence had been driven from the city, there was no organized government there, but rather a kind of ambitious anarchy, and public affairs had gone from bad to worse. Many of the popular party, seeing the ruin of the city and finding no explana-

tion for it, blamed it on the ambition of some powerful individuals who were encouraging disorder in order to create a government more to their own liking and thus take
away liberty. And such accusers stood around the loggias
and the piazzas speaking ill of many citizens, threatening
that if they ever became part of the Signoria they would
uncover this plot of theirs and punish them. It often happens that just such a man does rise to the highest magistracy; and when he arrives at the position he sees things
more closely: he realizes where disorders come from and
he recognizes the dangers they involve and the difficulty
of remedying them; and once he sees that the times, not
men, create disorder, he suddenly becomes a man of different character and kind, for the knowledge of particulars removes the misconception which he had taken for
granted when he considered matters in general terms.
Thus, those who heard him speak earlier, when he was a
private citizen, and now see him silent as he occupies the
highest office are convinced that this fact arose not from a
truer knowledge of affairs of state but rather, from some
trick or bribe by the powerful. And since this has happened to many men at many times, a proverb about the
matter has grown up among the people which states:
"They have one mind in the piazza and another in the
palace."

Considering everything that has been said in this section, we see that although the people can be deceived in
general terms, their eyes can be opened quickly if only a
means is found to show them the particulars, as Pacuvius
succeeded in doing in Capua and as the senate did in
Rome. I also believe it may be concluded that, regarding
the distribution of offices and honors, a prudent man
should never avoid the popular judgment in particulars,
for here alone do the people not deceive themselves; and
if they are sometimes deceived, the number of times is few
when compared to the many times that a few men are deceived when they have to make such appointments. Nor
does it seem superfluous for me to show, in the next chap-

ter, the means the senate employed to deceive the people in making its appointments.

CHAPTER XLVIII.   ANYONE DESIRING TO PREVENT A MAGIS-
TRACY FROM BEING GRANTED TO A MAN OF LOW RANK OR
TO A WICKED MAN SHOULD HAVE IT REQUESTED EITHER BY
A MAN OF VERY LOW RANK OR BY A VERY WICKED MAN OR
BY ONE OF TOO HIGH RANK, OR BY ONE WHO IS TOO GOOD

[The senate, fearing that the tribunes would be chosen from among the plebeians, had the most distinguished citizens present themselves or bribed the worst citizens to present themselves. In either case, the plebeians were shamed into giving the offices to the most honorable citizens. This demonstrates the truth of the preceding argument, namely, that the people may be deceived in general terms but are not so deceived in specific matters.]

CHAPTER XLIX.   IF CITIES WHICH HAD THEIR BEGINNINGS
IN LIBERTY, SUCH AS ROME, EXPERIENCE DIFFICULTY IN
FINDING LAWS TO PRESERVE THEIR FREEDOMS, THEN THOSE
CITIES WHOSE BEGINNINGS WERE SERVILE WILL FIND IT AL-
MOST IMPOSSIBLE TO DO SO

How difficult it is in organizing a republic to foresee all the laws required to keep it free is evident in the development of the Roman republic: for, notwithstanding the many laws that were instituted first by Romulus, then Numa, Tullus Hostilius, Servius, and finally by the decemvirs created for this task, new difficulties were nevertheless always appearing in the management of that city. It became necessary to establish new laws—as was the case when the Romans created the censors, a provision which helped keep Rome free for as long as she enjoyed her independence; for, since the censors became the arbiters of Roman morals, they served an important role in postponing Rome's corruption for a long time. The Romans made one error in the establishment of such an office: they created the office for a five-year term; but after a short time this was rectified through the prudence of the dictator, Mamercus, who, by means of a new law, reduced the term of office in the said magistracy to eighteen months. The censors who were then serving their term took this so badly that they deprived Mamercus of his place in the senate—an act which both the plebeians and the patricians strongly criticized. And if history does not show that Mamercus could have defended himself, either the historian is inadequate or Roman laws were not good enough in this respect, because it is not right for a republic to be organized in such a way that one citizen, without any recourse, can be harmed for promulgating a law conforming to free government. But, returning to the beginning of this discussion, let me say that in the creation of this new office one ought to bear in mind that if it is true that cities such as Rome, which have had their beginnings in liberty and already have self-government, experience great difficulty in finding laws to preserve their freedoms, then it is no wonder that those cities which have had servile beginnings find it not difficult but rather impossible ever to organize themselves in a way that will allow them to live in a civil manner and in peace.

This is evident in the case of Florence: because in her beginnings she was subject to Roman rule and had always lived under the control of others, she remained humble for a time and had no plans of her own; then, when the opportunity arose for her to breathe a bit, she began to establish her own laws, and these laws, since they were combined with old ones that were bad, could not possibly be good. And so, she had gone along managing her affairs for two hundred years (for which there are reliable documents) without ever having a government which could truly entitle her to be called a republic. And difficulties like hers have always existed in all those cities whose beginnings were similar to hers; while sufficient authority to reform her has been granted many times to a few citizens by means of public and free elections, nevertheless such citizens have organized her not for the common welfare but rather for the favor of their own faction—a fact which has caused not order but greater disorder in the city.

Now, to come to some specific examples, let me say that among other things that have to be considered by the founder of a republic is the necessity of scrutinizing carefully the men into whose hands he puts the power of life and death over his citizens. This was well done in Rome, for one could normally make an appeal to the people, and if something important did happen in which deferring action through an appeal was dangerous, the Romans found a remedy in the dictator, who acted immediately, a remedy they employed only in times of necessity. But Florence and the other cities which were founded as she was—as a slave—had this power vested in a foreigner who fulfilled this office as a prince's envoy; then, later on, when such cities as these gained their liberty, they continued to support this power vested in a foreigner and called him captain. Since he could easily be corrupted by powerful citizens, this was a very harmful practice, but later on, when this institution was modified by a change in governments, the Florentines set up eight citizens to fulfill the office of this captain; the result was that this institution went from bad to worse (for the reasons mentioned elsewhere), for these few men were always the servants of those few who were most powerful.

The city of Venice has protected herself from this danger by having ten citizens who possess the authority to punish any citizen without the right of appeal; since the ten might not be sufficient to punish the powerful, even though they have the authority to do so, the Venetians set up the Council of Forty; furthermore, they decided that their Council of the Pregadi, which is their greatest council, should have the power, in turn, to punish all of them—thus, if an accuser is not lacking, there is no lack of a judge to keep powerful men in check. And so, we see that if in Rome, organized by her own citizens and by so many prudent men, there sprang up every day new reasons for new laws to be passed in support of free government, then it is no wonder that in other cities with more disorderly beginnings so many problems appear that they can never be reordered properly.

CHAPTER L. NO SINGLE COUNCIL OR MAGISTRATE SHOULD BE ABLE TO HALT THE BUSINESS OF A CITY

[Examples from Roman history and from recent events in the Republic of Venice prove that no single council or magistrate should be able to hinder the smooth operation of a city's affairs; such councils or magistrates should be required to fulfill their offices until successors are chosen so that the republic remains safe.]

CHAPTER LI. A REPUBLIC OR A PRINCE SHOULD PRETEND TO DO OUT OF GENEROSITY WHAT MUST BE DONE OUT OF NECESSITY

[Prudent men make a virtue of necessity, as the Roman senate did when it pretended to pay the army from the public treasury out of generosity, while it actually did so in order to wage war more effectively. The people rejoiced at this in spite of the fact that the subsequent taxes levied to pay for this decision made the burden upon them even heavier.]

CHAPTER LII. THERE IS NO MORE SECURE AND LESS DANGEROUS MEANS OF PUTTING DOWN THE INSOLENCE OF A MAN WHO RISES TO POWER IN A REPUBLIC THAN TO BLOCK THOSE ROADS BY WHICH HE IS COMING INTO POWER

[If the enemies of Cosimo de' Medici had followed this rule, turning Cosimo's means to power against him by favoring the people as he did, they would have been more successful than they were in driving him out of the city. Piero Soderini might also have been successfully opposed in Florence if his adversaries had like Soderini, tried to gain the favor of the people.]

CHAPTER LIII.   THE PEOPLE, DECEIVED BY A FALSE APPEAR-
ANCE OF GOOD, OFTEN PRONOUNCE THEIR OWN RUIN; AND
HOW GREAT HOPES AND EXTRAVAGANT PROMISES EASILY
MOVE THEM

[The people are often deceived by a false appearance of
good unless they are persuaded otherwise by someone
worthy of their confidence. When the people have no one
to trust, ruin may sometimes ensue. Furthermore, it is always easier to convince the people to follow a proposal
which seems bold or certain, even if danger lurks behind
it, than to follow one which appears cowardly or uncertain, even if it conceals security. The truth of this statement is demonstrated by numerous examples, both
ancient and modern. Fabius Maximus, for instance, was
unable to convince the Romans that a prudent policy was
best in opposing Hannibal, and the result was the crushing defeat of Rome at Cannae, one which almost destroyed the republic. Furthermore, such a policy brings
ruin to the citizens who are charged with carrying it out,
for when victory seems certain to the people but defeat is
the result of their boldness, the commander is blamed for
the people's errors of judgment and is often punished.]

CHAPTER LIV.   HOW MUCH AUTHORITY A RESPECTED MAN
HAS IN CHECKING AN INCENSED CROWD

[When the populace is incensed or riotous, only a man of
reputation or influence can deal with them. Examples of
this can be found in both Roman and Florentine history.]

CHAPTER LV.   HOW EASILY MATTERS ARE CONDUCTED IN A
CITY WHERE THE POPULACE IS NOT CORRUPTED; WHERE
EQUALITY EXISTS, NO PRINCIPALITY CAN BE ESTABLISHED,
AND WHERE EQUALITY DOES NOT EXIST, A REPUBLIC CAN-
NOT BE ESTABLISHED

Although what is to be feared or expected from corrupt
cities has been amply discussed above, it does not seem
beside my purpose to consider one of the senate's deci-

sions concerning the vow made by Camillus to give Apollo a tenth part of the spoils taken from the Veienti. Since these spoils were already in the hands of the Roman people, with no way of keeping a record of them, the senate passed an edict ordering each man to give back to the public treasury the tenth part of what he had taken. And while this decision was not carried out—for the senate later found another means of satisfying Apollo by atoning for the people—it is nevertheless evident from such a decision how much the senate trusted in the goodness of the populace and how it judged that no one would fail to return exactly what the edict ordered. And, on the other hand, it is clear that the people did not think about cheating in regard to the edict by returning less than they should; instead, they decided to free themselves from the edict by openly demonstrating their indignation. This example, along with many others presented above, demonstrates how much goodness and religion there was in the Roman people and how much good was to be expected from them.

Truly, where this goodness does not exist nothing good can be expected, just as nothing good can be hoped for from those countries which, in our times, are clearly corrupt, as is Italy, above all others—and even France and Spain share some part of this corruption. If as many disorders do not seem to arise in those countries as they do daily in Italy, it is not so much because of the goodness of their people (which, in large measure, no longer exists) but rather because of their king, who keeps them united through his own ability and the still-unspoiled institutions of these kingdoms. It is most clear that in Germany this goodness and religion are still strong among the people, with the result that many republics flourish there in liberty and observe their laws in such a way that no one outside or inside these republics dares seize them. I should like to give an example, similar to that of the Roman senate and the populace discussed above, to show how true it is that a large portion of that ancient goodness still does exist in these kingdoms. When the need arises for these republics in Germany to spend a certain amount of money for the public good, the magistrates or councils who have the authority to do so assess every citizen of the city one or two percent of his wealth. After a decision has been reached, each man, according to the law of the land, appears before the tax collectors and, having first sworn to pay the proper sum, throws into a chest set aside for this purpose whatever his conscience tells him he should pay—a payment for which there is no other witness except the man who pays. From this one can see just how much goodness and religion there still is among these men. And one must assume that each man pays the correct sum, for if this were not the case the tax would not bring in the amount estimated on the basis of past collections made in this manner; such fraud would be revealed and, because of this, some other means would be put into use. Such goodness is all the more to be admired in these times, inasmuch as it is so rare; indeed, it seems to have survived only in that country.

This is the result of two things: first, they do not have many dealings with their neighbors, for their neighbors have not visited them, nor have they visited their neighbors; they have been content to enjoy the goods, to live on the foods, and to clothe themselves with the wool that their own country provides. As a result, the motive for any interchange and the beginning of any corruption has been removed, for they have had no opportunity to acquire the customs of France, Spain, or Italy—nations which, taken together, represent the corruption of the world. The second reason is that such republics as these, where a free and uncorrupted government has been maintained, do not allow any of their citizens to be or to live in the style of a gentleman; indeed, they maintain among themselves a complete equality and are most hostile to those lords or gentlemen who live in that country. And if, by chance, any such men fall into their hands, they kill them as instigators of corruption and the cause of all evil.

To clarify what the title of "gentleman" means, let me say that I call gentlemen all those who live off the revenue from their properties in a state of idleness and luxury, without paying any attention to the cultivation of land or to any other occupation necessary to make a living. Such men as these are pernicious in any republic or any country; but more pernicious than these men are those who, in addition to the aforementioned fortunes, possess castles and have subjects who obey them. The Kingdom of Naples, the papal states, Romagna, and Lombardy are full of these two kinds of men. As a result, in these lands no republic has ever arisen or any ordered political body survived, for men like these are completely opposed to any form of free government. And to introduce a republic into countries organized in such a fashion would not be possible; if someone who was their master wanted to reorganize them, there would be no other way than to establish a kingdom there. The reason is this: where the material is so corrupt that laws are not sufficient to check this corruption, one must establish, along with these laws, a source of greater force, that is, a kingly authority with absolute and all-inclusive power to check the excessive ambition and corruption of the powerful.

This statement can be verified with the example of Tuscany, where for a long time three republics have existed in a small territory: Florence, Siena, and Lucca; although they are subject to these three republics, the other cities of the province do maintain, or would like to maintain, their liberty—a fact demonstrated by their spirit and their institutions. This all comes from the fact that in that province there are no lords of castles and few or no gentlemen at all, but there exists so much equality there that a prudent man with a knowledge of ancient civilizations could introduce a civic form of government. But to her great misfortune this province has not, up to this time, been able to find a man with the understanding and power to do this.

And so from this discussion I draw these conclusions: anyone wishing to set up a republic where there are many gentlemen cannot do so unless he first does away with all of them, and anyone wishing to establish a kingdom or a principality where there is much equality will never do so unless he pulls out of that equal condition many ambitious and restless men and makes them gentlemen—and not in name only—by giving them castles and possessions and granting them favors in goods and retainers, so that when he is in their midst he maintains his power through their support, and they further their ambition through him, while the rest are obliged to endure the yoke that force and nothing else can ever make them endure. And since in this manner a proportion is established between those who apply force and those against whom it is applied, men remain fixed, each in his own rank. Since the establishment of a republic in a country suitable for a kingdom or a kingdom in a country suitable for a republic is a task for a man of rare intelligence and authority, there have been many who wished to do this but few who knew how to carry it out. This is so because the greatness of the task in part frightens men and in part hinders them so much that they fail at the very outset.

I know that this opinion of mine—that where gentlemen exist one cannot organize a republic—would seem to be in direct opposition to the Venetian republic, where no one may hold any rank except those who are gentlemen, but to this objection I answer that this example does not contradict my opinion; for the gentlemen in that republic are more so in name than in fact; they do not have great incomes from their possessions since their great wealth is founded upon trade and movable goods; furthermore, none of them own castles or have any jurisdiction over men. Hence, that title of gentlemen which they possess is one of dignity and reputation and not founded on any of those things which produce what are called *gentlemen* in other cities. And since other republics have their divisions under various names, Venice is thus divided into gentlemen and commoners; the Venetians allow only the former to hold (or rather, to be able to hold) all the offices; the others are completely excluded from them. This arrangement does not create trouble in that city for the reasons explained elsewhere; therefore, the founder of a republic should organize it where there already exists, or has existed, great equality; the founder of a principality, on the other hand, should organize it where there is great inequality—otherwise he will create something that is out of proportion and that is of short duration.

CHAPTER LVI.   BEFORE MOMENTOUS EVENTS OCCUR IN A CITY OR PROVINCE, THERE ARE SIGNS THAT FORETELL THEM OR MEN WHO PREDICT THEM

[The invasion of Italy by King Charles VIII of France was foretold by the priest Girolamo Savonarola. Before the death of Lorenzo de' Medici and the expulsion of Piero Soderini from Florence, the cathedral of the city was struck by lightning. In classical times, a voice announced to Marcus Caedicius that the Gauls were about to attack Rome. The explanation of this phenomenon is unclear, some philosophers claiming that the air is filled with spirits who take pity on men and warn them of impending disaster, but whatever the explanation, the phenomenon does exist.]

CHAPTER LVII.   THE PEOPLE ARE STRONG WHEN UNITED BUT WEAK AS INDIVIDUALS

After the ruin of their native city following the invasion of the Gauls, many Romans went to live in Veii despite the decree and order of the senate, which, in order to remedy this disobedience, commanded everyone by public edicts to return to live in Rome within a certain period of time and under prescribed penalties. At first these edicts were ridiculed by those against whom they were directed;

then, when the time to obey them drew near, everyone obeyed. Livy writes these words: "They were fierce when united, but when isolated the fear of each one rendered them obedient."[1] And, truly, nothing can demonstrate the nature of the masses better, in this respect, than what is shown in this passage. Many times the masses are bold in speaking out against the prince's decision; then, when they see the penalty is at hand, they do not trust one another and run to obey. Thus, it seems clear that you should not pay too much attention to what the people say about their own good or bad inclination, as long as your government is organized in such a way as to be able to maintain its good inclination or, if it is unfavorably disposed, to be able to provide that it will not harm you.

This refers to those unfavorable inclinations which the people possess, born from a cause other than having lost either their liberty or a prince they loved and who is still alive. The unfavorable inclinations that arise from these causes are, above all else, formidable and require strong remedies to check them; the other unfavorable inclinations of the people are easily remedied when the people have no leaders to whom they can turn. On the one hand, there is nothing more formidable than an unrestrained multitude without a leader, yet, on the other, there is nothing that is weaker; for in spite of the fact that it may have taken up arms, it is easy to put down provided you have a refuge where you can escape the first onslaught; for, when the people's spirits cool off a bit and each man sees that he must return home, they all begin to have doubts about themselves and start thinking about obtaining their own safety, either by escape or by coming to terms. Therefore, if the multitude, stirred up in this manner, wishes to avoid these dangers, it should immediately choose one man from its midst as a leader to direct it, to keep it united, and to make provision for its defense, as did the Roman populace when it left Rome after the

---

[1] Livy, VI, iv (cited by Machiavelli in Latin).

death of Virginia and chose twenty tribunes from among its number to provide for its safety. If this is not done, then what Livy says in the words cited above always happens: when united, the people are strong, but when each man later begins to think about his own personal danger, he becomes cowardly and weak.

CHAPTER LVIII.   THE MASSES ARE WISER AND MORE CONSTANT THAN A PRINCE

Nothing can be more unreliable and more inconstant than the masses, as our own Livy declares and as all other historians affirm. In the recounting of the actions of men, we often read that the masses condemn someone to death and then repent later, wishing that he were still alive, as is evident in what the Roman people did with Manlius Capitolinus, whom they first condemned to death and then wished to have back alive. And the words of the author are these: "As soon as he ceased to represent a danger, the people immediately were seized by remorse."[1] And elsewhere, when he is explaining the events in Syracuse after the death of Hieronymus, the grandson of Hiero, he declares: "Such is the nature of the masses—either to obey humbly or to rule arrogantly."[2]

I do not know whether, in undertaking to defend an argument which, as I have mentioned, all writers have attacked, I may not be taking on a task so difficult and so full of problems that I shall either have to abandon it in shame or follow it with great pains. But be that as it may, I do not, nor shall I ever, think it wrong to defend an opinion with reasons without employing either authority or force. Let me say, therefore, that all men, and especially princes, can be accused individually of that fault for which writers blame the masses: for anyone not regulated by law will make the same errors that the uncontrolled masses will make. And this is obvious, for there are, and

[1]Livy, VI, xx (cited by Machiavelli in Latin).
[2]Livy, XXIV, xxv (cited by Machiavelli in Latin).

have been, many princes who have been able to break the
bounds that could restrain them; nor shall we count
among these the kings who arose in Egypt when, in that
ancient time, the province was ruled by laws, nor those
who arose in Sparta, nor those in our own times who
arose in France, a kingdom more regulated by laws than
any other kingdom that we have any knowledge of in our
own day. The kings who arose under such constitutions
are not to be considered among those whose individual
nature we ought to consider here in order to see if it re-
sembles that of the masses, for they should be compared
to the masses regulated by laws in the same fashion as
they are; and we shall find in the masses that same goodness we discover in such kings and shall see that the
masses neither obey humbly nor rule arrogantly. The
Roman people were like this, for while the Roman republic endured without corruption, it never obeyed humbly nor ruled arrogantly; on the contrary, it held its
position honorably through its institutions and magistrates. And when it was necessary to band together
against some powerful man, as in the case of Manlius, the
decemvirs, and others who sought to oppress it, it did so;
when it was necessary to obey the dictators and the consuls for the public welfare, it did so. And if the Roman
people regretted the death of Manlius Capitolinus, it is
not surprising, for they regretted the loss of his virtues,
which were such that the memory of them aroused everyone's compassion; and it would have had the power to
produce the same effect in a prince, since all writers declare that ability is praised and admired even in one's enemies; and if Manlius had been resurrected because of
such an opinion, the people of Rome would have pronounced upon him the same sentence that they did when
they had him removed from prison and shortly thereafter
condemned him to death; nevertheless we see princes, reputed to be wise, who have had someone executed and
then wished him returned to life, as Alexander did in the
case of Clitus and his other friends and as Herod did with

Mariamne. But when our historian speaks of the nature of the masses, he does not mean those who are regulated by law, as the Romans were; he speaks of the uncontrolled masses, like those of Syracuse, which committed crimes typical of undisciplined and infuriated men, as did Alexander the Great and Herod in the instances mentioned. But the nature of the masses is no more to be condemned than that of princes, for both err when there is nothing to control them. There are many examples of this, in addition to the ones I have mentioned, both among the Roman emperors and other tyrants and princes; and in them we witness as much lack of stability and variation of behavior as may ever be found in any multitude.

Therefore, I come to a conclusion contrary to the common opinion, which declares that when the people hold power they are unstable, changeable, and ungrateful; I affirm, rather, that the people are no more susceptible to these sins than are individual princes. And if one were to blame both the people and princes alike, he might be telling the truth, but if princes are to be excluded from this charge, then he would be deceiving himself, because a people which have power and are well organized will be no less stable, prudent, and grateful than a prince; in fact, they may be more so, even though the prince is thought wise; and, on the other hand, a prince freed from the restraint of law will be more ungrateful, changeable, and imprudent than the people. And the changeability of their behavior does not arise from a different nature, for it is the same in all men, and if there is one better than the other, it is the people; it comes, rather, from having greater or lesser respect for the laws under which they both live. And anyone who considers the Roman people will see that they were opposed to the very title of king for four hundred years and were lovers of the glory and the common good of their city; and he will see many examples that testify to both characteristics. If anyone should cite, to the contrary, the ingratitude that the people showed toward Scipio, I would make the same reply I did earlier on this subject, where I showed that the people are less ungrateful than princes. But, concerning prudence and stability, let me say that the people are more prudent, more reliable, and have better judgment than a prince does. And it is not without reason that the voice of the people is likened to that of God: for it is evident that popular opinion has marvelous power in predicting, so much so that it would appear to foresee its own good and evil fortune through some occult ability. As for its judgment in various matters, when the people hear two equally able speakers, each arguing different opinions, only very rarely does it happen that they do not choose the better opinion and are incapable of understanding the truth of what they hear. And if they err in matters of courage or profit, as was mentioned above, a prince will often err because of his own passions, which are much stronger than those of the people. It is also evident that the people make better choices in electing magistrates than does a prince, for one can never persuade the people that it is good to elect to public office an infamous man of corrupt habits—something that a prince can easily be persuaded to do in a thousand ways; and when the people begin to feel an aversion for something, we see them persist in this aversion for many years—something we do not observe in a prince. For both of these characteristics I find it sufficient to cite the Roman people as evidence, for in so many hundreds of years, in so many elections of consuls and tribunes, the people did not make even four elections which they were forced to regret. And, as I have said, they so hated the very name of king that no amount of meritorious service rendered by one of their citizens seeking to gain the title could persuade the people to forget the just penalties he deserved for this ambition; furthermore, it is evident that cities in which people are the rulers increase their territories in a very short time, much more so than cities which have always been under a prince, just as Rome did after the expulsion of the kings and Athens did after she freed herself of Pisistratus. This is the result of nothing other than the fact that government by the people is better than government by princes. Nor do I wish everything that our historian says in the aforementioned passage and elsewhere to be cited against this opinion of mine, for if we were to discuss all the faults of the people and all those of princes, all the glories of the people and all those of princes, it would be evident that the people are far superior in goodness and in glory. And if princes are superior to the people in instituting laws, forming civic communities, and establishing statutes and new in- stitutions, then the people are so much more superior in maintaining the things thus established that they attain, without a doubt, the same glory as those who established them.

And, in short, to conclude this subject, let me say that just as the states of princes have endured for a long time, so too have the states of republics; both have needed to be regulated by laws, for a prince who is able to do what he wishes is mad, and a people that can do what it wishes is not wise. If, therefore, we are talking about a prince obe- dient to the laws or a people restricted by them, we shall observe more ability in the people than in the prince; if we are discussing either one or the other as being free from these restrictions, we shall observe fewer errors in the people than in the prince; moreover, they are less seri- ous ones and easier to remedy. For a licentious and un- ruly people can be spoken to by one good man and can easily be brought back to the right path; however, with an evil prince there is no one who can speak to him and no other remedy than the sword. From this fact one can draw a conclusion concerning the seriousness of their respective maladies: if words are enough to cure the malady of the people and the sword to cure that of the prince, there will never be anyone who will not conclude that the greater the faults, the greater the attention required. When a peo- ple is unrestrained, neither its mad actions nor the evil at hand need be feared, but rather the evil that may arise from them, since a tyrant may emerge from so much confusion. But with an evil prince the opposite happens: present evil is feared and one hopes for the future, since men persuade themselves that ending his evil life can result in an era of freedom. So you see the difference between the two: one concerns things as they are and the other concerns things that will be. The cruelties of the masses are directed against anyone who they fear might act against the public welfare; those of the prince are directed against anyone who he fears might act against his own interests. But the prejudice against the people arises because everyone speaks ill of them freely and without fear, even when they rule; one always speaks ill of princes only with great fear and apprehension. And this seems not to be beside the point, since this subject leads me ahead to discuss, in the following chapter, whether one may place more trust in alliances made with a republic or those made with a prince.

CHAPTER LIX. WHICH ALLIANCE, OR LEAGUE, IS MOST WORTHY OF TRUST: ONE MADE WITH A REPUBLIC OR ONE MADE WITH A PRINCE?

[An examination of the question reveals that in most cases there is little difference. Neither a prince nor a republic will honor agreements made by force; if one or the other feels that keeping the agreement will result in a loss of power, this party will not hesitate to break faith. However, republics will usually be more reliable than princes since they are slower to act and take more time in coming to a decision. Therefore, they are slower to break a treaty. Alliances are broken for profit, and a prince is more likely to break an agreement for a small advantage than is a republic. This discussion concerns agreements broken for improper motives, not those broken for legitimate reasons, such as nonobservance of terms.]

CHAPTER LX. HOW THE CONSULATE AND EVERY OTHER MAGISTRACY IN ROME WAS GRANTED WITHOUT REGARD TO AGE

[Merit, not age or birth, was always the qualification for office under the Roman republic, as is shown by the election of such men as Valerius Corvinus, Scipio, and Pompey while they were still very young. Any state that wishes to accomplish what Rome did should follow this example.]

BOOK II

INTRODUCTION

Men always praise ancient times and condemn the present, but not always with good reason; they are such advocates of the past that they celebrate not merely those ages which they know only through the memory of the historians but also those that they, now being old, remember having seen in their youth. And when this opinion of theirs is mistaken, as it is most of the time, I am persuaded that there are several reasons which lead them to make this mistake. First, I believe that we do not know the complete truth about antiquity; most often the facts that would discredit those times are hidden and other matters which bestow glory upon them are reported magnificently and most thoroughly. Most writers submit to the fortune of conquerors, and in order to render their victories glorious they not only exaggerate what they have ably achieved but also embellish the deeds of their enemies in such a way that anyone born afterward in either of the two lands—that of the victor or that of the vanquished— has reason to marvel at those men and those times and is forced to praise them and to love them to the greatest degree. Besides this, since men hate things either out of fear or envy, two very powerful reasons for hatred of things in the past are eliminated, for they cannot hurt you or give you cause for envy. But the contrary applies to those things you deal with and observe: they are known to you in every detail, you see in them what is good as well as the many things that displease you, and you are obliged to judge them most inferior to things of the past; while, in truth, those of the present may deserve even more glory and fame—I am not speaking of things pertaining to the arts here, for in themselves they possess so much brilliance that the times take away from them little and cannot bestow upon them much more glory than they intrinsically merit; I am speaking rather of those matters pertaining to the lives and customs of men, about which we do not witness such clear evidence.

I repeat, then, that this aforementioned custom of praising the old and condemning the new does exist, but it is not always wrong. Sometimes such a judgment has to be correct since human affairs are always in motion, either rising or declining. And so, one city or province can be seen to possess a government that was well organized by an excellent man; and for a time it may keep improving because of the ability of the founder. Anyone, then, who is born in such a state and praises ancient times more than modern times deceives himself, and his deception is caused by those things mentioned above. But those who are born afterward in that city or region, at the time of its decline, do not, then, deceive themselves. As I reflect on why these matters proceed as they do, I believe that the world has always been in the same state and that there has always been as much good as evil in it; but this evil and this good changes from country to country, as we can see from what we know of ancient kingdoms that were different from each other according to the differences in their customs, while the world remained the same as it always had been. There is only this difference: the world's talents first found a home in Assyria, then moved to Media, later to Persia, and, in time, came into Italy and Rome; and if, after the Roman empire, no succeeding empire has lasted, nor has there been one where the world has retained all its talents in one place, nevertheless we can still see them scattered among many nations where men live ably, as in the kingdom of the Franks, the Turks—that of the Sultan—and today among the peoples of Germany; earlier there was that Turkish group which achieved so many grand things and seized so much of the world once it had destroyed the Eastern Roman Empire. In all these lands, then, after the Romans came to ruin, and in all those groups of people, such talents existed and still exist in some of them where they are desired and truly praised. And anyone who is born there and praises past times more than present ones may be deceiving himself, but anyone who is born in Italy or Greece and has not become an Ultramontane in Italy or a Turk in Greece has reason to condemn his own times and to praise others, for in them there were many things that made them marvelous, but in the present ones there is nothing to be seen but utter misery, infamy, and vituperation. There is no observance of religion, laws, or military discipline; all is stained with every kind of filth. Furthermore, these vices are the more detestable as they are found among those who sit on tribunals, command others, and expect to be worshiped.

But, returning to our subject, let me say that if the judgment of men is unfair in deciding which is better— the present age or the past—the latter of which, because of its antiquity, men cannot have as perfect a knowledge of as they can of their own times, this should not corrupt the judgment of old men in assessing the time of their youth and their old age, since they have known and observed both one and the other equally well. This would be true if men were all of the same opinion and had the same desires in all phases of their lives; but since these desires change, and the times do not, things cannot appear to men to be the same, since they have other desires, other pleasures, and other concerns in their old age than they had in their youth. For as men grow older they lose in vigor and gain in judgment and prudence, and the things that seemed acceptable and good to them in their youth become, later on, as they grow older, intolerable and bad; and although they should place the blame for this on their own judgment, they blame the times instead. Besides this, human desires are insatiable, for we are endowed by Nature with the power and the wish to desire everything and by Fortune with the ability to obtain little of what we desire. The result is an unending discontent in the minds of men and a weariness with what they possess: this makes men curse the present, praise the past, and hope in the future, even though they do this with no reasonable motive. I do not know, therefore, if I deserve to be considered among those who deceive themselves if, in these discourses of mine, I am too lavish with my praise of ancient Roman times and condemn our own. And certainly, if the excellence that existed then and the vice that rules now were not clearer than the sun, I would speak more hesitantly for fear that I might fall into the same error of which I accuse others. But since the matter is clear enough for all to see, I shall boldly declare in plain terms what I understand of those ancient times and of our own times, so that the minds of young men who read these writings of mine may be able to reject the present and prepare themselves to imitate the past whenever Fortune provides them with an occasion. For it is your duty as a good man to teach others whatever good you yourself have not been able to do, either because of the malignity of the times or because of Fortune, in order that—since many will thus be made aware of it—someone more beloved by Heaven may be prepared to put your truth into action.

In the discourse of the preceding book I have discussed the decisions the Romans made in matters concerning their internal affairs; now, in this one, I shall discuss what it was that the Roman people did concerning the expansion of their empire.

CHAPTER I. WHETHER ABILITY OR FORTUNE WAS THE
MAIN REASON THE ROMANS CONQUERED THEIR EMPIRE

Many have held the opinion—among them Plutarch, a
most serious writer—that the Roman people, in acquiring
their empire, were favored more by Fortune than by their
own ability. And among the other reasons he brings forth,
he says that the people, by their own admission, attributed all their victories to Fortune, since they built more
temples to Fortune than to any other god. And it seems
that Livy holds this opinion, for he seldom has any
Roman deliver a speech in which he speaks of ability
without mentioning Fortune. But I do not accept this argument in any way, nor do I believe that it can be supported, for if no republic produced such results as Rome
did, it is obvious that there never has been a republic so
organized that she could acquire as Rome did. For the
ability of her armies caused her to acquire her empire,
and the institution of her conduct and her individual way
of living, which were discovered by her first lawgiver, allowed her to keep her conquests, as will be explained in
more detail in successive chapters.

These same writers declare that it was a consequence of
Fortune, and not because of the innate ability of the
Roman people, that they never had to fight two great wars
at the same time; that they never waged war on the Latins
unless they had completely vanquished the Samnites and,
in fact, were even waging war in their defense; they never
fought with the Tuscans unless they had first subjugated
the Latins and had almost exhausted the Samnites
through frequent defeats. However, if two of these powers
had united when they were fresh and at full strength,
without a doubt one might say that the ruin of the Roman
republic would have been inevitable. But no matter how
things turned out, they never waged two important wars
at the same time; on the contrary, the case was always
such that either one came to an end at the beginning of
another or the other was begun when one was finished.

This is surely evident from the order in which their wars took place: putting aside those wars waged before Rome was sacked by the Gauls, it is clear that while they fought with the Aequi and the Volsci—and those peoples were powerful—other nations never rose up against them. When they were defeated, the war against the Samnites broke out, and although the Latin peoples revolted against the Romans before the war ended, nevertheless, when this rebellion occurred the Samnites were allied with Rome; their army helped them to tame the Latin insolence. When the Latins were defeated, the war with Samnium broke out again, and when the Samnite troops were broken by the many defeats they suffered, the war against the Tuscans began; when this was settled, the Samnites again rose up because of the crossing of Pyrrhus into Italy. When he was repulsed and driven back into Greece, they instigated the First Carthaginian War; no sooner was that war over than all the Gauls, from both sides of the Alps, joined together against the Romans until, between Popolonia and Pisa, where the tower of Saint Vincent stands today, they were destroyed in a great slaughter. When this war was over, the Romans waged wars of little consequence over a space of twenty years, for they fought with no one except the Ligurians and the remainder of the Gauls, who were in Lombardy. And they continued in this manner until the Second Carthaginian War broke out, which kept Italy occupied for sixteen years. This war having ended with the greatest glory for Rome, the Macedonian War broke out; and, after that was over, there followed the war against Antiochus and Asia. After that victory, there remained in all the world neither prince nor republic that could, either by itself or together with others, oppose the Roman forces.

But before this last victory, one who carefully examines the order of these wars and the way the Romans proceeded will see in them good fortune mixed with great ability and prudence. Thus, if one looks for the cause of such good fortune one will discover it easily, for it is certainly true that when a prince or a people attains such a reputation that every prince or people nearby is afraid to attack singly and is in a state of fear, it always happens that none will ever attack unless driven to it by necessity; as a result, that power will have, as it were, the choice of waging war upon whichever of its neighbors it chooses, while keeping the others at peace with its diplomatic skill. And they will easily be kept at peace, partly because of their respect for this power and partly because they are deceived by the means employed to lull them to sleep. Other powers, which are far away and have no dealings with them, consider the matter a remote one, of no concern to them; they remain in this error until the fire draws near, and when it does, they have no remedy to extinguish it except their own forces, which, by then, will not suffice, since the other forces have become so very powerful.

I shall not discuss how the Samnites watched while the Roman people conquered the Volsci and the Aequi, and in order not to be too wordy I shall mention only the Carthaginians, who were very powerful and enjoyed a great reputation while the Romans were fighting with the Samnites and the Tuscans, for they already held all of Africa, Sardinia, and Sicily, and had conquered part of Spain. Their power, plus the fact that they were situated far from the borders of the Roman people, never made them think of attacking Rome or of giving aid to the Samnites and the Tuscans; on the contrary, they acted as a prosperous person would act when all goes well, making treaties with the Romans and seeking their friendship. They never realized their error until the Romans, having now conquered all the peoples between themselves and the Carthaginians, began to fight with the latter over the rule of Sicily and Spain. The same thing happened to the Gauls that happened to the Carthaginians, as well as to Philip, King of the Macedonians, and to Antiochus: all of them believed that while the Roman people were occupied with another power, the other power would defeat Rome and they would have the time to defend themselves against the Romans in either peace or war. Therefore, I believe that the Fortune the Romans enjoyed in this regard would have been possible for those rulers who acted in the same way as the Romans and possessed the same ability.

In this regard, I would talk about the method used by the Roman people in entering the territories of others if it were not for the fact that in my treatise on principalities I spoke of this at some length; this question is discussed fully in that work. To be brief, I shall say only this: they always tried to have some friend in a new province who might serve as a ladder to climb up or a gate through which to enter or as a means to hold onto it, as is evident when they entered Samnium with the aid of the Capuans, Tuscany with the support of the Camertines, Sicily with the assistance of the Mamertines, Spain with the help of the Saguntians, Africa with the aid of Masinissa, Greece with the Aetolians, Asia with the support of Eumenes as well as other princes, and Gaul with the assistance of the Aedui. And so, they never lacked support to facilitate their undertakings in acquiring and maintaining such provinces. The peoples who observe this practice discover that they have less need of Fortune than those who do not observe it well, and in order that everyone may better understand how much more effective was their ability than their Fortune in acquiring their empire, we shall discuss in the following chapter the characteristics of the peoples with whom they had to fight and how stubborn they were in defending their liberty.

CHAPTER II.   WITH WHAT KINDS OF PEOPLES THE ROMANS HAD TO FIGHT, AND HOW STUBBORNLY THOSE PEOPLE DEFENDED THEIR LIBERTY

Nothing made it more difficult for the Romans to conquer the peoples around them and the provinces some distance from them than the love such peoples had in those times for liberty, which they defended so stubbornly that they would never have been defeated except for the extraordinary amount of strength employed against them; and in many instances we know in what dangers they placed themselves in order to maintain or regain that liberty, and what revenge they took against those who had deprived them of it. We also learn from reading their histories about the harm servitude caused these people and their cities. Whereas in our own times there is only one country that can be said to contain within it free cities,[1] in ancient times there were in all lands many peoples who lived completely free. It is clear that in the times of which we are now speaking, from the Apennines which divided Tuscany from Lombardy all the way to the tip of Italy, all the peoples were free, as were the Tuscans, the Romans, the Samnites, and many others who inhabited that section of Italy. Nor do we ever read that any kings existed there besides the ones that reigned in Rome and Porsenna, King of Tuscany, the extinction of whose lineage history does not explain. But it is most clear that in the time when the Romans went to besiege Veii, Tuscany was free, and it enjoyed its liberty so much and so hated the very name of prince that when the people of Veii created a king for their protection and asked the Tuscans to help them against the Romans, the Tuscans, after holding many meetings, decided not to aid the people of Veii so long as they lived under a king, believing that it was not a good idea to defend the native city of those who had already subjected it to someone else.

It is an easy matter to understand the origin of this love for free government among peoples, for experience shows that cities have never enlarged their dominion nor increased their wealth except while they have existed in freedom. It is truly a marvelous thing to consider to what greatness Athens arrived in the space of one hundred years after she freed herself from the tyranny of Pisistratus; but, above all, it is even more marvelous to con-

[1] Here Machiavelli refers not to the republics of Italy, such as his native Florence, but to north European city-states in Germany and Switzerland.

sider the greatness Rome reached when she freed herself
from her kings. The reason is easy to understand, for it is
the common good and not private gain that makes cities
great. Yet, without a doubt, this common good is observed only in republics, for in them everything that pro-
motes it is practiced, and however much damage it does to
this or that private individual, those who benefit from the
said common good are so numerous that they are able to
advance it in spite of the inclination of the few citizens
who are oppressed by it.

The contrary happens when there is a prince; in general, what he does in his own interest harms the city and
what he does for the city's benefit harms him. For this
reason, when a tyranny replaces a free government the
least amount of evil that results in cities so affected is that
they no longer advance or increase in power and riches;
but, in most cases—in truth, always—they decline. And if
fate brings about the rise of an able tyrant who, through
courage and force of arms, increases his dominion, the republic derives no benefit from this; it is he who benefits,
for he cannot honor any of the brave and strong citizens
whom he tyrannizes unless he is willing to fear them. Nor
can he subjugate or make the cities he conquers tributaries to the city in which he is tyrant, for making the city
powerful does not benefit him; but it is in his interest to
keep the state disunited and to have each city and province acknowledge his personal rule. Thus, he alone profits
from his conquests and not his native city. And anyone
wishing to confirm this opinion with countless other arguments should read Xenophon's treatise entitled *On
Tyranny.*[2]

It is no wonder, then, that ancient peoples prosecuted
tyrants with so much hatred and loved free government,
and that the very name of liberty was so revered by them.
This was the case when Hieronymus, the grandson of

[2] The *Hiero,* an imaginary Socratic dialogue on tyranny with
Hiero of Syracuse, a figure frequently cited by Machiavelli,
serving as one of the interlocutors.

Hiero of Syracuse, was murdered in Syracuse, for when the news of his death reached his army, which was far from the city, the soldiers first began to riot and to take up arms against his murderers; but when they heard that in Syracuse the word liberty was being shouted, they calmed down completely and, delighted by that word, put aside their anger against the tyrannicides and began thinking about how a free government might be organized in their city.

It is also no wonder that the people take extraordinary revenge on those who deprive them of their liberty. There are many cases of this, but I will refer to only one of them: it happened in Corcyra, a Greek city, during the Peloponnesian War. Greece was at that time divided into two factions, one of which followed the Athenians, the other the Spartans; thus, in many cities that were so divided one faction sought the friendship of Sparta and the other that of Athens. And when it happened that in Corcyra the nobles prevailed and deprived the people of liberty, the popular party regrouped its forces with Athenian assistance, seized the nobles, and shut them up in a prison capable of holding all of them; then they took them out eight or ten at a time, and under the pretence of sending them into exile in various places they had them tortured in memorable fashion and then killed. When those still inside the prison became aware of this, they decided to escape this ignominious death if at all possible: armed with whatever they could find, they defended the entrance of the prison, fighting off all those who tried to enter. As soon as the people heard the noise, they removed the upper part of the building and smothered the prisoners with the debris. Many other events took place in that country of a similarly horrible and noteworthy nature; thus, it is evidently true that liberty that has actually been taken from you is avenged with greater ferocity than is liberty that someone tries to take from you.

Considering, therefore, why it is that in ancient times the people were greater lovers of liberty than in our own

times, I believe this arises from the same cause that makes
men less strong today—and this, I believe, is due to the
difference between our education and ancient education,
based upon the difference between our religion and ancient religion. Since our religion has shown us the truth
and the true path, it makes us value the honor of this
world less; whereas the pagans,[3] who valued it very much
and considered it the highest good, were more fierce in
their actions. This can be seen in many of their institutions, beginning with the magnificence of their sacrifices
as compared to the meagerness of our own. In our sacrifices there is some ceremony (more delicate than magnificent) but no act that is fierce or brave. Theirs lacked
neither pomp nor ceremonial magnificence; in addition,
there was the act of sacrifice, full of blood and ferocity,
involving the killing of a multitude of animals—this spectacle was awesome, and it produced similarly awesome
men. Besides this, ancient religion glorified only men who
were endowed with worldly glory, such as generals of
armies and rulers of republics; our religion has glorified
humble and contemplative men rather than active ones.
Furthermore, it has established as the supreme good humility, abjection, and contempt for human affairs, while
ancient religion defined it as grandeur of spirit, strength
of body, and all the other things likely to make men most
vigorous. If it is true that our religion also requires
strength, it is the kind of strength that makes you willing
to suffer rather than to undertake bold deeds.

So this way of living, then, seems to have rendered the
world weak and handed it over as prey to wicked men,
who can safely manage it when they see that most men
think more of going to Heaven by enduring their injuries
than by avenging them. If it would appear that the world
has become effeminate and Heaven disarmed, this, without a doubt, is the result of the cowardice of men who

[3] Machiavelli actually uses the Italian word *gentile* to mean
"pagan" here and elsewhere.

have interpreted our religion according to sloth and not according to strength. For if they would consider that religion permits us to defend and better the fatherland, they would see that it intends us to love and honor it and to prepare ourselves to be the kind of men who can defend it.

Such education and such false interpretations as these, then, explain the fact that there are not as many republics today as there were in ancient times and, as a result, that people do not have as much love for liberty now as they did then; yet I believe that the cause of this was, rather, that the Roman empire, with its forces and its greatness, wiped out all the republics and all the self-governing states. And although this empire was later dissolved, the cities have not yet been able to unite or to reorganize themselves in a self-governing body except for very few places in the empire; however this may be, the Romans did encounter in the very remotest part of the globe a confederation of extremely well-armed republics that were most stubborn in the defense of their liberty. This demonstrates that the Roman people would never have been able to overcome such republics without rare and immense ability.

And as an illustration of a member of these confederations, the example of the Samnites should suffice: it seems a marvelous thing (and Livy admits it) that because they were so powerful and their armies so strong they were able to resist the Romans until the time of Papirius Cursor, consul and son of the first Papirius—a space of forty-six years—after the many defeats, ruins, and massacres they had suffered in their country; especially when one observes that a country where there were once so many cities and men is now almost uninhabited; at that time there was such order and force there that it would have been unconquerable if it had not been for the skill of the Romans. It is easy to see where that earlier order came from and how this present disorder arose: it all resulted from living in freedom then and living in servitude now.

For, as I said above, all countries and provinces living in freedom make very great progress; for wherever there is a growing population marriages are freer and more desired by men, since every man willingly procreates the children he believes he can provide for without fear that this patrimony will be taken away; he is assured that they will be born free, not slaves, and that they may, through their own ability, become great men. Wealth derived from agriculture as well as from trade increases more rapidly in a free country, for all men gladly increase those things and seek to acquire those goods which they believe they can enjoy once they have acquired them. Thus, it comes about that men in competition with each other think about both private and public benefits, and both one and the other continue to grow miraculously.

The contrary of all these things occurs in countries that live in servitude: the further they move away from their accustomed good, the harsher is their servitude. And of all the harsh forms of slavery, the harshest is that which subjects you to a republic—first, because it is more lasting and there is less hope of escaping from it; second, because the goal of a republic is to enervate and weaken all other bodies in order to strengthen its own body. This is not done by a prince to whom you are subjugated unless the prince is some barbarian ruler or a destroyer of lands and a devastator of all human civilization, as are oriental rulers. But if he possesses humane and normal qualities, he is usually fond of all his subject cities and allows them all their industries and almost all their ancient institutions, so that if they cannot prosper like free men they will not come to ruin like slaves—and here I mean the kind of servitude which comes to cities subject to a foreigner, since I spoke earlier of those cities subject to one of their own citizens.

Anyone, then, who considers all that has been said will not wonder at the power of the Samnites when they were free and at their weakness when they later became slaves. Livy testifies to this fact in more than one passage, especially in his description of the war with Hannibal, where he shows that when the Samnites were oppressed by a legion of men stationed in Nola, they sent ambassadors to Hannibal begging him to come to their rescue. In their speech they said that they had fought with the Romans for a hundred years, using their own soldiers and their own generals; they had resisted two consular armies and two consuls on a number of occasions, and they had now come to such a shameful state that they could hardly defend themselves against one small Roman legion stationed in Nola.

CHAPTER III.   ROME BECAME A GREAT CITY BY DESTROY-
ING THE NEARBY CITIES AND BY FREELY ADMITTING
FOREIGNERS TO HER OFFICES

[A city must become populous to build a great empire, and this may be achieved either by attracting people to a city because of its advantages or by compelling them to go there to live. Rome did not commit the error of Sparta; she always allowed foreigners to take part in her government, thereby increasing her population as her empire grew. The actions of men resemble those of nature; thus, just as the great branches of a tree require a large trunk to support them, similarly a small republic cannot conquer and hold cities or states larger than itself unless it is allowed to grow.]

CHAPTER IV.   REPUBLICS HAVE USED THREE METHODS IN
ORDER TO EXPAND

Anyone who has studied ancient history knows that republics have used three methods in order to expand. One the ancient Tuscans employed, which consisted of associating together many republics in which none surpassed the other in authority or rank; as they conquered, they made the new cities their companions in the same manner as the Swiss do today or as the Achaeans and the Aetolians did in ancient Greece. And because the Romans waged many wars against the Tuscans, I shall present a rather lengthy account of them in order better to demonstrate the characteristics of this first method.

Before the creation of the Roman empire in Italy, the Tuscans were very powerful on both land and sea; and while there is no detailed historical account of their affairs, there still remains some small trace of their greatness. It is known that to the sea above them they sent a colony, called Adria, that was so noble that it gave its name to the sea the Latins still call the Adriatic; it is also known that their forces were obeyed from the Tiber River as far as the foot of the Alps, which circle the largest part of Italy, notwithstanding the fact that two hundred years before the Romans grew in strength the said Tuscans lost their rule over that land which today is called Lombardy; and that province was occupied by the Gauls, who, driven either by necessity or attracted by the sweetness of the fruits, and especially of the wine, entered Italy under their leader Bellovesus. After defeating and driving out the inhabitants of the province, they settled there and built many cities, and they called the province Gaul after the name they bore; they held this land until they were conquered by the Romans. The Tuscans, then, lived in equality and went about their conquests by employing the first method explained above, and there were twelve cities, among them Chiusi, Veii, Arezzo, Fiesole, Volterra, and other similar cities, which ruled their empire through a confederation; nor were they able to go beyond Italy with their conquests; the larger part of Italy remained intact for reasons that will be explained below.

The second method is to make allies for yourself—not to the extent, however, that you do not retain the position of command, the seat of the empire, and the glory of its undertakings—a method followed by the Romans. The third method is quickly to get subjects rather than allies for yourself, as the Spartans and the Athenians did.

Of these three methods, the last one is completely useless, as it was in the case of the two republics mentioned above, which came to ruin for no other reason than that they acquired more dominion than they were able to hold; for to undertake the task of governing cities by violence, especially those used to living in liberty, is a difficult and tiring matter. If you are not armed and equipped with strong forces, you can neither command nor rule them. If you wish to be in the position to do this, it is necessary to enlist allies who will give you aid. You should also increase the population of your cities. Because Athens and Sparta did neither of these things, their method of proceeding was useless.

But Rome, an example of the second method, rose to great power by doing both one and the other; and because she was the only city to operate in this way, she was the only one to become so powerful. She made many allies all over Italy who, in many ways, lived under laws similar to her own; on the other hand, as was mentioned above, since she always reserved for herself the seat of the empire and the glory of its undertakings, these allies of hers, without realizing it, found that they had subjugated themselves to her with their own labors and their own blood. For these allies marched with the Roman armies and reduced kingdoms to provinces outside of Italy, and they made subjects of those peoples who did not mind being subjects because they were accustomed to living under kings; these conquered peoples, having Roman governors and having been conquered by armies with the Roman name, recognized no other superior than Rome. As a result, the allies of Rome who were in Italy found themselves suddenly surrounded by Roman subjects and oppressed by such a very great city as Rome; and when they became aware of the deception under which they were living, it was too late to remedy it, for Rome had acquired so much authority with her overseas provinces and so much strength inside her own city, which was very large and very well armed. And although these allies of hers banded together against her to avenge themselves for their injuries, they lost the war in a short time, thereby

making their conditions worse, for instead of allies they
had now become subjects. This method of proceeding, as
was mentioned, has been followed only by the Romans,
yet a republic that wishes to expand can use no other
method, for experience has shown us no other way that is
more certain or more true.

The previously mentioned system of confederations,
under which the Tuscans, the Achaeans, and the Aetolians operated, and under which the Swiss operate today,
is the next best method after the one followed by the
Romans. Although with this method it is not possible to
grow very much, two good things result from it: first, you
do not easily draw wars down on your back; second, all
that you seize you can easily keep. The reason why it is
not possible to grow greater is that you are a federated republic with various seats of power, which makes it difficult for them to consult one another and arrive at
decisions. Moreover, it also means that the various parts
of the republic are not so eager to make conquests, since
the many communities participating in this dominion do
not regard such acquisitions as highly as a republic does,
which has hopes of enjoying them all alone. Besides this,
federated republics govern themselves through councils
and are bound to be slower in making every decision than
those who live within one and the same circle.

It is also clear from experience that this method of proceeding has a fixed limit, and there is no example demonstrating that this limit may be exceeded: the limit is a
confederation of between twelve and fourteen communities—after that they do not try to expand any further, for
when they arrive at the point where they believe they are
able to defend themselves from anyone, they seek no
greater dominion, both because necessity does not force
them to acquire more power and because they do not see
any usefulness in such acquisitions, for the reasons stated
above. The members of the confederation would have to
do one of two things: either continue to make allies for
themselves—the great number of which would cause con-

fusion—or make subjects for themselves, which they do not value for they judge it too difficult and not profitable enough. Thus, when they have arrived at such a number that they think may live in security, they turn to two procedures: first, they receive those who ask for their assistance and establish protectorates; by this means they obtain money from those around them which they can easily distribute among themselves; second, they wage war for others and get paid for this by the prince or whoever hires them for his undertakings, which is what the Swiss do today and what we read about the states mentioned above. Livy bears witness to this, saying that when Philip, King of Macedonia, came to parley with Titus Quintius Flaminius, speaking in the presence of a praetor of the Aetolians about an agreement, and the said praetor began talking with Philip, the king rebuked the Aetolians for their avarice and lack of faith, saying that they were not ashamed to fight with one man and later to send their men out into the service of his enemy, so that the banners of Aetolia were frequently seen flying in two opposing armies.

It is clear, then, that the system of confederations has always been the same and has always produced the same results. It is also clear that this method of acquiring subjects has always been weak and has resulted in little profit; when these confederations go beyond their limitations, they immediately come to ruin. And if this method of acquiring subjects is useless to armed republics, it is totally without value for republics that are unarmed, as the republics of Italy have been in our own times. Evidently, then, the true method is the one the Romans employed, and it is even more remarkable because there is no instance of it before Rome, and after Rome there has been no one who has imitated it. As for confederations, they are only found among the Swiss and the Swabian League which imitates them. As will be discussed at the conclusion of this subject, a great number of methods followed in Rome, as pertinent to domestic matters as to foreign affairs, are not only not imitated in our present times but are not even taken into account, for some people judge them as being untrue, others as impossible, and still others as inappropriate or unprofitable; as a result, while we stand here in this ignorance of ours we are the prey of anyone who wishes to overrun this country.

But, if the imitation of the Romans should seem difficult, the imitation of the ancient Tuscans should not appear so, especially to the Tuscans today; for if they were unable, for the reasons suggested, to establish an empire similar to that of Rome, they were still able to acquire in Italy the power that their method of proceeding allowed them. This power was secure for a long time, resulting in the utmost glory of empire and arms and the highest praises for their customs and religion. Their power and glory were first diminished by the Gauls and later destroyed by the Romans; and it was so totally destroyed that there is hardly any memory of it—in spite of the fact that two thousand years ago the power of the Tuscans was immense. This has made me think about why things are forgotten this way, and this will be discussed in the following chapter.

CHAPTER V. HOW THE CHANGES IN RELIGIOUS SECTS AND LANGUAGES, TOGETHER WITH THE OCCURRENCE OF FLOODS AND PLAGUES, ERASE THE MEMORY OF THINGS

[Historical records may be destroyed either by acts of Heaven or by man. Those committed by man involve changes of religion or language; whenever a new sect springs up, its first impulse is to destroy all vestiges of the sect that preceded it. Thus, the Christians attempted to erase the historical record of their pagan predecessors by burning their books and destroying their works of art. Acts of Heaven, such as floods, plagues, and famines, work upon the human race much as spontaneous purgation takes place in the human body; when nations become too populous and human wickedness becomes too great, such occurrences reduce the numbers of men, allowing the survivors to live more easily.]

CHAPTER VI. HOW THE ROMANS PROCEEDED IN WAGING WAR

[Since war is waged for the purpose of acquiring something at the least possible expense, the Romans always waged short and conclusive wars. Upon their victory, they forced the defeated enemy to cede some of his land, which they converted into private property or a colony; this land was on the enemy's frontier and the colonists protected Rome with no expense to the republic. Even when the Romans began to pay their soldiers to wage wars of longer duration farther away from Rome, they never stopped trying to limit their duration as much as possible, nor did they ever stop establishing colonies. By dividing the spoils of war and sending out colonies Rome was able to enrich herself and at the same time impoverish others.]

CHAPTER VII. HOW MUCH LAND THE ROMANS GAVE TO THEIR COLONISTS

[The precise amount is difficult to determine, but it seems to have been small, so that there would be more land to distribute to more colonists. Furthermore, since the Romans were poor at home, small quantities of land granted to colonists abroad would not allow them to be corrupted by wealth there.]

CHAPTER VIII. THE REASONS WHY PEOPLES LEAVE THEIR HOMELANDS AND OVERRUN THE LANDS OF OTHERS

[Two types of wars exist. The first, illustrated by the wars of Alexander the Great or the Romans against hostile powers, results from the ambition of a republic or a ruler to extend an empire abroad. The second type of war involves a whole people leaving its homeland, driven by

war, plague, or famine, to seek a new homeland not
merely for an extension of an empire but for the purpose
of dispossessing another population. This kind of war is
much more serious since each side fights for its very existence rather than for its freedom. The Romans experienced three of these wars and were victorious in all of
them, but when their armies lost their ancient valor under
the empire the Romans were defeated by invasions of
Goths, Vandals, and other foreign tribes.]

CHAPTER IX.   WHAT CAUSES COMMONLY PROVOKE WARS
BETWEEN POWERS

The cause that provoked war between the Romans and
the Samnites, who had been allies for a long time, is a
common cause among great powers. War either breaks
out by chance or it is provoked by the power wishing to
start the war. The war between the Samnites started by
chance, for the intention of the Samnites was not to wage
war against the Romans when they began fighting the Sidicines and the Campanians; but when the Campanians
were conquered, against the expectation of both the
Romans and the Samnites, they ran for aid to Rome, and
once the Campanians had entrusted themselves to the
Romans, the Romans were obliged to defend them as if
they were defending themselves and to wage a war which
they felt they could not honorably avoid. The Romans
thought it was reasonable not to defend their friends the
Campanians against their friends the Samnites, but they
also felt it would be shameful not to defend these peoples,
who were their subjects and under their protection, believing that if they did not undertake their defense they
would be closing the road to all those who might wish to
seek their protection in the future. And since Rome set
empire and glory, and not tranquillity, as her goal, this
undertaking could not be denied.

The same cause gave rise to the war against the Carthaginians: the Romans undertook the defense of the

Messinians in Sicily—again by chance. But later it was not by chance that the Second Punic War broke out, for the Carthaginian general, Hannibal, attacked the Saguntines, the allies of Rome in Spain, not in order to harm the Saguntines but rather to provoke the Roman armies and to have the opportunity to engage them in battle and cross over into Italy. This method of starting war has always been common among the powerful and among those who still have respect for both their own word and that of others. For if I wish to wage war upon a prince with whom I have long-respected treaties, I can attack one of his friends with more justification and excuse than I can attack the prince, knowing for a certainty that if I attack his friend he will either resent it (and I shall fulfill my intention of waging war upon him) or not resent it, in which case he will reveal his weakness or lack of faith by not defending one of his dependents. Either one of these two alternatives suffices to lessen his reputation and to facilitate my plans.

Concerning the provocation of wars, then, one should bear in mind what was said above concerning the surrender of the Campanians; furthermore, one should remember the remedy a city has when it cannot defend itself alone yet wishes to defend itself at any cost from anyone who attacks it: that remedy is for the city to give itself freely to the one it can count on to defend it, as the Capuans did with the Romans and the Florentines did with King Robert of Naples, who, although he did not want to defend them as his allies, subsequently did defend them as his subjects against the forces of Castruccio of Lucca, who was oppressing them.

CHAPTER X.   WEALTH DOES NOT REPRESENT THE SINEWS OF WAR AS POPULAR OPINION WOULD HAVE IT

Since anyone can begin but cannot end a war whenever he pleases, before he undertakes such action a prince should take stock of his forces and govern himself accordingly. But he should have enough prudence not to deceive himself about his forces; and he will deceive himself every time he measures them by wealth, by their location, or by their goodwill if he lacks troops of his own. For the aforementioned things surely increase your forces, but they certainly do not provide you with them, and by themselves they are nothing and are of no good whatsoever without faithful troops. For without them a great deal of money does you no good, the strength of the country does you no good, and the word and goodwill of men do not last, as they cannot be faithful to you if you cannot defend them. Every mountain, every lake, every inaccessible place becomes a plain when strong defenders are lacking. Wealth not only will not defend you, it will cause you to be plundered all the sooner.

Nothing can be more false than the popular conception that riches are the sinews of war. This maxim was uttered by Quintus Curtius in connection with the war between Antipater of Macedonia and the King of Sparta, where he described how the King of Sparta was forced to engage in battle and was defeated for lack of money; if he had postponed the battle for a few days, the news of the death of Alexander would have reached Greece, and as a result he would have been the victor without fighting; but since he lacked money and was afraid that his army might abandon him because of this, he was forced to tempt the fortunes of battle; thus, for this reason Quintus Curtius affirms that riches are the sinews of war. This maxim is cited every day and is practiced by princes who are not quite prudent enough to make use of it; because they base their actions upon it, they believe that possessing great riches is sufficient for their defense, and they do not realize that if riches were sufficient for victory Darius would have defeated Alexander; the Greeks would have vanquished the Romans; Duke Carlo would have beaten the Swiss in our times; and the Pope and the Florentines together would not have had any difficulty a few days ago in defeating Francesco Maria, the nephew of Pope Julius

II, in the war over Urbino. Nevertheless, all the aforementioned were conquered by those who thought good
soldiers, and not wealth, were the sinews of war.

Among the things that Croesus, King of the Lydians,
showed to Solon, the Athenian, was an immeasurable
treasure: when he asked Solon what he thought of his
power, Solon answered that he did not consider him more
powerful because of it, for war was waged with steel and
not with gold, and someone who had more steel than he
had could take his treasure away from him. Another example: after the death of Alexander the Great a number
of Gauls crossed Greece into Asia; when they sent envoys
to the King of Macedonia to draw up certain accords, that
king showed them a great amount of gold and silver in
order to demonstrate his power and to frighten them; as a
result, the Gauls—who, until that moment, had been set
on peace—broke the agreement because of the strong desire they now had to get the gold; and so, the king was despoiled of the very thing he had amassed for his defense.
A few years ago, the Venetians lost their entire state while
their treasury was still full of money, for they were unable
to defend themselves with it.

Hence, let me say that good soldiers, not gold, as common opinion proclaims, are the sinews of war, for gold is
not sufficient to find good soldiers but good soldiers are
more than sufficient to find gold. If the Romans had
wanted to wage war with wealth rather than with steel, all
the world's treasure would not have been sufficient, considering the greatness of the tasks they undertook and the
difficulties they encountered in them; but since they
waged their wars with steel, they never suffered a scarcity
of gold, for those who feared them carried it to them even
into their camps. And if that Spartan king had to tempt
the fortunes of war through a scarcity of money, what
happened to him because of money has often happened
for other reasons: for when an army lacks provisions and
must either die of hunger or fight in battle, it always
chooses to fight as the most honorable course and the one

in which Fortune can favor you in some way. It has also happened many times that when a general sees aid coming to the opposing army, he finds that he must engage in battle and tempt the fortunes of war immediately, for if he waits for his enemy to grow stronger, he will have to fight in any case, and with a thousand disadvantages. It has also been observed (as happened to Hasdrubal when he was attacked in the Marches by Claudius Nero together with the other Roman consul) that when a general is forced either to flee or to fight, he always chooses to fight, for he feels that this decision, while it may be most dangerous, can lead to victory, while the other one must in any event lead to defeat. There are, then, many necessities that force a general, contrary to his intention, to make the decision to fight; among them, sometimes, is a lack of money, but wealth should not, on this account, be judged the sinews of war any more than the other things that bring men to such straits.

I repeat again: not gold but good soldiers are the sinews of war. Money is certainly necessary as a secondary consideration, but it is a necessity that good soldiers supply by themselves; for it is as impossible for good soldiers to lack riches as it is for wealth to find good soldiers by itself. History demonstrates in a thousand places that what we are saying is true, notwithstanding the fact that Pericles advised the Athenians to wage war on the entire Peloponnesus, arguing that they would win the war because of their ingenuity and the power of their money. And although the Athenians sometimes succeeded in that war, they ultimately lost it, for the prudence and the good soldiers of Sparta were worth more than the ingenuity and wealth of Athens. But Livy is a better witness to the truth of this opinion than anyone else. In discussing the question of whether Alexander would have defeated the Romans if he had invaded Italy, he shows that three things are necessary in war: many good soldiers, prudent generals, and good fortune. In considering whether the Romans or Alexander would have prevailed in these matters, he then gives his conclusion without ever discussing riches. The Capuans, when they were requested by the Sidicines to take up arms with them against the Samnites, must have measured their strength by their wealth and not by their soldiers; for when they had taken the decision to assist them, they were forced after two defeats to become tributaries of the Romans in order to save themselves.

CHAPTER XI.   IT IS NOT A WISE POLICY TO FORM A FRIENDSHIP WITH A RULER WHO HAS MORE PRESTIGE THAN STRENGTH

[Alliances made with powers whose remoteness or internal conflicts make them unlikely to come to your assistance provide more prestige than protection. Examples of this erroneous policy can be found not only in Roman times but also in our own day. When, in 1479, the Florentines mistakenly relied upon the King of France since they were faced with opposition from the Pope and the King of Naples, they discovered that his aid was not forthcoming.]

CHAPTER XII.   WHETHER IT IS BETTER, UNDER THREAT OF ATTACK, TO ATTACK OR TO WAIT FOR THE OUTBREAK OF WAR

[Much debate has taken place on this issue. Some maintain that the only means of destroying an enemy is to take the war to his own territory, as both Hannibal and Scipio did in the Punic wars. Others affirm that the worst damage is inflicted upon an enemy when he is drawn away from his homeland, citing the defeats of the Athenians abroad as contrasted with their constant victories on their own territory, or the defeat of King Alfonso of Naples in Romagna by the King of France, Charles VIII.

My own opinion is based upon the distinction between well-armed countries and those that are not well armed, the former illustrated by the ancient Romans or the modern Swiss and the latter by the ancient Carthaginians or by modern France and Italy. A poorly armed country must keep the enemy at a distance, for its resources are financial and are weakened by the presence of the enemy within its borders. Thus, as long as Carthage's territory was undisturbed, its resources allowed a continuous war against Rome; in like manner, Florence was practically defenseless during the invasion of her territory by Castruccio Castracani of Lucca; but once he died and his forces were removed from Florentine territory, Florence was able to call upon her resources to attack the Duke of Milan in his own country. When countries are properly armed, as the Romans were or the Swiss are now, they become more difficult to attack the closer the enemy comes to their homeland, for their strength resides in their soldiers rather than in their wealth. Therefore, a ruler whose people are well armed and prepared should always wait for the invasion of a powerful enemy, while a ruler whose people are poorly armed and unaccustomed to warfare should always keep a war as far from his own territory as possible.]

CHAPTER XIII.   ONE RISES FROM A LOW TO A HIGH STATION MORE OFTEN BY USING FRAUD INSTEAD OF FORCE

I believe it to be very true that rarely or never do men of humble station rise to high ranks without force and without fraud, although others attain such rank either as a gift or by having it left to them as an inheritance. Nor do I believe that force by itself will ever suffice, although fraud alone surely can be enough: anyone who reads the life of Philip of Macedonia, Agathocles the Sicilian, and of many others like them will see this clearly, for from the lowest, or at least a very low, station they all acquired either a kingdom or great empires. Xenophon shows in his *Life of Cyrus* the necessity for deception: considering that the first expedition Cyrus made against the King of Armenia was full of deception and that he acquired his kingdom with cunning and not force, no conclusion can be drawn from this action other than that a prince who wishes to accomplish great things must learn to deceive. Xenophon also says that Cyrus tricked his maternal uncle, Cyaxares, the King of the Medes, in a number of ways and he demonstrates that without such fraud Cyrus would never have been able to attain the greatness he did. I do not believe that anyone who has been placed in a humble station has ever attained great authority by employing only open and guileless force, but this has certainly been the case for those who have employed only deception, as Giovanni Galeazzo Visconti did when he seized the government and the rule of Lombardy from his uncle, Messer Bernabò.

What princes have to do at the beginning of their expansion republics must also do—at least until they have become powerful and force alone is sufficient. And since Rome employed, in every instance, either by chance or by choice, all the methods necessary to attain greatness, she did not fail to use this one as well. She could not have chosen a better deception in the beginning than the method discussed above, that is, by making allies for herself, for under this title she made them her slaves, as were the Latins and the other peoples around her. For first she used their armies to subjugate the peoples near her and to gain the reputation of a state; then, after she had subjugated them, she became so great that she was able to defeat anyone. And the Latins never realized that they were completely enslaved until they saw that the Samnites were defeated twice and were forced to come to terms. This victory increased the reputation of the Romans among distant rulers, for through it they learned the Roman name but not about their armies; it also generated envy and suspicion in those who saw and heard about the armies, among whom were the Latins. And this envy and fear were so strong that not only the Latins but also the colonies they possessed in Latium, along with the Campanians, who had shortly before been defended by the

Romans, conspired against the Roman name. And the Latins waged this war in the manner in which most wars are waged, as was said above: they did not attack the Romans but defended the Sidicines against the Samnites, who were waging war against them with the permission of the Romans. And Livy shows that the Latins initiated the war because they recognized this deception when he has Annius Setinus, the Latin praetor, speak these words in their council: "For if we can still endure servitude under the pretense of an alliance of equals," and so on.[1]

Thus, it is evident that the Romans in their first conquests did not fail to use fraud, which must always be employed by those who from small beginnings wish to climb to sublime heights—and when such fraud is as concealed as it was in the case of the Romans, it is all the less worthy of criticism.

CHAPTER XIV.   MEN OFTEN DECEIVE THEMSELVES, THINKING THEY WILL CONQUER PRIDE WITH HUMILITY

[Humility may not only be of little use in some instances, it may even increase the insolence of an opponent. If a ruler must make a concession, it is always better to make that concession after actually encountering force rather than merely the threat of it. Yielding to a mere threat usually does not forestall war, but it certainly demeans a ruler. Preparing to meet force with force will at least cause you to be respected by both your enemy and your allies and may even increase the support of your allies.]

CHAPTER XV.   WEAK STATES ARE ALWAYS HESITANT IN MAKING DECISIONS, AND DELAYED DECISIONS ARE ALWAYS HARMFUL

[At some point in a discussion of policy a definite decision must be made without ambiguity or uncertainty. When the actions of a ruler or republic have been determined,

[1] Livy, VIII, iv (cited by Machiavelli in Latin).

the words to justify those actions will follow naturally and without need for much discussion. In the case of weak republics, like Florence, such hesitation and indecision have been just as damaging as delayed decisions, especially when the decision involves joining an ally in war. Hesitation in such instances—such as Florence's hesitation in joining the war of King Louis XII against Lodovico Sforza, Duke of Milan—can only be harmful. In this instance it cost Florence the goodwill of the victorious French king while it did nothing to aid the duke, who would have naturally resented the hesitation if he, and not the king, had been the victor.]

CHAPTER XVI.   HOW FAR SOLDIERS OF OUR TIMES HAVE TURNED FROM ANCIENT DISCIPLINE

[Modern commanders fail to follow the example of the ancient Romans, who drew up their troops in such a way that they were grouped together in three ranks and could resist repeated frontal attacks.[1] Instead, they are wont to form a long, thin line of troops which cannot resist more than one attack. Not one present-day commander has imitated ancient practices and reformed modern methods in the process. In general, they allege that the force of modern artillery prohibits them from initiating such a concentration of troops.]

CHAPTER XVII.   HOW MUCH VALUE SHOULD BE GIVEN TO ARTILLERY IN PRESENT-DAY ARMIES; AND IF THE OPINION GENERALLY HELD ABOUT ARTILLERY IS TRUE

[Some have argued that if artillery had existed in ancient times, the Romans would not have conquered so many countries as easily, nor would they have displayed the

[1] The technical aspects of this question, discussed at length by Machiavelli in *The Art of War,* are of little interest to the general reader. Selections from *The Art of War* included in this edition deal with the more general problem of the imitation of the ancients and the description of an ideal military leader.

courage they did; furthermore, they have argued that artillery complicates the order of battle and decreases the
value of other forms of weapons or troops. Since artillery
is more damaging to a defensive position than to an attacking army, and since their wars were aggressive and
not defensive, the Romans would have enjoyed even
greater advantage and success with artillery. As to
whether or not men can still display personal valor, exposure to artillery fire is not more dangerous than exposure
to other weapons, for few present-day commanders have
actually met death in this way. If modern men show less
courage, it is due more to their lack of discipline than to
the use of artillery. The claim that wars will now be
fought completely with artillery is entirely false, for a
well-trained army, one patterned after the ancients, will
emphasize the infantry rather than the cavalry, and this
sort of soldier can most easily avoid the dangers of artillery fire. Artillery is thus useful when employed by an
army composed of soldiers who match the Romans in
bravery, but without such bravery artillery is inefficient
when employed against valiant soldiers.]

CHAPTER XVIII. WHY, BASED UPON THE AUTHORITY OF
THE ROMANS AND THE EXAMPLE OF ANCIENT ARMIES, IN-
FANTRY SHOULD BE MORE ESTEEMED THAN CAVALRY

[The Romans always valued foot soldiers over cavalry, for
good troops on foot can always break a cavalry charge,
while only with much difficulty can cavalry break the
ranks of well-disciplined infantrymen. This has been the
greatest error committed by Italian rulers, for they have
constantly favored cavalry over infantry. The soldiers of
fortune they employed found it in their interest to command mounted troops rather than foot soldiers and thus
profited by spreading false rumors about the ineffectiveness of infantrymen. Nevertheless, numerous battles
today demonstrate the superiority of foot soldiers over
mounted troops, and even though many recognized this

superiority in ancient or modern times, nothing seems to persuade our princes to change their minds or to revive the military institutions of the ancients.]

CHAPTER XIX. CONQUESTS MADE BY REPUBLICS WHICH ARE NOT WELL ORGANIZED AND WHICH DO NOT PROCEED ACCORDING TO THE SKILL OF THE ROMANS BRING ABOUT THEIR RUIN INSTEAD OF THEIR PROSPERITY

Those opinions contrary to the truth and based upon the bad examples introduced by our own corrupt times prevent men from thinking about changing the ways to which they have grown accustomed. Who could have persuaded an Italian up to thirty years ago that ten thousand infantry could attack ten thousand cavalry and as many infantry on level ground and not only fight with them but defeat them, as is clear from what happened in Novara, a case cited more than once? And while histories are full of such examples, men would not place faith in them; and if they did believe in them, they would claim that men are better armed in these times and that a squadron of heavy cavalry should be able to charge a huge boulder, not to mention a group of infantry; and so, with these false excuses they would corrupt their judgment, nor would they consider how Lucullus, with just a few foot soldiers, routed 150,000 cavalry commanded by Tigranes; or how among those horsemen there existed a type of cavalry exactly like our own men-at-arms today; nor would they consider how this fallacy has been revealed by the example of those people on the other side of the Alps.

And since it is clear from this that everything histories tell us about infantry is true, all the other ancient institutions ought therefore to be accepted as true and useful. If this were the case, republics and rulers would make fewer errors and would be better able to resist any attack made against them; they would not put their trust in retreat; those who had a civic form of government in their hands would be better able to direct it, whether it be to expand it or to maintain it. They would realize that the true way to make a republic great and to gain power is by: increasing the inhabitants of one's city; making allies and not subjects; sending colonies out to look after conquered territories; profiting from the spoils of war; subjugating the enemy with raids and battles rather than with sieges; keeping the public treasury rich but the individual poor; and zealously supporting military training. And if this method of expansion does not please them, they should consider the fact that conquests by any other means result in the ruin of republics; this should check their every ambition, causing them to regulate their city well internally with laws and customs, check its expansion, and think only of self-defense and of maintaining their defenses in good condition—as do the republics of Germany, which live and have lived in freedom for some time.

Nevertheless, as I said elsewhere in discussing the difference between organizing for expansion and organizing to maintain things as they are, it is impossible for a republic to succeed in remaining tranquil and to enjoy its liberty within its own narrow confines, for if the republic does not harm others she will be harmed herself; and as a result of being harmed the desire and the necessity for expansion will arise. And when a republic does not have an enemy abroad, it will find one at home—it seems that this must happen to all the great cities. And if the republics of Germany have managed to exist in this fashion and have been able to endure for some time now, this comes from certain conditions existing in that country which do not exist elsewhere and without which a similar way of life could not be maintained.

The section of Germany of which I am speaking was, like France and Spain, subject to the Roman empire. But later, when that empire declined and its authority diminished in that province, the most powerful cities, as a result of the cowardice or the needs of the emperors, began to free themselves, ransoming themselves from the empire by reserving for it a small annual tribute; little by little, all those cities not directly dependent upon the emperor and subject to no other ruler purchased their liberty in a similar manner. It happened that at the same time these cities were buying their liberty certain communities subject to the Duke of Austria rebelled against him. Among them were Fribourg, the Swiss cities, and similar towns. These communities prospered in the beginning and gradually grew to such an extent that they not only refused to return under Austria's yoke but became feared by all their neighbors. These are the people we call the Swiss. This province, therefore, is divided among the Swiss, those republics called free cities, princes, and the emperor. And the reason wars do not start among so many different types of governments (or, if they do start, they do not last long) is due to the influence of the emperor; though unarmed, he nevertheless enjoys such a reputation among them that he serves as their conciliator, and with his authority he acts as a mediator, immediately putting an end to any quarrels. The greatest and longest wars that have been fought there have been those which took place between the Swiss and the Duke of Austria, and although the emperor and the Duke of Austria have been one and the same person for many years, he has not been able to overcome the bravery of the Swiss, with whom no agreement is ever possible without force. Nor has the rest of Germany given him much assistance, both because these communities do not wish to attack anyone who, like themselves, wishes to live in liberty and also because some of those princes cannot (for they are poor), while others will not (for they are jealous of his power). Therefore, these communities are content with their small dominion because they have no reason, on account of imperial authority, to wish it greater; they live united within their walls because there is a nearby enemy who would seize the opportunity to attack them whenever internal conflict arose. But if conditions were different in that province, they would find it necessary to expand and thus to disrupt their tranquillity.

But because such conditions are not present elsewhere, this way of life cannot be adopted: other states must either expand by means of confederations or expand as the Romans did. And anyone who does otherwise seeks not life but death and destruction, for conquests are dangerous in a thousand ways and for a thousand reasons; for one may acquire dominion but not necessarily strength, and anyone who acquires dominion without strength must come to ruin. One who is impoverished by wars cannot acquire strength even if he is victorious, for he spends more than he takes in from his conquests: the Venetians and the Florentines did this; as a result, they have been much weaker since the former held Lombardy and the latter Tuscany than when the one was content with the sea and the other with six miles of territory from their walls. All this comes from having wished to conquer without knowing how to choose the means; and these cities deserve even more blame inasmuch as they have less of an excuse—they were familiar with the means the Romans employed and could thus have followed their example, whereas the Romans, with their prudence, were able to discover the means and had no example to follow.

Furthermore, conquests sometimes do no small harm to any well-organized republic that acquires a city or a province full of dissipation; these bad habits can be picked up through one's dealings with them, as happened first to Rome after the conquest of Capua and later to Hannibal. If Capua had been further away from Rome, so that the remedy for the dissipation of her soldiers was not nearby, or if Rome herself had been corrupt in any way, the conquest of Capua, without any doubt, would have meant the downfall of the Roman republic. Livy bears witness to this with the words: "Capua, even then not very amenable to military discipline, and an instrument of every possible pleasure, turned away the weakened spirits of the soldiers from any thought of their fatherland."[1] Such cities or

[1] Livy, VII, xxxviii (cited by Machiavelli in Latin).

provinces truly take revenge upon the conqueror without battle or bloodshed, for, filling him with their own evil customs, they make him vulnerable to anyone who attacks him. Juvenal could not have put it better when, in treating this matter in his *Satires,* he says that as a result of their conquests of foreign lands foreign customs entered the Roman hearts, and in place of frugality and other excellent virtues "gluttony and luxury took over, avenging the conquered world."[2] If, then, the success of conquest was beginning to harm the Romans in those times during which they proceeded with so much prudence and ingenuity, what will happen to those whose actions are so different from theirs, and who, besides the other errors they commit (which I have discussed at length above), depend on soldiers who are either mercenary or auxiliary? As a result of this, they often suffer the kinds of harm that will be noted in the following chapter.

CHAPTER XX. WHAT SORT OF DANGER A PRINCE OR A REPUBLIC EMPLOYING AUXILIARY OR MERCENARY TROOPS INCURS

If I had not discussed at length in another work of mine the question of how useless mercenary or auxiliary troops are and how useful are one's own soldiers, I would extend my discussion in this chapter further than I plan to do, but since I have spoken of the matter elsewhere at length I shall be brief here. Yet I do not think that it is a matter to pass over lightly, since I have found so much concerning auxiliary troops in Livy. Auxiliary soldiers are those that a prince or a republic sends to your aid at their own expense and command. Turning to Livy's text, let me say that the Romans defeated two of the Samnites' armies in two different places by using their own troops, which they sent to the aid of the Capuans, and thus liberated the Ca-

[2] Juvenal, *Satires,* VI, 291–292 (cited by Machiavelli in Latin). Here, as elsewhere, Machiavelli generally cites from the classics in a less than scholarly fashion. In this instance he has added gluttony to Juvenal's text, which only mentions luxury.

puans from the war which the Samnites were waging
against them; then, wishing to return to Rome, they left
behind two legions in the city of Capua to defend them,
so that the Capuans would not again be deprived of a
garrison and again be the victims of the Samnites. Rotting
in idleness, these legions began to enjoy this city, so much
so that they forgot their fatherland and reverence for the
senate and began thinking about taking up arms and
making themselves the rulers of that land which they had
defended with their strength, since they felt that the inhabitants were not worthy to own property they did not
know how to defend. The Romans, who foresaw all this,
took measures to crush and correct it, as will be discussed
at length when I deal with conspiracies.

Let me say again that of all the many kinds of troops,
auxiliaries are the most harmful: for the prince or republic
that employs them has no authority over them whatsoever; only the one who sends them has authority over
them, for auxiliaries are troops sent to your aid by a
prince, as I have said, under his own generals, his own
flags, and are paid by him—as was the army that the
Romans sent to Capua. When they have conquered, such
soldiers as these in most cases plunder the one who has
hired them as well as the one against whom they are
hired, and they do this either because of the wickedness of
the prince who sends them or because of their own ambition. And while the intention of the Romans was not to
break the treaty and the other agreements they had made
with the Capuans, the conquest of the city nevertheless
appeared so simple to these soldiers that they were persuaded to consider taking from the Capuans their land
and their state. One could give many examples of this, but
I wish this one to suffice: that of the people of Reggio,
whose lives and city were taken by a legion that the
Romans had sent there as a garrison. A prince (or a republic) should therefore adopt any policy except that of
bringing auxiliaries into his state for his defense when he
has to rely completely upon them; for any pact or agree-

ment with the enemy, no matter how harsh, will be lighter on him when compared to the other means. And if past events are studied closely and present ones are reviewed, it will be discovered that for everyone who has succeeded in this, there are countless others who have been disappointed. And a prince or an ambitious republic cannot have a better opportunity to seize a city or a province than to be invited to send its own armies to the latter's defense. Therefore, anyone who is so ambitious that he calls in such assistance not only to defend himself but also to attack others seeks to acquire what he cannot hold and what can easily be taken from him by the very persons who acquire it for him. But the ambition of men is so great that in order to satisfy a desire of the moment they fail to consider the evil that may result from it in a brief period of time. Nor are they moved by ancient examples in this matter any more than in the others that have been discussed; for if they were moved by them they would see that the more generosity they show toward their neighbors and the less inclined they are to seize their territory, the more likely these neighbors are to throw themselves into their lap, as will be explained below by the example of the Capuans.

CHAPTER XXI. THE FIRST PRAETOR THE ROMANS SENT ANYWHERE WAS SENT TO CAPUA, AND THIS OCCURRED AFTER FOUR HUNDRED YEARS OF WAGING WAR

[Unlike other nations, the Romans imposed as few conditions as possible upon the cities they conquered when they did not destroy them. For instance, the first praetor sent abroad was sent to Capua, and this was four hundred years after the city came under Roman control and was done at the request of the city itself. Rome's success with this policy was due to the fact that the natives of the cities governed themselves and so there was no foreign government to arouse their anger. An example of such policy can be found in Florence today, for while the Pistoians have long been under Florentine control by their own free choice, such other cities as Lucca and Siena have resisted Florentine control. Had Florence treated these cities as she did Pistoia, all of Tuscany would have belonged to her.]

CHAPTER XXII.   HOW OFTEN THE OPINIONS OF MEN ARE WRONG IN JUDGING 'IMPORTANT MATTERS

[Men frequently hold erroneous opinions; and unless decisions are made by men of great ability, they will be based upon mistaken ideas. But such men are usually not in a position of authority in corrupt republics, for they are put out of office by envious and ambitious opponents, and their ability is recognized too late. An example of this is the decision of Pope Leo X to remain neutral during the invasion of the Duchy of Milan by Francis I, King of France, based upon his assumption that it would be to the Church's advantage to fall upon the victor of that struggle. However, after the king's victory over the Swiss at Marignano in 1515, the Pope did not dare attack the French. A victorious army should never be attacked on the supposition that the victory has weakened it enough to make it easy prey for another army, for the losses suffered are made up for by the reputation of the victory itself. Only if they could have been defeated before their victory should they be attacked afterward. The Latins made this mistake when Numicius, their praetor, urged them to attack Rome after a Roman victory, as a result of which they were defeated.]

CHAPTER XXIII.   HOW FAR THE ROMANS AVOIDED A MIDDLE COURSE IN PUNISHING SUBJECTS FOR SOME ACTION THAT REQUIRED PUNISHMENT

"The situation in Latium was now such that they could endure neither peace nor war."[1] Of all the unhappy situa-

[1] Livy, VIII, xiii (cited by Machiavelli in Latin).

tions, the most unhappy is that of a prince or a republic reduced to such a state that he or it can neither accept peace nor carry on war: reduced to such a state as this are those who are harmed by the conditions of a peace treaty to the point where in waging war they are either forced to become the prey of those who assist them or to remain the prey of the enemy. And one comes to all these extremes through bad advice, bad decisions, and from failing to measure well one's forces, as was mentioned above; for the republic or prince that does measure them well will only with difficulty be brought to the condition into which the Latins led themselves: when they should not have made an agreement with the Romans they did so, and when they should not have begun a war against them they did so; and thus they acted in such a manner that both the friendship and the enmity of the Romans were equally harmful to them. The Latins were therefore conquered and completely subjugated, first by Manlius Torquatus and later by Camillus; the latter forced them to surrender and to put themselves into the hands of the Romans; next, stationing garrisons in all the cities of Latium and taking hostages from all of them, he returned to Rome and announced to the senate that all of Latium was in the hands of the Roman people.

Because such punishment is noteworthy and deserves to be observed so that it may be imitated by rulers in similar cases, I should like to cite the words Livy placed in the mouth of Camillus, which bear witness both to the means the Romans employed in expanding and to the fact that in governmental decisions the Romans always avoided a middle course of action and took extreme ones. For a government is nothing more than the control of subjects in such a way that they cannot harm you or even wish to harm you. This is achieved either by making yourself completely safe against them, removing from them every means of doing you harm, or by doing good to them in such a way that it would not be reasonable for them to desire a change of Fortune. All this is quite clear both from Camillus's statement and from the judgment on it given by the senate. His words were these: "The immortal gods have made you so powerful that they have placed in your hands the power to decide whether or not Latium is to exist. Insofar as the Latins are concerned, you may obtain a perpetual peace either by acting cruelly or by pardoning them. Do you wish to be cruel to those who have surrendered and are conquered? In that case, you can destroy all of Latium. Do you wish, following the example of your ancestors, to increase Roman power by granting citizenship to the defeated? The material for increasing Rome's glory is at hand. Certainly the most stable government is that under which all are pleased to obey. Above all, while the Latins are still stunned with terror, you must subjugate their spirits either with punishment or with benefits."[2] The decision of the senate followed these remarks and was in accord with the words of the consul. City by city, all those citizens who were of importance were brought forth and were either granted favors or destroyed; the Romans bestowed exemptions, privileges, citizenship, and in every way assured the safety of those citizens who were favored, while they destroyed the cities of the others, sent colonies there, and led the citizens back to Rome, scattering them in such a way that they could never again do harm by means of arms or plots. The Romans, as I have said before, never employed a neutral course in such matters of importance.

Rulers should imitate this judgment. The Florentines should have adopted this policy when Arezzo and the entire Valdichiana rebelled in 1502. If they had done this, they would have made their empire secure and the city of Florence most great, and they would have given her those fields which she lacked for sustenance. But they employed that middle course, which is most harmful in judging men; some of the Aretines they banished and some they condemned to death; they took their offices and their an-

[2] Ibid.

cient ranks away from everyone in the city, and they left the city intact. And if, in the course of deliberation, any citizen advised that Arezzo be destroyed, those who appeared to be wiser said that to destroy her would bring little honor to the republic, for it would appear that Florence lacked the force to hold her. Such reasons as these are the kind that appear to be true but are not: for with this same reasoning one would never be able to execute a parricide or a wicked and infamous man, as it would be shameful for the ruler to demonstrate that he did not have the forces to keep a single man in check. And men who hold such opinions do not see that individual men and the city as a whole sometimes sin against a state to such a degree that, to set an example to others and for his own protection, a ruler has no alternative but to destroy them. Honor consists in having the ability and knowing how to punish them, not in holding them under control and incurring a thousand dangers: for a ruler who does not punish a man who errs in such a way that he cannot err again is considered either ignorant or cowardly.

The necessity of the judgment imposed by the Romans is also confirmed by the sentence they pronounced on the Privernates. Two things in Livy's text should be noted: first, as was said above, that subjects should either be given benefits or destroyed; second, how much generosity of spirit and speaking the truth avails in the presence of wise men. The Roman senate gathered to pass judgment on the people of Privernum, who, having rebelled, were afterward returned by force to Roman obedience. Many citizens were sent by the people of Privernum to implore the pardon of the senate; when, in their presence, one of the senators asked one of the people: "What punishment do you think the Privernates deserve?" the citizen of Privernum replied: "That which those who feel themselves worthy of liberty deserve." To this the consul answered: "But if we free you from punishment, what kind of peace can we expect to have with you?" To that the man replied:

"If you grant us a good one, a loyal and lasting peace; if you give us a bad one, not an enduring one." Whereupon the wisest part of the senate, in spite of the anger of many, said "that they had been listening to the words of a brave man worthy to be free, and that they did not believe it possible for any people, or any individual, to remain longer in the condition which he deplored. Peace would be certain when it was made by men who were pacified voluntarily, while loyalty could not be expected from anyone who was willing to reduce himself to servitude." On the basis of these words they decided that the Privernates should become Roman citizens and honored them with the privileges of citizenship, saying: "Only those who think of nothing but liberty are worthy of becoming Romans."[3] This true and noble response pleased their noble spirits, for any other reply would have been false and base; and those who believe otherwise about men, especially about those who are accustomed to being or appearing to be free, deceive themselves in this matter; and according to this deception they make decisions which are neither good for themselves nor likely to satisfy anyone. From this cause arise the frequent rebellions and the downfall of states.

But to return to our argument, let me conclude that because of the judgment pronounced on the Latins, when powerful cities accustomed to living in freedom are judged, it is necessary either to destroy them or to show them kindness—otherwise every judgment is made in vain. And what must be avoided above all is a middle course of action, which is harmful, as was the case with the Samnites when they trapped the Romans at the Caudine Forks and did not follow the advice of an old man who advised that the Romans either be allowed to leave with honor or that they all be killed; choosing the middle course of action, they disarmed them and put them under the yoke, thus allowing them to go away full of shame and

---

[3] Livy, VIII, xxi (cited by Machiavelli in Latin).

indignation. As a result, shortly thereafter they learned to their distress that the old man's counsel had been useful and that their own decision was damaging, as will be discussed at greater length in the proper place.

CHAPTER XXIV. FORTRESSES ARE GENERALLY MUCH MORE HARMFUL THAN USEFUL

It will perhaps seem to the wise men of our times a poorly considered matter that the Romans, in their desire to secure themselves from the peoples of Latium and the city of Privernum, did not think about building some fortresses there to serve as a check to keep these people faithful, especially since there is a saying in Florence, cited by our wise men, that Pisa and other cities like it must be held by fortresses. And if the Romans had been like them, they too would have considered building them; but because they were of different abilities, judgment, and power, they did not build them. While Rome lived in freedom and kept her laws and her strong institutions, she never built fortresses in order to hold on to either cities or provinces; she did, however, preserve some of those which were already built. Seeing, therefore, how the Romans proceeded in this matter, as well as how the rulers in our own times act, I should now like to consider the question of whether it is good to build fortresses and whether they bring harm or advantage to those who build them. First we must consider whether fortresses are built as defenses against the enemy or against one's own subjects.

In the first case they are not necessary, and in the second case they are harmful. So, beginning with the reasons why they are harmful in the second instance, let me say concerning a monarchy or a republic that is afraid of its subjects and of their rebellion, that such fear must arise from the hatred its citizens feel for their ruler—hatred for his evil conduct, which arises from his belief that he can hold them with force, or from his lack of prudence in governing them; and one of the things that makes him believe that he can rule by force is that he already possesses fortresses to hold his subjects in subjection. For the evil deeds that are the reason for their hatred arise, in good measure, from the fact that the prince or republic possesses fortresses which, when this is the case, are far more harmful than useful. First, as I have said, they make you more audacious and violent toward your subjects; and second, there is not the safety in them that you imagine. For all the force and violence employed to hold a people down is useless, except for two kinds: either you always maintain a good army ready to take to the field, as the Romans did, or you must scatter, destroy, disorganize, and disunite the people to such an extent that they cannot unite to attack you. If you reduce them to poverty, "to those despoiled, arms remain";[1] if you disarm them, "rage will provide them with weapons";[2] if you kill their leaders and continue to injure the others, their leaders are reborn like heads of the Hydra; if you build fortresses, they are useful in times of peace because they encourage you to mistreat your subjects, but in times of war they are most useless, for they are attacked both by the enemy and by your own people—nor is it possible for them to offer resistance to both one and the other. And if they were ever useless, they are especially so in our times because of artillery, for through its destructive force small places and those behind which embankments cannot be placed are impossible to defend, as was said earlier.

I should like to discuss this matter in more detail. Either you, prince, wish to hold the people of your city in check with these fortresses or you, prince or republic, wish to bridle a city taken in war. I shall now turn to the prince and say to him that nothing can be more useless in holding one's citizens in check than such fortresses, for the reasons given above; for it makes you readier and less hesitant in oppressing your people, and this oppression

[1] Juvenal, *Satires,* VIII, 124 (cited by Machiavelli in Latin).
[2] Vergil, *Aeneid,* I, 150 (cited by Machiavelli in Latin).

makes them so disposed to your downfall and fires them up in such a way that the fortress, which is the cause of this, can no longer defend you. Therefore, in order to keep himself good, a wise and good prince will never build a fortress so as not to give his sons a reason to become sorry; they will thus rely not on fortresses but on the goodwill of their subjects. Though Count Francesco Sforza was held to be wise when he became Duke of Milan, let me say that in this regard he was not wise, for the result of building such a fortress shows that it did harm to his heirs and did not provide for their security. Thinking that because of this fortress they could live securely and could oppress their citizens and subjects, they indulged in every sort of violence, making themselves so hated that they lost their state at the first attack of the enemy. Nor did that fortress defend or prove of any use to them in wartime; and in peacetime it did them a great deal of harm. If they had not possessed it and had, through lack of prudence, treated their citizens badly, they would have discovered the danger sooner and would have drawn back; they would then have been able to resist the French attack more courageously with their subjects as their friend (without the fortress) rather than as their enemy (with the fortress). These fortresses do not help you in any way, for they are lost either through the treachery of those who guard them, through the violence of those who attack them, or through starvation. And if you expect them to help you regain a state that has been lost where only the fortress remains in your hands, you must have an army with which you can attack the one who has driven you out of the city: and when you possess this army, you will recover your state in any case, just as if the fortress did not exist—even more easily, in fact, for the men will be friendlier to you than they would be if you had treated them badly on account of the arrogance which the fortress itself provokes. Experience has shown how the fortress of Milan has, in adverse times, done neither the Sforza family nor the French any good at all; on the contrary, it has brought much harm and damage to both of them, for because of the fortress they have not thought about a more honest means of holding onto that state. Guidobaldo, Duke of Urbino and son of Frederick, who was, in his times, an esteemed general, was driven out of his state by Cesare Borgia, son of Pope Alexander VI; later, when he returned as a result of an unforeseen event, he had all the fortresses in the province destroyed, judging them harmful. Since he was loved by his people, out of respect for them he did not want to have fortresses; as for the enemy, he saw that he could not defend his fortresses since they required an army in the field to defend them. He therefore decided to destroy all of them.

When Pope Julius II, after having driven the Bentivoglio family from Bologna, constructed a fortress in that city and allowed its people to be tormented by one of his governors to such an extent that they rebelled, he immediately lost the fortress; and thus the fortress was of no use to him and did him harm; although, if he had acted differently, it might have benefited him. Niccolò da Castello, father of the Vitelli family, returned to his native city, from which he had been exiled, and immediately demolished two fortresses which Pope Sixtus IV had built there, believing that not the fortresses but the goodwill of the people would have to maintain him in that state. But above all other examples, the most recent and most notable in every respect, and the most appropriate to demonstrate the uselessness of building fortresses and the usefulness of demolishing them, is that of Genoa in these times. Everyone knows how, in 1507, Genoa rebelled against King Louis XII of France, who came in person together with all his forces, to reconquer the city; and when he did so, he built a fortress, the strongest of all those that had been recorded up until the present, for it was impregnable in its site as well as in every other way, situated as it was on the top of the hills extending to the sea, called Codefà by the Genoese; and with it he dominated the entire port and a great part of the city of Genoa. Then, in 1512, when the French forces were driven out of Italy, Genoa, notwithstanding the fortress, rebelled, and Ottaviano Fregoso seized control of it; with great effort, he took the fortress at the end of sixteen months, because of starvation. Everyone believed, and many advised, that he ought to preserve it as his refuge for an eventual emergency; but as he was a most prudent man, he realized that the will of men (and not fortresses) maintains rulers in a state, and he destroyed it. And thus, not founding his state upon the fortress but rather upon his ability and prudence, he held it and still holds it now. And whereas to change the government of Genoa it was once sufficient to employ only a thousand foot soldiers, his adversaries have attacked him with ten thousand and have not been able to harm him. It is evident from this, therefore, that the demolition of the fortress did not harm Ottaviano and the construction of it did not defend the king. For if he had come into Italy with an army, he could have recovered Genoa, though he did not have a fortress there; but if he had not come into Italy with an army, he could not have held Genoa, even if he did have a fortress there. Consequently, it was expensive for the king to build it and shameful for him to lose it; for Ottaviano, its reacquisition was glorious and its destruction was profitable.

But let us come to republics that build fortresses not in their own country but in the lands they conquer. And to demonstrate the fallacy of this procedure—if the example of France and Genoa does not suffice—I am sure that of Florence and Pisa will. The Florentines built fortresses there to hold that city, not realizing that if they wished to hold the city—a city that had always been opposed to the very name of Florence, since it had lived in liberty, and had turned to rebellion as a last resort to preserve its freedom—it was necessary to follow the Roman method, that is, either to make her an ally or to destroy her. The strength of fortresses is shown by what occurred at the arrival of King Charles, to whom the fortresses surrendered, either because of the infidelity of those who guarded them or out of fear of a greater evil; if they had not existed there, the Florentines would not have based their possession of Pisa upon them, and the king would not have been able to deprive the Florentines of the city in that way. And the methods with which she had been held until that time would perhaps have been sufficient to hold her; without a doubt, they would have given no worse an account of themselves than the fortresses did.

I conclude, therefore, that to hold one's native city by means of a fortress is harmful, and for holding conquered lands fortresses are useless. I would have the authority of the Romans suffice, who tore down walls instead of building them in the lands they wished to hold by force. And if anyone, against this opinion of mine, would cite the example of Tarentum in ancient times or Brescia in modern times, places which were recovered from rebellious subjects, by means of fortresses, I reply that for the recovery of Tarentum, Fabius Maximus was sent at the beginning of a year with an entire army, which would have been sufficient to recover it even if there had been no fortress there; and though Fabius used that method, if the fortress had not existed he would have used some other which would have produced the same effect. And I do not know of what use a fortress is if, in retaking a city, you need a consular army and a Fabius Maximus as general. That the Romans would have retaken it anyway is evident from the example of Capua, where there was no fortress; yet, by virtue of their army, the Romans recaptured it.

But let us come to Brescia. What occurred in that rebellion rarely happens: that is to say, the fortress remains in your hands after the city has revolted, and you have a great army nearby, as was the army of the French; for when Monseigneur de Foix, the king's general, learned of the loss of Brescia while he was in Bologna with his army, he lost no time and left immediately for Brescia; arriving there in three days, he retook the city by means of the fortress. However, the fortress of Brescia, to do any good, needed a Monseigneur de Foix and a French army to provide aid for it in three days. So this example, as opposed to the contrary examples, is not sufficient since many fortresses have been taken and retaken in the wars of our day with the same fortune in which the countryside is taken and retaken, not only in Lombardy but also in Romagna, in the Kingdom of Naples, and in all parts of Italy. But as for building fortresses to defend oneself from foreign enemies, let me say that they are not necessary for those peoples and kingdoms that have good armies, and for those that lack good armies they are useless, for good armies are sufficient for self-defense, while fortresses without good armies cannot protect you. And this is seen through the experience of those who have been considered excellent in governmental affairs and in other matters as well, such as the Romans and the Spartans; for if the Romans did not construct fortresses, the Spartans not only refrained from doing so but did not even allow their city to have walls, for they wanted the ability of the individual—and no other defense—to protect them. This is the reason why, when a Spartan was asked by an Athenian if the walls of Athens seemed beautiful to him, he replied: "Yes, if they are inhabited by women."

The prince who has good armies, therefore, will find that fortresses on his shores and the frontiers of his state are sometimes able, perhaps, to hold the enemy off for a few days until order is restored; they can be useful, but they are not essential. But when a prince does not have a good army, having fortresses in his state or at his frontiers is either harmful or useless to him; harmful, for they are easily lost, and when they are lost they can be used to wage war against him; or if they are so strong that the enemy cannot occupy them, they are left behind by the hostile army and are of no benefit. For good armies enter enemy territory without regard for cities or fortresses, which are left behind them when they meet no determined resistance. This is evident from ancient history and from the actions of Francesco Maria, who, in recent

times, left ten enemy cities behind him without any hesitation in order to attack Urbino. Therefore, a prince who
can build a good army can do so without building fortresses, and a prince who does not have a good army
should not build them. He should fortify the city in which
he lives, keep it well supplied and its citizens well disposed in order to sustain an enemy attack long enough for
either an accord or outside assistance to free him. All
other plans are expensive in peacetime and useless in
wartime. And thus, anyone who considers all I have said
will see that the Romans, so wise in every other institution
of theirs, were also prudent in their judgment about the
Latins and the Privernates, for, giving no thought to fortresses, they made themselves secure with abler and wiser
methods.

CHAPTER XXV.   THAT AN ASSAULT UPON A CITY DIVIDED BY
INTERNAL STRIFE, IN ORDER TO OCCUPY IT AS A RESULT OF
THIS STRIFE, IS AN ERRONEOUS POLICY

[Roman history demonstrates that whenever Rome's enemies attacked her, hoping to capitalize on her internal
strife, the result was the unification of factions within the
city and Roman victory. A more intelligent policy would
have been to encourage such internal conflicts during
peacetime while acting as arbitrator among the factions.
Florence did this in Pistoia and acquired control of the
city in that way, but it never succeeded in gaining control
of Siena when it attempted to capitalize on that city's internal strife. Filippo Visconti, the Duke of Milan, consistently failed to defeat the Florentines when he tried to use
their disunity to his advantage, for his attacks always unified the city against him.]

CHAPTER XXVI.   INSULTS AND ABUSE AROUSE HATRED
AGAINST THOSE WHO EMPLOY THEM, WITHOUT PRODUCING
ANY BENEFIT

[Prudent men do not resort to threats or insults, for neither makes your enemy weaker but, rather, arouses his

suspicion or his hatred of you. The Romans always avoided this, and several instances in their history prove that they were correct in doing so.]

CHAPTER XXVII. PRUDENT PRINCES AND REPUBLICS OUGHT TO BE SATISFIED WITH WINNING, FOR WHEN THAT IS NOT ENOUGH THEY GENERALLY LOSE

The use of insulting language against the enemy arises, in most cases, from an insolence caused either by victory or by the false hope of victory, and this false hope makes men not only err in speaking but also in their actions. For when this hope enters men's breasts it causes them to go beyond their mark and, in most cases, to lose the opportunity of possessing a certain good by hoping to obtain a better one that is uncertain. And because this is a matter which merits consideration, for men often deceive themselves about it and thus damage their state, I choose to demonstrate it in detail with ancient and modern examples, since I am unable to give a clear demonstration solely with arguments.

After he had defeated the Romans at Cannae, Hannibal sent his envoys to Carthage to announce the victory and to ask for assistance. The senate debated over what was to be done. Hanno, an old and prudent Carthaginian citizen, advised them to use this victory wisely in making peace with the Romans, since they had conquered and they might obtain it with honorable conditions, but they could not hope to make such a peace after a defeat; for the intention of the Carthaginians should be to demonstrate to the Romans that defeating them was sufficient, and that after they had enjoyed a victory they did not seek to lose it in hopes of a greater one. This policy was not adopted, though it was later recognized as a very wise one by the Carthaginian senate—the opportunity had been lost. After Alexander the Great had taken the entire East, the Republic of Tyre—in those times a noble and powerful republic because its city was surrounded by the sea, like that of the Venetians—recognized Alexander's greatness and sent envoys to tell him that they wished to be his good servants and to give him the obedience he wanted, but that they were not ready to accept either him or his soldiers in the city; whereupon Alexander, outraged that one city wished to close against him those gates which the entire world had opened for him, rebuffed them and besieged the city, not accepting their conditions. Since the city was surrounded by water and well furnished with provisions and other munitions necessary for its defense, it resisted; after four months Alexander realized that one city, to its glory, was taking from him more time than many others he had conquered had taken from him, and decided to try agreement and to concede to them what they themselves had asked. But the people of Tyre had become arrogant, and not only would they not accept the agreement but they killed those who came to negotiate it. Angered by this, Alexander set himself to the siege with such force that he took and demolished the city and killed and enslaved its men.

In 1512 a Spanish army entered Florentine territory to restore the Medici in Florence and to levy a tribute upon the city. They had been brought there by citizens in the city who had given the Spanish hope that as soon as they were inside Florentine territory the inhabitants would take up arms in their favor; but once they entered the plain and no one showed himself, they tried to make a truce, since they were short of provisions; growing arrogant because of this, the people of Florence refused to accept it, and from this came the loss of Prato and the downfall of the Florentine state.

Rulers who are attacked cannot, then, commit a greater error than to refuse every agreement, especially when it is offered to them when the attack is carried out by men who are much more powerful than they are, for there will never be an offer so unfavorable that it will not, to some degree, ensure the well-being of him who accepts it and will not in some manner represent a partial victory for him. For it should have been enough for the people of

Tyre that Alexander accepted those conditions which he had originally refused, and their victory should have been great enough when they had forced such a man to condescend to their will with his arms in hand. It should have been enough, as well, for the Florentines—because it was a great victory for them—if the Spanish army acceded to some of their demands and did not fulfill all their own goals, since the aim of that army was to change the state in Florence, to shift it away from an alliance with France, and to get money from it. Since the army had achieved the last two of these three objectives and the people retained one of their objectives, namely, the preservation of their state, each side had obtained within the limits of the agreement a certain amount of honor and satisfaction. The people should not have cared about the two other things as long as they were left alive, nor should they have wished to place the matter in any way at the discretion of Fortune (although they foresaw an even greater and almost certain victory), thus risking their last stake, something which no prudent man ever risks unless he is forced to do so.

Hannibal, having left Italy, where he had won glory for sixteen years, was recalled by his Carthaginians to rescue his native city. He found Hasdrubal and Syphax defeated, the Kingdom of Numidia lost, and Carthage restricted to within the limits of her city walls, with no other refuge left her except himself and his army. Realizing that this was the last stake in the destiny of his fatherland, he did not wish to risk losing the city until he had tried every other remedy; and he was not ashamed to ask for peace, judging that if there was any remedy for his fatherland it was in peace and not in war. But when, later on, peace was denied him, he did not wish to avoid fighting even if he had to lose, believing that he might yet be able to win or, losing, lose gloriously. And if Hannibal—who was so able and whose army was intact—first sought peace rather than war when he realized that in losing the battle his native city would become enslaved, what should a man of

less ability and experience do? But men make this error
because they do not know how to limit their hopes; basing
themselves on these hopes, without measuring themselves
in other ways, they come to ruin.

CHAPTER XXVIII.   HOW DANGEROUS IT IS FOR A REPUBLIC
OR A PRINCE NOT TO AVENGE A PUBLIC OR PRIVATE INJURY

[Offenses committed against private individuals, like
those committed against an entire people, are dangerous,
for if the injured man does not receive satisfaction he will
seek to avenge himself. An excellent example of this is the
assassination of Philip, King of Macedonia and the father
of Alexander the Great, by Pausanias, a man who requested justice from Philip but to whom it had been
denied.]

CHAPTER XXIX.   FORTUNE BLINDS MEN'S MINDS WHEN SHE
DOES NOT WANT THEM TO OPPOSE HER PLANS

If we consider carefully how human affairs proceed, we
will see that many times things happen and incidents
occur against which the heavens do not wish any provision to be made. And if what I am discussing happened in
Rome, where there was so much ability, religion, and
order, it is no wonder that it occurs much more frequently
in a city or province that lacks these three above-mentioned qualities. Since this instance is very noteworthy in
illustrating the power of Heaven over human affairs, Livy
explains it at length and with the most effective language,
saying that since Heaven, for some reason, wanted the
Romans to recognize its power, it first caused those Fabii
who went to the Gauls as envoys to make a mistake, and
as a result of their action the Gauls were incited to wage
war upon Rome; then it commanded that nothing worthy
of the Roman people be done in Rome to stop that war;
before this it had arranged for Camillus, perhaps the sole
remedy for such a great evil, to be exiled to Ardea; then,
when the Gauls came toward Rome, those who had

created a dictator many times to deal with the attack of the Volscians and other nearby enemies of theirs failed to do so on this occasion. Also, in choosing their soldiers they did so in a feeble manner, without much care, and they were so slow in taking up arms that they barely managed to meet the Gauls on the river Allia, only ten miles away from Rome. There the tribunes set up their camp without any of their usual caution: without first inspecting the spot or surrounding it with a trench or stockade; not using any precautions, human or divine. And in drawing up the order of battle they allowed their ranks to be thin and weak so that neither the soldiers nor the generals accomplished anything worthy of Roman discipline. Then they fought without bloodshed, for they fled before they were attacked; the greater part of them went to Veii, while the rest retreated to Rome, where, without even going to their homes, they immediately entered the Capitol; the senate, not thinking of defending Rome, did not even close the city gates—not to mention anything else—and part of the people fled while others went with the soldiers to the Capitol. Yet, in defending the Capitol they used methods that were not disorderly, for they did not burden it with useless people; they stocked it with all the grain they could so that they might survive during a siege. As for the useless crowd of old people, women, and children, the greater number fled to surrounding cities and the rest remained inside Rome at the mercy of the Gauls. Thus, one who reads about the deeds accomplished by the Roman people so many years earlier and then reads about these later times would not, under any circumstance, believe that it was the same people. When Livy described all the aforementioned disorders, he concluded with these words: "Fortune blinds men's minds to such an extent when she does not wish them to oppose her gathering might."[1] This conclusion could not be more true; thus, men who normally live under great adversity, or with suc-

[1] Livy, V, xxxvii (cited by Machiavelli in Latin).

cess, deserve less praise or blame, for in most cases it is evident that they have been driven to a grand or a disastrous action by a great opportunity that the heavens have granted them by giving or taking away from them the chance to act effectively.

Fortune certainly does this, for when she wishes to bring about great things she chooses a man of such spirit and ability that he recognizes the opportunities she offers him. In like manner, when she wishes to bring about great disasters, she puts men there who will contribute to that downfall. And should there be someone present who could oppose her, she either kills him or has him deprived of all means to achieve anything good.

We see from this passage that in order to make Rome greater and to lead her to the grandeur she attained, Fortune found it necessary to strike her down (as we shall discuss at length in the beginning of the following book) even though she did not wish to ruin her completely. Therefore, we see that she had Camillus exiled but not executed; she had Rome, but not the Capitol, taken; she commanded the Romans not to think of any good measure to protect Rome, but later not to overlook any good preparation in the defense of the Capitol. In order that Rome might be taken, she arranged for the majority of the soldiers who had been defeated at the river Allia to go to Veii, thus cutting off all avenues for the defense of the city of Rome. Yet in arranging this she prepared everything for Rome's recovery, having brought an entire Roman army to Veii and Camillus to Ardea in order to be able to achieve a great undertaking under a general untarnished by any disgrace of defeat and with a reputation intact for the recovery of his native city.

In confirmation of the things discussed, some modern examples might be cited, but we shall omit them, not judging them necessary, as this should be enough to satisfy anyone. Again, let me affirm as true, according to what is evident from all the histories, that men can assist Fortune but not oppose her; they can weave her schemes but they cannot break them. They should never give up, for not knowing her goals as she travels through crooked and unknown roads, men always have hope, and with hope they should never despair in whatever fortune and whatever difficulty they find themselves.

CHAPTER XXX. TRULY POWERFUL REPUBLICS AND PRINCES DO NOT BUY FRIENDSHIPS WITH MONEY BUT RATHER WITH THEIR ABILITY AND THE REPUTATION OF THEIR FORCES

The Romans were being besieged in the Capitol, and although they were expecting assistance from Veii and Camillus, as a result of hunger they came to an agreement with the Gauls to ransom themselves for a certain amount of gold. Just as they were in the process of weighing out the gold, according to the agreement, Camillus arrived with his army: Fortune brought this about, the historian says, "so that the Romans might not survive by having ransomed themselves with gold."[1] This is worthy of note not only in this instance but also in the course of this republic's history, where it is clear that cities were never bought with money nor peace ever purchased with money but always by force of arms—something, I believe, which has never been true of any other republic. Among the other signs by means of which the power of a strong state is recognized is the way in which it lives with its neighbors. And when it governs itself in such a way that its neighbors, in order to keep it as a friend, become its tributaries, then this is a certain sign that that state is powerful; but when these same neighbors get money from her, even if they are inferior to her, then this is a great sign of weakness.

Read all the Roman histories and you will see that the Massilians, the Aedui, the Rhodians, Hiero of Syracuse,

---

[1] A reference to Livy, V, xlix (although Machiavelli adds the remark about Fortune to his paraphrase of Livy's original Latin).

Eumenes, and Masinissa—all near the borders of the Roman empire—competed in payment and tribute for the empire's needs in order to have its friendship, seeking nothing from it but to be defended. The contrary is seen in weak states: beginning with our own Florence, in past times, when her reputation was highest, there was no insignificant lord in Romagna who did not receive some payment from her; moreover, she gave this to the Perugians, the inhabitants of Città di Castello, and to all her other neighbors. If this city had been armed and vigorous, everything would have been the opposite: those cities would have given money to her to obtain her protection and would not have sought to sell their own friendship but to purchase hers. Nor did the Florentines alone live in this cowardice, but also the Venetians and the King of France, who, with so great a kingdom, lived as a tributary to the Swiss and to the King of England. All this came from having disarmed his people and from the fact that this king and the other rulers named earlier preferred to enjoy the immediate benefit of being able to despoil the people (and to avoid a danger more imaginary than real) rather than to accomplish things that would make them secure and their states happy forever. This disorder, even if it gives rise to tranquillity for a while, is always, in time, a cause of emergencies, damage, and incurable disasters. It would take too long to recount how often the Florentines, the Venetians, and the Kingdom of France have bought themselves out of wars and how often they have been subjected to a disgrace to which the Romans were subjected only once. It would take too long to recount how many cities the Florentines and the Venetians bought in which disorder could later be seen, for things bought with gold cannot be defended with steel. The Romans observed this noble attitude and this way of living as long as they lived in freedom, but later, when they came under the rule of emperors and the emperors began to be evil and to love the shade more than the sun, the Romans also began to buy themselves off—first from the

Parthians, then from the Germans, then from other
nearby peoples—and this was the beginning of the downfall of so great an empire.

Similar difficulties, then, arise from having disarmed
your people, and from this results another, still greater,
difficulty: the closer the enemy gets to you, the weaker he
will find you; for anyone who lives in the way mentioned
earlier treats those subjects inside his empire badly and
those on the borders of his empire well in order to have
men well disposed to keeping the enemy at a distance.
From this it follows that in order to keep his enemy at a
distance, he pays those lords and people close to his borders. The result is that these kinds of states put up a mini-
mum amount of resistance on their borders, but when the
enemy has crossed them they have no remedy whatsoever. And they do not realize that their method of proceeding is contrary to any good institution, for the heart
and the vital organs of a body, not its extremities, should
be protected, since without the latter the body lives, but if
the former is harmed it dies; and these states do not protect the heart, but keep their hands and feet protected
instead.

What this error has brought about in Florence has been
seen and is still seen every day: for when an army passes
her borders and enters her body near the heart, she has no
other remedy left. A few years ago the same thing was
true with the Venetians; if their city had not been protected by the seas, it would have seen its end. This has not
been the case so often in France, for that kingdom is so
large that it has few superior enemies; nevertheless, when
the English attacked that kingdom in 1513, the entire
country trembled; the king himself, as well as everyone
else, felt that a single defeat might take the kingdom and
his government from him. The opposite was true with the
Romans, for the closer the enemy approached to Rome,
the more powerful it found that city in resisting him. And
this is evident from Hannibal's invasion of Italy, for after
three defeats and so many slain generals and soldiers, the

Romans were able not only to hold out against the enemy but also to win the war. All this arose from the fact that they had protected their heart well and had been less concerned with their extremities: the foundation of Rome's state was the people of Rome, the associated Latin cities, and the other allied cities in Italy and their colonies; from them they drew enough soldiers to fight and to hold the world. And that this is true is evident from the question that Hanno, the Carthaginian, posed to the envoys of Hannibal after the defeat of Cannae. After they had glorified Hannibal's exploits, they were asked by Hanno if anyone had come from the Roman people to ask for peace, and if any of the cities of the Latin nations or the colonies had rebelled against the Romans; when both questions were answered in the negative, Hanno said: "This war is still as undecided as it was before."[2]

We see, therefore, both from this discussion and from what we have said many times elsewhere, what a difference there is in the method of proceeding between present republics and ancient ones. We also see miraculous losses and gains because of this, for where men possess little ability Fortune demonstrates her power all the more; and since she is changeable, republics and states often change, and they will continue to do so until someone arises so devoted to antiquity that he will rule Fortune in such a way that she will have no reason to demonstrate, with every revolution of the sun, how powerful she can be.

CHAPTER XXXI.   HOW DANGEROUS IT IS TO BELIEVE EXILES

It does not seem beside the point to discuss, somewhere in these discourses, how dangerous a thing it is to believe those who have been driven from their native city, for such men as these have to be dealt with every day by those in authority. And I am doing this especially since it can be demonstrated with a memorable example cited by

[2] Livy, XXIII, xiii (an Italian paraphrase of the Latin original).

Livy in his history—even though it is outside the topic of his argument. When Alexander the Great passed over into Asia with his army, Alexander of Epirus, his brother-in-law and uncle, came with his men into Italy, called there by the exiled Lucanians, who led him to believe that he could take possession of that country with their assistance. Whereupon, on the basis of their word and in that hope, he came into Italy and was killed by them after their fellow citizens promised to take them back into their native city if they killed him. Therefore, it should be clear how vain are the words and promises of those who find themselves shut out of their native city. As far as their loyalty is concerned, one has to realize that anytime they find they can return to their native city by some means not requiring your support, they will abandon you and ally themselves with others, notwithstanding any promise they may have made to you. And as for their vain promises and hopes, their burning desire to return home is so great that they naturally believe many things that are false, and to these they skillfully add many more, so that between what they believe and what they say they believe they fill you with so much hope that, should you base a decision on this, either you incur useless expenses or you undertake an enterprise that leads you to ruin.

I should like the example of Alexander to suffice, along with that of Themistocles of Athens, who, after being declared a rebel, fled to Darius in Asia; there he made such promises if the king would attack Greece that Darius undertook the invasion. When, later on, Themistocles could not keep these promises, he poisoned himself, either out of shame or because he feared punishment. And if this error was committed by Themistocles, a most excellent man, what must one think of those of lesser ability who more readily allow themselves to be drawn by their desire and passion to commit even greater errors. Therefore, a prince should be slow to undertake actions based upon the report of an exiled man, for in most cases he will either end up in shame or suffer grave damage. Furthermore, since cities are seldom taken by stealth or through information supplied by those from the inside, it does not seem beside my subject to discuss this matter in the following chapter, adding to this the many methods used by the Romans in conquering cities.

CHAPTER XXXII. ON THE MEANS EMPLOYED BY THE ROMANS IN TAKING CITIES

[The Romans always believed that laying siege to a city was the least practical means of taking it. When they took a city, they preferred to take it by assault or persuade it to surrender by means of a combination of force and deceit. Using treachery is the least desirable method since the slightest error can result in failure. The Romans preferred to force cities to surrender, not by long sieges, but by defeating the enemy in the field and by raids upon his surrounding territories; for a victory on the battlefield produced immediate results, while the outcome of a long siege was always doubtful and, even when successful, might take many years.]

CHAPTER XXXIII. HOW THE ROMANS BESTOWED GREAT AUTHORITY UPON THEIR MILITARY LEADERS

[Although the Roman senate reserved for itself the right to begin wars and to ratify treaties, it granted much discretionary power to the commanders in the field. This was a wise policy, for if the senate had controlled every aspect of a war it would have forced the commander to be more cautious and to act more slowly; furthermore, the glory of the final victory would have to be shared with the senate. But the senate wisely decided that the commander's love of glory would be sufficient to regulate his conduct. Today, however, the republics of Venice and Florence act in precisely the opposite manner, for if their military men have merely to set up an artillery piece, they want to know all about it, and this mistaken policy has led us to our present difficulties.]

BOOK III

CHAPTER I.   IN ORDER FOR A RELIGIOUS GROUP OR A RE-
PUBLIC TO EXIST FOR A LONG TIME, IT IS NECESSARY OFTEN
TO BRING IT BACK TO ITS BEGINNINGS

It is a sure fact that all things of this world have a limit
to their existence; but those which complete the entire life
cycle ordained for them by Heaven are those which do
not let their bodies fall into disorder but, rather, keep
them in an orderly fashion so that no change occurs, or, if
it does, it is a healthy change and not a damaging one.
And since I am speaking of mixed bodies, such as republics and religious groups, let me say that those changes are
healthy which bring such bodies back to their beginnings.
It follows that among such states or groups, those having
the best organization and longest life span are those that
can often renew themselves through their own institutions
or can arrive at such a renewal through some incident
outside their own operation. And it is clearer than the
light of the sun that without such renewals these bodies
do not endure.

The means of renewing them is to bring them back to
their beginnings, for all the origins of religious groups, republics, and kingdoms contain within themselves some
goodness by means of which they have gained their initial
reputation and their first growth. Since, in the course of
time, this goodness becomes corrupted, if nothing inter-
venes that may bring it up to the proper mark, that body
is, of necessity, killed by such corruption. And doctors of
medicine say, when speaking of the body of man: "Every
day it absorbs something that requires a remedy from
time to time." This return to beginnings, in the case of republics, is accomplished either by an external event or as
a result of internal foresight. As for the first method, it is
evident that Rome had to be captured by the Gauls in
order for her to be reborn; and in being reborn she had to

take on new life and new strength and adopt once more
the observance of religion and justice, both of which were
becoming corrupt. This point is made very clear in Livy's
history, where he demonstrates that in calling out their
army against the Gauls, and in creating tribunes with
consular authority, the Romans observed no religious
ceremony. And, in the same way, they not only failed to
punish the three Fabii, who had fought against the
Franks "contrary to the law of nations," but they made
them tribunes. And one may presume, too, that they were
taking less account of the good laws instituted by Romulus and other prudent rulers than was reasonable and
necessary for maintaining a free government. This external reversal occurred so that all the institutions of that city
might be revived, as well as to show the people that it was
not only necessary to maintain religion and justice but
that they should also honor their good citizens and count
their abilities for more than those conveniences which
they felt were lacking on account of their actions. We see
that this was precisely what occurred: for as soon as Rome
was recaptured, the Romans renewed all the institutions
of their ancient religion and punished the Fabii who had
fought "contrary to the law of nations"; they then honored the ability and virtue of Camillus, so much so that
the senate and the others put their envy aside and placed
in his hands all the responsibility of the republic. It is necessary, therefore, as has been mentioned, that men living
together under any kind of institution should often come
to know themselves, either because of such external
events or because of internal ones. As for the latter, they
usually arise either from a law, which often obliges the
men who reside in that body to examine their affairs, or,
more often, by one good man born among them who,
with his exemplary deeds and his able works, produces
the same effect as does that law.

This benefit, then, arises in republics either through the
ability of one man or through the strength of a law; as for
the latter, the institutions that brought the Roman repub-

lic back toward its beginnings were the tribunes of the plebeians, the censors, and all the laws that checked the ambition and the insolence of the citizens. Such laws needed to be given life by the ability of one citizen who would courageously fight for their application against the power of those who might transgress against them. Concerning the application of such laws before the capture of Rome by the Gauls, the most notable examples were the death of the sons of Brutus, the death of the decemvirs,[1] and the death of Spurius Melius, the grain dealer. After the taking of Rome, we may cite the death of Manlius Capitolinus, the death of the son of Manlius Torquatus, the punishment by Papirius Cursor of Fabius, his master of cavalry, and the accusations brought against the Scipios. Because of their extraordinary and striking nature, the occurrence of each of these events made men return to their proper position; and as they became more rare, they gave men more time to become corrupted and to behave in a more dangerous and disorderly fashion. For this reason, not more than ten years should pass between one act of enforcement of the law and the next because after that amount of time has elapsed men begin to change their habits and to break the laws; and if nothing arises that recalls the penalty to their minds and renews the fear in their hearts, the delinquents will multiply in such a short time that they will not be punishable without danger. Those who governed the Florentine state from 1434 until 1494 used to say, in this regard, that it was necessary to reorganize the state every five years; otherwise it would be very difficult to maintain it; and by "reorganizing the state" they meant striking that same terror and fear into the hearts of men that they had instilled when they first constituted it, at which time they punished those men who, according to that old way of ruling, governed badly. When the memory of such punishment disappears, men grow bold and attempt to devise new plans to spread se-

[1] The decemvirs were actually exiled, not put to death.

dition; it is therefore necessary to make provision against this by bringing the state back toward its beginnings.

This return to origins in republics also arises from the simple ability of one man, without the necessity of any law moving people to action; his conduct will be of such renown and of such an exemplary character that good men will desire to imitate it and evil men will be ashamed to lead a life contrary to it. Those in Rome who provided particularly good examples were Horatius Cocles, Scaevola, Fabricius, the two Decii, Regulus Atilius, and several others; with their unusual and virtuous examples, these men created almost the same effect in Rome that its laws and institutions had created. And if the aforementioned punishments, together with these individual examples, had occurred at least every ten years in that city, it would have necessarily followed that the city would have never been corrupted; but since both of these occurred less frequently, the corrupting influences began to multiply, for after Marcus Regulus no similar example was witnessed in the city; and although there were the two Catos in Rome, there was such a space of time between Marcus Regulus and the two of them, and then between the two of them themselves, and they remained so isolated, that they could not achieve any good effect with their good examples—especially the last Cato, who, finding the better part of the city corrupted, could not, with his example, improve the citizens. And this should suffice as far as republics are concerned.

As for religious groups, these renewals are still seen to be necessary, as is evident from the example of our own religion, which would have been completely extinguished if it had not been brought back to its beginnings by Saint Francis and Saint Dominic: for with their poverty and the example of the life of Christ these two saints restored religion to the hearts of men whence it had vanished; and their new institutions were so powerful that they prevented the dishonesty of priests and the heads of the reli-

gion from ruining it. They continued to live in poverty
and had such a reputation with the people in the confessional and in their preaching that they made them understand that it is evil to speak evil of what is evil and that it
was good to live in obedience under the priests' control,
and that the errors of priests should be left for God to
punish: and thus, these church rulers do their worst, for
they can have no fear of a punishment they do not see and
in which they do not believe; therefore, this renewal has
maintained, and still maintains, our religion.

Kingdoms also need to be renewed and to bring back
their laws to their beginnings. What a good effect this
achieves can be seen in the Kingdom of France, which
lives under laws and regulations more than any other
kingdom. The parliaments are the upholders of these laws
and regulations, especially that of Paris, which is renewed
every time it takes an action against a prince of that kingdom or goes against the king in its judgments. And it has
maintained itself until now by being the obstinate opponent of the nobility of that kingdom; but should it, at any
time, fail to punish the nobility and allow such offenses to
increase, then the consequence will doubtless be that
either these offenses will have to be corrected amidst great
disorder or the kingdom will fall apart.

It may be concluded, then, that there is nothing more
necessary in a political community, whether it be a religious group, a kingdom, or a republic, than to restore to it
the reputation that it had at its beginnings and to strive to
see that there are either good laws or good men to produce this effect without having to resort to external forces;
although this may sometimes be the best remedy, as it was
in Rome, it is such a dangerous one that there is no reason
to desire it. In order to demonstrate to everyone to what
extent the accomplishments of individual men made
Rome great and brought about many good effects in that
city, I shall now narrate and discuss these actions: this
third book and last section of the commentary on these

first ten books of Livy will conclude within the framework of this topic. Although the actions of kings were great and noteworthy, since history treats of them in great detail I shall nevertheless leave them aside, discussing them only when kings did something pertaining to their own personal interests; we shall begin, then, with Brutus, the father of Roman freedom.

CHAPTER II. HOW IT IS A MOST WISE POLICY TO PRETEND TO BE MAD AT THE RIGHT TIME

[From the example of Junius Brutus, who feigned madness to protect himself until he could arouse the citizens of Rome against their tyrannical kings, we see that all those who are dissatisfied with their rulers but are too weak to oppose them openly should either pretend to be their supporters or feign madness.]

CHAPTER III. HOW NECESSARY IT WAS TO KILL THE SONS OF BRUTUS IN ORDER TO MAINTAIN A NEWLY ACQUIRED FREEDOM

[Brutus's severity in judging his own sons and in condemning them to death was most unusual but most beneficial to the maintenance of the freedom Rome had acquired through his deeds. Everyone should realize from the study of ancient history that when a government changes it is necessary to make examples of those who oppose the new regime. In our own day, Piero Soderini thought he could appease the opponents of his new regime in Florence by doing good deeds. He was mistaken about this, and he should have taken more drastic measures against his enemies, for the good results of such actions would have revealed them to be motivated not by personal ambition but by a concern for the common good. Because he was unable to imitate Brutus, he lost both his prestige and his position as gonfaloniere of Florence.]

CHAPTER IV. A PRINCE CANNOT LIVE SECURELY IN A PRIN-
CIPALITY WHILE THOSE FROM WHOM HE HAS TAKEN IT ARE
STILL ALIVE

[Old offenses are never canceled by new benefits, particularly when the gains are less important than the offenses
previously suffered. Tarquinius Priscus and Servius Tullius lost their kingdoms because they did not know how to
protect the kingdoms they had usurped from others.]

CHAPTER V. WHAT CAUSES A HEREDITARY RULER TO LOSE
HIS KINGDOM

[When Tarquinius Superbus murdered Servius Tullius,
he should have experienced no difficulty in maintaining
his rule, for the dead man had no heirs. But he failed to
respect ancient customs, ruled as a tyrant, and disregarded the senate's authority. The fact that his son,
Sextus, raped Lucretia was not, as some claim, the cause
of his downfall, for any other event would have eventually aroused the spirit of rebellion against him. Princes
should learn from this that they begin to lose their kingdom when they show little regard for the customs and ancient traditions of their subjects. Conspiracies will be
discussed at length in the next chapter, for they are of
great importance both to rulers and to private citizens.]

CHAPTER VI. CONSPIRACIES

I think it would not be proper for me to omit a discussion of conspiracies, since they are a matter of grave danger both to princes and to private citizens; for it is evident
that many more princes have lost their lives and their
states through conspiracies than through open warfare.
While the ability to wage open warfare against a prince is
granted to just a few people, being able to conspire
against a prince is granted to everyone. On the other
hand, private persons will not find a more dangerous or

more reckless undertaking than this one, for it is difficult and most dangerous at every stage. The fact is that many conspiracies are attempted but very few reach their desired goal; therefore, in order that princes may learn to guard themselves from these dangers and private persons may enter into them with more caution—or, rather, that private persons may learn to live content under the rule assigned to them by fate—I shall discuss conspiracies in great detail, without omitting any noteworthy case useful to the instruction of either kind of person. And truly golden is this maxim of Cornelius Tacitus, which states: men must honor past things and obey present ones; they should wish for good princes, but they should endure whatever sort they have. And truly, anyone who does otherwise generally brings ruin upon himself and his native city.

In treating this subject, we must first consider against whom conspiracies are formed. We find that they are made either against one's native city or against a prince. I should like to discuss these two kinds at present, for the kinds that are formed to hand a city over to the enemies besieging it, or those that have some similarity to this for whatever reason, have been sufficiently discussed above. In this first part we shall treat of conspiracies against a prince, examining first the causes of such conspiracies, which are many. One, however, is much more important than all the rest, namely, being hated by all his subjects; for when a prince has aroused a universal hatred, it follows that there are some private individuals who have been severely harmed by him and who desire revenge. This desire is increased in them by that universal hostile feeling they see aroused against him. A prince, therefore, should avoid such private hatreds; how he should act in order to avoid them I do not wish to discuss here, since I have treated this problem elsewhere; but if he guards himself against this, the simple individual offenses will create less opposition for him. The first reason is that rarely will he encounter men who value one injury so much that they place themselves in great danger to avenge it; the second is that even when they possess the courage and strength to do it, they are held back by that universal goodwill they see the prince enjoy.

Injuries must affect either property, life, or honor. Insofar as threats to one's life are concerned, they are more dangerous than their execution—that is, threats are most dangerous, but when they are carried out there is no danger whatsoever, for one who is dead cannot think about a vendetta, and those who remain alive, in most cases, leave the thinking to you. But anyone who is threatened and is forced by necessity either to act or to suffer becomes a very dangerous man to the prince, as will be discussed in detail in its proper place. Apart from this necessity, property and honor are the two things concerning which men take offense more than anything else, and the prince ought to be cautious in such matters, for he can never take away from a man so much that there is not left to him a dagger for avenging himself, and he can never dishonor a man so much that he does not retain a spirit determined on revenge. And of the honors that may be taken from a man, women are the most important; after that, personal disgrace. This kind of dishonor armed Pausanias against Philip of Macedonia and has armed many others against many other princes; in our times Luzio Belanti conspired against Pandolfo, tyrant of Siena, for no other reason than that Pandolfo had given his daughter to Luzio as his wife and then had taken her away, as we shall discuss in its proper place. The main reason that moved the Pazzi to conspire against the Medici was the estate of Giovanni Bonromei, which was taken away from them by the Medici. There is another cause, a most important one, which makes men conspire against a prince—the desire to free their native city after it has been seized by him. This reason moved Brutus and Cassius against Caesar; it moved many others against Phalaris, Dionysius, and other usurpers of their native city. Nor can any tyrant guard himself from this passion except by abandoning his tyranny. And since there is no one who will do this, there are few tyrants who do not come to a bad end; hence this verse from Juvenal: "Few kings descend to the realm of the son-in-law of Ceres without wounds or slaughter, and few tyrants die a bloodless death."[1]

The dangers that are incurred in conspiracies, as I said above, are great and continue throughout all their phases: for in such matters there is danger in planning them, in executing them, and even after they are carried out. There may be one conspirator or many, although a single person cannot be said to constitute a conspiracy; rather, he represents the firm determination of one man to kill the prince. Of the three kinds of danger risked in conspiracies, this single man avoids the first, for before the execution of the conspiracy he runs no danger whatsoever, since others do not share his secret, nor does he run the risk that his plan will come to the prince's ear. Such a determination on the part of one man can arise in any man of whatever rank—great, small, noble, common, close to or at a distance from the prince—for everyone is permitted to speak to him at some time, and anyone who is allowed to speak to him may give vent to his feelings. Pausanias, about whom I have spoken above, killed Philip of Macedonia on his way to the temple, surrounded by a thousand armed men and standing between his son and his son-in-law. But he was a nobleman and known to the prince. A poor and abject Spaniard gave King Ferdinand of Spain a blow in the neck with a dagger; the wound was not a mortal one, but it is evident from this that he had the courage and the opportunity to carry this out. A dervish (Turkish priest) with a scimitar struck at Bajazet, father of the present Turk; he did not wound him, although he nevertheless had the courage and the opportunity to do so. I believe many men with like dispositions can be found who have a similar wish, for in the wish there is neither penalty nor any danger whatsoever; but there are few who do so, and of those

[1] *Satires*, X, 112–113 (cited by Machiavelli in Latin).

who do very few or none escape being killed on the spot; for this reason you do not find people who wish to go to a sure death. But let us leave aside these single cases and turn to conspiracies among many people.

Let me say that, according to the history books, all conspiracies have been formed by those great men closest to the prince; for others, if they are not actually mad, cannot conspire, since weak men and men not close to the prince lack all those hopes and opportunities which are required for the execution of a conspiracy. First, weak men cannot find supporters who will keep faith with them, for a man cannot consent to their intention without some of those hopes that cause men to incur great dangers; if, therefore, they increase their number to two or three persons, they find themselves an accuser and come to ruin. Even when they are so lucky as to avoid the accuser, they are surrounded by such difficulty in the execution—for they do not have easy access to the prince—that it is impossible for them not to come to ruin; if noblemen and those who enjoy easy access to the prince are hindered by the difficulties explained below, the difficulties of the weak must increase without end. Therefore, since men are not completely insane in matters concerning life and property, when conspirators see they are weak they are cautious; and when they are tired of a prince they turn to cursing him and wait for others who have greater power than they possess to avenge them; indeed, if there is anyone who has ever attempted such a thing, we can only praise his intentions but not his prudence.

It is evident, then, that those who have conspired have all been noblemen or men close to the prince; of these, many were led to conspire as a result of too many favors rather than too many injuries—as was Perennius against Commodus, Plautianus against Severus, and Sejanus against Tiberius. All these men were set up by their emperors with so much wealth, honor, and rank that they felt they lacked nothing for the perfection of their power but the empire itself; unwilling to forgo that, they began to conspire against the prince, and all their conspiracies met the end that their ingratitude deserved. Yet in more recent times similar attempts have met with success, such as that of Jacopo di Appiano against Messer Piero Gambacorti, Prince of Pisa, who had raised and nourished Jacopo and had given him a reputation—then Jacopo took his state away from him. The conspiracy of Coppola against King Ferdinand of Aragon in our day was of this kind: when Coppola had reached such greatness that he felt he lacked only the kingdom, he lost his life attempting to get that as well; and truly, if any conspiracy against princes made by noblemen should have been successful, it was this one— undertaken by another king, one might say, by one who had good opportunity to fulfill his plan. But the lust for power that blinds conspirators also blinds them in carrying out their undertaking; for them failure would be impossible if they knew how to accomplish their evildoing with prudence. A prince, therefore, who wishes to guard himself against conspiracies must fear those for whom he has done too many favors more than those upon whom he has inflicted too many injuries; for if the latter lack opportunities the former have them in abundance; and their desires are similar, since the desire for power is as great as or greater than that of revenge. Therefore, princes should bestow as much authority upon their friends as will leave a gap between their power and that of the principality, preserving something desirable in between; otherwise it would be unusual if they did not come to the same end as the aforementioned princes. But let us return to our order of argument.

Since men who conspire must be nobles who have easy access to the prince, let me discuss the successes of these undertakings of theirs and then examine the reasons for their success or failure. As I said above, there are three periods of danger in conspiracies: before the deed is done; while the deed is being done; and afterward. Few conspiracies can be found that have enjoyed a successful conclusion, for it is almost impossible to get through all three periods successfully. Now, discussing the dangers that exist before the execution of the deed—the most important—let me say that one must be very prudent and very lucky if the conspiracy is not to be revealed in the course of its planning. Conspiracies are uncovered either because of denunciations or because of suspicion. The denunciation arises from encountering treachery or lack of prudence among the men with whom you discuss the conspiracy. Treachery is easily encountered, for you cannot communicate your plan to anyone but your trusted friends, who will risk death for love of you, or to men who are unhappy with the prince. One can find one or two trusted friends, but when you try to extend yourself to many it is impossible to find them; then, the love they have for you must indeed be very great if the danger and fear of punishment do not seem greater to them. Moreover, with regard to the love you think a man has for you, men commonly deceive themselves in this matter; you can never be sure of his love without testing it, and, in the case we speak of, testing is very dangerous. And although you may have tested such men in some other dangerous matter where they have been faithful to you, you cannot measure this case by that loyalty, for it is charged with far greater danger than any other situation. If you measure loyalty by how discontent a man feels with the prince, you can easily deceive yourself in this matter, too, for as soon as you have revealed your intention to the malcontent, you give him the means to content himself, and his hatred must be great or your authority very powerful if either is to keep him loyal.

The fact is that many conspiracies are uncovered and suppressed in their initial stages, and when one has been kept secret among many men for a long time, it is considered something unusual—as was the conspiracy of Piso against Nero and, in our own times, that of the Pazzi against Lorenzo and Giuliano de' Medici, which was known to more than fifty men and yet was discovered only at the moment of its execution. As for uncovering one's intention through lack of prudence, this happens when a conspirator speaks without caution in such a way that a servant or some other third person overhears—as happened to the sons of Brutus, who were overheard by a servant who later accused them as they planned the affair with the envoys of the Tarquins. Or you may carelessly reveal it to a woman or a boy you love or to some other foolish person, as did Dymnus, one of the conspirators, with Philotas, against Alexander the Great, who revealed the conspiracy to Nichomachus, a young boy whom he loved, who immediately told it to Cebalinus, his brother, who told the king. As for uncovering one's intention through suspicion, there is an example of this in the conspiracy of Piso against Nero, in which Scaevinus, one of the conspirators, made his will the day before he was to murder Nero, ordered Milichus, his freedman, to sharpen one of his old, rusty daggers, freed all his servants and gave them money, and had bandages for binding wounds made. Through these suspicious acts Milichus became aware of the matter and denounced him to Nero. Scaevinus was seized together with Natalis, another conspirator, for the day before they were seen talking together at length and in secret, and when their depositions did not agree they were forced to confess the truth; in this way the conspiracy was uncovered, resulting in the downfall of all the conspirators.

Concerning the discovery of conspiracies, it is impossible to protect oneself from malice, imprudence, or carelessness so that the plot will not be revealed whenever the participants in it exceed the number of three or four. And when more than one of them are caught, it is impossible not to expose the conspiracy, since two men cannot agree in all their explanations. When only one of their number is caught he can, if he is a strong and courageous man, keep silent as to the identities of the other conspirators, but they must show no less courage by standing firm and not revealing themselves by fleeing, for the conspiracy can be revealed by whichever party lacks courage—either the one who is imprisoned or the one who is free. The example brought forward by Livy of the conspiracy against Hieronymus, King of Syracuse, is an unusual one: when Theodorus, one of the conspirators, was arrested, he concealed with great strength all the conspirators' identities and accused, instead, the friends of the king; on the other hand, the conspirators trusted so much in Theodorus's courage that no one left Syracuse or gave any sign of fear. In organizing a conspiracy, then, all these dangers must be surpassed before the execution of it is reached. If these dangers are to be avoided, these are the measures to take: the first and truest, or, rather, to put it better, the only remedy is not to give your fellow conspirators time to accuse you but to communicate the plan to them the moment it is to be executed—and not before. Those who have done this have certainly avoided the dangers involved in preparing the conspiracy and, in most instances, the other ones as well; indeed, all of the conspiracies that were carried through in this way achieved a successful conclusion; any prudent man should take the opportunity of conducting himself in this manner. I believe it is sufficient to cite two examples.

Nelematus,[2] unable to stand the tyranny of Aristotimus, tyrant of Epirus, gathered together in his home many relatives and friends, and when he had urged them to free their native city, some of them asked for time to deliberate and to organize; whereupon Nelematus had his servants lock the house and said to those who had made the request: "Either you swear now to carry this out or I shall deliver you all as prisoners to Aristotimus." Moved by these words, they so swore, and without delay they left and successfully carried out Nelematus's plan. When a Magian, through trickery, had seized the Kingdom of the Persians, Ortanes,[3] one of the noblemen of the kingdom,

---

[2] The historical accounts of Justin and Plutarch credit this conspiracy to Hellanicus and do not mention a Nelematus.

[3] Herodotus credits this plot to Otanes, not Ortanes.

overheard and discovered the fraud. When he conferred with six other princes of that state, saying that he was going to rid the kingdom of the tyranny of that Magian, some of them asked for more time. Darius, one of the six men called on by Ortanes, rose and said: "Either we go now to carry this out or I go to accuse you all." Thus, in full agreement, they rose without giving anyone time to change his mind and successfully carried out their plans. Also akin to these two examples is the method the Aetolians used in killing Nabis, the Spartan tyrant: they sent their fellow citizen Alexander with thirty horsemen and two thousand footsoldiers to Nabis under the pretense of sending him aid; they communicated the secret only to Alexander, and they obliged the others, under penalty of exile, to obey him in any and everything. Alexander went to Sparta and did not communicate his mission until he was ready to complete it; he therefore succeeded in killing Nabis. And so, these men, employing these methods, avoided the dangers risked in planning conspiracies; and anyone who imitates them will always avoid such dangers.

And, to show that anyone may do as they did, I give the example of Piso, cited above: Piso was a very great and renowned man, close to Nero, who greatly trusted him. Nero often went to his gardens to dine with him. Piso, then, was able to make friends with men of courage and spirit whose characters were suited to such a conspiracy (which is very easy for an important man). When Nero was in Piso's gardens, he could tell his friends the plan and, with the proper words, encourage them to undertake what they did not have the time to refuse and which could not fail to succeed. And thus, if we examine all the other conspiracies, few will be found that could not have been carried out in the same manner. But men are usually so deficient in understanding the ways of the world that they often commit the gravest of errors, and so much greater ones do they commit in those matters which are most extraordinary, as, for example, conspiracies. The conspiracy, then, should never be revealed until the moment of its execution; and if you must reveal it, do so to a single person with whom you have had long experience or who is motivated by the same causes as you are. To find one person like this is much easier than to find more than one, and because of this there is less danger in it; then, even if he does deceive you, there still remains the remedy of defending yourself—something which does not exist when there are many conspirators involved. I have overheard some prudent man say that to one person one can say anything—if you do not put it into writing—for the "yes" of one man is worth as much as the "no" of the other; and everyone should guard himself from writing as if from a reef, for there is nothing that can convict you more easily than your own handwriting. When Plautianus wanted to murder the Emperor Severus and Antoninus, his son, he entrusted the secret to the tribune Saturninus, who—wishing to accuse him and not obey him, yet fearing that if it came to an accusation Plautianus would be more likely to be believed than he would—asked Plautianus for a written order to validate this command. Plautianus, blinded by ambition, did so; whereupon he was accused by the tribune and was convicted; without that note and certain other evidence Plautianus would have emerged the winner, so audaciously did he deny the charges. Thus, against the accusation of a single man there is some defense, provided that you cannot be convicted by something in writing or other kinds of evidence; against such evidence one must guard oneself.

There was a woman in Piso's conspiracy named Epicharis, who had once been Nero's mistress. She thought it would be helpful to have among the conspirators a captain of some of the triremes Nero kept as his guard, so she told him about the conspiracy without naming the conspirators. Then, when that captain broke faith with her and accused her to Nero, the audacity of Epicharis was so great in her denials that Nero was confused and did not condemn her. In revealing the conspiracy to one person, therefore, there are two dangers: first, that he may accuse you directly, and, second, that he may accuse you after he is convicted and is forced to do so under torture, having been arrested because of suspicion or some sign of guilt he has betrayed. But from one and the other of these two dangers there is some recourse: the first accusation can be denied by citing the hatred that the man has for you, and the second can be denied by citing the torture used to make him tell lies. It is, therefore, prudent not to reveal the matter to anyone, but rather to act according to the examples given above; or if you do reveal it, do not go beyond one person, for even though there is some danger in this course of action, there is much less than in revealing it to many. Similar to this situation is one in which you are forced to do to the prince what you see that the prince would like to do to you—an emergency so great that it does not give you any time except to think of protecting yourself. This kind of urgency almost always brings the conspiracy to its desired end, and to prove this I need cite no more than two examples.

The Emperor Commodus had among his first and closest friends Laetus and Eclectus, the leaders of the Praetorian guards. And Marcia was among the first of his concubines or mistresses. Because he was often reproached by them for the manner in which he disgraced himself and his imperial office, he decided to have them killed, so he wrote out a list containing the names of Marcia, Laetus, and Eclectus, along with several others that he wanted to have killed the following night, and put the list under the pillow of his bed. After he had left the room to wash himself, one of his favorite young boys, who was playing around the bedchamber and on the bed, came upon the list; as he was leaving the bedchamber with the list in hand, he ran into Marcia, who took it from him. As soon as she read it and saw its contents, she immediately sent for Laetus and Eclectus; after all three realized the danger they were in, they decided to prevent it and without delay murdered Commodus that night.

The Emperor Antoninus Caracalla, who was stationed with his armies in Mesopotamia, had as his prefect Macrinus, a man more like a civilian than a soldier. Since evil rulers always fear others will act against them in a way that they themselves feel they deserve, Antoninus wrote to his friend Maternianus in Rome, asking him to learn from the astrologers if there was anyone who aspired to the empire and to let him know about it. Maternianus wrote him that Macrinus was the person who aspired to it; but the letter first fell into the hands of Macrinus, not the emperor; Macrinus, realizing the necessity of either killing him before a new letter came from Rome or of dying himself, commissioned Martial, his trusted centurion (whose brother had been put to death a few days earlier by Antoninus), to kill him. And Martial did so successfully. So it is clear that the emergency that allows no time produces almost the same effect as the method, mentioned above, that Nelematus of Epirus employed. What I stated near the beginning of this discourse is also clear—that threats do more harm to princes and are the cause of more effective conspiracies than injuries; a prince should guard himself against making threats, for men should either be befriended or the prince should secure himself against them and never reduce them to the point where they are obliged to think that either they must die or the prince must be killed.

As for the dangers risked during the execution of the conspiracy, these arise either from a change in the plan, a lack of courage on the part of the person who carries it out, an error he makes as a result of a lack of prudence, or from not bringing the matter to a perfect conclusion so that some of those whom he had planned to kill remain alive. Let me say, then, that nothing disturbs or impedes the actions of men more than to have to change a plan quickly, without sufficient time, and to modify it from what had been planned earlier. And if change creates confusion in anything, it does so especially in matters of war and in things similar to those of which we are speaking; for in such actions there is nothing more necessary than for men to resolve to accomplish the part assigned to them; and if men have focused their imaginations upon one method and one plan for many days and are suddenly required to change it, it is impossible for this not to upset everyone and to ruin everything. Thus, it is much better to carry out something according to the given plan, even when some inconvenience is seen in it, than to enter into a thousand inconveniences by trying to remove the problem. This applies whenever there is no time to replan, for when there is time a man can control things in his own way.

The conspiracy of the Pazzi against Lorenzo and Giuliano de' Medici is well known. The established plan was to serve a meal for the Cardinal of San Giorgio and to kill them at that meal. Certain men were assigned to kill them, others to seize the palace, and still others to run through the city proclaiming liberty to the people. It happened that when the Pazzi, the Medici, and the cardinal were in the cathedral church of Florence hearing a solemn service, it became known that Giuliano would not take breakfast with them that morning. This forced the conspirators to assemble; what they had planned to do in the Medici home they now decided to do in church. This changed the whole plan, and Giovambattista da Montesecco did not want to take part in the murder, declaring that he did not wish to do this in a church. In this way they had to entrust every deed to new agents, who, not having had time to prepare themselves, committed such errors that they were put down while carrying out the plan.

Failure of courage in carrying out a conspiracy results either from respect for the victim or from the assassin's personal cowardice. And the majesty and reverence that follows the presence of a prince is so great that it is a simple matter for it to weaken or terrify the assassin. When Marius was taken by the Minturnians, a slave was sent to kill him; terrified by the presence of that man and the memory of his name, the slave became cowardly and lost all power to kill him. And if this power resides in a man tied up in prison and overcome by bad fortune, how much more is it to be feared in a prince who is free, accompanied by the majesty of his office and the splendor of his followers! Such ceremony as this can frighten you or truly weaken you when accompanied by a pleasant greeting. Some men were conspiring against Sitalces, King of Thrace.[4] They decided on the day of execution, gathered together at the appointed place where the prince was, but none of them made a move to harm him. They departed without having attempted anything and without knowing what had prevented them, and each blamed the other. They fell into this error many times, so that when the conspiracy was discovered they suffered the penalty for the crime they could have committed but did not have the will to complete. Alfonso, Duke of Ferrara, had two brothers who conspired against him; they employed as their intermediary Giannes, a priest and the duke's cantor. At their request he often brought the duke among them so that they had the opportunity to kill him. Nevertheless, neither of them ever dared to do it, so that when they were discovered they suffered the punishment for their wickedness and lack of prudence. This negligence could not have come from anything else but the fact that the duke's presence frightened them or the kindness of this ruler humbled them. In such undertakings a difficulty or error arises either from a lack of prudence or a lack of courage, for when either of these two things possesses you, and you are carried away by confusion of the brain, you either say or do something that you should not.

And how men are possessed and confused cannot be better demonstrated than by Livy, where he describes Alexamenes the Aetolian when he wanted to kill Nabis the Spartan, of whom we have spoken above. When the

---

[4] Machiavelli may here have confused Sitalces with Cypselus, tyrant of Corinth.

time for the deed had arrived, and he had revealed to his
followers what had to be done, Livy says: "Even he had to
regain his courage, as he was disturbed by so serious an
act."[5] It is, indeed, impossible for anyone—even one who
is strong-minded and used to the killing of men, and familiar with the use of steel—not to be confused. Therefore, experienced men should be chosen for such
operations, and no others should be trusted, even if they
are reputed to be extremely brave. For where courage in
great undertakings is concerned, no one can promise a
certain outcome unless he has had experience in such
matters. This confusion, then, can make you drop the
weapons from your hands or make you say things that
produce the same effect. Lucilla, the sister of Commodus,
planned for Quintianus to kill the emperor. He waited for
Commodus at the entrance to the amphitheater, and,
drawing near him while holding a bare dagger, cried:
"The senate sends you this." These words caused him to
be arrested before he had brought down his arm to strike.
Messer Antonio da Volterra, chosen, as was mentioned
above, to kill Lorenzo de' Medici, while drawing near to
him shouted: "Ah, traitor!" This exclamation was the salvation of Lorenzo and the downfall of that conspiracy.

A conspiracy can fail to reach completion when it is
directed against one ruler, for the reasons already given,
but it can fail to reach completion more easily when it is
directed against two rulers. Indeed, this kind of conspiracy is so difficult that it is almost impossible for it to succeed, since to carry out two assassinations at the same
time in different places is almost impossible; yet two such
acts cannot be carried out at different times if the first is
not to spoil the second. Thus, if conspiring against one
prince is an uncertain thing, one that is dangerous and
imprudent, to conspire against two princes is completely
vain and foolhardy. And if it were not for the respect I
hold for the historian, I should never believe what Hero-

[5] Livy, XXXV, xxxv (cited by Machiavelli in Latin).

dian says of Plautianus to be possible; that is, when he says that Plautianus entrusted to the centurion Saturninus the charge that he alone should kill Severus and Antoninus, who lived in different places; for this matter is so far removed from what is reasonable that anyone other than this authority would not persuade me to believe it.

Certain young Athenians conspired against Diocles[6] and Hippias, tyrants of Athens; they murdered Diocles, but Hippias, who survived, avenged him. Chion and Leonidas of Heraclea, disciples of Plato, conspired against Clearchus and Satirus, who were tyrants; they killed Clearchus, but Satirus, who remained alive, avenged him. The Pazzi, whom we have cited many times, only succeeded in killing Giuliano. Thus, everyone should avoid similar conspiracies against more than one leader, for they do not benefit oneself, one's country, or anyone; on the contrary, the survivors who remain become more insufferable and harsher, as is well known to Florence, Athens, and Heraclea, which I mentioned previously. It is true that although the conspiracy Pelopidas organized to liberate Thebes, his native city, met with all these difficulties, it nevertheless had a most happy ending; for Pelopidas did not conspire against two tyrants but against ten, and not only was he not intimate with them, so that access to these tyrants was not easy for him, but he was also a rebel. Nevertheless, he was able to come into Thebes, murder the tyrants, and liberate his native city. However, he did all this with the aid of one Charon, adviser to the tyrants, from whom he obtained easy access for his undertaking. Despite this, no one should follow his example, for it was an impossible undertaking whose success was miraculous—it was so viewed by historians at that time, and still is, for they praise it as a rare thing almost without parallel. Such an action can be interrupted by a false suspicion or by an unforeseen accident occurring during the course of the execution. On the morning

[6] Hipparchus, not Diocles, ruled Athens with Hippias. Machiavelli here repeats an error found in Justin, his source.

when Brutus and the other conspirators decided to kill Caesar, it happened that Caesar was seen speaking at length to Gaius Pompilius Lenas, one of the conspirators; the others, observing this long conversation, were afraid that the said Pompilius had revealed the conspiracy to Caesar, so they decided they would kill Caesar right there and not wait for him to go to the senate; and they would have done so if, after the conversation was over, they had not been reassured by the fact that Caesar made no unusual move. These false suspicions are to be considered and prudently respected, so much the more so as they are easily aroused, for anyone who has a guilty conscience can easily be led to believe that people are talking about him. A word with another meaning is overheard which shakes your courage and makes you think it was said with respect to your plans. The result is that you either reveal the conspiracy yourself by fleeing or you confuse the undertaking by acting at the wrong time. And this occurs more easily when there are many people aware of the conspiracy.

As for accidents, since they are unexpected I can only demonstrate them by examples, in the hope of making men accordingly cautious. Luzio Belanti, of Siena, of whom we have made mention earlier, because of the anger he felt against Pandolfo, who had taken away from him the daughter he had earlier given him as his wife, decided to kill him and chose his time as follows: Pandolfo went almost every day to visit one of his sick relatives. On the way he would pass Luzio's home. Hence, when Luzio saw this, he planned to have his conspirators in the house, ready to kill Pandolfo on command when he passed. They were all armed and placed inside the entrance; Luzio put one conspirator at the window, so that when Pandolfo passed by he could make a sign to indicate that he was approaching. It happened that as Pandolfo approached and the man had given the sign, Pandolfo encountered a friend, who stopped him, and some of those who were with him continued to walk ahead. Hearing the noise made by the weapons, they uncovered the ambush. In this way Pandolfo was saved while Luzio and the conspirators were forced to flee from Siena. This accidental meeting prevented that action and made Luzio fail in his undertaking. Since they are rare, no remedy can be provided against such accidents. It is, nevertheless, still essential to study all the possibilities that may arise and to guard against them.

There now only remains for us to discuss the dangers incurred after the execution, and these amount only to one—that is, when someone remains to avenge the dead prince. Those remaining can be his brothers, his sons, or other supporters in a position to inherit the principality. Either because of your negligence or for the reasons given above, there may remain those who will undertake this vendetta. This happened to Giovanni Andrea da Lampognano, who, together with his co conspirators, killed the Duke of Milan; but since they left the duke's son and two of his brothers alive, in time the latter avenged the dead man. And truly, in such instances the conspirators are to be excused, for they have no other remedy; but when someone is left alive because of their lack of prudence or negligence, then they deserve no excuse. Some conspirators from Forlì killed Count Girolamo, their lord, and took his wife and small children. Since they felt they could not live securely unless they had command of the fortress—and the castellan would not surrender it to them—Madonna Caterina, as the countess was called, promised the conspirators that if they allowed her to go into the fortress she would deliver it up to them and they could keep her children as hostages. With this promise, they allowed her to enter the place; when she was inside, she reproached them for the death of her husband and threatened them with every kind of revenge. And to show that she had no concern for her children, she showed them her genitals, declaring that she still had the means to produce more offspring. Thus, the conspirators, lacking a plan and realizing their error too late, paid the penalty for their lack of prudence in the form of perpetual exile. But of all the dangers that can arise after the execution of a conspiracy, there is none more certain nor more to be feared than when the people have loved the prince you have killed: against this danger conspirators have no remedy whatsoever and can never secure themselves. As an example there is Caesar, whose death was avenged by the Roman people, who loved him. The reason why the conspirators, subsequently driven out of Rome, were all killed at various times and in various places stems from this fact.

Conspiracies against one's own city are less dangerous for those who undertake them than are those against princes because in organizing the former there are fewer dangers and in carrying them out there are only the same dangers; and after the execution there is no danger at all. In organizing them there are not many dangers, for a citizen can prepare himself for the acquisition of power without revealing his intention and plan to anyone. If these plans of his are not interrupted, his undertaking can be carried out successfully; but if his plans should be interrupted by some law, he can wait and try another way. This, let it be understood, applies to a republic where some corruption already exists, for in one which is not corrupted, where no evil has taken root, these thoughts cannot occur to one of its citizens. Thus, the citizens can aspire to the principality through many ways and means without undergoing the danger of being suppressed, both because republics are slower and less careful than princes and because they have more respect for their important citizens; such men, therefore, are bolder and more courageous in acting against them. Everyone who has read about the conspiracy of Catiline, which Sallust described, will remember how, after the conspiracy was discovered, Catiline not only remained in Rome but went to the senate and spoke offensively both to it and to the consul—so great was the respect that this city had for her citizens. And after he had left Rome and was already with his armies, Lentulus and those others would not have been arrested if there had not been letters in their own handwriting that clearly implicated them. Hanno, a very important citizen of Carthage who aspired to the tyranny, planned to poison the entire senate during the wedding of one of his daughters and then to make himself prince. When this became known, the senate did nothing except pass a law that limited the expenses of banquets and weddings—so great was the respect it had for this man's qualities. It is certainly true that in carrying out a conspiracy against one's own city there are more and greater difficulties because rarely do your own forces suffice in conspiring against so many; and everyone is not the leader of an army, as was Caesar or Agathocles or Cleomenes, and men like them, who, with a single blow and with their own forces, occupied their native cities. For men such as these, the way is most easy and secure, but others who do not possess so many additional forces must do things either through deception and ingenuity or with foreign troops. As for deceit and ingenuity, when Pisistratus the Athenian had defeated the inhabitants of Megara and had, as a result, won the favor of the people, he went outside one morning, wounded, declaring that the nobility had injured him out of envy and he asked to have armed men with him as a bodyguard. With this authority, he easily rose to such greatness that he became tyrant of Athens. Pandolfo Petrucci returned with other exiles to Siena, and he was entrusted with the guardianship of the public square, something the others refused as a thing of little importance; nevertheless, in time his armed guards gave him such a reputation that in a short while he became prince of the city. Many others, using other plans and methods, have, in the course of time and with danger, achieved their goal. Those who have conspired to occupy their native city with their own forces or with foreign armies have experienced different results, depending on Fortune. The previously cited Catiline was ruined in this way. Hanno, of whom we made mention above, when the poison did not succeed, armed his partisans, who numbered many thousands, and both he and they were killed. Some of the first citizens of Thebes called to their aid a Spartan army in order to make themselves tyrants, and the Spartans seized the tyranny of that city. Thus, when all the conspiracies directed against one's own city are examined, you will find few if any that were suppressed at the stage of being organized, but all either succeeded or failed while being carried out. After they are carried out, no dangers are involved other than those inherent in the nature of the principality itself, for when a man has become a tyrant he experiences the natural and routine dangers that tyranny brings upon him, against which he has no other remedies than those discussed above.

This is as much as I intend to write about conspiracies, and if I have discussed those which are carried out with steel and not with poison, this comes from the fact that they are all subject to the same laws. It is true that those which make use of poison are more dangerous because they are more uncertain, for everyone does not have the means, and it is necessary to entrust them to those who do, and this necessity of depending upon others makes it dangerous for you. Then again, a drink of poison may not be fatal for many reasons, as happened to those who killed Commodus; for after he had vomited the poison that they had administered to him, they were forced to strangle him to kill him. Princes, therefore, have no greater enemy than a conspiracy, for when a conspiracy against them is carried out, it either kills them or disgraces them: if it succeeds they die; if it is uncovered and they kill the conspirators, it is always believed that the plot was an invention of that prince to give vent to his avarice and his cruelty against the lives and property of those whom he had put to death. I do not wish, however, to fail to warn that prince or that republic against whom a conspiracy is organized to take this precaution: when a conspiracy is uncovered, before deciding to avenge it they should seek to understand very well its characteristics and measure carefully the conditions of the conspirators as well as their own; and when they find the plotters to be great and powerful, they should never reveal the conspiracy to the public until they are prepared to suppress it with sufficient force—doing otherwise would result in their downfall. Hence, with all their skill, they should pretend to know nothing, for when the conspirators see that they are discovered they will act without hesitation, driven by necessity. An example is provided by the Romans: after they left two legions of soldiers to guard the Capuans against the Samnites, as we have said elsewhere, the leaders of these legions conspired to subjugate the Capuans. When this became known in Rome, the Romans sent Rutilius, the new consul, to prevent this from happening. In order to lull the conspirators to sleep, he spread the news that the senate had confirmed the assignments of the Capuan legions. Believing this to be true, these soldiers thought they had time to carry out their plan and did not try to hasten the matter; and so, they remained unaware until they began to realize that the consul was separating one legion from the other, and this aroused their suspicion and caused them to reveal and to implement their plans. There cannot be a better example than this on either side, for it shows how slow men are in matters when they believe they have time and how swift they are when necessity drives them to it. Nor can a prince or a republic that wishes to put off the uncovering of a conspiracy to his or its advantage employ a better method than to offer guilefully an opportunity in the near future to the conspirators so that in waiting for that moment they will think they have time, whereas they are actually giving that prince or republic time to punish them. Anyone who does otherwise hastens his downfall, as did the Duke of Athens and Guglielmo de' Pazzi. After the duke had become tyrant of Florence and had learned that he was being conspired against, without studying the matter carefully, he had one of the conspirators seized. This immediately caused the others to take up arms and seize the state from him. When, in 1501, Guglielmo was commissioner in the Valdichiana, he had heard that there was a conspiracy in Arezzo favoring the Vitelli to take away that city from the Florentines. He immediately went to that city and, without considering either his own forces or those of the conspirators, and without preparing himself with any force, he had one of the conspirators seized on the advice of his son, the bishop. Following this arrest, the others immediately took up arms and wrested the city away from the Florentines, and Guglielmo the commissioner became a prisoner. But when conspiracies are weak, they can and should be suppressed without hesitation.

Two methods have been used but should never be imitated in any way: the one used by the aforementioned Duke of Athens, who, in order to show that he felt he enjoyed the goodwill of the Florentine citizens, put to death a man who revealed a conspiracy to him; the other followed by Dion of Syracuse, who, in order to test the intentions of someone he suspected, allowed Callippus, whom he trusted, to pretend to organize a conspiracy against him. Both of these rulers ended badly: the first discouraged informants and encouraged those who wanted to conspire, while the other provided an easy road to his death, or, rather, was himself the actual head of his own conspiracy—the event proved that Callippus, able to conspire against Dion without opposition, did so with such success that he deprived his master of his state and his life.

CHAPTER VII. HOW REVOLUTIONS FROM FREEDOM TO SLAVERY AND FROM SLAVERY TO FREEDOM SOMETIMES OCCUR WITHOUT BLOODSHED WHILE AT OTHER TIMES THEY ABOUND IN IT

[The outcome of such revolutions depends upon whether or not they take place by violent means, for when they are accompanied by violence many people are inevitably hurt. If, however, they occur with the common consent of the people, there is no reason to harm anyone other than the heads of these governments. Change without bloodshed occurred with the expulsion of the Tarquins, or the expulsion of the Medici from Florence in 1494. Revolutionary changes in governments brought about by men who seek vengeance, however, are bound to be bloody.]

CHAPTER VIII.   ANYONE DESIRING TO CHANGE THE GOVERNMENT OF A REPUBLIC SHOULD CONSIDER ITS SUBJECTS

[An evil citizen can do little harm in a republic that is not yet corrupt, as can be seen from Roman history in the examples of Spurius Cassius and Manlius Capitolinus. Such men must, if they wish to come to power, employ means in a corrupt city which differ from those necessary in one that is not yet corrupt. Manlius would have succeeded if he had applied his methods during the more corrupt times of Marius or Sulla. Therefore, if a man wishes to seize power in a republic and impose upon it an evil form of government, he must do so after a period of gradual corruption has set in; such a period of gradual decay will inevitably occur if some man of exceptional ability does not restore the government to its original principles at some time. Thus, before attempting an alteration in the government of a republic, a man should consider the nature of its citizens.]

CHAPTER IX.   HOW IT IS NECESSARY TO CHANGE WITH THE TIMES IN ORDER ALWAYS TO ENJOY GOOD FORTUNE

I have often observed that the reason for the bad as well as good fortune of men is to be found in the way in which their way of working fits the times: for it is clear that in their actions some men proceed with impetuosity, others with care and caution. And since men go beyond the proper limits in both these methods, they make errors in both, not being able to follow the true path. But that man whose method of procedure, as I have said, fits the times makes fewer mistakes and enjoys a prosperous fortune, for you always act as Nature inclines you. Everyone knows how Fabius Maximus proceeded carefully and cautiously with his army, refraining from every act of impetuosity or Roman boldness, and good fortune caused this method of his to fit well with the times. At the time Hannibal came into Italy as a young man with fresh fortune, having already twice defeated the Roman people, and while that republic was almost totally deprived of her good soldiers and was terrified, no better fortune could arise for her than to have a general who, with his hesitation and caution, might delay the enemy. Nor could Fabius have found times more suitable to his methods, which caused him to become famous. And that Fabius did this naturally and not by choice is evident, for when Scipio wished to cross over into Africa with his armies to end the war, Fabius spoke out against it, as a man who was unable to give up his methods and his practices. In fact, if it had been left to him, Hannibal would still be in Italy, for Fabius was a man who did not understand that the times had changed and that it was also necessary to change the methods of warfare. And if Fabius had been king of Rome, he could have easily lost that war, for he would not have known how to change his ways to suit the times; however, since he was born in a republic where there were different citizens and different opinions, just as Rome once had Fabius as the best leader in times requiring that the war be drawn out, so later she had Scipio in times suitable for winning it.

Therefore, the truth is that a republic is of longer duration and has a much better fortune than a principality, for a republic, by virtue of its diverse citizenry, can better accommodate itself to the changeability of conditions than can a prince. For, as I have said, a man who is used to acting in one way never changes; he must come to ruin when the times, in changing, no longer are in harmony with his ways.

Piero Soderini, cited on other occasions, proceeded in

all his affairs with humanity and patience. He and his native city prospered when the times were in harmony with his way of acting; but later, when the time came for him to put aside his patience and humility, he did not know how to do so, and the result was that, together with his native city, he came to ruin. Pope Julius II proceeded with impetuosity and haste throughout the entire span of his pontificate; and because the times went along with him every one of his undertakings succeeded. But if other times requiring different methods had come, he would have necessarily come to ruin, for he could not have changed either his method or his way of governing. And there are two reasons why we cannot change ourselves: first, because we cannot oppose the ways in which Nature inclines us; second, because once a man has truly prospered by means of one method of procedure it is impossible to convince him that he can benefit by acting otherwise. As a result, it happens that Fortune varies for a single man, for she changes the times while he does not change his ways. The downfall of cities also arises from this fact, for republics do not modify their methods with the times (as we have discussed above at length); rather, they are slow since it is more difficult for them to change. For change results from times in which the entire republic is shaken; and for this to occur, it is not sufficient for one man alone to modify his method of procedure.

And since we have mentioned Fabius Maximus, who kept Hannibal at bay, it seems appropriate for me to discuss, in the following chapter, whether a general eager to give battle to the enemy at any cost can be prevented from doing so by the enemy.

CHAPTER X. A COMMANDER CANNOT AVOID A BATTLE WHEN HIS ADVERSARY WISHES TO FIGHT AT ANY COST

[If there has been a departure from ancient practices in modern times, this departure is most notable in military

matters. This is because most princes and republics entrust these affairs to others; and when they do order a
commander to the field, they tell him to avoid battle at all
costs, thinking to imitate, in this fashion, the policies of
Fabius Maximus, who saved Rome from the Carthaginians. But this is wrong, for if the enemy is determined to
fight, a field commander cannot avoid it; and so, to avoid
battle at all costs really means to fight on the enemy's
terms. In any case, it would be more accurate to say that
Fabius Maximus, when he enjoyed an advantage, preferred to fight rather than to hesitate. Many examples
from the campaigns of Hannibal, Scipio, and Gaius Sul-
picius underline the truth of this position.]

CHAPTER XI.   ONE WHO MUST FIGHT MANY ENEMIES, AL-
THOUGH HE MAY BE INFERIOR TO THEM, MAY STILL WIN IF
ONLY HE STANDS UP TO THE FIRST ONSLAUGHTS

[A single power, although weaker than the sum of its enemies, may still be able to emerge victorious if it is able to
break up the coalition. Numerous examples from present times will bear out the truth of this proposition; for
example, the Italian alliance against Venice in 1483 eventually resulted in an improvement of the Venetian position. The same thing occurred a few years ago when all of
Europe formed an alliance against France; as a result of
the defection of Spain, however, all of the allies were
forced to come to terms with France. The crucial factor
here is the ability to withstand the first onslaughts of such
a confederated attack; if this is done, some means can
eventually be found to weaken the coalition and to
achieve eventual victory.]

CHAPTER XII.   HOW A PRUDENT COMMANDER IMPOSES
EVERY NECESSITY OF FIGHTING UPON HIS OWN SOLDIERS
BUT DOES NOT DO SO TO THE ENEMY

[Necessity plays a great role in human affairs and may
lead men to glorious achievements. Thus, a prudent com

mander may leave an escape route open to his enemy while closing such an avenue to his own troops. When attacking a city, a commander should dispel all reason for an obstinate defense on the part of its citizens, promising them a pardon if they fear punishment and, if they fear the loss of their freedom, insisting that the attack is aimed only at a few of their number. Roman history is full of examples of enemy soldiers fighting more bravely and to greater effect once all means of escape were cut off; for necessity, as Livy notes, is the last and best of weapons.]

CHAPTER XIII.   ON WHICH IS MORE TRUSTWORTHY: A GOOD COMMANDER WITH A WEAK ARMY, OR A GOOD ARMY WITH A WEAK COMMANDER

[Since there are many instances in which the ability of troops has saved the day while in others, the ability of the commander has done so, it must be concluded that one has need of the other. According to Julius Caesar, neither a good army poorly commanded nor a poor commander with good soldiers is worth much. Whether it is easier for a good army to make a good commander, or vice versa, it is obvious that many men can select one good man more easily that a single man can select many good men. Commanders who have had not only to defeat the enemy but also to train their own soldiers display a twofold ability and deserve twice as much glory.]

CHAPTER XIV.   WHAT EFFECTS ARE PRODUCED BY NEW INVENTIONS THAT APPEAR OR NEW SOUNDS THAT ARE HEARD IN THE MIDST OF BATTLE

[Such occurrences have a great effect upon a well-trained army and are even more effective in one without discipline. Good discipline is absolutely essential in warfare, so that small rumors, cries, or disturbances do not cause your troops to flee.]

CHAPTER XV. ONE MAN, AND NOT MANY, SHOULD BE
MADE COMMANDER OF AN ARMY; AND HOW A NUMBER OF
COMMANDERS CAN BE HARMFUL

[Numerous ancient and modern examples prove the
harmful effects of dividing a military command among
many men. The Romans·learned the evil results of such a
policy, but this mistake is still the cause of most of the
military disasters that have befallen French and Italian
armies in our times. Rather than improving the quality of
command, sending more than just one above-average
commander to the field only produces confusion and is
less beneficial than sending a single commander of only
average ability.]

CHAPTER XVI. TRUE ABILITY IS SOUGHT IN DIFFICULT
TIMES; IN EASY TIMES MEN WITH WEALTH OR FAMILY
CONNECTIONS, NOT ABLE MEN, ARE MOST POPULAR

It always was and always will be the case that great and
exceptional men are neglected in a republic during times
of peace; because of the envy the reputation arising from
their ability creates, there are many citizens in such times
who wish to be not just their equals but their superiors.
There is a good passage about this in Thucydides, the
Greek historian, who shows that when the Athenian republic had gained the upper hand in the Peloponnesian
War and had checked the pride of the Spartans, subjugating almost all the rest of Greece, she gained so much
renown that she planned to seize Sicily. This undertaking
came under debate in Athens. Alcibiades and some other
citizens argued in favor of the plan, for they gave less
thought to the public welfare than to their own reputation
(since they planned to be the leaders of such an undertaking). But Nicias, who was one of the most famous men of
Athens, advised against it. In addressing the people, the
best reason he brought forward to persuade them to trust
him was this: that in advising them not to wage this war,

he was advising them in a matter that was not in his own interest, for with Athens at peace he realized that there were countless citizens who wanted to get ahead of him, but if they waged war he knew that no citizen would be superior or even equal to him.

It is evident, then, that in republics the people have little esteem for their able men in times of tranquillity. This causes such men to feel indignant on two counts: first, they see themselves as not having reached their proper rank; second, they see themselves in the company of associates and superiors who are unworthy men and men of less ability than they. This disorder in republics has brought about many downfalls. The citizens, feeling that they have been undeservedly rebuffed and recognizing that the reason for this lies in the fact there is peace and not turmoil, set about to stir up the times by instigating new wars to the detriment of the republic. Considering the possible remedies for this, I find that there are two: first, keeping the citizens poor so that they cannot corrupt either themselves or others with riches; second, organizing oneself in such a way that one can always wage war and, as a consequence, there will always be need of reputable citizens—which was the Roman practice. Because that city always maintained armies in the field, there was always a need for able men; hence, she could not take away a rank from one who deserved it and give it to one who did not; if Rome sometimes did this by mistake or as a test, the immediate consequence was such disorder and such danger that she quickly returned to the true way. But other republics which are not organized as she was and only wage war when necessity requires it cannot defend themselves from such a problem; on the contrary, they will always encounter it and disorder will always arise from it, especially when the neglected and able citizen is vengeful and has some reputation and following in his city. Rome had protected herself against this at one time; but when she conquered Carthage and Antiochus (as was described elsewhere) and no longer feared wars, she, too, ceased to pay as much attention to ability as to the other qualities which gain favor with the people, believing that she could entrust her armies to whomever she wished. We see that Paulus Emilius was frequently defeated for the consulship, nor was he made consul before the Macedonian War broke out; but since this was judged a dangerous war, it was entrusted to his care by the entire city.

After 1494, in our city of Florence, when there had been many wars in which the Florentine citizens had made a bad showing, the city chanced upon a man who demonstrated how one ought to command armies. He was Antonio Giacomini. So long as dangerous wars had to be waged, the ambition of the other citizens abated; in the election of the commissioner and the leader of the armies he had no competitor whatsoever. But when a war was to be waged wherein the outcome was in no doubt and there was promise of very great honor and high rank, then he discovered so many competitors that when three commissioners had to be chosen to attack Pisa he was left out. Although it is not immediately evident that failing to send Antonio resulted in harm to the republic, nevertheless, it can easily be conjectured; since the Pisans no longer had anything to defend themselves with or to live on, if Antonio had been present they would have been so tightly squeezed that they would have surrendered themselves to the Florentines' discretion. But since they were besieged by generals who knew neither how to blockade them nor how to attack them with force, they held out for so long that Florence finally had to buy them off where she could have taken them by force. It was likely that such disdain for Antonio might have affected him greatly; he must have been very patient and good not to want to take revenge for it—either through the downfall of the city, if he could bring it about, or through the injury of some individual citizens. A republic ought to guard itself against this, as will be discussed in the following chapter.

CHAPTER XVII. A MAN SHOULD NOT BE OFFENDED AND THEN ASSIGNED TO AN IMPORTANT GOVERNMENTAL POST

[Men who have been offended sometimes attempt to use another governmental post to make up for their previous experiences, as Claudius Nero did when he attacked Hasdrubal in Italy after being reviled for failing to defeat him in Spain, thereby risking his army in a dangerous engagement which he was lucky to win. If such a great man was aroused to such lengths by offenses during a time when Rome was still free from corruption, one can well imagine what others in corrupt cities would attempt. Since it is impossible to foresee all such dangers to a republic, it would be impossible to design one that would last forever.]

CHAPTER XVIII. NOTHING IS MORE WORTHY OF A COMMANDER THAN FORESEEING THE PLANS OF THE ENEMY

[Military matters are difficult to understand, for it is hard to understand or foresee the enemy's plans, actions, or even if and when a battle is won or lost.]

CHAPTER XIX. WHETHER INDULGENCE OR PUNISHMENT IS MORE NECESSARY IN CONTROLLING A MULTITUDE

The Roman republic was disturbed by the enmities of the nobles and the plebeians; nevertheless, when war was upon them they sent forth their armies with Quintius and Appius Claudius in command. Since Appius was cruel and harsh, his troops obeyed him so badly that, on the brink of defeat, he fled from his province. Quintius, on the other hand, was kind and humane; he was obeyed by his soldiers and carried off the victory. Thus, it seems that it is better in controlling a multitude to be humane rather than arrogant, merciful rather than cruel. Nonetheless, Cornelius Tacitus, with whom many other writers agree, arrives at the opposite conclusion in one of his maxims when he says: "In governing a multitude, punishment is more valuable than indulgence."[1] And in considering how both of these opinions can be maintained, let me say that you either have to rule men who are usually your companions or men who are always your inferiors. When they are your companions, punishment simply cannot be used, nor that severity described by Tacitus; and because the Roman plebeians had authority in Rome equal to that of the nobility, a man who became ruler for a limited period of time could not control them with cruelty and harshness. And it is clear that those Roman captains who made themselves loved by their armies and who managed them with indulgence frequently achieved better results than those who made themselves extraordinarily feared—unless they were endowed with exceptional ability, as was Manlius Torquatus. But if you command subjects such as those Tacitus describes, you must lean toward punishment rather than indulgence if they are not to become insolent and tread on you because of your excessive kindness to them. But this, too, must be moderated in a way that does not arouse hatred; for making oneself hated benefits no prince. The way to avoid this is to leave the property of subjects alone. No prince is eager to spill blood except when he is driven to do so by necessity, unless he does so to hide his greed, and this necessity seldom arises. But when this eagerness is combined with greed, the necessity always appears, and a reason is never lacking to do away with these subjects, as was discussed at length in another treatise.[2] Quintius, therefore, deserved more praise than Appius, and the maxim of Tacitus deserves to be approved within its limits and not in the instances experienced by Appius.

And because I have discussed punishment and indulgence, it does not seem superfluous to demonstrate how

[1] *Annals*, III, lv (cited by Machiavelli in the original Latin).
[2] *The Prince*, XVII.

an act of kindness toward the Faliscians could accomplish more than weapons.

CHAPTER XX. ONE EXAMPLE OF KINDNESS MADE A GREATER IMPRESSION ON THE FALISCIANS THAN DID ALL OF ROME'S FORCE

[When Camillus refused the offer of a group of the city's most noble youths, an offer made to him by the schoolmaster of the city he was about to capture, the inhabitants were so impressed by his kindness that they decided to surrender to him, proving that violence can sometimes accomplish less than humane actions. Xenophon shows how much esteem Cyrus gained by such actions, while Hannibal gained fame and victory through opposite methods, as the next chapter will show.]

CHAPTER XXI. HOW IT CAME ABOUT THAT HANNIBAL, WHOSE METHOD OF PROCEDURE WAS DIFFERENT FROM SCIPIO'S, ACHIEVED THE SAME RESULTS IN ITALY THAT SCIPIO ACHIEVED IN SPAIN

I believe that some people will be amazed to see how some generals, though they led different kinds of lives, have nevertheless achieved results similar to those who have lived in the manner described above. It is thus clear that the causes of their victories are not dependent upon the previously mentioned causes. On the contrary, it appears that these methods do not bring you more power or Fortune if contrary methods can enable you to acquire glory and fame. In order not to pass over the above-mentioned men and to clarify what I am trying to say, let me point out that when Scipio entered Spain, with that kindness and compassion of his he quickly made the province his friend, and he was adored and admired by its people. On the other hand, when Hannibal entered Italy by means of completely opposite methods—that is, with cruelty, violence, plundering, and every sort of perfidy—he achieved the same result Scipio had achieved in Spain, for all the cities of Italy revolted in his favor and all its people followed him.

And in considering what might have caused this, there could be a number of reasons. The first is that men desire novelty to such an extent that those who are doing well wish for change as much as those who are doing badly; for, as was mentioned earlier—and it is true—men become bored in good times and complain in bad ones. This desire, then, opens the gates to anyone who puts himself at the head of some innovation in a province: if he is a foreigner, everyone runs to follow him; if he is a native, they crowd around him, increase his strength, and grant him their favor to such an extent that in whatever manner he proceeds he succeeds in making great progress in those places. Besides this, men are driven by two major impulses: either by love or by fear. And so, people can be commanded by someone who makes himself loved just as easily as they can be led by someone who makes himself feared; but in most cases a man who makes himself feared is better followed and more readily obeyed than one who makes himself loved.

And so, it is of little importance which of these roads a general chooses to travel as long as he is an able man and his ability gives him a reputation among the people. When his ability is great, as it was with Hannibal and Scipio, it cancels all those errors he made while making himself either loved or feared too much. From both of these methods great difficulties can arise that can bring about the downfall of a prince, for anyone who wishes to be loved too much becomes hated every time he deviates from the true path, and anyone who wishes to be feared too much becomes hated every time he exceeds the norm. And to keep within a middle course is not possible precisely because our nature does not allow us to do so; one who oversteps the middle course must atone for his excess with a great amount of ability, as Hannibal and Scipio did. Nevertheless, it is evident that although both men were harmed by their way of acting, at the same time their reputations were also enhanced.

I have already mentioned the heights to which both these men were raised. The harm that came to Scipio in Spain was that his soldiers rebelled against him, together with part of his allies, a matter which arose from nothing other than the fact that he was not feared. For men are so restless that as soon as the smallest door is opened to their ambition, they immediately forget all the love they give their prince, who had shown them such kindness—as did these soldiers and allies I just mentioned, to such an extent that in order to remedy this problem Scipio was forced to employ some of the cruelty he had always avoided. As for Hannibal, there is no particular instance where his cruelty and his lack of faith caused him harm; but it can safely be said that Naples and many other cities that remained faithful to the Roman people did so out of fear of his particular qualities. It is certainly clear that his merciless manner made him more hated by the Roman people than any other enemy Rome ever had. And while Pyrrhus was in Italy with his army, the Romans pointed out to him the man who wanted to poison him, but they never forgave Hannibal, even when he was disarmed and exiled, and in the end they brought about his death. These difficulties came to Hannibal, then, because he was reputed to be merciless, perfidious, and cruel; but, on the other hand, this also resulted in a great advantage for him, for because of this he was admired by all historians: there never arose in his army, although it was made up of different kinds of men, any dissension among the men or against himself. This could not have come from anything other than the terror his character inspired, for it was so great that when it was combined with the reputation his ability had earned him, it kept his soldiers quiet and united.

I conclude, then, that it is of little importance which method a general practices, provided that he possess enough ability to provide a good seasoning to either one of the two ways of behaving. As I have said, there are defects and dangers in both ways when they are not corrected by an extraordinary ability. If Hannibal and Scipio achieved the same result—the one with praiseworthy deeds and the other with detestable ones—it seems to me that a discussion of two Roman citizens who attained the same glory by both different and praiseworthy means should not be omitted.

CHAPTER XXII.   HOW THE HARSHNESS OF MANLIUS TOR-
QUATUS AND THE KINDNESS OF VALERIUS CORVINUS
EARNED THE SAME GLORY FOR EACH MAN

There were two excellent generals living in Rome at the same time: Manlius Torquatus and Valerius Corvinus, equal in ability, victories, and fame, and each had acquired his reputation with equal skill insofar as facing the enemy was concerned. But as for managing armies and soldiers, they differed drastically in their methods: Manlius commanded his men with all severity, never permitting them any pause in their labor or fatigue; Valerius, on the other hand, treated them pleasantly, with every form and manner of human kindness and intimate friendliness. We see that in order to obtain the obedience of his soldiers one killed his son while the other never harmed anyone; nevertheless, in using such different methods each achieved the same result, both against their enemies and in favor of the republic and themselves. For no soldier ever refused to fight, rebelled, or acted in any way contrary to their wishes, although the commands of Manlius were so harsh that all commands that went beyond the normal measure were called "Manlian commands."

Here we should consider: first, what obliged Manlius to act in such a rigid manner?; second, why was Valerius able to act so kindly?; third, how did these different methods produce the same result?; and finally, which of them is best and most useful to imitate? If one carefully examines the nature of Manlius from the time Livy first mentions him, he will find him a most powerful man, respectful toward his father and his country and most respectful to his superiors. These things are clear from the killing of the Gaul, the defense of his father against the tribune, and from what he said to the consul before he went to fight the Gaul: "Without your order, I shall never fight the enemy, even if I see a certain victory."[1] So, when a man such as this comes into command, he wants to find all men like himself; his strong spirit makes him give strong orders, and that same spirit wants his commands to be obeyed once they are given. And it is a very sound rule that whenever harsh orders are given it is necessary to be harsh in having them executed; otherwise you will find yourself deceived. That is to say, if you want to be obeyed you must know how to give orders; for those men who know how to command will compare their qualities with those who have to obey, and when they see a correspondence there they will then give orders, but when they see a lack of correspondence, they will refrain from commanding.

Therefore, a prudent man has said that in order to hold a republic with force there must be a correspondence between the man who exerts the force and those against whom this force is applied; whenever this proportion exists, it can be believed that this force will last, but when the man subject to the force is more powerful than the man who employs it, we can assume that this force will end at any day.

But, to return to our topic, let me say that to order strong measures it is necessary to be strong; and the man who possesses this strength and orders these measures cannot then have them obeyed with softness. But anyone who does not possess this strength of spirit ought to guard against unusual commands; he may employ his kindness in normal commands, for normal punishments are not

[1] Livy, VII, x (cited by Machiavelli in the original Latin).

blamed upon the commander but rather upon the laws and their institutions. We should believe, then, that Manlius was obliged to proceed so rigidly by the extraordinary character of his orders, to which his nature inclined him; such orders are useful in a republic, for they lead its institutions back to their beginnings and their ancient vigor. And if a republic were fortunate enough to have, as we said above, someone who could renew her laws by means of his example, who would not only keep her from running to her ruin but would pull her back from it, such a state would endure forever. Thus, Manlius was one of those who maintained military discipline in Rome with the severity of his orders; he was obliged to first by his nature and then by his desire that what his natural inclination made him do should be put into effect. Valerius, on the other hand, was able to act humanely, like a man to whom the observance of the things usually observed in Roman armies was enough. Because this was a good practice, it was sufficient to bring him honor, for it was not difficult to observe and did not oblige Valerius to punish the transgressor, both because there were none and because if there had been any, they would have blamed their punishment, as was mentioned, upon the institutions and not upon the cruelty of the commander. In this way Valerius was able to show every kind act as having come from himself, as a result of which he gained the gratitude of the soldiers and made them happy. Thus, since both commanders possessed the same authority, they were able to achieve the same result by acting in different ways. Those who might wish to imitate them could fall into the vices of contempt and hatred, both of which I described above in discussing Hannibal and Scipio—something that can only be avoided if you possess unusual ability.

It remains now to consider which of these two methods is the more praiseworthy. This is open to dispute, for writers praise both methods; nevertheless, those who write about how a prince should act favor Valerius more than

Manlius. In giving many examples of the humanity of Cyrus, Xenophon (cited previously) agrees closely with what Livy says about Valerius. For when Valerius was made consul in the war against the Samnites and the day of battle came, he spoke to his soldiers with the same kindness he had always practiced. Concerning this speech Livy has this to say: "Never was a commander more friendly with his soldiers, since he did not hesitate to carry out his duties among the soldiers of the lowest ranks without complaining. Also, in military games, when equals competed as equals in contests of speed or in tests of strength, he won or lost with the same kind attitude, nor was anyone ever despised who presented himself as an equal; he was kind in his actions when the circumstances permitted; and in conversation he was no less mindful of the freedom of others than of his own dignity; and he exercised his command (and nothing was more popular) with the same skills with which he had acquired it."[2] Livy speaks honorably of Manlius in the same manner, demonstrating that his severity in the matter of the death of his son made the army so much more obedient to the consul that it resulted in a victory for the Roman people against the Latins. He goes so far in praising him that, after reporting such a victory, having described the complete order of the battle and pointed out all the risks the Roman people ran and the difficulties they encountered in winning it, he draws this conclusion: only the ability of Manlius gave the victory to the Romans. And in a comparison of the forces of both armies, he affirms that the side which had Manlius as consul would have conquered. Therefore, considering everything the historians have said about these men, it would be difficult to choose between them. Nevertheless, so as not to leave this question undecided, let me say that for a citizen who lives under the laws of a republic, I believe the procedure of Manlius to

[2] Livy, VII, xxxiii (cited by Machiavelli in the original Latin).

be more praiseworthy and less dangerous. This method works entirely for the well-being of the public and in no way involves private ambition, for a man cannot acquire partisans by such a method since he always shows himself to be stern toward everyone and to love only the common good. And by acting this way he acquires no special friends (what we call partisans, as was mentioned above). No other method of proceeding can be more useful or more desirable in a republic, for it is not lacking in public benefit and there can be in it no suspicion of private power. But in the method used by Valerius the contrary happens: though it is true that this method produced the same results insofar as the public is concerned, nevertheless, many doubts arise from it because of the particular goodwill that the man acquires among his soldiers, which might produce bad results contrary to freedom in a long period of rule.

And if these bad effects did not arise with Publicola, the reason for this was that Roman spirits were not yet corrupted and he had not ruled continuously for a long enough time. But if we have to consider a prince, as Xenophon did, we should follow faithfully the example of Valerius and abandon that of Manlius; for a prince ought to seek obedience and love in his soldiers and subjects. Observing the institutions and being considered skillful bring him obedience; affability, kindness, mercy, and the other qualities Valerius possessed—and that Xenophon said Cyrus also possessed—bring him love. For a prince to be individually well liked and to have the army as his partisan is in conformity with all the other demands of his position, but when a citizen has the army as his partisan, this does not at all conform to those demands which oblige him to live under the laws and to obey the magistrates.

Among the ancient records of the Venetian republic, it appears that when the Venetian galleys returned to Venice a certain dispute arose between the men of the galleys and the people. This led to rioting and fighting, and the matter could not be quieted by the force of government officials or through respect for the citizens or fear of the magistrates. Then, suddenly, before those sailors a gentleman appeared who had been their leader the year before, and out of love for him they departed and abandoned the fight. This obedience generated such suspicion in the senate that a short time later the Venetians secured themselves against this man either by imprisonment or by death. I conclude, therefore, that the procedure of Valerius is useful in a prince but pernicious in a citizen, not only to his country but to himself—to his country since these methods prepare the way for tyranny; to himself since in suspecting his method of procedure his city is forced to secure itself against him, thereby causing him harm. And, on the contrary, I affirm that the procedure of Manlius is harmful in a prince and useful in a citizen—and especially useful to his country—for it rarely causes harm, unless the hatred that your severity brings you has not already been increased by the suspicion which, as a result of your great reputation, your other virtues bring upon you, as will be shown below in the case of Camillus.

CHAPTER XXIII.   WHY CAMILLUS WAS EXILED FROM ROME

[Imitating Valerius does harm to a man's country and to himself, while imitating Manlius assists one's country although it may result in personal harm. Camillus acted much like Manlius, and it was his practice of being more severe in his punishments than he was generous in his rewards which caused him to become hated. This example shows what a ruler must do in order to avoid being despised. His worst mistake would be to deprive his subjects of whatever they value most. A second error is to be arrogant and proud.]

CHAPTER XXIV.   THE PROLONGATION OF MILITARY AU-
THORITY ENSLAVED ROME

[Two causes brought about the destruction of the Roman
republic: the disputes connected with the Agrarian Law
and the prolongation of military authority. This latter
practice became more common as the Romans waged war
farther abroad. The results were twofold: first, only a
small number of men acquired a military reputation; second, the men who held command for long periods were
able to use it to gain political power, as did Sulla, Marius,
and, eventually, Julius Caesar. If the Romans had not
prolonged the terms of military command, they would not
have won so great an empire in such a brief time, but neither would they have lost their liberty in such a short
period.]

CHAPTER XXV.   ON THE POVERTY OF CINCINNATUS AND
MANY ROMAN CITIZENS

Elsewhere we have discussed how the most useful thing
that can be instituted in a free state is to keep the citizens
poor. And while it is not clear which institution produced
this result in Rome, especially since the Agrarian Law encountered so much opposition, nevertheless, experience
shows that four hundred years after Rome had been built
there was still a great deal of poverty there; nor can it be
believed that any other condition produced this effect
than the knowledge that the avenue to whatever rank or
office you wished to obtain was not closed to you on the
basis of your wealth, and that Ability was sought after in
whatever home she lived. This method of living made
wealth less desirable. For example, when Minutius, the
consul, and his army were besieged by the Aequi, Rome
was so filled with the fear that the army might be lost that
they decided to appoint a dictator—the last resource in
any difficult situation. They selected Lucius Quintius
Cincinnatus, who at that time was on a small farm that he
worked with his own hands. The event is celebrated by

Livy with these golden words: "This should be heeded by
all who disparage every human thing in comparison to
riches and who have no use for honor or skill unless
wealth flows in abundance."[1] Cincinnatus was plowing
his little farm, which was not longer than four *jugers*,
when the legates of the senate arrived from Rome to advise him of his election to the dictatorship and to show
him in what danger the Roman republic found itself. He
put on his toga and went to Rome, where he gathered together an army and went off to free Minutius; after defeating and despoiling the enemy and freeing the consul,
he forbade the besieged army to take part in the pillaging,
saying these words to them: "I do not want you to take
part in the pillaging of those by whom you were almost
despoiled." He took the consulate away from Minutius
and made him a legate, saying to him: "You will remain
in this rank until you learn to know how to be consul."[2]
And he made Lucius Tarquinius his master of horse, who
fought on foot because of his poverty. And so it is evident
that poverty was honored in Rome, and that for a good
and valiant man like Cincinnatus four *jugers* of land were
enough to support him. Evidence of poverty also appears
in the times of Marcus Regulus, for when he was in Africa
with his army he asked leave of the senate to return to
care for his farm, which was being ruined by his workers.
There are two noteworthy points here: first, poverty, and
how the Romans were content with it; and that winning
honor from war was enough for these citizens, who left all
the profit to the public. If Regulus had thought of making
himself rich from the war, he would have paid little heed
to the fact that his fields were being ruined. The other
thing to note is the generosity of spirit of these citizens,
whose greatness of mind rose above a prince when they
were placed at the head of an army; they feared neither
kings nor republics; nothing frightened or confused them,
and once they returned to being private citizens, they be-

[1] Livy, III, xxvi (cited by Machiavelli in the original Latin).
[2] Ibid., III, xxix (cited by Machiavelli in the original Latin).

came frugal, humble, careful of their small means, obedient to the magistrates, and respectful toward their superiors to such an extent that it seemed impossible that one and the same spirit might undergo such a transformation. This poverty endured until the times of Paulus Emilius, which were virtually the last happy times of the republic, when a citizen whose triumph enriched Rome nevertheless remained poor himself. And poverty was still regarded so highly that in honoring a man who had conducted himself well in war Paulus gave a son-in-law of his a silver cup, which was the first piece of silver in his house. I could enter a long discussion of how poverty has produced much better fruits than riches—how the former has honored cities, provinces, and religions while the latter has ruined them—if this subject had not already been celebrated by other men countless times.

CHAPTER XXVI.　HOW A STATE IS RUINED BECAUSE OF WOMEN

[In Livy we read how the offense against Lucretia by the Tarquins brought about the event that ended their rule and how the offense committed against Virginia cost the decemvirs their authority. Furthermore, Aristotle lists the injuries done to women as one of the most important causes of a tyrant's downfall. Since this topic has been discussed in the chapter on conspiracies, I shall only say here that rulers should pay attention to this problem in governing a state.]

CHAPTER XXVII.　HOW UNITY MAY BE RESTORED TO A DIVIDED CITY, AND HOW THE OPINION THAT DIVIDED CITIES MUST BE KEPT DIVIDED IN ORDER TO HOLD THEM IS NOT TRUE

[The example of the Roman consuls shows that of the three methods of dealing with a divided city—killing the leaders of the factions, expelling them from the city, or forcing them to make peace with each other—the first is the most reliable and the last the most dangerous. Florence attempted to control Pistoia by the third method, but was finally forced to use exile to control the city; it would have been safer to have killed the leaders of the city's factions, but the Florentine republic was too weak to follow such a policy. Although it was a commonly held belief that fostering divisions in subject cities enabled Florence to govern them more effectively, such factions, in fact, always offered an enemy a means of taking these cities, as it is impossible to defend a city with enemies both without and within. Thus, such a policy may be of some use in peacetime, but it could be disastrous in time of war.]

CHAPTER XXVIII.   THE DEEDS OF THE CITIZENS SHOULD BE SCRUTINIZED CAREFULLY, FOR THE BEGINNING OF TYRANNY IS OFTEN CONCEALED BENEATH A PIOUS ACT

[While a republic cannot survive without outstanding citizens, it is also true that the reputation such citizens acquire in a republic may also be the cause of tyranny. Because of this, there must be some check upon their reputations so that these citizens will benefit and not harm the republic and its freedom. A citizen may acquire reputation by either public or private means. While the first means is never harmful, private means are always very dangerous, for they create factions and partisans and encourage those who are favored to become corrupt. Any well-organized republic, such as Rome, will encourage citizens to gain fame by public rather than private means.]

CHAPTER XXIX.   THAT THE SINS OF THE PEOPLE COME FROM THEIR PRINCES

A prince should not complain of any sin committed by the people he governs, for such sins of necessity come either from the prince's negligence or from the fact that

he is stained with similar defects. Anyone examining the
people, who, in our times, have been reputed to be totally
engaged in robberies and like crimes, will see that this
comes solely from those who govern them, who are of a
similar nature. Romagna, before Pope Alexander VI did
away with the lords who ruled it, was an example of the
most wicked way of life, for there murder and looting
would take place on a grand scale at the slightest pretext.
This arose from the sorry nature of the princes, not from
the sorry nature of the inhabitants, as those rulers
claimed. Since those princes were poor yet wanted to live
as if they were rich, they were forced to engage in frequent robberies, and they did so by various means.
Among their most dishonest methods was the making of
laws prohibiting certain actions; then they were the first to
provide reasons for the nonobservance of these laws. Nor
did they ever punish those who did not observe them except when they saw that many others had become involved in the same practice; then they turned to
punishment—not out of their zeal to uphold the law they
had made but rather out of their greed to collect the fines.
Many problems arose from this situation, and one above
all: the people became impoverished and were undisciplined; those who had become poor sought to enrich
themselves at the cost of those who were less powerful.
From this sprang all those evils described above, of which
the prince is the cause.

And that this is true is shown by Livy when he recounts
how the Roman legates, while carrying the Venetian gift
of booty to Apollo, were captured by the pirates of Lipari
in Sicily and taken to that city. When Timasitheus, their
prince, learned what kind of gift it was, where it was
going, and who had sent it, he comported himself like a
Roman (although he was born in Lipari) and showed his
people how impious it would be to steal such a gift. With
the consent of the crowd, he allowed the legates to depart
with all their possessions. The words of the historian are
these: "Timasitheus instilled religious fear into the crowd,

which is always like its ruler."[1] And Lorenzo de' Medici, in confirmation of this maxim, said: "What the ruler does, many do afterward, / because all their eyes are fixed on their ruler."[2]

CHAPTER XXX.   ANY CITIZEN WHO WISHES TO EMPLOY HIS INFLUENCE IN DOING GOOD FOR HIS REPUBLIC MUST FIRST PUT DOWN ENVY; AND HOW, WHEN THE ENEMY ATTACKS, THE CITY'S DEFENSE MUST BE ORGANIZED

[Envy may be overcome either because an impending disaster forces everyone to turn to a man of obvious ability to save them from it or when a man's natural rivals are removed either by violence or in the normal course of events. When an able man can rid himself of those who envy him by natural means, this is most fortunate, but when this is not the case he must find some other method of removing them. Moses was forced to kill a great number of men in order to establish his laws and institutions, for they opposed him out of envy. Both Girolamo Savonarola and Piero Soderini of Florence recognized the danger of envy surrounding their positions, but Savonarola was unable to obtain enough authority to remove his opponents while Soderini felt his goodwill would lessen the opposition of his opponents. Both men came to ruin because they could not overcome envy. In defending a city, one should avoid relying upon a mob and give authority and arms only to a select group of men.]

CHAPTER XXXI.   STRONG REPUBLICS AND EXCELLENT MEN RETAIN THE SAME SPIRIT AND THE SAME DIGNITY IN EVERY SITUATION

[Great men like the Roman Camillus never alter their characters with a change in their fortunes and are so resolute in their undertakings that Fortune can have no hold over them. Weak men behave in the opposite manner, for

[1] Livy, V, xxviii (cited by Machiavelli in the original Latin).
[2] *Rappresentazione di San Giovanni e Paolo.*

they become elated with success and terrified by failure. Republics act like men in this regard, as can be seen by examining Rome and Venice. The Romans never despaired in adversity, nor did they become arrogant in victory. The Venetians, on the contrary, feel that their good luck is due to admirable qualities they do not actually possess, and when they are defeated they become despondent and lose their spirit. Although I have already noted that a state's security depends upon military discipline, and that there can be no good laws or institutions without it, it is not superfluous to repeat this again. If a city is well trained and well armed, as Rome was, her character will be unchangeable and will not depend upon the whims of Fortune, as does the character of the Venetian republic.]

CHAPTER XXXII.   WHAT MEANS SOME HAVE EMPLOYED TO UPSET A TREATY OF PEACE

[There is no surer means of disturbing a peaceful settlement than to commit an outrageous action against the party with which you do not wish to uphold the settlement.]

CHAPTER XXXIII.   TO WIN A BATTLE IT IS NECESSARY TO INSPIRE AN ARMY'S CONFIDENCE IN ITSELF AND IN ITS COMMANDER

[An army's confidence depends on whether it is well armed and well organized and whether the soldiers know each other. To achieve this, the troops must be natives of the same area and must have lived together. Their commander must also possess qualities which inspire confidence, such as bravery, alertness, and dignity. The Romans inspired confidence in their men by means of religion.]

CHAPTER XXXIV.   WHAT KIND OF FAME, RUMOR, OR OPIN-
ION MAKES THE PEOPLE FAVOR ONE CITIZEN; AND WHETHER
THE PEOPLE DISTRIBUTE OFFICES WITH GREATER PRUDENCE
THAN A PRINCE

[In choosing leaders, the people usually rely upon gossip
and upon the reputation of men when they have no actual
knowledge of their deeds, as well as upon some precon-
ception of their worth. Such men are thus judged by their
family, by their behavior, and by the company they keep.
A reputation based upon family standing is unreliable;
that derived from one's company is better, but still not as
good as fame gained from honorable actions of a private
nature. Men in a republic ought to strive to rise above the
mean through extraordinary deeds. Such feats should be
the basis for appointing men to high office, but mistakes
can also be made in estimating the greatness of a man's
deeds. Therefore, well-organized republics encourage
other citizens to proclaim publicly a candidate's faults in
order to warn the people before they make their choice.
When the people has enough information, it judges men
running for offices better than princes do.]

CHAPTER XXXV.   WHAT RISKS ARE RUN WHEN ONE TAKES
THE LEAD IN COUNSELING AN UNDERTAKING, AND HOW
MUCH GREATER THESE RISKS ARE WHEN THE ENTERPRISE
IS AN EXTRAORDINARY ONE

[Since men judge actions by their results, a man who
counsels a difficult undertaking will suffer the consequences if failure results, but if it is successful his rewards
will not be proportionately as great. The advisers of a
prince or republic find themselves in a difficult position,
for if they hesitate to give their honest counsel they may
fail to fulfill the duties of their offices, but if they are honest they risk losing their position and possibly even their
lives. The only answer is to offer and defend your views
without undue emotion, so that if they are accepted by a
ruler or a republic they will appear to be the will of the

majority and will not cause undue disgrace if they result
in disaster. If, however, you have insisted upon your
views against a majority and disaster results, your downfall will ensue. Advocating a minority opinion that might
have prevented a catastrophe is one means of acquiring
glory, and although it is not a happy means of obtaining a
reputation, it is nevertheless worthy of mention.]

CHAPTER XXXVI.   THE REASONS WHY THE FRENCH HAVE
BEEN, AND STILL ARE, CONSIDERED BRAVER THAN MEN AT
THE OUTSET OF A BATTLE AND LESS THAN WOMEN
AFTERWARD

[Livy describes the French in this manner, but it does not
necessarily follow that their nature could not be disciplined so as to prolong their bravery until a battle's end.
There are three kinds of armies. The first kind has both
bravery and discipline, for from order arises both bravery
and ability, as was the case in the Roman army. The army
of the French, on the other hand, had bravery without
discipline. Since it lacked a method in fighting, unless it
succeeded during an initial attack it was usually defeated.
The third kind of army is the kind we see in Italy today,
which lacks both bravery and discipline.]

CHAPTER XXXVII.   WHETHER SMALL SKIRMISHES BEFORE
THE MAIN BATTLE ARE NECESSARY; AND HOW TO FIND OUT
ABOUT A NEW ENEMY AND AVOID SUCH SKIRMISHES

[In human affairs there is one constant problem: in per-
fecting one thing we always produce another thing that is
evil, and the two are so inseparable that one cannot exist
without the other. This is true of anything men undertake,
and it is for this reason that you can only attain the good
you seek with Fortune's assistance. A good commander,
therefore, should do nothing, no matter how insignificant,
which would adversely affect his army. Skirmishing can
achieve good results as well as bad ones, for without testing a new enemy by means of such encounters you will

never know how to fight him; if you fail to gain the upper hand in these skirmishes, however, your troops may be afraid to face the enemy. If a commander is forced to skirmish, he must do so only when he has such an advantage that he is not likely to be defeated.]

CHAPTER XXXVIII.   WHAT A COMMANDER SHOULD BE LIKE TO GAIN THE CONFIDENCE OF HIS ARMY

[Before Valerius Corvinus went into battle against the Samnites, in addition to skirmishing with the enemy he addressed his army, asking his men to follow him, not because of his brilliant oratory, but rather because of his valiant deeds. Men who command others should follow his practice, for a man's deeds bestow honor upon his titles, while titles alone do not make a man famous. It is more difficult to meet an enemy with an inexperienced army than with an army composed of veterans. To do this, great generals of the past have exercised their troops for several months before the battle to accustom them to obeying orders and accepting discipline. No ruler with a sufficient number of men should despair of lacking soldiers, for if he is unable to train them adequately it is a sign of his own shortcomings and not the cowardice of his subjects.]

CHAPTER XXXIX.   THAT A COMMANDER SHOULD BE FAMILIAR WITH VARIOUS TERRAINS

[A military leader must be familiar with various kinds of terrains and countries, for without such knowledge he cannot perform his duties well. Such knowledge is acquired only through much practice, hunting being an excellent exercise to achieve this. Ancient writers note that great heroes of the past were raised in the forests and were avid hunters. Xenophon suggests that a hunting expedition is very much like a war and that great men should practice this sport. A knowledge of many kinds of terrains in one country can be applied to others as well, for there is a certain uniformity in all countries.]

CHAPTER XL.   HOW EMPLOYING FRAUD IN WAGING A WAR IS A GLORIOUS AFFAIR

Although the employment of fraud in all of one's actions is detestable, it is a praiseworthy and glorious affair in waging a war; and anyone who overcomes the enemy with fraud is to be praised as much as a man who overcomes the enemy by sheer strength. This is evident from the judgment passed by many who have written about the lives of great men: they praise Hannibal and the others who have been outstanding in the use of such methods. Since one can read about many examples of this, I shall not cite any. I shall say only this: I am not implying that the fraud which makes you break your promises and established agreements is a glorious thing, for this kind of fraud—even if it sometimes gains you a state or a kingdom, as has been discussed above—will never win you glory. But I am speaking of the kind of fraud that is used against an enemy who does not trust you, the kind involved in waging war, as was Hannibal's fraud when he pretended to retreat at the Lake of Perugia in order to encircle the consul and the Roman army, or the time he lit up the horns of a cattle herd in order to escape from the hands of Fabius Maximus.

The fraud that Pontius, general of the Samnites, employed to encircle the Roman army at the Caudine Forks is the kind I mean. When he had stationed his own army behind the mountains, he sent some of his soldiers, dressed as shepherds, to the plain with a large flock. When they were taken by the Romans and asked where the Samnite army was, they all agreed to say, following Pontius's orders, that it was at the siege of Nocera. This was believed by the consuls, who enclosed themselves inside the Caudine cliffs, where they were immediately attacked by the Samnites. This victory, achieved by means of fraud, would have been most glorious for Pontius if he had followed the advice of his father, who wanted the Romans either to be allowed to survive in liberty or to all be killed, and who advised that a middle course should not be taken, "for it neither wins friends nor eliminates enemies."[1] This course is always pernicious in matters of state, as I have discussed above.

CHAPTER XLI. ONE'S COUNTRY MUST BE DEFENDED, WHETHER WITH SHAME OR WITH GLORY, AND IT IS WELL DEFENDED IN ANY MANNER

As was mentioned above, the consul and the Roman army were besieged by the Samnites, who had imposed upon the Romans the most disgraceful of conditions: namely, putting them under the yoke and sending them back to Rome disarmed. Because of this, the consuls were stunned and the army was desperate, when Lucius Lentulus, the Roman legate, announced that he did not believe any plan for saving their country should be rejected. Since the survival of Rome depended upon the survival of the army, he believed in saving it by any means, for one's country is well defended by any means which defends it, whether by disgrace or glory. If that army were saved, Rome would have time to erase the disgrace, but if it were not saved, even if it died gloriously Rome and her freedom would be lost. And so his advice was followed. This thought deserves to be noted and put into practice by any citizen who has occasion to advise his country, for when the entire safety of one's country is at stake, there should be no consideration of just or unjust, merciful or cruel, praiseworthy or disgraceful; on the contrary, putting aside every form of respect, that decision which will save her life and preserve her liberty must be followed completely. This course of action is imitated in word and deed by the French in order to defend the majesty of their king and the power of their kingdom, for no voice is heard more

[1] Livy, IX, iii (cited by Machiavelli in the original Latin).

impatiently than the one which says: "This decision is disgraceful for the king," for they say that their king cannot suffer shame in any of his decisions, whether they be made in good or adverse fortune, for, win or lose, it is a kingly affair.

CHAPTER XLII.   PROMISES EXACTED BY FORCE SHOULD NOT BE KEPT

When the consuls returned to Rome with their army disarmed and the disgrace they had suffered, the first in the senate to say the peace made at Caudium should not be observed was the Consul Spurius Postumius, who said that he and the others who had made the peace, not the Roman people, were obligated to keep it, and that if the people wished to free themselves from any obligation they had only to surrender himself and the others who had made the agreement as prisoners into the hands of the Samnites. And he maintained this conclusion with such conviction that the senate was finally convinced; they sent him and the others to Samnium as prisoners, protesting to the Samnites that the peace was not valid. And Fortune was so favorable to Postumius in this instance that the Samnites decided not to keep him. After he had returned to Rome, he enjoyed more fame among the Romans as a result of having lost than Pontius ever did among the Samnites for having won. There are two things to note here. First, that glory can be acquired from any kind of action. For in victory it is acquired in the normal course of things; in defeat it may be won either by showing that such a defeat was not occasioned through your fault or by immediately doing some great deed that cancels the defeat. Second, it is not shameful to break promises you have been forced to make. Promises involving public matters that are made under duress are always broken without disgrace to anyone who breaks them when the force is removed. Various examples of this can be found in all the histories; we encounter them every day in our own times. And not only are forced promises never kept among princes when the force is removed, but all other promises are also broken when the causes for such promises are removed. Whether or not this is a praiseworthy thing, and whether or not similar methods ought to be observed by a prince, is discussed at length in my treatise, *The Prince.* I shall therefore, say nothing about this at the moment.

CHAPTER XLIII. THAT MEN BORN IN ANY GIVEN PROVINCE ALWAYS DISPLAY ALMOST THE SAME NATURE

Prudent men often say, neither casually nor groundlessly, that anyone wishing to see what is to come should examine what has been, for all the affairs of the world in every age have had their counterparts in ancient times. This is because these affairs are carried on by men who have, and have always had, the same passions and, of necessity, the same results come from them. It is true that their actions are more effective at one time in this province than in another, and more in that than in this one, according to the kind of education from which those peoples have taken their way of living. Knowing future affairs is also facilitated by knowing past ones, especially when a nation has maintained the same customs for a long time—for example, being continuously greedy or fraudulent or having some other similar vice or virtue. And anyone who reads about the past affairs of our city of Florence and considers those which have occurred most recently will find the German and French people full of avarice, pride, ferocity, and treachery, for these four things, in different times, have all greatly harmed our city. As for treachery, everyone knows how many times Florence gave money to King Charles VIII, and how he promised to surrender the fortresses of Pisa to her but never did. In this, that king demonstrated his treachery and his great greed. But let us pass over recent matters. Everyone knows what happened in the war which the

Florentine people waged against the Visconti, dukes of Milan. When Florence had no other remedy, she thought about bringing the emperor, with his prestige and armed forces, into Italy to attack Lombardy. The emperor promised to come with many men to wage this war against the Visconti and to defend Florence from their power if the Florentines would pay him one hundred thousand ducats when he assembled his armies and one hundred thousand ducats upon his arrival in Italy. The Florentines agreed to these terms and paid him the first amount, followed by the second. When he arrived at Verona, he turned back without doing anything, protesting that he stopped because the Florentines had not respected the agreements they had made with him. Thus, if Florence had not been constrained by necessity or conquered by passion, and if she had read about and recognized the ancient customs of the barbarians, never would she have been deceived by them at this or at any other time, for they have always acted the same way and have always employed the same means everywhere and with everyone. This is evident from what they did to the Tuscans in ancient times. The latter, being oppressed by the Romans and having been defeated by them many times and put to flight, agreed to give the Gauls, who lived in Italy on the other side of the Alps, a sum of money with the proviso that they would unite their armies with the Tuscan army and march against the Romans. The result was that once the Gauls had taken the money, they no longer wanted to take up arms on behalf of the Tuscans, declaring that they had received the money, not for waging war against their enemies, but for refraining from plundering the Tuscan countryside. And thus, as a result of the avarice and treachery of the Gauls, the Tuscan people were, at a single stroke, deprived of their money and the assistance they had hoped for. Thus, it is clear from this example of the ancient Tuscans and that of the Florentines that the French have always employed the same methods; and from this it can easily be inferred how much faith princes can put in them.

CHAPTER XLIV.   ONE OFTEN OBTAINS WITH IMPETUOSITY AND AUDACITY WHAT COULD NEVER BE OBTAINED BY ORDINARY MEANS

[When one ruler wishes another ruler to do his bidding, he should not allow him time for deliberation; rather, he should act in such a way as to precipitate a swift decision. Pope Julius did this when he marched against Bologna, calling upon the Venetians to remain neutral and requesting assistance from France after he had begun his campaign. He thus left Venice and France little choice but to honor his requests.]

CHAPTER XLV.   WHETHER, IN BATTLES, IT IS BETTER TO SUSTAIN THE ENEMY'S ATTACK AND THEN TO COUNTER-ATTACK OR TO ATTACK HIM FIRST WITH FURY

[Decius and Fabius, two Roman consuls, fought the armies of the Samnites and the Etruscans at approximately the same time but with different methods. Whereas Decius attacked first, Fabius allowed the enemy to attack and then counterattacked. Fabius was the more successful of the two, and his tactics are thus safer and more worthy of imitation.]

CHAPTER XLVI.   HOW IT HAPPENS THAT A FAMILY IN A CITY MAINTAINS THE SAME CUSTOMS FOR A PERIOD OF TIME

[The characteristics which families exhibit differ not only from city to city but also within cities; some families produce men who are stern and determined, while others living in the same city have different attributes. Since most families intermarry, such a phenomenon cannot be due to heredity; it is caused, instead, by the different ways in which the families educate their children. A man's conduct is influenced by what is valued or despised by his family during his childhood.]

CHAPTER XLVII.   THAT A GOOD CITIZEN OUGHT TO FORGET PRIVATE INJURIES FOR THE LOVE OF HIS NATIVE CITY

[The example of Fabius, who, as consul, named his enemy, Papirius Cursor, dictator in order to save Rome in the war with the Samnites, is one that should be followed by all good citizens, who should put aside private injuries in order to protect their native city.]

CHAPTER XLVIII.   WHENEVER ONE OBSERVES AN ENEMY COMMITTING A GROSS ERROR, ONE SHOULD ASSUME THAT THERE IS A TRICK BENEATH IT

[A commander should never accept an obvious mistake by his enemy without questioning it, for it is not likely that the enemy lacks caution in this manner. But men are so avid for victory that they allow themselves to be blinded to the possibility of treachery.]

CHAPTER XLIX.   IF A REPUBLIC IS TO BE KEPT FREE, IT REQUIRES NEW ACTS OF FORESIGHT EVERY DAY; AND, FOR WHAT GOOD QUALITIES QUINTUS FABIUS WAS CALLED MAXIMUS

As I have already said many times, emergencies requiring a physician inevitably arise every day in a great city, and the more important these incidents are, the more useful it is to find the wisest physician. And if ever such emergencies arose in a city, they did so in Rome—both strange and unforeseen ones; as, for example, the one in which it seemed that all Roman women had conspired to murder their husbands: many were found to have poisoned their husbands and many had already prepared the poison for doing so. The conspiracy of the Bacchanals, discovered during the Macedonian War, was another example involving thousands of men and women. If it had not been uncovered, or if the Romans had not been accustomed to punishing great numbers of wrongdoers, the city would have been in great danger. For, if the greatness of that republic and the power of her actions were not evident in other countless ways, they certainly were evident from the quality of the punishments she imposed on those who went astray. She never hesitated to put to death an entire legion or an entire city at one time, nor to banish eight or ten thousand men with penalties so unusual that they could not be carried out by one man, let alone by so many of them. This was the case with those soldiers who had fought so unsuccessfully at Cannae: they were banished to Sicily and were required to take up lodgings outside the cities and to eat while standing.

But of all her other punishments, the most terrible was the decimation of an army, in which one out of every ten men in that army was put to death by lot. Nor could one find a more terrifying punishment in chastising a multitude than this one: for when a large group does wrong and the instigator is not evident, all cannot be punished, for there are too many. To punish a part of them and leave another part unpunished would wrong those who were punished, and the unpunished would retain the courage to do wrong at another time. But in killing by lot a tenth part of them—when all of them deserve it—he who is punished suffers his fate and he who is not punished lives in fear that the next time it may be his turn and is thus careful not to go astray.

And so, the poisoners and the Bacchanals were punished according to the nature of their sins. Although these sicknesses produce evil effects in a republic, they are not fatal, for there is almost always time to cure them; but in those sicknesses which concern the state, there is no time, and unless they are cured by a prudent man, they bring the city to ruin. In Rome, as a result of the generosity the Romans practiced in granting citizenship to foreigners, so many new children were born that they soon possessed such a proportion of the vote that the government began to change, moving away from the policies and the men it was accustomed to. When the censor Quintus Fabius saw this, he put all these new families, the cause of this disorder, into four tribes; thus, reduced to such a small area, they were no longer able to infect all of Rome. This matter was well understood by Fabius, and he provided a suitable remedy for it without changing the government; it was so acceptable to that civic body that he deserved to be called "Maximus."

A FABLE: BELFAGOR, THE DEVIL WHO TOOK A WIFE

EDITORS' NOTE

The popularity of the novella form, a literary genre similar to the short story, began with the appearance of Boccaccio's Decameron *in the fourteenth century. Following this model, a number of Renaissance writers in Italy, France, England, and Spain (Anton Francesco Grazzini, Matteo Bandello, Marguerite de Navarre, Cervantes, and others) made the novella the most popular fictional genre of the age. In general, each of these writers employed a frame story to open the collection of stories, which described how, as a result of some special event (a plague in Boccaccio's work; a festival, carnival, or storm in other novellas), a number of narrators gathered to tell stories in order to pass the time. Thus, most of these works combined the opening frame with many different tales, on a variety of topics, told by a number of different narrators. Part of the charm of this genre was due to the urbane and witty commentaries on the various stories that the frame characters provided. However, a few novellas existed as individual, autonomous stories with no frame or companion pieces. One of these single stories was Luigi da Porto's tale of Romeo and Juliet, which eventually made its way to England and Shakespeare through a number of translations and versions. Another such masterpiece was Machiavelli's* Belfagor, *the only novella of his we have preserved. It is the equal of any other single story that Renais-*

*sance Europe produced. Moreover, from an anecdote which
Bandello recounts in his own collection of such tales (I, xl),
it seems clear that Machiavelli enjoyed a reputation as a
skillful storyteller among his close friends and associates.
Scholars date the composition of this novella between 1515
and 1520; it was first published in the 1549 edition of Machiavelli's complete works.*

It is written, in the old chronicles of Florentine history,
how a most holy man, whose life was well known to those
who lived at that time, prayed with religious fervor and
saw that, among the countless number of miserable souls
who die outside God's grace and go to Hell, all (or the
greatest portion of them) complained that it was only because of their wives that they had been brought to such
misery. Whereupon Minos and Rhadamanthos, along
with all the other judges of Hell, were very perplexed.
They were not able to believe that these accusations
against the fairer sex were true, but the complaints increased daily. So they made an appropriate report to
Pluto, who decided to make a thorough investigation of
the matter with the help of all the princes of Hell, and to
take whatever action might be deemed best in order to
discover the falsity or truth of this question. Having called
them all to a council, Pluto spoke in this manner:

"My very dear friends, since by heavenly decree and
unchangeable destiny I am the owner of this kingdom, I
cannot be obliged to submit to any earthly or heavenly
judgment; nevertheless, because the ultimate proof of
prudence in those who hold great power is to submit
themselves to the rule of law and to value the opinions of
others, I have decided to ask your advice on how to act in
a matter that could bring shame to our rule. Since the
souls of all the men who come into our kingdom say that
their wives were the cause, and since this seems impossi-

ble to us, I am afraid that if we accept their explanations
we might very well be accused of being too credulous, yet
if we do not we might be accused of not being stern
enough and, hence, poor friends of justice. Now, since
one is the vice of the frivolous and the other that of the
unjust, and since we wish to avoid being accused of either,
we have—being unable to find the means—called you together so that you may aid us with your advice in order
that this realm, which has always lived free from scandal
in the past, may continue to do so in the future."

Each of the princes believed the matter to be of the utmost importance and worthy of much consideration; all
concluded that it was necessary to get to the bottom of the
issue, but none could agree on how it should be done.
While some felt that one, and others that several, of their
number should be sent into the world in human shape to
discover the truth in person, many others felt it could be
done without so much fuss by forcing a number of souls
to reveal the truth under various kinds of torture. Since
the majority was of the opinion to send someone back to
earth, that course of action was adopted. Unable to find
anyone who would undertake this task of his own free
will, they decided that lots should be drawn. The lot fell
upon Belfagor, an archdevil, formerly an archangel before his fall from Heaven. Although Belfagor was reluctant to carry out this task, he was nevertheless compelled
by the authority of Pluto to follow the council's instructions and agreed to heed those conditions which they had
solemnly decided upon among themselves. They were:
that a hundred thousand ducats would be disbursed immediately to whoever was chosen for the mission; with
this money he was to go into the world and, disguised in
the body of a man, he was to take a wife and to live with
her for ten years; then he was to pretend to die and return
to his superiors in order to report on the burdens and discomforts of marriage based on his experience. It was further agreed that during this period he was to be subject to
all the inconveniences and evils that men suffer, including

poverty, imprisonment, disease, and every other kind of misfortune that men experience—unless he could avoid all this by means of his own wit or trickery.

So, Belfagor accepted the conditions and the money and entered the world. Accompanied by his retinue of servants and horsemen, he entered Florence with a flourish. He chose to live in this city above all others because he felt it was the most likely place to live for anyone who was fond of usury. He took the name Roderigo of Castile and rented a house in the Ognissanti district; and in order not to reveal his true identity, he said that he had left Spain as a child and had gone to Syria, and that he had made a fortune in Aleppo, whence he had departed for Italy in order to take a wife in a place that was more civilized, more urbane, and more in keeping with his own character. Roderigo was a very handsome man and looked about thirty years old. Having demonstrated in only a few days how rich he was, and having given evidence of his humanity and liberality, many noble Florentines with a number of daughters (but little money) offered them to him. From among all these Roderigo chose a very beautiful girl named Onesta, the daughter of Amerigo Donati, who had three other daughters of marriageable age as well as three sons. And although Amerigo came from a very noble family and was highly respected in Florence, in proportion to the size of his family and his nobility, he was nevertheless very poor.

Roderigo organized a magnificent, splendid wedding; he omitted nothing that one might desire in a celebration of this kind. And since he was subject to all human passions (because of the rule imposed upon him before he left Hell), he began to take pleasure in the pomp and circumstance of the world and to enjoy being praised by other men—a thing that was by no means inexpensive. Moreover, he had not lived long with Madonna Onesta before he fell madly in love with her; he could not bear to see her unhappy or displeased. Now, Onesta brought with her to Roderigo's house, together with her nobility and her beauty, more pride than Lucifer ever had, and Roderigo who had experienced them both, judged his wife's pride to be the greater. And her pride increased when she discovered how much her husband loved her; since she thought she could dominate him in every way, she ordered him about without pity or respect, nor did she hesitate to speak to him in injurious or vile terms when he refused to give her something. All of this was, for Roderigo, the cause of much misery. Nevertheless, respect for his father-in-law, her brothers, relatives, the obligation of matrimony, and, above all, the great love he had for her made him patient. I shall not even mention the extravagant expenses incurred to make her happy: dressing her in the newest fashions and keeping her in the latest novelties which our city habitually changes. In addition, to keep peace with her it was necessary to help her father marry off the other daughters, and great sums of money were consumed in this project. Besides this, since he wished to be on good terms with her he was obliged to send one of her brothers to the East with cloth, another to the West with silks, and to open a jewelry shop for the third in Florence. In these ventures he spent the greater part of his fortune. In addition to all this, during carnival time and St. John's Day, when the entire city customarily made merry and many rich and noble citizens honored each other with sumptuous banquets, Madonna Onesta, so as not to be inferior to other women, wanted her Roderigo to surpass all the others in giving such parties. Roderigo bore all these tribulations for the reasons already given; nor would they have seemed onerous if he had been rewarded with peace and quiet at home and if he had been able to await the day of his ruin in tranquillity. But the opposite occurred, for in addition to these crushing expenses, Onesta's arrogant nature brought him countless problems. As a result, there was not a servant who could stand being in his house for more than a few days; and Roderigo was sorely inconvenienced by not having a faithful servant to whom he could entrust his af-

fairs; even those devils that Roderigo had brought with
him as part of his retinue preferred to return to the fires of
Hell rather than to live in the world under Onesta's
authority.

Thus, living such a tumultuous and unsettled life and
having already consumed all his ready cash in extravagant expenditures, Roderigo began to live in the hope of
the profits he expected from his Eastern and Western investments. Because his credit was still good, he kept up
his standard of living by signing promissory notes, and it
soon became obvious to those who deal in that kind of
business that a great many of these notes were in circulation. When his situation was already precarious, news
suddenly arrived from the East and the West: one of Madonna Onesta's brothers had gambled away all of Roderigo's goods, and the other, returning on a boat laden
with his uninsured merchandise, had gone down with the
cargo.

No sooner had this news leaked out than Roderigo's
creditors met and declared him bankrupt. Unable to take
legal action against him, since his notes were not yet due,
they concluded that it would be a good idea to keep an
eye on him so that he might not run away in secret. Roderigo, on the other hand, seeing no way out of his dilemma, and knowing that his infernal powers were
limited by his agreement, decided to flee at all costs; one
morning he escaped on horseback through the Gate of
Prato, which was near where he lived. No sooner was his
departure discovered than a great commotion arose
among the creditors, who ran to the magistrates and dispatched couriers after him, as well as a mob of people.
When the alarm was sounded, Roderigo had not gotten
more than a mile from the city; so, seeing himself in trouble, he decided to leave the main road and set off across
the fields in order to flee more secretly. But he was prevented from doing so by the many ditches that crossed the
countryside. Since he could no longer go on horseback, he
left the animal on the road and began to flee on foot,

crossing field after field covered with those vines and canes so abundant in the countryside until he arrived above Peretola, at the house of Gianmatteo del Brica, a workman of Giovanni Del Bene. As luck would have it, he found Gianmatteo coming home to feed his oxen. He asked for his help, promising him that if he would save him from the hands of his enemies (who were chasing him to let him rot in prison), he would make him a rich man, and that he would either give him proof of this before he left or he would put himself in the hands of his own pursuers if his friend was not satisfied. Gianmatteo, although a peasant, was no fool; realizing that he had nothing to lose by saving Roderigo, he agreed and pushed him under a pile of manure in front of his house, covering him with reeds and other garbage he had collected there for burning.

No sooner had Roderigo been hidden than his pursuers arrived. In spite of their threats they were unable to force Gianmatteo to say that he had seen him. And so, they continued on and, having searched in vain that day and the next, they returned dead tired to Florence. When the noise had died away, Gianmatteo released Roderigo from his hiding place and asked him to fulfill his promise. In reply Roderigo said: "My brother, I am deeply in your debt and want to satisfy you in every way; and so that you may believe what I can do, I shall tell you who I am." And then he told him about the kind of being he was and about the laws governing his stay outside of Hell and about the wife he had taken; furthermore, he explained how he was going to make Gianmatteo rich. The method was to be this: whenever he heard that some woman had become possessed, he should count on the fact that it was Roderigo possessing her and that he would never leave the woman unless Gianmatteo came to exorcise him. This way he could get as much money as he wished from the girl's parents. When this agreement was reached, he left.

Not many days passed before word spread through all of Florence that a daughter of Ambruogio Amidei, mar-

ried to Bonaiuto Tedalducci, was possessed; the family
tried all the remedies that are normally used in such cases:
placing the head of St. Zanobius and the cloak of Saint
Giovanni Gualberto on her head, all of which merely
made Roderigo laugh. And in order to make it clear that
the girl's illness was due to a spirit and not to some imaginary fantasy, he spoke in Latin, debated philosophical
questions, and uncovered the sins of many, one of which
concerned a friar who had kept a woman in his cell
dressed as a novice for more than four years. Such things
amazed everyone. Messer Ambruogio, as a result, was
very unhappy. He had tried every remedy in vain and had
lost all hope of curing his daughter when Gianmatteo
came to him and promised him the health of his daughter
if he would give him five hundred florins to buy a farm at
Peretola. Messer Ambruogio accepted the offer. Whereupon Gianmatteo, after having first said some masses and
performed some ceremonies to dress up the operation,
approached the girl's ear and said: "Roderigo, I have
come to find you so that you can keep your word." To
which Roderigo answered: "I am happy to do so. But this
is not sufficient to make you rich. Therefore, when I leave
here I shall possess the daughter of King Charles of
Naples and will never leave her but for you. You can then
get anything you wish. After that, don't bother me any-
more." Having said that, he left the girl, to the pleasure
and admiration of all Florence.

Not long after that, all Italy heard about the tragedy
that had befallen the daughter of King Charles. Being
unable to find a cure, and having received word of Gianmatteo, the king sent to Florence for him. Gianmatteo,
upon arriving in Naples, cured the girl after a few ceremonies. But Roderigo, before he left the girl, said: "See,
Gianmatteo, I have fulfilled my promises to make you
rich. Now we are even and I am bound to you no longer.
Therefore, I would be happy if you did not cross my path
again, for I shall harm you in the future just as I have
helped you in the past." Therefore, when Gianmatteo re-

turned to Florence a very rich man (he had received more than fifty thousand ducats from the king), he thought of enjoying those riches peacefully, never dreaming that Roderigo meant to harm him. But his intentions were abruptly upset by the news that arrived: a daughter of King Louis VII of France was possessed. Gianmatteo found this news most disturbing, considering both the power of that king and the words of warning from Roderigo. Being unable to find a cure for his daughter and hearing about Gianmatteo, the king first asked for his aid by messenger. But when Gianmatteo claimed that he was indisposed, the king was forced to turn to the city government, which obliged Gianmatteo to obey. So he went, disheartened, to Paris, where he first explained to the king that even though he had cured a few women possessed by devils in the past, this did not mean that he knew how, or would be able, to cure all such cases, for there were some demons of such a treacherous nature that they did not fear threats, incantations, or any religious power; but in spite of all that he was ready to do his duty, and he begged the king's pardon and forgiveness if he failed. To this the troubled king replied that he would hang him if he failed to cure her. Gianmatteo was greatly disturbed by this; nevertheless, he screwed up his courage and had the possessed girl brought forward. Leaning close to her ear, he humbly asked Roderigo's aid, reminding him of the service he had rendered him and what an example of ingratitude it would be if he abandoned him now in his hour of need. To this Roderigo replied: "What, you vile traitor? Do you dare come before me? Did you think you could boast about having made yourself rich by my work? I am going to show you and everyone else how I, too, can give and take away as I please. Before you leave here I shall see that you are hanged."

Since Gianmatteo saw no other way out, he decided to try his luck in another way. The possessed girl having been taken away, he said to the king: "Sire, as I told you, there are many demons so malevolent that one cannot deal with them, and this one is of that type. Nevertheless, I would like to try one last experiment; if it succeeds, Your Majesty and I shall obtain our end; if not, I am at your mercy and you can grant me such compassion as my innocence merits. Meanwhile, have a huge scaffold built in the square, before the church of Notre Dame, of sufficient size to hold all the lords and the clergy of this city; have it covered with cloth of silk and gold, and have an altar built above it. Next Sunday morning I want you and the clergy and all your princes and barons to assemble on it with regal pomp and with magnificent robes. After the celebration of a solemn mass, have the possessed girl brought forward. Furthermore, I want there to be in one corner of the square at least twenty men with trumpets, horns, drums, bagpipes, flutes, cymbals, and any other instrument that makes noise. When I raise my hat, they are to play on their instruments as they advance toward the scaffold. I believe that all of these things, together with certain other secret remedies, will make this spirit depart."

The king ordered everything to be done at once. When Sunday morning arrived, the scaffold was full of important people and the piazza teeming with commonfolk. After the mass had been celebrated, the possessed girl was brought forward by two bishops and many noblemen. When Roderigo saw such a crowd gathered together and such preparations, he was almost stupefied, saying to himself: "What does this lazy peasant think he is doing? Does he think he can frighten me with these ceremonies? Doesn't he know that I am used to seeing the glories of Heaven and the furies of Hell? Whatever happens, I shall punish him!"

As Gianmatteo approached him and begged him to leave, he answered: "What a fine idea you have! What did you expect to accomplish with all these displays of yours? Did you think you could escape my power and the king's wrath? Base peasant, I'll surely have your neck." While Gianmatteo repeated his pleas and the devil continued his insults, the former, deciding not to lose any more time, made a sign with his hat; all those who were designated to make noise began to sound their instruments, moving toward the scaffold with a clamor that rose all the way to Heaven. At the sound of this Roderigo pricked up his ears and, not knowing what it was and being very much amazed and stupefied, asked Gianmatteo what was going on. To this Gianmatteo replied excitedly: "Alas, Roderigo! It is your wife coming to reclaim you!"

What a marvel it was to behold the shock that the mere mention of his wife produced in Roderigo. It was so great that, without thinking about whether it was possible or probable for her to be there, and without a word, he fled in terror, leaving the girl cured, for he preferred to return to Hell to give an explanation of his actions rather than to live again with the many problems, dangers, and discomforts that marriage imposed upon him. Thus, Belfagor, on his return to Hell, testified to the evils that a wife brought into a household. And Gianmatteo, who knew more about such things than the devil, returned home a happy man.

THE MANDRAKE ROOT

EDITORS' NOTE

Machiavelli's interest in comedy was a sustained and serious one. In 1504, the year in which the action of The Mandrake Root *unfolds, he composed a comedy entitled* The Masks, *which was based upon* The Clouds *by Aristophanes. Unfortunately, his grandson destroyed the only manuscript because of its trenchant criticism of certain Florentine political figures of the day. Some time later, Machiavelli turned his attention to the comedy of classical Rome, composing a prose version of* The Girl from Andros *by Terence. After the completion of* The Mandrake Root, *he found sufficient inspiration in* Casina, *by Plautus, to create another comedy of his own entitled* Clizia, *a work set in the Florence of his own time (1506) and first performed in 1525. The attempt to establish the date of composition of* The Mandrake Root *has aroused a good deal of argument and is still open to dispute. Although 1518 seems to be the most plausible date, there may be no accurate means of dating the work precisely; it is possible that it was composed anytime between 1504 and 1519, the date on the only extant manuscript copy of the play.*

Judging from the letters written to Machiavelli by friends and from the remarks of many of his contemporaries, The Mandrake Root *was a spectacular success. At one performance, in 1522, the play could not continue past the fourth act because of the press of the enthusiastic crowd. In Venice it was staged in competition with the* Menaechmi *of Plautus; the general impression of the audience was that Plautus's work was a "dead thing" compared to Machiavelli's comedy. Traditionally considered the greatest Italian dramatic work of the Renaissance, it was read with admiration by authors as diverse as Carlo Goldoni and Voltaire, who were influenced by its infectious humor. For a special performance of the play at Faenza, organized in 1526 by Francesco Guicciardini, Machiavelli composed several songs which were meant to be inserted after the prologue and the first four acts. These canzoni have been omitted from this translation since they were not part of the original comedy.*

Although some critics have attempted to reduce this marvelous comedy to the status of a political allegory, wherein Callimaco represents Duke Lorenzo de' Medici, Lucrezia is Florence, and Nicia stands for the ill-fated Piero Soderini, Machiavelli's patron in the Florentine chancery, none of Machiavelli's contemporaries (i.e., those best qualified to notice any allegorical intent) viewed the play in this light; they all considered it as an exemplary neoclassical comedy, intended solely to delight without containing a political message. The work employs the five-act structure Renaissance critics attributed to the Roman theater, and its scenes are divided by the entrance or exit of one of its characters. Moreover, the unities of time, place, and action are followed to the letter. Many of the comedy's characters have strong links with the stock figures of the Roman stage—the parasitic servant, the pedantic lawyer, the star-crossed lover. However, Machiavelli has given such familiar figures new life in Renaissance garb. Ligurio and Timoteo, moreover, are superior to any of the classical antecedents one might consider to be their models.

In spite of the prologue's clear statement concerning the title of the comedy ("Our story has the title Mandrake Root*"), the first two printed editions of the play, in 1518 and 1522, were somewhat mysteriously entitled* The Comedy of Callimaco and Lucrezia. *Furthermore, in much of the au-*

thor's correspondence with friends the play is referred to as *"the comedy of Messer Nicia."* Only with the third edition of 1524 did the title mentioned in the prologue become standard. Machiavelli's use of the motif of the mandrake root combines several distinct legends with an original twist of his own invention. In the play (II, 6), we learn, first, that a potion made from the mandrake root is the surest means of rendering a woman pregnant; second, that any man who sleeps with a woman who has taken this potion will die within eight days; and, finally, that the only remedy for this danger is for another man to sleep with the woman for an entire night so as to draw out the mandrake's poison.

The legend of a poisoner girl, raised on snake venom, whose embraces killed her lovers, can be traced as far back as the twelfth century to a book of Arabic origin. The mandrake's powers as a narcotic and an aphrodisiac were proverbial. According to tradition, the plant's root possessed a human shape and meant death for the person who uprooted it. In order to procure the plant it was necessary to tie a hungry dog to its root and to urge the dog forward with a bit of food, thus uprooting the plant, killing the dog, yet leaving its master unharmed and in possession of the miraculous herb. In his comedy, Machiavelli transfers the structure of this legend to the play itself, replacing the dog with the poor, unfortunate man who is destined, so Messer Nicia believes, to die after a night of bliss with his wife, Lucrezia. Moreover, Machiavelli has combined the legend of the poisoner girl with that of the mandrake. By inventing the "remedy" wherein the first man must spend the night with the woman to spare the life of Messer Nicia, he has also managed to create a natural situation permitting him to observe the unities of time, place, and action without the slightest hint of any pedantic adherence to the so-called rules of dramatic structure that mar many of the other neoclassical dramatic works produced during this same period.

THE PLAYERS

CALLIMACO, a young Florentine in love
SIRO, his manservant
LIGURIO, a clever parasite and rascally go-between
MESSER NICIA, a foolish lawyer
LUCREZIA, his beautiful wife
SOSTRATA, her mother
BROTHER TIMOTEO, a priest whose services are for sale
A LADY

PROLOGUE

God save you, gracious audience,
since all your graciousness, it seems,
depends upon your being entertained.
If you will just keep quiet for a while
we would like you to hear about
a strange event that happened in this land.
See this setting,
right here on stage?
Today it is the Florence you live in,
tomorrow, Rome or Pisa, if you like.
You're going to split your sides with laughter.

On my right there stands the house
of a doctor of the law
who learned a lot by reading his Boethius.
That street there in the dim-lit corner
is the street of Love—
whoever falls there cannot rise again.
You will also get to know,
if you stay with us for a while,
a certain friar,
a kind of abbot or a prior
of the church across the street.

A young man named Callimaco Guadagni
who just got back from Paris
lives there, in that house on the left.
He is known among his friends
as a worthy, noble fellow
both in looks and deeds.
He loved too much
a certain clever girl,
and how she was deceived by him
our comedy will explain—
how nice for you if you could be
tricked in the way she was!

Our story has the title *Mandrake Root*.
Why call it this?
The play will tell you why as it unfolds.
Its author isn't very famous,
but if you find you're not amused,
he'll stand you to a glass of wine.
To entertain you here today, we have
one poor, unhappy lover,
a scholar, not too bright,
a friar who lived a wicked life,
and evil's favorite parasite.

And if all this seems unimportant,
too trivial to come
from a man who is wise and serious,
excuse the author; he is only trying
with these little trifles
to brighten up his miserable life.
There is no other thing
that he can turn to—
for it has been impossible
to show his worth in other arts,
since no one will reward him for his labors.

He expects that his reward will be for all
to jeer and snicker and speak badly
of all they see and hear.
It is to this condition, with no doubt,
throwing our ancient code of valor out,
we have degenerated totally.
No wonder, then, that men
who see their efforts scorned
do not exert themselves to do,
no matter what the hardships,
the work the snow conceals and wind destroys.

And if by speaking badly of this author
you think you've got him by the hair,
frightened and dismissed him,
I warn you that he, too, knows how
to be just as malicious—
in fact, he is an expert at the art!
And, although he owes
respect to no man
in all of Italy,
gladly would he serve
a man who is his better.

But let's ignore those who speak evil,
and get back to our comedy
before it is too late—
Anyway, one should not put too much faith
in what a bunch
of foolish people say.
But, now, here comes Callimaco
and with him is his faithful servant, Siro.
They'll fill you in on everything.
Pay close attention now and don't wait
for me to give you further explanations.

ACT I

SCENE 1

CALLIMACO, SIRO

CALLIMACO: Siro, don't leave. I want you a moment.

SIRO: Here I am.

CALLIMACO: I believe you were amazed by my sudden departure from Paris, and you are probably wondering right now why I have been here almost a month without doing anything.

SIRO: That is very true.

CALLIMACO: If I haven't told you before what I am about to tell you now, it is not because I don't trust you, but rather because I feel that the best way to keep a secret is to say nothing unless you absolutely have to. Now, since I believe I shall be needing your help, I want to tell you everything.

SIRO: I am your servant, and servants should never question their masters or judge their motives; they should, when taken into the confidence of their master, serve faithfully. That's what I have always done and am still ready to do.

CALLIMACO: I realize that. I think you have heard me say a thousand times (so one more time won't matter) that I lost my family at the age of ten and that my guardians sent me to Paris, where I lived for twenty years. And when King Charles started those disastrous wars that destroyed Italy, I decided not to come home but to live in Paris, judging life there to be more secure than here in Italy.

SIRO: That is true.

CALLIMACO: And having sold all my belongings except this house, I lived in France for ten very happy years . . .

SIRO: Yes, I know that.

CALLIMACO: . . . spending my time partly studying, partly enjoying myself, and partly dealing in business. And I did not let any one occupation interfere with the others. And for this reason, as you know, I lived peacefully, offending no one and pleasing all. I managed to get along with everybody—merchants, nobles, foreigners, townspeople, rich and poor alike.

SIRO: That's the truth.

CALLIMACO: But Fortune felt I was too lucky; she saw to it that one Camillo Calfucci ran into me in Paris.

SIRO: I am beginning to see your problem.

CALLIMACO: I often entertained him, as I did other Florentines, and in speaking to him one day it happened that we began to argue about whether the most beautiful women lived in France or in Italy. Since I could not argue about Italian women, having left the country as a small boy, another Florentine at this gathering defended the French, while Camillo took the Italian side. After much discussion on both sides, Camillo got angry and claimed that he had a relative whose beauty alone could win the argument, even if every other Italian girl were an ugly monster.

SIRO: Now I know what you want to say.

CALLIMACO: He said her name was Madonna Lucrezia, the wife of Messer Nicia Calfucci, about whom he spoke so highly, praising her beauty and her manners so much that all of us were dumbfounded; and his praise filled me with such a great desire to see her that, forgetting all my other plans and no longer caring whether Italy was at war or peace, I set out to see her: and after my arrival, I found that the fame of Lucrezia's beauty was nothing compared to her real beauty (something that rarely occurs), and I want her so badly that I am nearly out of my mind.

SIRO: If you had mentioned it to me in Paris, I would have known how to advise you, but now I don't know what to say.

CALLIMACO: I'm telling you, not because I want your advice, but because I need to get this off my chest; and I also want you to be ready to help me if necessary.

SIRO: I am more than ready, but do you have any hope of success?

CALLIMACO: Ah, little or none. I'll explain: in the first place, she is not the type to go along with the plans I have for her; she is extremely virtuous and not given to thoughts of love. She has a rich husband who lets her dominate him, and though he is no longer young he is certainly not over the hill yet. Nor does she have neighbors or relatives who can escort her to soirées, parties, or to the other usual social occasions for young people. No workmen are allowed in the house, and all her servants fear her. Her character has not the slightest speck of corruption in it.

SIRO: Well, then, what are you going to do?

CALLIMACO: Nothing is ever so impossible that there isn't a way to do it. Even though such hope may be fragile and vain, a man's desire and determination to accomplish a difficult task will blind him to the chances of failure.

SIRO: Well, then, what is it that gives you hope?

CALLIMACO: Two things. The first is the stupidity of Messer Nicia, who is the dumbest, most foolish man in Florence (in spite of his law degree); the second is the desire of both Nicia and Lucrezia to have children, for they have been married six years without any. They are rich and do not want to die without heirs. A third reason comes to mind as well—Lucrezia's mother was not exactly a saint in her younger days. She's rich now and I'm not sure how to handle her.

SIRO: Have you made a move yet?

CALLIMACO: Yes, I have, but nothing serious.

SIRO: What do you mean?

CALLIMACO: You know Ligurio, who often comes to eat with us. He used to be a marriage broker; now he simply begs his meals. Because he is good company, Messer Nicia has taken a liking to him, and Ligurio uses him. Though he never gets invited to supper, he does get a bit of money from time to time. I've become his friend and have told him of my passion, and he has agreed to help me in any way possible.

SIRO: Be careful that he doesn't trick you, too; these spongers are not to be trusted.

CALLIMACO: I know that. But when you need somebody, you have to trust him. If we succeed, I have promised him some money; if not, he will at least earn a meal, since I do not like eating alone!

SIRO: What has he agreed to do so far?

CALLIMACO: He has promised to persuade Messer Nicia to go with Lucrezia to the mineral baths this May.

SIRO: How does that fit in with your plans?

CALLIMACO: What do you mean? Why, such a locale could change her prudish nature, since all one does at a place like that is to have a good time. I would go there myself and arrange all sorts of amusing things to do in order to show myself off in the best way; perhaps I could even become friendly with both of them. Who knows? Only time will tell, but one thing does lead to another.

SIRO: It just might work.

CALLIMACO: Ligurio left this morning to speak to Messer Nicia about it, and he will let me know how things turn out.

SIRO: Here come both of them.

CALLIMACO: I'll keep out of sight so I can speak to Ligurio when Messer Nicia has left him. In the meantime, go about your duties. If I need you for something, I'll let you know.

SIRO: I'm off. (*Exit Siro; enter Messer Nicia and Ligurio.*)

SCENE 2

MESSER NICIA, LIGURIO

NICIA: I think your advice is sound, and I spoke to my wife about it last night. She promised to give me an answer today; but, to tell you the truth, I, for one, am not very excited about going.

LIGURIO: Why?

NICIA: Because I am basically a homebody. And then, to

have to move my wife, servants, and baggage with me does not suit me. Besides this, last night I spoke to several doctors. One says to go to San Filippo, another to Porretta, a third to La Villa—I think they are a bunch of frauds. To tell you the truth, these doctors don't know their business.

LIGURIO: You are probably disturbed more for the first reason you mentioned: you are used to having the dome of Santa Maria del Fiore in view.

NICIA: You are mistaken! When I was younger, I was quite the roamer. There wasn't a fair in Prato that I didn't visit, and there is not a castle around here that I have not been to. What's more, I have even been as far as Pisa and Livorno. What do you say to that!

LIGURIO: You must have seen the Carrucola of Pisa.

NICIA: You mean the Verrucola.[1]

LIGURIO: Ah, yes, the Verrucola. Did you see the sea at Livorno?

NICIA: I certainly did see it.

LIGURIO: How much bigger is it than the Arno?

NICIA: Than the Arno? It's four—no, more than six—no, more than seven times bigger. You don't see anything but water and water and more water.

LIGURIO: Well, I certainly am amazed that you see so much difficulty in going to a spa, since you have pissed in so many other different places.

NICIA: Don't be childish. Do you think moving an entire household is nothing? Nevertheless, I want children so much, I am ready to do anything. You talk to these doctors about it and find out where they would advise me to go. Meanwhile, I'll go home to my wife and then you and I will meet there.

LIGURIO: As you wish. (*Exit Nicia.*)

[1]The Verrucola is a mountain range near Pisa.

SCENE 3

LIGURIO, CALLIMACO

LIGURIO: I don't think there is anyone in the whole world as stupid as he is; yet Fortune has been so good to him. He's rich, he's got a beautiful wife who is wise, has good manners, and is fit to govern a kingdom. Only rarely does a marriage bear out the proverb about marriage which says that God makes men but they find their own mates. Usually it is the excellent man who ends up with some beast or, on the contrary, the fine lady who marries a fool. But from Nicia's stupidity some good may come: Callimaco has hope. (*Enter Callimaco*.) But here he comes now! What are you doing here, Callimaco?

CALLIMACO: I saw you with Messer Nicia, and I was waiting until you got rid of him to hear what you decided.

LIGURIO: He is exactly the kind of man you think he is: of little prudence or courage. He would only leave Florence reluctantly. However, I have encouraged him, and finally he told me that he was ready to do anything. I think we could get him to leave if we wanted to, but I'm no longer sure that it suits our needs.

CALLIMACO: Why?

LIGURIO: It's like this. You know that all kinds of people go to those baths, and it is possible that someone might show up who would be attracted to Lucrezia as you are, and he might be richer and more handsome than you. Thus, our efforts might benefit others; competition might make her even more reluctant, or, should she be willing, she might well turn to someone else.

CALLIMACO: I realize that what you are saying is true, but what am I to do? What choice do I have? Where am I to turn? I have to try something, grandiose or dangerous, ruinous or infamous. It's better to die than to live like this. If only I could sleep at night, if I could eat, if I could just converse, if I could get pleasure from something—then I wouldn't mind waiting. But there seems to be no way out, and without any hope I shall die. And if I am to die, then nothing will stop me, no matter how violent or vicious I have to be.

LIGURIO: Don't talk like that; control yourself.

CALLIMACO: I conjure up schemes like this to keep calm, can't you see? Either we go on with our plan to send them to the baths or else we have to come up with another plan just to keep me from so much torment.

LIGURIO: You are right, and I'm the one to do it!

CALLIMACO: I believe it, though I know that people like you live by deception; however, I don't think you'll trick me because, if you do, and I catch you, I'll do everything to get even with you, and you would then lose my hospitality and the hope of what I promised you in the future.

LIGURIO: You can trust me, for even if my reward—which I am eager to get—is not forthcoming, I am a part of this scheme and I want you to consummate your desire almost as much as you do. But let's leave it at that. Messer Nicia gave me the task of finding a doctor and of discovering which of the baths would be the best one to choose. Now do as I tell you: say that you have studied medicine and have practiced in Paris. He'll have no trouble believing it—he's a simpleton; and you are learned and can recite a few words to him in Latin.

CALLIMACO: How will this help?

LIGURIO: It would help us send him to whichever bath we choose and enable me to try another plan I have in mind, one which would be quicker, more certain, and more likely to succeed than the trip to the baths.

CALLIMACO: What are you saying?

LIGURIO: If you keep your courage up and put your trust in me, I'll see to it that you have your wish before this time tomorrow. And even if he were able to tell whether or not you were a real doctor (which is not the case), my plan won't give him time to think or, if he does figure it out, he won't be in time to spoil my work.

CALLIMACO: You are reviving me. This is too great a promise, and I now have too great a hope. How will you do it?

LIGURIO: You'll learn it all in due time. I have told you enough for now; we have little enough time for action, much less for talk. You go home and wait for me there, and I'll go find Messer Nicia. And when I bring him to you, take your cue from me and fit your words to mine.

CALLIMACO: I'll do just as you say, but I am afraid that the hope you have given me will go up in smoke.

Curtain

ACT II

SCENE 1

LIGURIO, MESSER NICIA, SIRO

LIGURIO: As I was telling you, I believe God has sent us this man to help you fulfill your wish. He has had a great deal of experience in Paris, but do not be surprised if he has not practiced medicine in Florence. He does not need to for two reasons: first, he is rich; and second, he may be returning to Paris at any time now.

NICIA: That's what concerns me—I don't want him to get me in a pickle and then leave me holding the bag.

LIGURIO: Don't worry about that; just worry about the possibility of his not taking your case. But if he does take it, he will not abandon you until he sees it through to the end.

NICIA: I'll leave that problem to you. As for his qualifications, as soon as I speak to him I shall be able to tell if he is competent or not. I am not the kind of man that can be taken in!

LIGURIO: It's precisely because you are the person I know you to be that I am taking you to meet him. And if you do not think that he is an able man after examining him, his learning, and his manner of speech, then I am no longer an honest man!

NICIA: Well, for God's sake, let's get on with it! Where does he live?

LIGURIO: He lives right here in this square, through that door facing you.

NICIA: Good. You knock.

LIGURIO (*knocks*): There you are.

SIRO: Who is it?

LIGURIO: Is Callimaco in?

SIRO: Yes, he is.

NICIA: Why don't you call him Doctor Callimaco?

LIGURIO: He's not concerned with such trifles.

NICIA: Don't say that! Use his proper title. If he doesn't like it, that's tough!

SCENE 2

CALLIMACO, MESSER NICIA, LIGURIO, SIRO

CALLIMACO: Who is it that wants to see me?

NICIA: *Bona dies, domine magister.*[1]

CALLIMACO: *Et vobis bona, domine doctor.*[2]

LIGURIO: What do you say to that?

NICIA: Christ, what a doctor!

LIGURIO: If you two want me to stay here, speak so that I can understand you; otherwise we won't get anywhere.

CALLIMACO: What brings you here?

NICIA: I don't know where to begin. I am looking for two things that most men would avoid—to bring trouble to myself and to others. I don't have children and I want them, and to bring this trouble on myself I have come to trouble you.

CALLIMACO: It never troubles me to serve men of merit and breeding like yourself. I did not spend so many years in Paris learning my art for any other reason than to serve you and your peers.

NICIA: I am very grateful. Whenever you need my professional skill I'll help you gladly. But let us return *ad rem*

[1] Good day, professor.
[2] A good day to you, counselor.

nostra.[3] Have you decided which bath would be good to encourage my wife to become pregnant. I know that Ligurio here has told you our problem.

CALLIMACO: That is true, but in order to fulfill your desire it is first necessary to know why your wife is sterile, since there are many possible causes. *Nam causae sterilitatis sunt: aut in semine, aut in matrice, aut in instrumentis seminariis, aut in virga, aut in causa extrinseca.*[4]

NICIA: My God, this is the best doctor in the world!

CALLIMACO: Besides these possibilities, her sterility could be caused by your own impotence; if this were the case, there would be no remedy.

NICIA: Me, impotent? Don't make me laugh. I'm the healthiest and most virile man in Florence.

CALLIMACO: If that is true, then rest assured that we shall find a remedy.

NICIA: Can't we find something besides the baths? I don't want the inconvenience, and my wife will leave Florence only against her will.

LIGURIO: Yes, there is one—I'll answer that question myself. The good doctor is sometimes so polite that he never gets down to business. Callimaco, haven't you told me that you can mix certain potions that guarantee pregnancy?

CALLIMACO: Yes, I have. But I am careful about discussing them with people I don't know well, since they might take me for a charlatan.

NICIA: You can rely on me—you have impressed me so much that I would believe anything you say or do.

LIGURIO: I think you will have to take a urine sample.

CALLIMACO: Of course, you can't do without that.

LIGURIO: Call Siro. He can go home with the counselor and get it; we'll wait for him here. (*Enter Siro.*)

---

[3] to our business
[4] The various causes of sterility can reside either in the semen, in the womb, in the testicles, in the penis, or in some extrinsic cause.

CALLIMACO: Siro, go with him. Messer Nicia, come back as soon as possible, if it suits you, and we'll think of a solution to the problem.

NICIA: What do you mean "if it suits me"? I'll be back in no time at all. I have more faith in you than a Hun in his sword! (*Exeunt Callimaco and Ligurio.*)

SCENE 3

MESSER NICIA, SIRO

NICIA: Your master is truly a worthy man.

SIRO: More than you know.

NICIA: The King of France must hold him in great esteem.

SIRO: Indeed.

NICIA: That must make him happy to live in France.

SIRO: Yes, it does.

NICIA: He has the right idea. Here all we have are blockheads who have no idea how to appreciate talent. If he lived here, no one would even notice him. I know what I'm talking about—I had to shit blood to learn a few legal terms; if I had to live on that I'd be in bad trouble, I tell you!

SIRO: Do you earn a hundred ducats a year?

NICIA: Ducats—not even a hundred lire! Listen—if you're not working for the government in this town you won't even find a dog that'll bark at you! Here men of learning are good for nothing but funerals, weddings, or hanging around all day at the courthouse. But I'm not dependent on anyone, and it doesn't bother me, since others are worse off than myself. I wouldn't want what I am saying to get around, or I might get some new tax slapped on me or some other trouble that would really make me sweat.

SIRO: Don't worry about me.

NICIA: We're home—wait here. I'll be right back.

SIRO: Go right ahead. (*Exit Messer Nicia.*)

SCENE 4

SIRO

SIRO: If all educated men were like that one, we would all go mad! It looks like that rascal Ligurio and my crazy master are leading Messer Nicia to disaster. I'm all for it, as long as I know we'll get away with it; but if we get caught, my skin is in danger as well as my master's life and goods. He has already become a doctor of medicine—who knows what his plan is or where it will lead. But here's the lawyer with a urine bottle in his hand. Who wouldn't laugh at this trick?

SCENE 5

MESSER NICIA, SIRO

NICIA (*talking to himself as if to Lucrezia*): I always did everything your way; now I want you to do it my way. If I had known I wouldn't have children when I married you, I would have chosen a peasant woman. Oh, Siro, there you are! Follow me. What a job it was to get that silly woman to give me this urine! I don't mean that she doesn't want children—she wants them more than I—but whenever I try to do something about it, she gives me a hard time!

SIRO: Have patience—with sweet words you can make a woman do anything you want.

NICIA: Sweet words, you say? She's driving me crazy! Get going, and tell your master and Ligurio I'm here.

SIRO: Here they are now. (*Enter Ligurio and Callimaco.*)

SCENE 6

LIGURIO, CALLIMACO, MESSER NICIA

LIGURIO (*aside to Callimaco*): The lawyer will be easy to persuade, but his wife will be a problem. I think I have a way.

CALLIMACO: Do you have the specimen?

NICIA: Siro has it covered.

CALLIMACO: Give it here. Ah, this urine shows a weak kidney.

NICIA: It does look a bit cloudy, but she just passed it a moment ago.

CALLIMACO: Don't be surprised by its appearance. *Nam mulieris urinae sunt semper maioris grossitiei et albedinis et minoris pulchritudinis quam virorum. Huius autem, in caetera, causa est amplitudo canalium, mixtio eorum quae ex matrice exeunt cum urina.*[1]

NICIA: Oh, in the name of Saint Puccio's cunt! This fellow really knows how to talk—the more I know him, the smarter he gets!

CALLIMACO: I am afraid that your wife is not well covered at night, and that's why her urine is cloudy.

NICIA: She usually wears a long nightgown, but before she comes to bed she's like an animal out in the cold—four hours on her knees muttering "Our fathers."

CALLIMACO: Well, counselor, either you trust me or you don't; either I give you a sure cure or not. If you trust me, you'll take the cure, and if your wife doesn't have a son in her arms within the year, I'll give you two thousand ducats.

NICIA: Go on and tell me. I'll do anything you say. I trust you more than my confessor.

CALLIMACO: Then you have to understand this: nothing is more certain to make a woman pregnant than to give her a potion to drink made from the mandrake root. This is a tried and true remedy I've used several times and have always found successful, and if it were not so the Queen of France would still be sterile, not to mention an infinite number of other noble ladies of that country.

NICIA: Is this possible?

[1] The urine of the woman is always heavier and off-white and less limpid than that of the man. This fact is due to the greater width of her urinary tract and the presence of materials in the liquid that leave the womb along with the urine.

CALLIMACO: It's a fact. And Fortune has smiled on you, for I just happen to have with me all that I need to mix the potion, and you can have it anytime.

NICIA: When should she drink it?

CALLIMACO: This evening after supper, since the moon is just right and there couldn't be a better moment.

NICIA: Prepare the potion, and I'll make her take it—there won't be any problems.

CALLIMACO: There's only one catch—the man who first sleeps with a woman who has taken this medicine will die within eight days, and nobody can save him.

NICIA: Oh bloody shit! I won't touch that crap! You're not going to pull that on me. You've really fixed me up fine!

CALLIMACO: Calm yourself—there is a way.

NICIA: What is it?

CALLIMACO: Make someone else sleep with her so that, being with her one night, he will draw out the poison of the mandrake on himself.

NICIA: I wouldn't do that.

CALLIMACO: Why?

NICIA: Because I don't want to turn my wife into a whore and myself into a cuckold.

CALLIMACO: What are you saying, counselor? I took you for a smarter man. You mean to say that you hesitate to follow the King of France and most of the French nobility in these affairs?

NICIA: But who do you think I could find to do such a crazy thing? If I warn him, he won't agree; if I don't say anything, I shall trick him and commit a criminal offense. I don't want to get into any trouble.

CALLIMACO: If that's all that worries you, leave everything to me.

NICIA: How will you arrange it?

CALLIMACO: I'll tell you. I'll give you the potion this evening after supper; you give it to her to drink and put her to bed immediately, about four hours after dark. Then you, Ligurio, Siro, and I will disguise ourselves and go looking in the New Market and the Old Market and around here for the first likely young loafer to come along. We'll gag him and force him into your house and into your bedroom in the dark. Then we'll put him in the bed, tell him what to do, and there won't be any trouble at all. Then in the morning we'll send him off before dawn, wash up your wife, and you can use her as you wish without danger.

NICIA: I'm glad that you say kings and princes and noblemen use this method, but, more than that, I'm glad that no one will find out about it.

CALLIMACO: Who would tell?

NICIA: One important obstacle still remains.

CALLIMACO: What's that?

NICIA: To persuade my wife. I'm not sure she'll ever agree to it.

CALLIMACO: You are right. But I wouldn't call myself a husband if I couldn't dominate my own wife.

LIGURIO: I have thought of a solution.

NICIA: What is it?

LIGURIO: Her confessor.

CALLIMACO: But who will convince him?

LIGURIO: You, me, money, human nature, and the way priests are.

NICIA: I'm afraid that if I suggest it she won't go to talk to her confessor.

LIGURIO: There is even a remedy for that.

CALLIMACO: Tell me.

LIGURIO: Have her mother take her.

NICIA: She trusts her mother.

LIGURIO: And I know that her mother thinks the way we do. Come on, let's hurry—it's getting late. Callimaco, you take a walk, but be sure to meet us with the potion at home two hours after dusk. Messer Nicia and I shall go to persuade her mother, since I know her well. Then we'll go see the priest and let you know what we have done.

CALLIMACO (*aside to Ligurio*): Please, don't leave me alone.

LIGURIO: You really seem in bad shape.

CALLIMACO: Where can I go at this hour?

LIGURIO: Here, there, anywhere—Florence is a big place!

CALLIMACO: I can't stand it.

Curtain

ACT III

SCENE 1

SOSTRATA, MESSER NICIA, LIGURIO

SOSTRATA: I have often heard that a wise man chooses the lesser of two evils. If there is no other way to have children, then you must choose this method if it does not bother your conscience.

NICIA: That's right.

LIGURIO: You go find your daughter, and your son-in-law and I will find Brother Timoteo, her confessor, and tell him of the problem so that you will not have to. Then we'll see what he tells you.

SOSTRATA: Let's do that. You go that way, and I'll look for Lucrezia and take her to speak to the priest and see what happens. (*Exit Sostrata.*)

SCENE 2

MESSER NICIA, LIGURIO

NICIA: Perhaps you are surprised, Ligurio, that I have to go to so much trouble to persuade my wife, but if you knew everything you wouldn't be.

LIGURIO: I think it's because women are suspicious by nature.

NICIA: It's not just that. She used to be the sweetest, most docile person in the world, but since one of her neighbors told her that if she vowed to hear the first morning mass for forty days in a row she would conceive, she swore to do so and she attended mass about twenty times. Well, then—one of those horny priests began to pester her so much that she didn't want to go back. It's too bad that those who should set us good examples are like that. Don't you think I'm right?

LIGURIO: You're right as the devil!

NICIA: Since that time she has been as nervous as a hare. Suggest something to her and she'll find a thousand objections.

LIGURIO: I'm not surprised, but how did she fulfill her vow?

NICIA: She had herself dispensed from it.

LIGURIO: Good. But tell me, do you have twenty-five ducats, because in these matters you have to spend a bit in order to make this priest our friend and to encourage him to hope for more.

NICIA: Take them—money's no problem; I'll get them back somewhere else.

LIGURIO: These priests are astute and very clever; it's only natural, since they know both our sins and their own. If you're not experienced and if you don't know how to get them to help you, they can trick you. I don't want you to spoil everything by talking, because a man of your learning may spend all day in his study with his books, but he may not know how to manage more worldly affairs. (*Aside*): This guy is such an idiot that I am afraid he'll spoil everything.

NICIA: Just tell me what I should do.

LIGURIO: Leave the talking to me, and don't say anything unless I give you a sign.

NICIA: Agreed, but what sign will you give me?

LIGURIO: I'll wink and bite my lip. No, that won't work. Say, how long has it been since you spoke to this priest?

NICIA: More than ten years.

LIGURIO: Good. I'll say that you have become deaf, and you are not to answer or to say anything unless we shout at you.

NICIA: I'll do just that.

LIGURIO: Don't get upset if I say something that appears to be beside the point; I know what I'm doing.

NICIA: Well, until then. (*Exeunt Nicia and Ligurio.*)

SCENE 3

BROTHER TIMOTEO, A LADY

TIMOTEO: If you want to confess, I am ready to serve you.

LADY: Not today, thanks. I have an appointment. I just wanted to get a few things off my chest by chatting with you this way. By the way, have you said those masses to Our Lady?

TIMOTEO: Yes, I have.

LADY: Take this florin and say the mass of the dead every Monday for two months in the name of my late husband. Even though he was a brute, the flesh is weak, and when I remember him sometimes I can't help but feel a shiver . . . But do you really think he is in purgatory?

TIMOTEO: Beyond any shadow of a doubt.

LADY: I'm not so sure. You know very well what he did to me sometimes. Oh, how tired I am of bothering you about him! I kept away from him as much as I could, but he was so insistent. Oh, Our Lord in Heaven!

TIMOTEO: Don't worry. Great is God's mercy: if a man's will is not lacking, there is always time for him to repent.

LADY: Do you think the Turks will invade Italy this year?

TIMOTEO: They will if you don't say your prayers.

LADY: My faith! God preserve us from those devils! I have a very great fear of being impaled by these Turks! I see a friend of mine here in church who has something for me. I'll have to go meet her. Good day to you. (*Exit.*)

TIMOTEO: Go in God's name.

SCENE 4

TIMOTEO, LIGURIO, MESSER NICIA

TIMOTEO: Women are the most charitable creatures in the world—and also the most troublesome. If you avoid them, you avoid problems, but you also avoid certain advantages; but if you deal with them, you have both the advantages and the problems. I suppose it is true that you cannot have honey without flies. (*Enter Nicia and Ligurio.*) But what brings you here, gentlemen? Don't I recognize Messer Nicia?

LIGURIO: Speak louder. He has become so deaf that he can't hear a word.

TIMOTEO: Welcome, sir!

LIGURIO: Louder!

TIMOTEO: Welcome!!!

NICIA: I'm glad to be here.

TIMOTEO: What brings you here?

NICIA: I'm fine, thanks.

LIGURIO: Talk to *me,* father; for him to hear you, you'd have to bring down the square!

TIMOTEO: What do you seek of me?

LIGURIO: Messer Nicia here, and another fine gentleman whom you will hear about later, have several hundreds of ducats to distribute as alms.

NICIA: Oh, blood and shit!

LIGURIO (*to Messer Nicia*): Shut up, damn it—we won't give him much. Father, don't be surprised at what he says. He doesn't hear, but sometimes he thinks he does and answers without making sense.

TIMOTEO: Go on and let him say what he wishes.

LIGURIO: Of these alms, I have a portion with me, and they have decided that you are the man to distribute them.

TIMOTEO: I shall be happy to do so.

LIGURIO: But before we give you the money, you must help us with a strange case concerning Messer Nicia; only you can help us. It is a question concerning the honor of his entire household.

TIMOTEO: Tell me about it.

LIGURIO: I don't know if you know Camillo Calfucci, Messer Nicia's nephew.

TIMOTEO: Yes, I know him.

LIGURIO: A year ago he went to France on some business. Having lost a wife earlier, he left his daughter in the care of a convent—whose name I'd rather not divulge now.

TIMOTEO: What happened?

LIGURIO: What happened was that either because of the carelessness of the sisters or the stupidity of the girl she now finds herself four months pregnant; so that unless we patch things up with prudence, not only Messer Nicia, the nuns, the daughter, and Camillo but the entire Calfucci family will be disgraced. And Messer Nicia is so worried about the scandal that he vowed to give three hundred ducats for the Lord's work if this is kept secret.

NICIA: That's ridiculous!

LIGURIO (*to Nicia*): Shut the hell up! And he will put them into your custody; it's a matter that only you and the abbess can remedy.

TIMOTEO: How do you mean?

LIGURIO: Persuade the abbess to give the girl something to make her miscarry.

TIMOTEO: This is something I shall have to think about.

LIGURIO: Just think how much good would come from this act: you will preserve the honor of the convent, of the girl, and of her relatives; you will return a maiden to her father, satisfy Messer Nicia here and all his family, and distribute alms to the amount of three hundred ducats. On the other hand, you're only doing away with a piece of unborn flesh without feelings, a thing that might die in a thousand other ways, for I think that whatever pleases the majority is a good in itself.

TIMOTEO: So be it in God's name. May everything you wish be done and all of it for God's sake and for the sake of charity. Give me the convent's address, the potion, and, if you want, the money so that it can start doing some good.

LIGURIO: Now you are beginning to be the priest I thought you were. Take this portion of the money. The convent is . . . Wait a moment, a woman here in church is calling me. I'll return in a moment—don't leave Messer Nicia alone. I only have a couple of words to say to her. (*Exit.*)

SCENE 5

BROTHER TIMOTEO, MESSER NICIA

TIMOTEO: How much time does the girl have left?

NICIA: I'm furious.

TIMOTEO: I said, how much time does the girl have left?

NICIA: Goddamn him!

TIMOTEO: Why?

NICIA: I hope he breaks his neck.

TIMOTEO: I'm really in a mess. I'm dealing with a madman and a deaf man. One runs away, the other doesn't hear. But if there's a profit here somewhere, I'll be shrewder than they are. Ligurio is coming back.

SCENE 6

LIGURIO, BROTHER TIMOTEO, MESSER NICIA

LIGURIO (*to Messer Nicia*): Shut up. Father, I have wonderful news.

TIMOTEO: What is it?

LIGURIO: This woman I spoke to told me that the girl aborted herself.

TIMOTEO: Good. These alms will go into the general account.

LIGURIO: What do you mean?

TIMOTEO: I mean that now you have even better reason to give alms.

LIGURIO: The alms will be given in due course, but first there is something else you must do to help Messer Nicia.

TIMOTEO: What is it?

LIGURIO: Something less pressing, less scandalous but more acceptable to us and more profitable to yourself.

TIMOTEO: What is it? We are on such good terms and are so agreeable that there is nothing I would not do for you.
LIGURIO: I'll tell you about it in church privately, and Messer Nicia will be happy to wait for us here. We'll be right back.
NICIA: Don't do me any favors.
TIMOTEO: Let's go. (*Exeunt Timoteo and Ligurio.*)

SCENE 7

MESSER NICIA

NICIA: Is it day or night? Am I awake or dreaming? Am I drunk? No, I haven't been able to touch a drop because of all these goings-on. We arrange to say one thing to the priest, and then he says something else. First he wanted me to pretend I was deaf, and I had to stuff my ears so that I couldn't hear all the stupid things he said, to God knows what end! I'm out twenty-five ducats, we haven't even begun discussing my problem, and now they've left me standing here like a dumb prick! Oh, here they are again, and a pox on them if they haven't discussed my business.

SCENE 8

BROTHER TIMOTEO, LIGURIO, MESSER NICIA

TIMOTEO: Have the ladies come ahead. I know what I have to do, and if my authority has any influence we'll conclude this little family problem tonight.
LIGURIO: Messer Nicia, Brother Timoteo is willing to do everything he can. Make sure that the women come.
NICIA: You certainly have taken a burden off my mind. Will it be a boy?
LIGURIO: Yes, a boy.
NICIA: I'm so happy, I'm crying.
TIMOTEO: You two go ahead into the church, and I'll wait

for the ladies here. Stay out of sight, and when they have gone I shall tell you what their reaction was. (*Exeunt Ligurio and Nicia.*)

SCENE 9

BROTHER TIMOTEO

TIMOTEO: I don't know who's fooling who. That rascal Ligurio came to me with that first story to test me, so that if I refused to help him in that first affair he would have said nothing about the other in order not to reveal their plans, and the false pretext doesn't even concern them. It's true that I have been tricked, but this ruse can still be profitable to me. Messer Nicia and Callimaco are rich, and I should be able to get quite a bit out of both of them for different reasons. The affairs must be kept secret, since that is as much in my interest as in their own. Come what may, I'll have no regrets. There will probably be difficulties, since Madonna Lucrezia is clever and kind, but I shall play on her kindness. And, anyway, women aren't too bright. If a woman is capable of putting a few words together, she is considered a genius—in the land of the blind a one-eyed man is king. Here she is with her mother—who is really capable of anything. She will be of use to me in convincing her daughter. (*Exit.*)

SCENE 10

SOSTRATA, LUCREZIA

SOSTRATA: I'm sure you realize, Lucrezia, that I value your reputation as much as anyone in the world, and I wouldn't advise you to do anything that wasn't right. I've told you before, and I am telling you now, that if Brother Timoteo tells you there is nothing to burden your conscience about, you can do it without further thought.
LUCREZIA: I've always been afraid that Nicia's desire to have children would get us into trouble; because of this, I

am always suspicious whenever he comes up with a new scheme—especially after my bad experience in church, as you know. But of all the things he's dreamed up, this is the strangest—to have to submit my body to this outrage, to be the cause of a man's death because of such a disgrace. If I were the last woman on earth and the future of the human race depended on me, I don't think I could go through with it.

SOSTRATA: I don't know how to explain certain things to you, daughter. Speak to the priest, see what he has to say, and then do what he advises and what we, who love you, advise you to do.

LUCREZIA: I'm sweating with excitement.

SCENE 11

BROTHER TIMOTEO, LUCREZIA, SOSTRATA

TIMOTEO: Welcome, both of you! I know what you want me for, since Messer Nicia spoke to me. To tell you the truth, I've been paging through my books for more than two hours to study this case, and after much thought I have found numerous entries, both in particular and in general, that seem made for us.

LUCREZIA: Are you speaking the truth or just joking?

TIMOTEO: Oh, Madonna Lucrezia! Are these matters one jokes about? Don't you know me yet?

LUCREZIA: Yes, I know you, Father, but this is the strangest thing I have ever heard.

TIMOTEO: Madonna, I believe you, but I don't want you to carry on this way. Many things appear terrible, unsupportable, and strange from a distance; but when you approach them they become normal, bearable, and quite common—that's why they say that fear itself is worse than the evil that you fear. This is such a case.

LUCREZIA: I hope to God it is!

TIMOTEO: Let me return to what I said before. As far as your conscience is concerned, you should take this as a general rule, that where there is a certain good and an

uncertain evil the good should never be avoided for fear
of the evil. Here we have a certain good—you will conceive and bear a child, producing a soul for Our Lord.
The uncertain evil is that the man who sleeps with you
after you take the mandrake potion may die, but it is also
possible that he will not die. But since there is some danger, it is best that Messer Nicia not run this risk. As for the
act itself, whether or not it is a sin is foolish to discuss, for
it is the will that sins, not the body; the true sin is to displease your husband—but you will be pleasing him—or
to take pleasure in the act—but it will displease you. Besides this, in all things one must look to the result: the
outcome of your act is to fill a seat in paradise and to
please your husband. The Bible says that the daughters of
Lot, believing themselves to be alone in the world, lay
with their father; and because their intent was good they
did not sin.

LUCREZIA: What counsel do you give me, then?

SOSTRATA: Just let yourself be counseled, daughter. Don't
you see that a childless woman has no security? If her
husband dies, she is left like a stray animal, abandoned by
everyone.

TIMOTEO: I swear to you, Madonna Lucrezia, by this holy
cloth I wear, that humoring your husband in this matter
will cause you no more spiritual grief than would eating
meat on Wednesday, and that is a sin that can be removed
with holy water.

LUCREZIA: Where are you leading me, Father?

TIMOTEO: I'm leading you toward something for which
you will always thank me in your prayers—and you will
be even more satisfied about a year from now.

SOSTRATA: She will do what you wish. I'll put her to bed
tonight myself. Silly girl, what are you afraid of? There
are fifty girls in town who would thank God to be in your
place.

LUCREZIA: I agree, but I don't think I shall be alive tomorrow morning.

TIMOTEO: Have no fear, my child. I shall pray to God for you and shall ask the angel Raphael to comfort you. Go now with my blessing and prepare yourself for this holy miracle.

SOSTRATA: Peace be with you, Father.

LUCREZIA: God and Our Lady protect me from harm! (*Exeunt Lucrezia and Sostrata.*)

SCENE 12

BROTHER TIMOTEO, LIGURIO, MESSER NICIA

TIMOTEO: Ligurio, come out now!

LIGURIO: How did it go?

TIMOTEO: Very well. They went home prepared to do everything, and there won't be any problems since her mother went with her and will put her to bed herself.

NICIA: Are you telling the truth?

TIMOTEO: Jesus, you are cured of your deafness!

LIGURIO: Saint Clement has granted him this miracle.

TIMOTEO: You will naturally want to place an ex-voto here to spread the word; this way I, too, can make a profit.

NICIA: Let's not get off the track. Will she give us any trouble in doing what I wish?

TIMOTEO: No, I tell you.

NICIA: I'm the happiest man in the world.

TIMOTEO: I believe it. You'll soon be the father of a fine boy, and to hell with those without your luck!

LIGURIO: Father, go back to your devotions. If we need anything else, we'll come to see you. Messer Nicia, you should follow your wife to keep her from changing her mind, and I shall find Doctor Callimaco and get him to send the potion. Let's meet after dark in order to arrange what we have to do later.

NICIA: That's fine. Goodbye.

TIMOTEO: Go with God's blessing.

Curtain

ACT IV

SCENE I

CALLIMACO

CALLIMACO: I certainly would like to know what the others have done. When will I see Ligurio again? It must be eleven o'clock—no, almost midnight! What agony I've been through and still have to put up with! It's true that Nature and Fortune balance their accounts—you never get something good without having to pay for it by misfortune. The higher my hopes, the greater are my fears. Poor me! How can I continue living in anguish like this, with so many hopes and fears to upset me? I am like a ship blown by two contrary winds—the closer I come to port, the more likely it is that I will sink. The stupidity of Messer Nicia gives me hope, but the cleverness and resoluteness of Lucrezia give me pause. Ah, if I could only rest. Sometimes I try to calm myself and reproach my frenzy by telling myself: "What are you doing? Are you mad? When you win her, what then? You will see the mistake you have made and repent of the bother and the anguish it cost you. Don't you realize how little satisfaction men find in things they desire as compared with what they hope to find in them? On the other hand, the worst that can happen to you is to die and go to hell, and many others have suffered the same fate—many gentlemen, too! Are you ashamed to be damned with such company as they? Face your fate—flee danger; but if you cannot, then confront it like a man. Don't cringe like a woman!" In this way I try to raise my spirits, but it doesn't last long, for my desire to possess the woman I love only once overtakes me so that I feel weak from head to toe: my legs shake; my stomach turns; my heart is in my throat; my arms hang heavy; my tongue is mute; my eyes are dazzled; my brain is dizzy. If I could just find Ligurio, I would have someone to tell this to. His report will either give me life a while longer or strike me dead. (*Enter Ligurio.*)

SCENE 2

LIGURIO, CALLIMACO

LIGURIO: I never wanted to see Callimaco more than now and never had more trouble in finding him. If I were bringing him bad news, I would have met him immediately. I've been to his home, to the piazza, to the market, to the Spini Works, to the loggia of the Tornaquinci, and I haven't found him. These lovers are like cats on a hot roof—they just can't keep still.

CALLIMACO: Why am I waiting? He looks happy. Ligurio, Ligurio!

LIGURIO: Oh, Callimaco. Where have you been?

CALLIMACO: Any news?

LIGURIO: Good news.

CALLIMACO: Really good?

LIGURIO: The best.

CALLIMACO: Has Lucrezia agreed?

LIGURIO: Yes.

CALLIMACO: The priest did his job?

LIGURIO: He sure did.

CALLIMACO: Oh, what a blessed friar! I'll always pray to God for him.

LIGURIO: That's a good one—as if God granted the prayers of the evil as well as those of the good. This priest will want something besides your prayers!

CALLIMACO: What does he want?

LIGURIO: Cash!

CALLIMACO: Give it to him. How much did you promise?

LIGURIO: Three hundred ducats.

CALLIMACO: You did well.

LIGURIO: Messer Nicia forked over twenty-five of them.

CALLIMACO: Messer Nicia?

LIGURIO: Don't worry about details. Just be happy that he did.

CALLIMACO: What did Lucrezia's mother do?

LIGURIO: Almost everything. When she understood that her daughter could have this pleasant evening without sin, she didn't stop praying, ordering, and comforting Lucrezia until she led her to the priest and worked it out so that Lucrezia consented.

CALLIMACO: Oh, God, what have I done to deserve such good fortune? I'm so happy I could die!

LIGURIO: What kind of guy is he? First he's dying of grief, then of happiness. He seems to want to croak any way he can. Have you got the potion ready?

CALLIMACO: Yes, it's here.

LIGURIO: What are you sending?

CALLIMACO: A glass of hippocras tea. Just the thing to calm her stomach and to warm the heart. Oh my god, oh my god, I'm ruined.

LIGURIO: What is it? What are you talking about?

CALLIMACO: There's no way out.

LIGURIO: What the hell is going on?

CALLIMACO: We haven't gotten anywhere. And I've painted myself into a corner.

LIGURIO: Why? Tell me what's the problem. Take your hands away from your face.

CALLIMACO: Don't you see the problem? I told Messer Nicia that you, he, Siro, and I would get someone to lie with his wife.

LIGURIO: So what?

CALLIMACO: What do you mean, so what? If I'm with you, I can't be the one who is kidnaped, and if I'm not with you, he'll discover the trick.

LIGURIO: You're right. But isn't there a way around this?

CALLIMACO: I don't think so.

LIGURIO: Yes there is.

CALLIMACO: What is it?

LIGURIO: Let me think a bit.

CALLIMACO: You really had everything figured out, didn't you? I'm really cooked if you have to start thinking at this point!

LIGURIO: I've got it.

CALLIMACO: What is it?

LIGURIO: I'll see to it that the priest takes care of this, since he's helped us this far.

CALLIMACO: How?

LIGURIO: We all have to disguise ourselves. I'll dress the priest—we'll change his voice, his face, and his clothes. I'll tell the counselor that he is you, and he'll believe it.

CALLIMACO: That's fine, but what must I do?

LIGURIO: Be sure to wear a short cloak and come by his house with a lute in your hand, singing a little tune.

CALLIMACO: Without a mask?

LIGURIO: Of course. If you wore a mask he would suspect something.

CALLIMACO: Then he'll recognize me.

LIGURIO: No, he won't, because you are going to distort your features. Twist your face with your mouth open, gnash and grind your teeth, and close one eye. Try it right now.

CALLIMACO: Like this?

LIGURIO: No.

CALLIMACO: This way?

LIGURIO: Not enough.

CALLIMACO: Is this better?

LIGURIO: Yes, yes, remember how to do that. I have a false nose at home; you can put that on, too.

CALLIMACO: Okay, but what next?

LIGURIO: When you arrive at his block, we'll be there to grab you and your lute; we'll spin you around, bring you inside, and put you in bed. You have to do the rest on your own!

CALLIMACO: But that's where the difficult part begins!

LIGURIO: That's your worry. Only make sure that you can get back again—that we cannot arrange for you.

CALLIMACO: What do you mean?

LIGURIO: That you should take her tonight. Before you leave, let her know who you are, explain the trick to her, show her your love, tell her how much you care for her, how, without any scandal whatever, you can be her lover, and how scandalous it would be to become your enemy. It's impossible that she won't see the light and that she will want tonight to be the last night.

CALLIMACO: You really believe this?

LIGURIO: I'm sure of it. But let's not lose any more time— it's already ten o'clock. Call Siro, send the potion to Messer Nicia, and wait for me at home. I'll get the priest, disguise him, and bring him here. Then we'll find Messer Nicia and do whatever still has to be done.

CALLIMACO: Fine. Get going. (*Exit Ligurio.*)

SCENE 3

CALLIMACO, SIRO

CALLIMACO: Siro!

SIRO: Sir?

CALLIMACO: Come here.

SIRO: Here I am.

CALLIMACO: Take that silver goblet inside the dresser in my room, cover it with a piece of cloth, bring it here, and don't spill anything on the way.

SIRO: It's as good as done. (*Exit Siro.*)

CALLIMACO: Siro has been with me for ten years and has always served me faithfully. I believe I can trust him in this case as well; although I haven't explained everything to him, he is very shrewd and will figure it out; he seems to be going along with it.

SIRO: Here it is.

CALLIMACO: Very good. Now go to Messer Nicia's and tell him that this is the medicine his wife has to take right after supper—the sooner she eats, the better. And inform him that we'll all be at our assigned posts—at the time he is to meet us there. And hurry up.

SIRO: I'm going.

CALLIMACO: And listen, if he wishes, wait and come back

with him; if not, return here immediately after giving him the goblet. Do you understand?

SIRO: Yes, sir. (*Exit.*)

SCENE 4

CALLIMACO

CALLIMACO: Here I am, waiting for Ligurio to return with the priest. Whoever said that waiting is a hard thing surely told the truth. I seem to be losing ten pounds an hour, thinking about where I am now and where I could be in two hours, and being afraid all the time that something may interfere with my plans. If that happens, it will be my last night on earth, because I'll hang myself, jump into the Arno, throw myself out of those windows, or even cut my own throat in her doorway! I'll do something, because I couldn't live any longer. But is that Ligurio I see? It *is* Ligurio, and he has someone with him who looks like a lame hunchback—that must be the priest in disguise. Oh, these friars—when you've known one, you've known them all! Who is the other guy with them? It looks like Siro, already back from Messer Nicia's. It's he. I'll wait here to meet them.

SCENE 5

SIRO, LIGURIO, CALLIMACO, BROTHER TIMOTEO IN DISGUISE

SIRO: Who's that with you, Ligurio?

LIGURIO: A very worthy man.

SIRO: Is he lame or just pretending?

LIGURIO: Mind your own business!

SIRO: He has the face of a real crook!

LIGURIO: For Christ's sake, shut up or you'll ruin everything! Where's Callimaco?

CALLIMACO: Here I am. Welcome to all of you.

LIGURIO: Callimaco, warn this idiot Siro; he's about to spill the beans.

CALLIMACO: Listen, Siro. Tonight you must do everything Ligurio tells you just as if it were I ordering you; and whatever you see and hear you must keep very secret if you value my property, my honor, and my life as well as your own interests.

SIRO: Consider it done.

CALLIMACO: Did you give the goblet to Messer Nicia?

SIRO: Yes, sir.

CALLIMACO: What did he say?

SIRO: That he'll be at your service shortly.

TIMOTEO: Is this Callimaco?

CALLIMACO: Yes, I am Callimaco, at your service. Our contract is drawn—you have myself and my fortune at your disposal just as if it were your own.

TIMOTEO: I understand everything and believe in it; therefore I have done for you what I would not have done for another person in the world.

CALLIMACO: You will not be sorry.

TIMOTEO: It is enough that you wish me well.

LIGURIO: Enough with all these polite exchanges! Siro and I are going to disguise ourselves. Callimaco, you come with us and get ready to play your role. The priest will wait for us here. We'll return immediately, then go to find Messer Nicia.

CALLIMACO: Fine. Let's go.

TIMOTEO: I'll wait here. (*Exeunt Callimaco, Siro, and Ligurio.*)

SCENE 6

BROTHER TIMOTEO

TIMOTEO: It certainly is true what people say: bad company leads men to the gallows, and one can end just as badly by being too credulous or too good as one can by being too evil. God knows that I never intended to hurt anyone. I was in my cell saying my office and looking after my flock, when along comes this devil Ligurio, who first made me dip my finger into mischief, then my arm, and then all of me, and I still don't know where it will end. But one thing consoles me: when something involves a number of people, no one person in particular can be blamed. Ah, I see Ligurio and that servant returning. (*Enter Ligurio and Siró.*)

SCENE 7

BROTHER TIMOTEO, LIGURIO, SIRO

TIMOTEO: Welcome back!

LIGURIO: How do we look?

TIMOTEO: Perfect.

LIGURIO: The lawyer is missing. Let's head toward his house. It's already past eleven. Hurry!

SIRO: Someone is opening his door. Could it be a servant?

LIGURIO: No, it's Messer Nicia. Hah, hah, hah!

SIRO: You're laughing?

LIGURIO: Who wouldn't? He's wearing some kind of crummy old cloak that doesn't even cover his ass. What the devil does he have on his head? It looks like something worn by churchmen; and he even has a little sword underneath. Hah, hah, hah! He's muttering something or other. Let's keep out of sight and listen to what his wife has to put up with.

SCENE 8

MESSER NICIA

NICIA: What a lot of problems my crazy wife creates! She sent the maids to her mother's and the butler to our country villa. I approve of that, but I don't approve of all the fuss she made before she agreed to be put to bed—"I don't want to!" "What will I do?" "What are you making me do?" "Oh mamma mia!" And if her mother had not told her what would happen to her if she didn't change her mind she would never have gone to bed. A pox on her! I don't mind if a woman is a bit bothersome, but not that much! She's driving me out of my mind, that chicken

brain! If you were to say to her, "Hang me if you're not
the finest woman in Florence!" she would say, "What
have I done to you?" And even though I'm sure the sword
will wound her tonight, before I leave the battlefield I'm
going to inspect everything with my very own hands. I
really look rather handsome. Who would recognize me? I
look taller, younger, slimmer, and there isn't a woman in
Florence who would charge me to sleep with her tonight.
But where are the others?

SCENE 9

LIGURIO, MESSER NICIA, BROTHER TIMOTEO, SIRO

LIGURIO: Good evening, counselor!

NICIA: Oh, ah, O my . . .

LIGURIO: Don't be afraid, it's only us.

NICIA: Oh, you're all here. If I hadn't recognized you, I'd
have given you all a whack with my sword! Are you Ligurio? And you Siro? And this other is your master?
Good.

LIGURIO: Yes, counselor.

NICIA: Let's take a look. Oh, he's disguised so well that not
even the sheriff would know him!

LIGURIO: I had him put two nuts in his mouth so that no
one would recognize his voice.

NICIA: You are stupid.

LIGURIO: Why?

NICIA: Why didn't you tell me about that? I would have
put some in my mouth as well; you know how important
it is for people not to recognize our voices.

LIGURIO: Here, put this in your mouth.

NICIA: What is it?

LIGURIO: A ball of wax.

NICIA: Give it here . . . ugh, phew! May you burn in Hell,
you dirty bastard!

LIGURIO: Oh, excuse me, I gave you the wrong one by
accident.

NICIA: Ugh, yech, phew! (*He spits violently.*) What, what—what was it?

LIGURIO: Bitter aloes.

NICIA: God damn you! (*He spits again.*) Doctor, aren't you going to say anything?

TIMOTEO: I'm angry with Ligurio for doing that.

NICIA: Oh, how well you disguise your voice!

LIGURIO: We're losing time here. I'll be the general and draw up the army for the battle. At the right horn will be Doctor Callimaco, I'll be on the left, and between the horns will be Messer Nicia. Siro will be rear guard and will help anyone who falls back. The password will be Saint Cuckold.

NICIA: Who is Saint Cuckold?

LIGURIO: He is the most venerated saint in France. Let's be off. Set our ambush at this corner. Be quiet. I hear a lute playing.

NICIA: It's a man. What should we do?

LIGURIO: We'll send a scout to the front to find out who he is and, depending on what he reports back to us, we'll take it from there.

NICIA: Who will go?

LIGURIO: You go, Siro. You know what you have to do. Make inquiries, investigate, then return immediately and report to us.

SIRO: I'm on my way.

NICIA: I don't want to make a mistake here by picking up somebody who is weak or sick, or we'll have to repeat this operation tomorrow night.

LIGURIO: Don't worry. Siro can handle this. He's on his way back now. What did you find out, Siro?

SIRO: He's the handsomest young rake you ever saw—not more than twenty-five years old, alone, shabbily dressed, and playing a lute.

NICIA: If you are right, he's just what we need. But be sure not to spoil this stew; otherwise I'll dump it all on you.

SIRO: He's just the way I described him to you.

LIGURIO: Let's wait until he turns the corner, and then we'll all jump him at once.

NICIA: Doctor, come over here—you've been so quiet all evening. Here he comes! (*Enter Callimaco, disguised and singing.*)

CALLIMACO: "May the devil go to bed with you, since I cannot be there."

LIGURIO: Hold him tight. Give us that lute!

CALLIMACO: Hold on—what have I done?

NICIA: You'll soon see. Cover his head. Gag him!

LIGURIO: Spin him around!

NICIA: Give him another turn, another. Now put him in the house!

TIMOTEO: Messer Nicia, I'm going home for a nap; my head is killing me. And, if you won't be needing me, I will not be back tomorrow morning.

NICIA: Fine, Doctor Callimaco, don't come back; we can handle everything ourselves. (*Exeunt all save the priest.*)

SCENE 10

BROTHER TIMOTEO

TIMOTEO: Now that they've all gone inside, I'll return to the monastery. And you, in the audience, don't worry: nobody will sleep tonight, for the comedy's action will not be interrupted by an interval of time. I shall say my prayers. Ligurio and Siro will eat, since they didn't have time to eat today. The lawyer will go from room to room, keeping his eye on things. Callimaco and Madonna Lucrezia won't sleep, because I know that if I were he and you were she, we wouldn't sleep either!

Curtain

ACT V

SCENE 1

BROTHER TIMOTEO

TIMOTEO: I was so anxious to know how Callimaco and the others made out last night that I didn't get any sleep. I've tried to pass the time of day in various ways: I said morning mass, read one of the lives of the church fathers, went into the church and lit a lamp that had burned out, and changed the veil on one of our Madonnas who works miracles. How many times have I told these friars to keep it clean! And they wonder why devotion is declining. I remember when she had five hundred ex-votos around her, and today there are less than twenty; this is our fault because we haven't kept up her reputation. We used to go there every evening after the services in procession and have litanies sung to her every Saturday. We even made our own ex-votos so that there were always fresh ones there; we used the confessional to encourage men and women to make offerings to her. Now we no longer do anything like this, and then we wonder why things have cooled down! Oh, what little brains these brothers of mine have! But I hear a great commotion coming from Messer Nicia's place. There they are. They're throwing their prisoner out the door. I'm just in time. It's almost dawn. The lovers must have enjoyed themselves to the last drop. I want to hear what they are saying, but they must not see me, so I'll hide.

SCENE 2

MESSER NICIA, CALLIMACO, LIGURIO, SIRO

NICIA: You grab him here, I'll hold him on this side, and Siro, you take him by his cloak from behind.
CALLIMACO: Don't hurt me!

LIGURIO: Don't be afraid, just be on your way.

NICIA: We'd best not go further.

LIGURIO: You're right. Let's leave him here. Give him another two turns so he won't know where he came from. Spin him around, Siro!

SIRO: There.

NICIA: Again!

SIRO: It's done.

CALLIMACO: My lute!

LIGURIO: Go on, you wretch, beat it! If I hear you talking about this, I'll cut your throat! (*Exit Callimaco.*)

NICIA: He ran off. Let's remove these disguises. We all have to be out of our houses early so that it doesn't look like we have been up all night.

LIGURIO: You're right.

NICIA: You and Siro go to find Doctor Callimaco and tell him everything went well.

LIGURIO: What can we tell him? We don't know anything. You know we arrived at your house, and that we went into the cellar to drink. You and your mother-in-law handled him, and we didn't see you again until just now, when you called us to get rid of him.

NICIA: That's true. Oh, can I tell you some fine stories! My wife was in bed in the dark. Sostrata was waiting for me by the fire. I arrived with that guy. In order not to have any doubts about anything, I led him over to a little room where there was a weak light so that he could not see my face.

LIGURIO: How very wise.

NICIA: I made him strip. That bothered him, but I turned on him like a mad dog so that he tore off his clothes in a flash and was completely naked. He had an ugly face, a horrible nose, and a twisted mouth, but you never saw such beautiful skin—white, soft, tender. As for the rest, you needn't ask.

LIGURIO: Some things are best not discussed. But did you have to see everything?

NICIA: Are you kidding? Once I had put my hand in the

flour, I had to knead the dough. I wanted to see if he was healthy. Suppose he had the pox; where would that leave me? Of course I checked everything.

LIGURIO: Yes, you are right.

NICIA: When I saw he was healthy, I had him follow me and led him into the bedroom in the dark. I put him in the bed. Then, before I left I decided to feel with my own hands how things were getting along. I'm not one to take fireflies for lanterns!

LIGURIO: My, my—with what wisdom you arranged this whole affair!

NICIA: When I had touched and felt everything, I left the room, locked the door, and returned to Sostrata at the fireplace. We stayed up all night talking.

LIGURIO: What did you talk about?

NICIA: About Lucrezia's stupidity, and how it would have been better if she had agreed to this without so much fuss. Afterward we talked about the baby which I could already feel in my arms—the little brat!—until I heard the clock strike. Thinking it was almost dawn, I returned to the bedroom. What do you think of this—I could hardly wake that wretch up!

LIGURIO: I believe it!

NICIA: He really enjoyed his sauce! Finally he got up, I called you, and we brought him outside.

LIGURIO: It went very well.

NICIA: You know, something worries me.

LIGURIO: What's that?

NICIA: That poor young man who has to die so soon; this one night cost him so dear.

LIGURIO: Oh, you don't have to worry about that—it's his problem.

NICIA: I guess you're right. But I can't wait to see Doctor Callimaco and to congratulate him.

LIGURIO: He'll be out within an hour. But the sun is already up. Let's change our clothes. What about you?

NICIA: I'm going home, too, for clean clothes. I'll get my wife up and have her wash, and then I'll bring her to

church to have her purified again. I would like you and
Doctor Callimaco to be there, and we should speak to the
priest to thank him and to reward him for the good that
he has done us.

LIGURIO: Well said. That's just what we'll do. (*Exeunt all
but Brother Timoteo.*)

SCENE 3

BROTHER TIMOTEO

TIMOTEO: I'm pleased with the way things went, considering how stupid that lawyer is, but the thing that pleased
me most was what he said about my reward. I shouldn't
stay here since they will be looking for me at my place. I'll
wait for them in church, where my services bring a higher
price. But who is coming out of that house? It looks like
Ligurio, and that must be Callimaco with him. I don't
want them to see me, as I explained. If they don't come to
me, I can always find them. (*Exit.*).

SCENE 4

CALLIMACO, LIGURIO

CALLIMACO: As I told you, Ligurio my friend, at first I was
rather uneasy for a number of hours, and although I enjoyed myself very much, things didn't seem right. But
when I told her who I was, and about my love for her, and
how easily the stupidity of her husband might allow us to
love happily without any scandal, and how I would marry
her as soon as God had made other plans for Messer
Nicia—and when, in addition to these facts, she had felt
the difference between the way I made love and how
Nicia did, and the difference between the kisses of a
young lover and those of an old husband, after sighing a
few times she said: "Since your cunning, the stupidity of
my husband, the unscrupulousness of my mother, and the
evil nature of my confessor have made me do what I

would never have done on my own, I shall have to believe that it is some divine power that causes me to act in this way! And since I am not capable of resisting Heaven's wishes, I accept. Therefore, I take you for lord, master, and guide: you must be everything good; for me you will be my father, my defender; and what my husband wanted for one night I now want him to have forever. Become his close friend, then. Be in church this morning, and from there you can come to dine with us here; you can come and go as you will, and we can be together constantly and without suspicion." Hearing those words, I was about to die from happiness. I could not express even a small part of what I felt. I am the happiest and most satisfied man in the world, and if time or death does not take this happiness from me, I shall be more blessed than the blessed, more saintly than the saints.

LIGURIO: I am content if you are happy, and everything went just as I told you it would. But what do we do now?

CALLIMACO: Let's go to the church, since I promised to be there to see Lucrezia, her mother, and Messer Nicia.

LIGURIO: I hear the door opening. They are over there with Messer Nicia behind them.

CALLIMACO: Let's go to the church and wait for them there. (*Exeunt Ligurio and Callimaco.*)

SCENE 5

MESSER NICIA, LUCREZIA, SOSTRATA

NICIA: Lucrezia, I think everything should be done prudently and not haphazardly.

LUCREZIA: Now what is your complaint?

NICIA: Look how she answers—just like a proud cock!

SOSTRATA: Don't be too surprised; after all, she is a bit excited.

LUCREZIA: What do you mean by that?

NICIA: I'd better go ahead to speak to the priest and tell him to meet you at the door of the church to purify you. It is truly fitting that you be reborn this morning.

LUCREZIA: Well, aren't you going then?

NICIA: You are really something this morning. Last night you seemed almost dead.

LUCREZIA: That's thanks to you.

SOSTRATA: Go on and find the priest. No need—there he is outside the church.

NICIA: You're right.

SCENE 6

BROTHER TIMOTEO, MESSER NICIA, LUCREZIA, CALLIMACO, LIGURIO, SOSTRATA

TIMOTEO: I am outside because Callimaco and Ligurio told me that Messer Nicia and the ladies are coming to church. Here they come now.

NICIA: *Bona dies,* Father!

TIMOTEO: Welcome, all of you. May Fortune smile on all of you, and may God grant you a handsome son, Madonna Lucrezia.

LUCREZIA: May God grant it.

TIMOTEO: Oh, He will, He certainly will grant it.

NICIA: Are Ligurio and Doctor Callimaco coming to church as well?

TIMOTEO: Of course.

NICIA: Call them.

TIMOTEO: Come over here! (*Enter Callimaco and Ligurio.*)

CALLIMACO: God save you all!

NICIA: Doctor, give my wife your hand.

CALLIMACO: Most happily.

NICIA: Lucrezia, this is the man who will provide us with a stout support for our old age.

LUCREZIA: I am most grateful for that support, and I hope that he will become our close friend.

NICIA: God bless you! I want you and Ligurio to dine with us this morning.

LUCREZIA: Of course.

NICIA: I am going to give them the key to the ground floor of the loggia so that they can come and stay there whenever they like; they have no women to care for them, poor beasts.

CALLIMACO: I accept with pleasure, and I'll make use of it whenever my need arises.

TIMOTEO: Will I receive the monies for the alms?

NICIA: You certainly will, Father. They will be sent today.

LIGURIO: Won't someone remember Siro?

NICIA: Let him ask. Whatever I have is his. Lucrezia, how much should we give the priest for cleansing you?

LUCREZIA: Give him ten large ducats.

NICIA: Oh, my God!

TIMOTEO: Lady Sostrata, you seem to be younger today.

SOSTRATA: I'm happy. Who wouldn't be today?

TIMOTEO: Let's all go into the church, and I'll say the required service. Afterward you can go off to eat at your leisure. You in the audience—don't wait for us to come out this time. The service is long, and I shall remain in church. The others will leave by the side door for their homes. Farewell!

Curtain

From *THE ART OF WAR*

EDITORS' NOTE

Many of the general ideas contained in this work on war and military life are essential for an understanding of the most important concepts in Machiavelli's political theory. The Art of War *is not without errors of judgment or fundamental conceptual flaws. Machiavelli's distrust of cavalry and his belief in the ineffectiveness of artillery in a modern army led him to make serious tactical blunders and to ignore the actual developments evident in the armies of his own time. His hatred of mercenary troops was motivated more by his humanistic preoccupation with the concept of civic virtue fostered by a citizens' militia than by a reasoned and dispassionate study of the actual military institutions of his day. For example, the armies of Cesare Borgia, which he praised, were composed not of the duke's own subjects, as he imagined, but of professional mercenaries. Moreover, the bloodless battles he described with contempt in several of his works, and which he attributed to the use of mercenary troops, were not, in fact, as bloodless as he imagined. His empirical observations were often distorted by the ideas he discovered in the classical texts on warfare and military leaders by Livy and Tacitus, as well as other writers, and his evaluation of military science in Renaissance Italy was colored by ideological concerns and political preferences. But if his essentially literary and humanistic views hindered an empirical study of military institutions in his time, they also* allowed him to envision a more fundamental theoretical relationship between politics and warfare, which resulted in a concept of civic humanism that would be an integral part of the republican legacy in years to come.

The gap between practice and theory in Machiavelli's discussion of the art of war was evident even when the work first appeared in print. In the preface to one of his Novelle (*I, xl*), Matteo Bandello tells a humorous story about Machiavelli's futile attempts to drill some troops under the command of the brilliant Medici condottiere, Giovanni delle Bande Nere (*1494–1526*). After more than two hours in the hot Milanese sun, Machiavelli had failed to implement his own advice in the field, yet with only the sound of a drum and the force of his personality the condottiere restored order and corrected Machiavelli's mistakes in the twinkling of an eye. Yet Machiavelli's political duties in the Florentine chancery did provide him with some limited practical military experience, for his first official mission in 1498 involved the war with Pisa. In 1505 he was authorized to raise a body of militiamen from among the Florentine citizenry. His faith in a nonprofessional army was strengthened when his troops took Pisa in 1509. However, his militiamen were no match for the seasoned professional soldiers who attacked Florence in 1512 and restored the Medici to power. His discussion of the essential unity of politics and military science in The Art of War has always appealed to great military thinkers, including Frederick the Great, Napoleon, and von Clausewitz.

The Art of War *is divided into a preface and seven books. It is written in the form of a dialogue, a form popular among many humanists of the period, and the discussion of the art of war is set within a conversation among various friends who have gathered, in 1516, at the Orti Oricellari (the gardens belonging to Cosimo Rucellai, a Florentine gentleman) to welcome a well-known mercenary commander, Fabrizio Colonna. After the preface has underlined the essential interdependence of political and military affairs, the succeeding sections of the dialogue deal with: the*

*problems of the citizen soldier (I); arms and military train-
ing (II); the role of artillery and the ideal army in battle
(III); advice to military leaders (IV); spoils, supplies, and
tactics in hostile territory (V); setting up camp, winter campaigns, strategy, and psychological warfare (VI); the defense and siege of cities, rules for war, a portrait of the ideal
general, and the hope for a rebirth of ancient military valor
in modern Italy (VII). Many of the technical sections will
be of interest only to specialists and military historians, but
the pages reprinted in this translation—consisting of the
complete preface, a major portion of the first book on the
citizen soldier, a crucial section from the second book on the
relationship of* virtù *and* Fortuna, *and that part of the
seventh book enumerating the qualities of the ideal military
leader and calling for a renaissance of classical military
skill in modern Italy through an imitation of ancient military institutions—represent fundamental statements that
shed light on these and related topics in Machiavelli's major
political works.* The Art of War *was published in 1521,
being only one of two works by Machiavelli that appeared in
print before his death. It received Renaissance translations
into French (1546), English (1563 and 1573), Spanish (1536
and 1541), and German (1623), and continued to be widely
read throughout the nineteenth century.*

PREFACE TO *THE BOOK OF*
THE ART OF WAR
BY NICCOLÒ MACHIAVELLI,
CITIZEN AND FLORENTINE SECRETARY

*To Lorenzo di Filippo Strozzi,
Florentine Patrician*

Many, Lorenzo, have held and still hold this opinion:
that no two things have less in common or differ more
from each other than a civil and a military life. Hence,

one often notices that if a person plans to excel in military life, he not only immediately changes his way of dressing but also his habits, his customs, and his voice, thus setting himself apart from every civilian custom. For he cannot believe that he who seeks to be ready for any sort of violence can wear civilian clothes; nor can civilian habits and practices be followed by one who judges these practices to be effeminate and these customs to be useless to his profession; nor does it appear suitable to retain normal behavior and speech when he wishes to terrify other men with his beard and his curses. This makes such an opinion in these times seem to be very true.

But if ancient institutions are taken into consideration, one will find no two things more united, more alike, and, of necessity, more interrelated than these two; for all of the arts that have been instituted in a civil society for the common good of mankind and all of the institutions established to make men live in fear of the laws and of God would be vain if they were not provided with defenses; such defenses, if they are well organized, will preserve these institutions even if they are poorly organized. And thus, on the contrary, good institutions without military backing undergo the same sort of disorder as do the rooms of a splendid and regal palace which, adorned with gems and gold but lacking a roof, have nothing to protect them from the rain. And if in any other institution of city-states and kingdoms one uses every care to keep men loyal, pacified, and full of the fear of the Lord, in the army this care should really be doubled. For in what man can a country seek greater loyalty than in him who has promised to die for her? In whom should there be more love for peace than in him who can only be harmed by war? In what man should there be more love of God than in him who, submitting himself daily to countless dangers, has more need of His aid? When this necessity was well considered by those who governed empires and were in charge of armies, it caused military life to be praised by other men and to be followed and imitated with great diligence.

But since military institutions are completely corrupted and have, for a long period, diverged from ancient practices, bad opinions about them have arisen, causing the military life to be despised and encouraging men to avoid associating with those who follow this profession. And since I am of the opinion, because of what I have seen and read, that it would not be impossible to restore this profession to ancient methods and to revive in it some measure of its past strength, I have decided, in order to do something of worth and not to waste my leisure time, to write for the satisfaction of those men who love ancient deeds about the art of war as I understand it. And although it is a daring thing to discuss a subject that others have made a profession, nevertheless I do not believe it is wrong to occupy with words a rank which many with greater presumption have held with deeds, for the errors that I commit in writing can be corrected without harm, but those which others have committed in practice cannot be recognized except through the downfall of their governments. Therefore, Lorenzo, please consider the qualities of these labors of mine and, utilizing your judgment, bestow upon them the blame or praise you deem they merit. I send them to you both to show you how grateful I am for the benefits I have received from you—although my capabilities may not equal them—and also because it is the custom to honor with such works those who shine forth in their nobility, their wealth, their intelligence and their generosity—and how well I know that you have few equals in wealth and nobility, fewer still in intelligence, and none in generosity.

BOOK I

Because I believe that one can praise every man after his death without being blamed, since suspicion of flattery no longer exists, I shall not hesitate to praise our Cosimo Rucellai, whose name I shall never be able to recall to mind without tears, for I recognized in him those qualities desired in a good friend by his friends and in a citizen by his native city. I do not know what he considered to be so much his own (not excepting his soul, to mention nothing else) that he would not spend it willingly for his friends; nor do I know what undertaking would have frightened him if he had perceived the good of his native city in its accomplishment. And I freely confess that I have never met a man, among the many men I have known and have had dealings with, who was more ardent for grandiose and magnificent affairs. Nor did he complain of anything to his friends on his deathbed other than having been born to die young in his home, unhonored, not having been able to assist anyone the way he would have liked to. For he knew that no one could say anything about him other than that a good friend had passed away. Even if his deeds did not materialize, however, that is no reason for us or others who knew him not to bear witness to his praiseworthy qualities. Still, it is true that Fortune was not so completely unfriendly to him that she did not leave some brief reminder of the force of his intelligence, as some of his writings and his love of poetry demonstrate; for although he was not in love, in order not to waste time waiting for Fortune to lead him to higher thoughts he composed such works in his youth. Clearly, from these one can learn with what felicity he expressed his ideas and how greatly he might have been honored in the profession of poetry if he had followed it as his calling. However, since Fortune has deprived us of the presence of such a friend, there appears to be no other remedy than to enjoy his memory as much as possible and to repeat whatever he cleverly stated or wisely argued. And because there is nothing fresher of his memory than the recent conversation he had with Fabrizio Colonna in his gardens (where that captain discussed many affairs of war and Cosimo keenly and wisely addressed many questions to him), it seems fitting to me, since I was present with some of our mutual friends, to preserve it for posterity so that those friends of Cosimo who were also present can, as they read, refresh their memory of his exceptional qualities. Others may lament the fact that they were not present, but they will still learn many things useful not only for military life but also for civilian life, wisely treated by a very intelligent man.

I say, therefore, that when Fabrizio Colonna had returned from Lombardy, where he had fought for some time, with great glory to himself, for the Emperor Charles V, he decided, while passing through Florence, to rest there several days in order to visit His Excellency the Duke of Urbino and to see again several gentlemen with whom he had been friendly in the past. Whereupon Cosimo decided to invite him to his gardens, not so much to demonstrate his generosity as to have cause to speak with him at length, and to hear and learn from him the many things one can hope to learn from such an individual—for Cosimo it represented an opportunity to pass the day discussing those matters which gave his mind the most satisfaction. Fabrizio came, as Cosimo desired, and was received by Cosimo together with several other intimate friends, among whom were Zanobi Buondelmonti, Batista della Palla, and Luigi Alamanni, all young men beloved by him and steeped in the same studies, whose good qualities we shall leave unsaid, for they speak for themselves every day and every hour.

Fabrizio, therefore, was honored (according to the times and the place) by all of them with the greatest possible honors; but when the pleasures of the meal were over and the tables were cleared and all celebrating was done with—something which occurs quickly among great men whose minds are turned toward honorable thoughts—Cosimo, using the pretext of avoiding the heat in order better to satisfy his desire, felt that it was best that they retire to the most private and shaded part of his garden. When they had arrived there and had taken their seats, some on the grass, which is very cool in that place, others upon seats placed in the shadow of the tallest trees, Fabrizio praised the spot as delightful. Looking closely at the trees and not recognizing some of them, he was perplexed. Noticing this, Cosimo said: "Perhaps you do not know some of these trees; but do not be surprised, for there are some here more famous among the ancients than they are among us today." And when he had told him their names and had described how Bernardo, his grandfather, had worked extremely hard in cultivating them, Fabrizio replied: "I had thought as much; this place and this pursuit remind me of several princes of the Kingdom of Naples who delight in these ancient groves and shades."

Pausing at this point in his speech, while sitting pensively there for a moment, he continued: "If I thought I would offend you, I would not give you my opinion on such matters; but I could not offend you, for I am speaking with friends and for the sake of argument, not in order to criticize. How much better off those princes would have been (God rest their souls) had they tried to equal the ancients in strong and rugged matters instead of delicate and soft ones, in those things done in the heat of the sun and not in the shade, taking their course of action from a true and perfect antiquity, not from that of a false and corrupted one; for when such activities began to please my Romans, my country fell into ruin." To this Cosimo replied—to avoid the inconvenience of having to repeat constantly "he said" and "the other answered," only the names of the speakers will be noted, without repeating anything else. Therefore:

COSIMO: You have opened the way to an argument that I had hoped for, and I beg you to speak without restraint, since I shall question you without reservations; and if in questioning or responding I excuse or blame anyone, it will not be for the sake of excusing or blaming but to learn the truth from you.

FABRIZIO: And I shall be very happy to tell you what I

know about all you ask; as to whether what I say is true or not, I leave that to your judgment. And I shall be very happy if you ask, for I am as ready to learn from your questions as you are from my replies; for a wise interrogator often causes one to reflect upon a number of things and to learn about many others which, without the benefit of questions, one might never have learned.

COSIMO: I'd like to return to what you said first, that my grandfather and those princes of yours would have been wiser to imitate the ancients in manly matters rather than in delicate ones; for I wish to make excuses for my ancestors, leaving excuses for the others to you. I do not believe that there ever was, in his time, a man who detested soft living so much as my grandfather did, or who was ever so fond of that rugged life about which you spoke; nevertheless, he recognized that neither he nor his sons could follow such a life, having been born in a corrupt century where anyone who wished to depart from common customs would be criticized and villified by everyone. For if a man stretched out naked on the sand in the summer under the noonday sun, or upon the snow in the coldest of winter months, as Diogenes did, he would be considered mad. If anyone, like the Spartans, reared his children in the country, making them sleep in the open, go about with their heads uncovered and without shoes, bathe in cold water to induce them to bear up under stress and to make them love life less and to fear death less, he would be ridiculed and considered more of an animal than a man. If anyone, moreover, lived on vegetables and despised gold, as Fabricius Luscinus did, he would be praised by few and followed by none. Therefore, although disgusted by current ways of living, my grandfather abandoned the examples of the ancients in this and followed them only in matters that would attract less attention.

FABRIZIO: You have defended him admirably in this matter, and you certainly speak the truth; but I was not talking so much about such severe ways of life as about other, more humane ways that have more in common with the life of today; these, I believe, would not be difficult for anyone who is counted among a city's leading citizens to introduce. I shall never depart from my Roman friends in recommending examples for anything. If one considers their life and the organization of their republic, one will see that many things there could be introduced into a government that is not totally corrupt.

COSIMO: What are these things that you would like to introduce in imitation of the ancients?

FABRIZIO: To honor and reward ability; not to despise poverty; to value the methods and the institutions of military discipline; to make citizens love one another; to live without factions; to value the public interest over private interests; and other similar principles that could easily suit our times. It is not difficult to be persuaded about these matters when one thinks about them enough and studies them in the correct way, for so much truth can be seen in them that any common intelligence may grasp it. Anyone who institutes such a way of life plants trees under whose shade one can live with greater happiness and prosperity than under this one.

COSIMO: I shall not reply to what you have said in any way (I would rather leave this to the judgment of those who can easily judge it); rather, I shall address myself to you, who accuse those who are not imitators of the ancients in serious and important matters, for I believe that in this manner my intention will be more easily fulfilled. I should like, therefore, to know from you why it is that, on the one hand, you castigate those who do not follow the ancients in their actions while, on the other, in your own art of war, in which you are reputed to be most excellent, you evidently have not made use of any ancient methods or anything similar to those methods.

FABRIZIO: You have landed just where I thought you would, for my remarks deserved no other question, nor did I desire any other one. And although I could save myself with a facile excuse, I would rather, since the time

is right, engage in a longer argument for the greater satisfaction of both of us. Men who wish to accomplish an undertaking ought first to prepare themselves with care so
that when the opportunity arises they will be able to carry
out what they have proposed to do. Since preparations, if
they are made carefully, remain unknown, no one can be
accused of negligence if his plan is not discovered before
that opportunity arises; but when it arrives and he does
not act, it becomes obvious that he either did not prepare
himself enough or did not have enough foresight. And
since I have not yet had the opportunity to be able .to
demonstrate the preparations I have drawn up to lead
military arts back to their ancient institutions, if I have
not led them back I cannot be criticized either by you or
by others. I believe that this excuse should suffice as a
reply to your accusation.

COSIMO: It would more than suffice if I were certain that
the opportunity had not arisen.

FABRIZIO: But since you question whether or not this opportunity has arisen, I wish, if you will bear with me, to
discuss at length what kind of preparations should be
made first, what sort of opportunity must arise, and which
difficulties keep the preparations from working and the
opportunity from arising. This matter is both very difficult and extremely easy to accomplish, although it may
seem to be a contradiction.

COSIMO: You could not please me and these others more
than by doing this; and if it does not bother you to talk, it
will never annoy us to listen to you. But since this discussion must be lengthy, I ask, with your permission, that
these friends of mine assist me; we ask only one thing of
you: that you will not be irritated if, from time to time, we
interrupt you with some important questions.

FABRIZIO: I would be very happy if you, Cosimo, and
these other young men question me, for I believe that
youth is more amenable to military affairs and is more inclined to believe what I shall say. Older men, with white
hair and blood frozen in their veins, are usually partly

averse to war and partly beyond correction, for they believe that the times, not defective institutions, force men to live as they do. Therefore, feel free to ask questions of me; I wish you would, not only because it would give me a chance to rest, but also because it pleases me not to leave any doubts in your minds. I'd like to begin with your own words: you told me that in war, my profession, I had not used any of the methods of the ancients. On this topic I maintain that since this is a profession by means of which men cannot live honestly at all times, it cannot be carried on as a profession except in a republic or in a kingdom; neither of these governments, when it is well organized, has ever allowed any of its citizens or subjects to practice it as a profession; nor has any good man ever taken it up as his own particular profession. For a man will never be judged good who, in his work—if he wants to make a steady profit from it—must be rapacious, fraudulent, violent, and exhibit many qualities which, of necessity, do not make him good. Nor can men who practice war as a profession—great men as well as insignificant men—act in any other way, since their profession does not prosper in peacetime. Therefore, such men must either hope for no peace or must profit from times of war in such a manner that they can live off that profit in times of peace. Neither of these thoughts is found in a good man, for the desire to be able to support oneself at all times leads to theft, acts of violence, and the murderous deeds that such soldiers perpetrate on their friends and foes alike. From not desiring peace come the treacherous deeds that military leaders commit against their employers to keep a war going; and if peace does come, it often happens that the leaders, having been deprived of their salary and their living, set up their standards as soldiers of fortune and illegally sack a province without mercy. Do you not remember, in your own affairs, how countless numbers of soldiers, finding themselves unemployed in Italy after the end of the wars, joined together in many brigades, which were called companies, and went about holding up towns for ransom and sacking the countryside, and no one was able to find a remedy? Have you not read that the Carthaginian soldiers, at the end of the first war with the Romans—under Matho and Spendius (two leaders chosen by them from the mob)—waged a more dangerous war against the Carthaginians than they had just finished waging against the Romans? In the times of our fathers, Francesco Sforza, in order to live honorably in times of peace, not only tricked the Milanese who hired him but also took away their liberty and became their prince. All the other professional soldiers of Italy have been like him; and if they have not, through their evil deeds, become dukes of Milan, they deserve to be blamed even more, for without so much profit they all have the same drawbacks as he—this is evident if one examines their lives. Sforza, the father of Francesco, forced Queen Giovanna of Naples to throw herself into the arms of the King of Aragon when he abandoned her suddenly and left her unarmed in the midst of her enemies, his only purpose being to satisfy his ambition and to extort money from her or to take the kingdom away from her. Andrea Braccio da Montone sought to occupy the Kingdom of Naples by the same means; had he not been routed and slain at Aquila, he would have succeeded. Similar disorders are born from no other reason except that there have been men who used the trade of a soldier as their profession. Do you not have a proverb that reinforces my arguments? "War produces thieves and peace hangs them." For those who do not know how to live by another means and cannot find anyone who will hire them, not having enough ability to join together to commit an honorable act of evil, are forced by necessity to become highway robbers, and justice is forced to execute them.

COSIMO: You have made this military profession of yours seem worthless, and I had thought it to be the most excellent and the most honorable profession there was. Therefore, if you do not explain yourself better, I shall remain unsatisfied, for if what you say is true, I do not know from whence arises the glory of Caesar, Pompey, Scipio, Marcellus, and so many other Roman leaders who are celebrated as gods.

FABRIZIO: I have not yet finished what I proposed to say regarding two matters: first, that a good man cannot make this trade his profession; second, that a republic or a kingdom that is well organized has never permitted her subjects or citizens to make it their profession. Concerning the first statement, I have said all that has come to my mind. There remains the second, and with it I shall respond to your last question. Let me say that Pompey, Caesar, and practically all those leaders after the last Carthaginian war acquired fame as brave men, not as good ones; and those who lived before them acquired glory as both brave and good men. This came about because the latter did not take up the exercise of war as their profession, while the former did make it their profession. While the republic thrived in an uncorrupted state, no great citizen ever presumed, by such a means, to increase his power during peacetime, to break the laws, despoil the provinces, usurp and tyrannize his country or in any manner to increase his station; nor did anyone of low rank think of violating his oath, entering into private conspiracies, not fearing the senate, or perpetrating some tyrannical injury in order to be able to live at all times by means of the art of war. Those who were leaders, content with their triumphs, returned willingly to private life; and those who were regular soldiers laid down their arms more willingly than they had taken them up; and each man returned to the profession that had earned him his living before; nor was there anyone who hoped to make his living by plundering or by means of a military profession. One thinks, when talking about great citizens, of the obvious case of Regulus Atilius, captain of the Roman armies in Africa, who, after nearly defeating the Carthaginians, demanded permission from the senate to return home in order to take care of his lands, which had been ruined by his workers. Now, it is clearer than the sun that if that man had practiced war as his profession, and had thought to make a profit by means of it, having in his grasp so many provinces, he would never have asked permission to return home to care for his fields; for on any one day he could have made much more money than the total worth of all his lands.

But since these good men, who did not practice war as their profession, did not wish to gain anything from it but toil, dangers, and glory, when they had become renowned enough they only wanted to return to their homes and to their professions. And as for men of lower estate and common soldiers, it is clear that they followed the same practice, for each of them gladly left such an occupation; when he was not fighting, he was willing to do so, and when he was fighting, he wanted not to fight. This can be proved in a number of ways, particularly when we observe how among the major privileges the Roman people bestowed upon its citizens was that of not being forced, against one's will, to become a soldier. As long as she was well organized (which she was until the time of the Gracchi), Rome did not have a single soldier who assumed that duty as a profession; because of this she had few bad soldiers, and those who were bad were severely punished. Therefore, a well-organized city must desire that this study of warfare be pursued as an exercise in peacetime and as a necessity and for glory in wartime; it must allow only its citizens to practice it as a profession, as Rome did. And any citizen who, in practicing this profession, does so with another purpose in mind, is not a good citizen; and any city that is governed otherwise is not well organized.

COSIMO: I am very pleased and satisfied with what you have said until now, and this conclusion which you have drawn pleases me as well; as far as a republic is concerned, I believe that your opinion is correct, but as far as kings are concerned, I am uncertain, for I would suppose that a king might wish to have around him men who would make just such a pursuit their profession.

FABRIZIO: A well-instituted kingdom should avoid such

professional soldiers even more, since they alone are the source of the corruption of its king and, in sum, the ministers of tyranny. And do not cite as a contrary example any present kingdom, for I shall deny that those are well-organized kingdoms. Kingdoms that have good institutions do not give absolute authority to their kings except in the command of their armies; for only in this institution are sudden decisions necessary; because of this, a single individual must be in charge. In other matters the king cannot do anything without advice, and his advisers would have to live in fear that he has around him in times of peace those who desire war, for they make their living from it.

But I want to consider this question at greater length. I do not wish to select a kingdom that is completely good but one that is like some we have today, where those who practice war as their profession are still to be feared by kings. Since the nerve of any army, without question, lies in the infantry, if a king does not arrange things in such a way that his infantrymen are content to return home and to live off their trades during times of peace, he will of necessity come to ruin; for there exists no more dangerous sort of infantry than one composed of men who make war their profession, since you are forced either to make war constantly and repeatedly pay these men, or run the risk that they will take your kingdom from you. To wage war constantly is not possible; one cannot pay them repeatedly either; therefore, of necessity one runs the risk of losing the state.

As I have mentioned, as long as my Roman friends were wise and good, they never permitted their citizens to choose this activity as their profession, notwithstanding the fact that they would have been able to employ them continuously since they constantly made war. But in order to avoid the dangers that can arise from the continuous practice of war, they varied the men, since the circumstances did not vary, and acted in such a fashion that every fifteen years they rotated the ranks of their legions;

thus, they took advantage of men in their prime, which lasts from eighteen to thirty-five years of age, during which time their legs, hands, and eyes are in perfect accord; nor did they wait until their strength grew weaker and their maliciousness grew stronger, as they did later during corrupt times. For first Octavian, and after him Tiberius—both of whom were concerned more for personal power than for the public welfare—began to disarm the Roman people in order to be able to command more easily and to keep those same armies at the frontiers of the empire. And since they thought that such measures as these would not be sufficient to keep the people and the Roman senate in check, they instituted another army, called the Praetorian Guard, which stayed close to the walls of the city and turned it into a stronghold. And because they allowed the men who were selected for this army to make it their profession, these men immediately became insolent and posed a threat to the senate as well as a danger to the emperor. As a result of the guards' unruly nature many emperors were put to death, for these men could give the empire to, or take it from, whomever they chose; and sometimes it would happen that a number of emperors were created by various armies at the same time. These things first led to the division of the empire and finally to its ruin. Therefore, if kings want to live securely, they must be sure that their foot soldiers are made up of men who go to war of their own accord and, when the time comes, return home when peace arrives even more willingly than when they left. This will always occur when the king chooses men who know how to live better by any profession other than a military one. Thus, he must want his subordinates to come back to rule their own people when peace returns, his gentlemen to return to the administration of their properties, and his foot soldiers to return to their own particular trades; and each of these groups will willingly wage war in order to have peace and will not seek to disturb the peace in order to wage war.

COSIMO: This argument of yours truly appears to be well founded; nevertheless, since it is almost the contrary of what I thought until now, my mind is still not purged of every doubt; for I see how many lords and gentlemen live during peacetime by means of the military profession, like yourself, who are hired by princes and by cities. I also see that almost all these professional soldiers regularly receive their wages; I see many foot soldiers still guarding cities and fortresses—and it would appear to me that there is ample employment for everyone in time of peace.

FABRIZIO: I do not think that you believe that every man has his own position during peacetime; for, assuming that no other reason can be put forward, the small number of those troops who remain in those places you mentioned would respond to you. What proportion of the foot soldiers needed in wartime are necessary in peacetime? For fortresses and cities which are guarded in peacetime are guarded even more in time of war; and to them are added the soldiers who are kept in the field, whose numbers are numerous and who are disbanded in peacetime. And concerning garrisons of states (which are small in number), Pope Julius and you Florentines have demonstrated to everyone how much those who only know how to practice the profession of war are to be feared; you have thrown such men out of your guards and have replaced them with Swiss men, since the latter were born and raised in obedience to the law and were selected by their communities by means of an honest election. So, from now on you should not maintain that there is employment for every man in peacetime. As for horsemen, it appears that a solution may be more difficult to find, since they continue to be paid during peacetime. Nevertheless, anyone who carefully considers the whole problem will find the answer easy, for this means of keeping men-at-arms is a corrupt method and is not good. The explanation is that they are men who make a profession of warfare, they would cause a thousand problems every day in the states in which they reside if they were supported by a body of

men of sufficient size; but since there are few of them and
they are unable to constitute an army by themselves, they
are not often able to cause serious damage. Nevertheless,
they have done so many times, as I remarked about Francesco Sforza, his father, and of Braccio da Montone.
Therefore, I do not approve of this custom of keeping
men-at-arms—it is corrupt and can cause serious problems.

COSIMO: You would do without them? Or, if you kept
them, how would you do so?

FABRIZIO: By means of a citizens' militia: not like that of
the French king, since it is as dangerous and as arrogant
as our own, but like those of the ancients, who created the
cavalry from among their own subjects and who, in
peacetime, sent them home to live by their own professions, as I shall explain in more detail before this argument is ended. If this sector of the army can live from
such activity during peacetime, this is the result of a corrupt institution. As for the appropriations reserved for
myself and other military leaders, I say that this, in like
manner, is a very corrupt institution; for a wise republic
must not grant this to anyone; on the contrary, it must use
its own citizens as its military leaders in wartime and must
want them to return to their professions in peacetime.
Likewise, a wise king ought not to pay such salaries or, if
he does pay them, he should do so either as a reward for
some distinguished deed or in order to assure himself of
the services of a man both in peacetime and in wartime.

And since you cite my own case, I want to use myself as
an illustration: I maintain that I have never followed war
as a profession, since my profession is to govern my subjects and to defend them, and, in order to defend them, to
love peace and to know how to wage war. My king rewards and esteems me not so much for my knowledge
about warfare as for my advice during peacetime. No
king, therefore, if he is wise and wishes to rule prudently,
should want to have around him anyone who is not of the
same feelings; for if he has around him either too many

lovers of peace or too many lovers of war, they will make him err. According to my proposals here in my first discourse, I cannot speak further on this matter; and if what I have said does not suffice, you should seek someone else to satisfy you further. You can well begin to understand what difficulties there are in bringing ancient methods back into present wars and what preparations a wise man must make, and what opportunities one must hope for, in order to bring such plans to fulfillment; but you will gradually come to understand these matters better, if my argument does not tire you, when you compare any part of ancient institutions to modern methods.

COSIMO: If we wished, at the outset, to hear you discuss such matters, what you have said about them up to this moment has truly doubled our wishes; therefore, we thank you for what we have received and we beg you for the rest.

FABRIZIO: Since this pleases you, I wish to treat this subject from the beginning so that you may understand it better, for it is possible in this way to explain more completely. The goal of anyone wishing to wage war is to be able to do battle with any enemy in the field and to be able to win the day. To wish to do so necessitates the institution of an army. To institute the army, it is necessary to find men, arm them, organize them, drill them in both small and large groups, quarter them, and confront the enemy with them, either marching or taking up a fixed position. In these matters resides all the labor of a field campaign, the most necessary and most honorable kind. For anyone who understands how to draw up his troops for battle, any other errors he may commit in conducting the war will be tolerable; but anyone who lacks this discipline, even if he excels in other particulars, will never conduct a war with honor, for winning one battle cancels out all of your other mistaken actions; thus, in the same manner, all of the good works you previously accomplished are useless when a battle is lost.

Since men must first be found, however, it is necessary

to come to the matter of conscription of soldiers, which
the ancients called the *delectus*. We refer to it as the draft,
but in order to call it by a more honorable title, I should
like to retain the name of conscription. Those who set up
rules for warfare wanted the men to be selected from temperate climates, so that they would possess both spirit and
prudence; for a warm climate produces prudent but less
courageous men, while a cold climate produces brave but
foolhardy men. This rule is very useful for a prince who
governs many lands, for he is permitted to choose his men
from the places that will best serve him; but, in order to
provide a rule on this topic that will be of use to anyone, it
is necessary to state that every republic and every kingdom must select troops from its own territories, either hot,
cold, or temperate. For we witness from ancient examples
how in every country with an army one can produce good
soldiers; for where natural talent is lacking, perseverance
(a quality that, in this instance, is more valuable than natural talent) can provide a remedy. Choosing them from
other places cannot be called conscription, since this
means taking the best from a province and having the authority to select those who are unwilling to serve as well as
those who are willing to serve. One cannot, however,
make such a choice except in regions under one's own
rule, since you cannot force those who are not in your
own domain to serve you.

COSIMO: And it is still possible, from among those who
wish to volunteer, to choose some and to reject others;
and because of this it can still be called conscription.

FABRIZIO: You are correct to a certain extent, but consider
the defects inherent in conscription, since many times it is
not even conscription at all. The first problem: those who
are not your subjects and who serve as volunteers are not
the best; on the contrary, they are the worst soldiers of a
province. For if there are any men who are scandalous,
lazy, uncontrollable, atheists, fugitives from paternal authority, swearers, gamblers, or poorly bred, they are those
who wish to serve in the army. Their customs cannot be

more contrary to a true and good militia. When so many of these men offer themselves to you that you can choose more than you need, you may select them; but with such poor material, it is not likely that this type of conscription will be of any use. But in many instances there are insufficient numbers of men to meet your needs, so that you are forced to take them all; for this reason you cannot call this a conscription but rather a hiring of soldiers. Today, by means of this poor system, all of the armies of Italy and elsewhere are being formed, except for Germany, for no one there is taken on by the prince's orders, but only according to the wish of whoever volunteers to serve as a soldier. Consider for yourselves, then, which methods of those ancient armies can be introduced into an army of men assembled in such a fashion.

COSIMO: What method would you employ, then, to raise an army?

FABRIZIO: The one I mentioned: select them from the prince's subjects and with his authority.

COSIMO: Among those selected in this fashion, could you introduce any ancient procedures?

FABRIZIO: Of course, if he who commanded them were their prince or their established lord in a principality; or if he were a citizen and temporarily a captain in a republic; otherwise it is difficult to accomplish anything of value.

COSIMO: Why?

FABRIZIO: I shall explain this in time; now let it suffice for me to say that it is not possible to operate in any other way.

COSIMO: Since, therefore, this conscription must be made in one's own territories, where do you deem it best to choose your men, from the cities or from the countryside?

FABRIZIO: Those who have written about this problem are all in agreement that it is best to choose them from the countryside, since they are men used to hardships, brought up in toil, accustomed to being in the sun and to avoiding the shade; they are men who can use tools, dig

ditches, carry burdens, and who are without guile and
without malice. But in this regard, my opinion would be
that since soldiers are of two kinds, infantrymen and cavalry, one should select infantrymen from the countryside
and cavalry from the towns.

COSIMO: At what age would you take them?

FABRIZIO: If I had to create a new militia, I would choose
my men from seventeen to forty years of age; if the militia
were already established and I had to renew it, I would always take them at seventeen.

COSIMO: I do not fully understand this distinction.

FABRIZIO: I shall explain it to you. If I had to institute a
militia where there was none, it would be necessary to select all those men who were most qualified, provided that
they be of military age, in order to train them in the manner I shall shortly explain; but if I had to make a selection
in places where this militia was already instituted, I would
take men of seventeen as supplementary soldiers, for the
older men would already be chosen and in service.

COSIMO: Therefore, you would want to establish a citizen's
militia similar to that which we have here.

FABRIZIO: That is correct. But I would arm them, set up
their leaders, train and organize them in a manner which
I am not sure you follow here.

COSIMO: You are then praising the citizens' militia?

FABRIZIO: Why would you wish me to condemn it?

COSIMO: Because many wise men have always criticized it.

FABRIZIO: You contradict yourself when you say that a
wise man criticizes the militia; while such a man may be
reputed wise, he can easily be otherwise.

COSIMO: The poor showing it has always made will force
us to retain such an opinion.

FABRIZIO: Be careful that the shortcoming is not yours
rather than the militia's, as you will come to realize before
this discussion is finished.

COSIMO: If you can convince us of this, you will be doing a
very good thing; yet I wish to tell you why others criticize
it in order that you may justify yourself better. They say

this: that it will either be useless—in which case to trust in the militia will cause us to lose the state—or it will be effective—in which case whoever commands the militia will easily be able to take the state from us. The Romans are cited as examples of people who, using these kinds of soldiers, lost their liberty. The Venetians and the King of France are cited: the former used the arms of others in order to prevent any of their own citizens from seizing power, while the king disarmed his own people in order to be able to govern them more easily. But they fear its inefficacy more than this. They cite two principal reasons for this inefficacy: first, that the soldiers are inexperienced; second, that the men are forced to serve as soldiers. They claim that men seldom learn anything and that force never does any good.

FABRIZIO: All these reasons you mention are put forward by shortsighted men, as I shall clearly demonstrate to you. First, as for the inefficacy of the militia, I say to you that no militia can be more efficacious than your own, nor can anyone's own militia be organized except in this manner. And because this allows no room for argument, I do not wish to lose time dwelling on it—let all of the examples from ancient history be sufficient. And since they cite inexperience and force, I say that it is true that inexperience produces fear and that force produces discontent; but courage and experience can be instilled in them by arming, drilling, and organizing them, as you will see in the course of this argument. But, as for force, you have to understand that the men who are brought into the militia by order of the prince have to enter neither under force nor completely voluntarily. For if they were all volunteers, the inconveniences I mentioned above would arise; that is, there would not be a conscription and there would be few who would go. In like manner, compulsion would bring about bad results. Therefore, one must choose a middle path where neither compulsion nor free will is the sole operative, but where the men are attracted by a respect they have for the prince and where they fear his anger more than their immediate inconvenience. And it always turns out to be a force formed by means of free will in such a way that no discontent, which might lead to bad effects, will come of it. I do not, however, because of this, say that it cannot be defeated, for the Roman armies were defeated many times and the army of Hannibal was beaten; it is clear that no one can organize an invincible army. However, these wise men of yours must not measure the inefficacy of this sort of army by a single defeat; they should believe that just as it can be defeated, it can similarly conquer and remedy the cause of its defeat. And when they search for this remedy, they will discover that it will not have resulted from a defect in method but rather from the imperfection of its organization. And, as I said, they ought to make provisions for this, not by accusing the citizens' militia but by correcting it. You will learn how this must be done as we go along.

As for your fears that such an institution may deprive you of your state by means of the individual who becomes its captain, I reply that arms carried by one's citizens or subjects, when they are bestowed by law and are well organized, never do harm; on the contrary, they are always useful, and cities are maintained without corruption by means of them better than they are without them. Rome remained free for four hundred years and was armed; Sparta, for eight hundred; many other cities were unarmed and remained free for less than forty years. Cities need military forces, and when they do not have their own they hire foreigners. These foreign soldiers are more likely to harm the public good than are one's own men, since such men are more easily corrupted and more likely to be used by some citizen seeking power; such a man has easier material to manage, since he wishes to oppress men who are unarmed. Besides this, a city will fear two enemies more than one. A city that uses foreign troops simultaneously fears the foreigner it hires as well as the citizen. To prove that this fear does exist, let me remind you of what I said earlier concerning Francesco Sforza. A city that uses its own troops fears only its own citizens. In spite of the many reasons I can bring to bear, I would have this one suffice: no one ever established a republic or a kingdom who did not believe that the same people who lived there would also defend it with their arms.

And if the Venetians had been as wise in this matter as in their other institutions, they could have set up a new monarchy in the world. They deserve even more blame since they had been armed by their first lawgivers. Not possessing any territory on land, they were armed at sea, where they carried out their wars with great skill and, through their own arms, increased their homeland. But when the time came for them to wage war on the mainland in order to defend Vicenza, instead of sending one of their citizens to fight on land they hired the Marquis of Mantua as their leader. This was the unfortunate policy that cut off their legs and kept them from climbing to Heaven's greatness. And if they did this out of the belief that they knew how to fight at sea but were unsure as to how to do so on land, this was an unwise move; for a sea captain, experienced in fighting the winds, the waters, and men, can become a leader on land more easily than a captain on land can become a sea captain. My Roman friends, knowing how to fight on land but not on the sea, did not hire Greeks or Spaniards familiar with the sea when they fought the Carthaginians, who were powerful on the ocean; rather, they imposed that duty on the citizens they usually used to fight on land—and they triumphed. If the Venetians hired foreign soldiers lest one of their citizens could become a tyrant, this was a senseless fear; for, besides the arguments on this matter that I advanced a while ago, if a citizen with naval forces had never made himself a tyrant in a city situated on the sea, he would have had even less chance with ground forces. If they had considered this, they would have seen that it is not arms in the hands of one's citizens that produce tyrants but rather the evil institutions of the government that tyrannize a city; and if a city has a good government, it need not fear its armies. Therefore, they chose an imprudent policy which caused them to lose much glory and much peace of mind. As for the error the King of France committed in not keeping his own people disciplined in warfare (a case those citizens of yours cite as an example), no one who sets aside his own private feelings will judge that this is not a defect in that kingdom and not the sole cause of its weakness.

But I have made too great a digression, and perhaps I have strayed from my topic; yet I have done so in order to reply to you and to show you that one cannot build one's foundation on forces other than one's own, and one cannot organize one's own forces in any fashion other than by means of a citizens' militia, nor can one introduce other kinds of armies or military discipline by any other means. If you have read about the institutions established by the first kings in Rome, especially by Servius Tullius, you will discover that the organization of the classes was nothing other than a regulation permitting the quick assembly of an army for the defense of the city. But let us return to conscription. I repeat, if I had to recruit for an existing army, I should pick men of seventeen; but if I had to create a new one, I should choose men between the ages of seventeen and forty in order to be able to make use of them immediately.

COSIMO: Would you distinguish among the professions of the men you select?

FABRIZIO: These writers I have cited do so, for they do not wish us to choose fowlers, fishermen, cooks, whoremongers, and anyone who makes a profession of pleasure; they suggest, rather, that we select farmers, blacksmiths, farriers, carpenters, butchers, hunters, and other similar trades. But I would make very little distinction between men and their quality based upon their professions, although I would do so regarding their usefulness. Peasants who are accustomed to working the fields are more useful than anyone, since of all trades this is the most frequently used in the army. After them come blacksmiths, carpenters, farriers, and stonemasons, of whom it is useful to have a great many, since their trades serve in many areas; it is always a good thing to have a soldier from whom you can require double service.

BOOK II

COSIMO: I should like to learn from you, if you have pondered the matter, how it is that so much cowardice, so much lack of order, and so much neglect of these military matters exist in our times?

FABRIZIO: I shall gladly tell you what I think about the matter. You know that although there have been many famous warriors in Europe, there have been few in Africa and even fewer in Asia. This comes about because these last two regions of the world have had only one or two principalities and few republics; Europe alone has had several kingdoms and countless republics. Men become excellent and demonstrate their ability to the extent that they are employed and are advanced by their prince, their republic, or their king; therefore, it follows that where there are many rulers, there are many valiant men; and where there are few rulers, these men are few in number. In Asia one finds Ninus, Cyrus, Artaxerxes, Mithridates—very few others are fit to be in their company. In Africa, leaving aside the ancient Egyptians, we can name Masinissa, Jugurtha, and the leaders produced by the Carthaginian republic; when compared with those of Europe, however, these are few, for in Europe there are countless excellent men, and there would be many more if, together with those already known, we could name the others who are lost to us because of the malevolence of time. For the world has been more distinguished in those areas where the existing states have favored ability, either because of necessity or because of some human characteristic. In Asia, then, there arose few such men since that region was completely under a single kingdom, which, because of its size, remained listless for much of the time;

it could not produce men distinguished in what they do. In Africa the same thing occurred; yet more great men were produced there because of the Carthaginian republic. For more great men spring from republics than from kingdoms, since in republics ability is usually revered while in kingdoms it is feared, so it is that in republics great men are encouraged while in kingdoms they are destroyed.

Anyone who examines Europe will find it to be full of republics and principalities which, out of the fear they have for each other, are obliged to keep alive their military institutions and to honor those who have distinguished themselves in service. In Greece, besides the kingdom of the Macedonians, there were many republics, and in each of them very great men rose up. In Italy there were the Romans, the Samnites, the Tuscans, and the Cisalpine Gauls. France and Germany were full of republics and princes, as was Spain. And although in comparison to the Romans few other men of this caliber are named, this is the result of malicious historians who follow Fortune and usually limit themselves to praise of the victors. It is not reasonable to suppose that among the Samnites and the Tuscans, who fought 150 years with the Roman people before being subdued, there did not exist a great number of excellent men. And the same is true for France and Spain. But that ability which historians do not praise in individual men they praise in a general way in their race, when they exalt to the stars the obstinacy that such people displayed in defending their freedom.

Since it is therefore true that where there are more states there are more able men, it must follow that if these states are done away with, their ability is likewise done away with, for what has produced the able men has been removed. Therefore, when the Roman empire later grew and destroyed all of the republics and the principalities of Europe and Africa and, for the most part, those of Asia, it left no path for ingenuity other than Rome. Then, as time passed, able men became as few in number in Europe as in Asia; and this type of ability reached a final decline when all ability was concentrated in Rome. When Rome was corrupted, almost the entire world came to be corrupted. The Scythian peoples were able to plunder that empire which had destroyed the abilities of others without knowing how to maintain its own. Even though that empire, as a result of the flood of these barbarians, was subsequently divided into many parts, this ability was not reborn there. One explanation for this is that it is a difficult matter to restore institutions after they have been destroyed. Another is that the manner of living today, as a consequence of the Christian religion, does not force one to defend oneself as it did in ancient times. For then men defeated in war were either killed or sold into perpetual slavery, where they led miserable lives; captured territories were either devastated or their inhabitants were driven out; their possessions were seized and they were scattered all over the world, so that those who were overcome in warfare suffered every form of misery. Terrorized by this fear, men kept military training alive and honored those who excelled in it.

But today this fear has, for the most part, been lost; few defeated men are killed and none are kept prisoner for a long time, for they can easily free themselves. Cities, even when they rebel a thousand times, are not leveled. Men are permitted to keep their property, so that the worst evil one fears is a tax. Men therefore do not wish to submit themselves to military institutions and to exert themselves therein in order to avoid those dangers that they do not actually fear. Furthermore, these European territories are under the rule of very few rulers as compared with the past; for all of France obeys one king, all of Spain obeys another, and Italy has few territories. Weak cities consequently defend themselves by joining anyone who conquers, and powerful states do not fear a complete defeat for the reasons mentioned above.

COSIMO: And yet we have witnessed many cities sacked during the last twenty-five years and some kingdoms lost.

These examples ought to teach others how to live and to revive a number of these ancient institutions.

FABRIZIO: You are correct; but if you will note which towns have been sacked, you will discover that they have not been the capitals of states but less important towns: it was Tortona that was sacked, not Milan; Capua and not Naples; Brescia and not Venice; Ravenna and not Rome. These examples are not enough to make anyone who rules change his policy; on the contrary, they make him more obstinate in the belief that he can buy off his liberty with a ransom; and because of this, such rulers do not wish to submit themselves to the hardships of military training, since they regard such matters as partly unnecessary and partly a matter about which they have no understanding. Those others who are enslaved peoples and to whom such examples ought to instill fear do not have the power to remedy their situation; and those princes who have lost their states have no time to do so; those who still retain them do not understand and have no desire to do so, for they would rely upon Fortune without any inconvenience rather than upon their own ability. They see that Fortune governs everything, since little ability exists there, and they want her to rule them and not them her. And to show that what I say is the truth, just consider Germany, where there are many principalities and republics that contain much ability; all that is good in the military methods of the present day comes from those peoples who, being very jealous of their states and fearing slavery (which is not feared elsewhere), all maintain themselves as free and independent people. I wish this to suffice concerning my opinion on the causes of the present decadence. I do not know if you are in agreement with me or if this discussion has given rise to some doubts.

COSIMO: Not at all! On the contrary! I remain completely convinced.

* * *

BOOK VII

FABRIZIO: Would you, perhaps, also like to learn what qualities a military captain must possess? I shall be able to satisfy you, and in few words, on that question, for I know of only one man who would know how to accomplish all the things that we have discussed together today; yet the knowledge of these alone would not be sufficient if he did not know how to learn on his own, for no one without inventiveness was ever a great man in his profession; and if invention in other kinds of work honors the man, in this one especially it brings praise. And it is seen that every invention, no matter how insignificant, is celebrated by historians; for it is obvious that they praise Alexander the Great because, in order to break camp more secretively, he did not give the signal by trumpet but with a hat hoisted on a spear. He is also praised for having taught his soldiers to kneel upon the left knee when encountering the enemy in order to withstand their assault more bravely; this new idea not only gave him the victory, it also bestowed upon him such fame that all of the statues erected in his honor were sculpted in that position.

But since it is time to conclude this discussion, I wish to return to my subject, and in so doing I shall escape that penalty usually incurred in this city by those who fail to do so. If you remember, Cosimo, you asked me the reason why I was, on the one hand, an admirer of antiquity and a critic of those who do not imitate it in important matters, and why, on the other hand, I myself did not imitate antiquity in affairs of war which I have made my profession—you could see no reason for this. To this I replied that men who wished to accomplish things should first prepare themselves to learn the art of war in order to be able to put it into operation when the occasion arises. Whether or not I know how to return the militia to its ancient practices I wish you (who have heard me discuss this question at length) to decide. From what I said, I feel cer-

tain that you understand how much time I have spent on
these thoughts, and you can imagine, I think, how very
much I should like to put these thoughts of mine into action. That I have been able to do so, or have even had the
opportunity to do so a single time, you can easily determine. To convince you all the more, as well as for my own
justification, I now wish to present the reasons. In so
doing, I shall partly keep my promise to you by demonstrating how difficult it is, and how easy it could be at this
time, to practice the imitation of the ancients. Therefore,
let me say that no activity practiced by men today can
more easily be brought back to ancient practices than
warfare, but it can only be done by those princes who can
raise an army, from among the subjects of their state, of
between fifteen and twenty thousand young men. On the
other hand, nothing is more difficult than this when the
prince does not possess this ability.

And in order that you may better understand this part
of my argument, you should know that there are two
kinds of military leaders who have been praised. One
kind includes those leaders who have accomplished great
deeds with an army already organized according to its
normal discipline; the majority of the Roman citizens and
others who have commanded armies are examples of
these leaders—men who have not had any other problem
except to keep up the training of their men and see that
they are well led. Another kind includes those leaders
who have not only had to overcome an enemy but who,
before reaching that point, were forced to produce a good
and well-disciplined army of their own; these men, without a doubt, deserve more praise than those who operated
with good and disciplined armies. Examples of this second group of leaders include Pelopidas, Epaminondas,
Tullus Hostilius, Philip of Macedonia (the father of Alexander the Great), Cyrus (king of the Persians), and Tiberius Sempronius Gracchus. All these men first had to
establish a good army and then wage war with it. They
were all able to accomplish this, both because of their

wisdom and because they had subjects fit to receive such training. It would never have been possible for one of them, however great his ability, to accomplish such a praiseworthy deed if he had been a mercenary in a foreign country, full of corrupt men unaccustomed to any sort of honorable obedience.

Therefore, in Italy it is not enough to know how to command a previously established army; it is first necessary to know how to create one, and then how to command it. And to do this there must be princes who, possessing much territory and many subjects, have the capacity to do so. I cannot be counted among these, for I have never commanded, nor can I command, unless it is in an army of foreigners and men obligated to others than myself; whether or not it is possible to introduce among such men some of the things we discussed today I leave to your judgment. How can I make one of these soldiers who bears arms today carry more arms than he usually does; and, in addition to his arms, rations for two or three days and a shovel? How can I make him dig or keep him every day, and for many hours, practicing drills so that I can use him in real battles? How will he keep himself from gambling, whoring, swearing, and from the general insubordination of today's army? How can he be brought back to such a degree of discipline, obedience, and respect that a tree full of apples in the middle of the camp would remain untouched? We have read how many times this occurred in ancient armies. What can I promise them that will make them fear me or respect me if, after the war, they know they will have nothing further to do with me? How can I make them feel shame when they are born and raised without it? Why should they obey me when they do not know me? By what God or saints should I have them swear: by those they worship or by those they curse? The saints they worship I do not know, but I certainly know the ones they curse. How can I believe that they will keep the promises they made to those they continuously despise? How can those who have contempt for God honor

men? What good form, therefore, could possibly be
stamped on this raw material?

And if you tell me that the Swiss and the Spanish are
good soldiers, I will confess to you that they are a good
deal better than the Italians; but if you pay attention to
my argument and the practice of these two peoples, you
will see how they both lack many things required to attain
the perfection of the ancients. The Swiss became good
soldiers as a result of one of their customs, which I described to you today, while the others were made good out
of necessity. Waging war in a foreign land and believing
themselves to be faced with a choice of either victory or
death, the Spanish became good soldiers because they
had no place to flee. But it is a goodness defective in many
parts, for the only good thing in it is their common practice of meeting the enemy with the point of their pike or
sword. Nor is there anyone capable of teaching them
what they lack—even less, one who does not speak their
language.

But let us return to the Italians, who, in not having wise
princes, have not accepted any good institutions; and because they have not experienced the necessity that the
Spanish felt, they have not adopted any for themselves.
They therefore are scorned by the rest of the world. It is
not the people who are to blame, but rather their princes,
who have been punished and who, because of their ignorance, have received the fitting penalty of losing their
states ignominiously and without having done a single admirable deed. Do you wish to test whether what I have
said is true? Consider, then, how many wars have been
fought in Italy since the invasion of King Charles VIII
until the present day. Although wars usually make men
warlike and renowned, the longer and more savage these
wars were, the more they caused a loss of reputation, both
of the subjects and their rulers. This came about because
the traditional institutions were not, and are still not,
good; and there is no one here who has known how to
adopt any new institutions. Nor should you ever believe

that a reputation can be won for Italian arms except through the means that I have enumerated and through the deeds of those who possess the greatest states in Italy; for this form can only be stamped upon simple, rough, and independent men, not upon evil, badly governed, and foreign ones. Nor has any good sculptor ever been found who believes that he can make as beautiful a statue from a piece of poorly blocked marble as he can from one that is rough.

Before they had felt the blows of the Transalpine wars, our Italian princes believed that a prince need only know how to dream up witty replies in his study; write a beautiful letter; display intelligence and readiness in his conversation and his speech; weave a fraud; adorn himself with gems and gold; sleep and eat in a more splendid style than others; surround himself with a large number of courtesans; conduct himself in a miserly and arrogant manner with his subjects; rot in laziness; give military positions as favors; despise anyone who had shown them any praiseworthy path; and expect that their pronouncements be taken as oracles. Nor did these wretched men realize that they were preparing themselves to become the prey of anyone who assaulted them. This resulted in the great terrors, the sudden flights, and the miraculous losses of 1494; thus, three very powerful states of Italy were sacked and despoiled many times. But what is worse is that those princes who still remain persist in the same errors and live in the same disorder; they do not consider that those who, in ancient times, wished to maintain their states did, and had done, all of the things that I have discussed—their goal was to prepare the body for hardships and the mind not to fear danger. Thus it came about that Caesar, Alexander, and all those excellent men and princes were foremost in their soldiers' ranks and went about in armor on foot; they would rather lose their lives than their states; in such a manner they lived and died valiantly. One could, perhaps, condemn some of them for being overambitious for power, but one could never accuse any of them of being too soft or of any other characteristic that makes a man delicate and unwarlike. If these things were read and believed by Italian princes, it would be impossible for them not to bring about a change in their way of life and in the fortune of their nations.

And since you complained of your militia in the beginning of our discussion, let me say that if you had organized it as I have explained above, and it had subsequently not proved itself, you would have cause to complain; but if it was not organized and trained in the manner I suggested it could place the blame on you for having produced an abortion instead of a perfect figure. The Venetians, as well as the Duke of Ferrara, tried this method but were unable to carry it through—because of their own defects and not as a result of those of their men. And I can assure you that any of those rulers who possess a state in Italy today and who try this path will be ruler of this province before anyone else. Things will develop in that state as they did in the Kingdom of Macedonia, which, under the rule of Philip—who had learned the manner of organizing armies from Epaminondas the Theban—became so powerful by means of this kind of organization and these practices that it could occupy all of Greece in a few years. While the rest of Greece remained at ease and occupied herself with reciting comedies, Philip left such a foundation to his son that he was able to make himself prince of the entire world.

Therefore, anyone who despises these thoughts despises his principality, if he be a prince; if he be a citizen, he despises his native city. And I complain about Nature, which either should not have made me aware of this or should have given me the means of putting it into practice. Nor can I dream of ever having another opportunity, since I am old; and because of this, I have been very frank with you. Since you are young and qualified, if the things I have said please you, you can, at the proper time and to the profit of your princes, mention them and suggest that they adopt them. I would not have you be afraid or dismayed for this province of Italy, for it seems it was born to revive dead things, as we have seen in its poetry, painting, and sculpture. But as for myself, because I am along in years, I have no hope of seeing this come about. And yet, if Fortune had, in the past, conceded me as great a state as is sufficient for such an enterprise, I believe that I would have shown the world in a very short time how much ancient institutions are worth; and, without a doubt, I would have added to the glory of my state or lost it with no shame.

THE LIFE OF CASTRUCCIO CASTRACANI OF LUCCA

EDITORS' NOTE

In July of 1520 Machiavelli traveled from Florence to nearby Lucca on private business. While there, he composed a brief work on the affairs of Lucca and read in Latin a biography by Niccolò Tegrimi on the life of Castruccio Castracani (1281–1328), the town's most illustrious citizen and a medieval condottiere. Machiavelli's interest in writing a biography of Castruccio was more than a passing fancy, for this warrior-prince was one of Florence's cleverest adversaries, and Machiavelli would treat him again in The History of Florence (II, 25–26, 29–30). *While the biography gave Machiavelli the opportunity to sharpen his talents as a historian, it nevertheless left his creative imagination unfettered by the demands of the larger work and allowed him to create a biography closer in spirit to literature than to history, the portrait of an archetypal prince akin to Cesare Borgia in* The Prince, *whose military tactics reflected some of the concepts embodied in* The Art of War.

No contemporary reader of this work ever expected precise historical accuracy from it. Instead, the author was supposed to fashion his biographical sketch in such a way that its literary structure would underscore the protagonist's greatness. Thus, when Zanobi Buondelmonti wrote to Machiavelli to thank him for the gift of the work, he praised it highly while at the same time recognizing that the many witty sayings Machiavelli attributed to Castruccio were taken from other literary works (primarily Diogenes Laertius's Lives and Opinions of Eminent Philosophers). *Far from criticizing Machiavelli for including this essentially false information, however, Buondelmonti noted that Machiavelli might have done a better job of making the sayings correspond to his character's otherwise admirable qualities. For Machiavelli's readers, then, the demands of modern historical research were no more compelling than the need to find aesthetically pleasing patterns and politically relevant examples in the text.*

The biography first appeared in the 1532 edition of Machiavelli's Prince. *For many years thereafter, in both Italian editions and foreign translations, the life of Castruccio was often included with Machiavelli's more famous discussion of the ideal ruler. Men of letters admired its literary qualities, and Henry Fielding was even moved to imitate its structure in one of his novels,* Jonathan Wild. *Until very recently, however, its importance as a case study of the impact of mercurial Fortune on a great leader's political and military career was often overlooked.*

Written by Niccolò Machiavelli and
Sent to His Very Dear Friends
Zanobi Buondelmonti and Luigi Alamanni

Those who think about it, my dearest Zanobi and Luigi, are amazed to find that all men, or the majority of them, who have accomplished great deeds in this world, and who have been outstanding among the men of their day, have both in their origins and their birth been humble and obscure, or have been afflicted by Fortune in an extraordinary manner. Because all of them have either been exposed to wild beasts or have had such base parents that, being ashamed of them, they have made themselves sons of Jupiter or some other god. Since many of them are known to all of us, it would be boring and not very acceptable to my readers to give their names again; therefore, we shall consider their names superfluous and omit them. I believe that Fortune, wishing to demonstrate to the world that it is she, and not Prudence, who makes men great, begins to show her influence at a time when Prudence can have nothing to do in the matter, in order that she may claim credit for everything.

Castruccio Castracani was one of those men; like the others, he had neither a happy nor a renowned birth, as will be clear in the narration of the course of his life. Having discovered in this biography many things that are truly exemplary concerning the power of ingenuity and of Fortune, I thought I should recall it to the memory of men. And I wanted to dedicate it to you, since more than any men I know, you delight in noble deeds.

Let me continue. The Castracani family was numbered among the noble families of Lucca, although at present, being subject to our changing world, it no longer exists. Into this family was born one Antonio, who took Holy Orders, was named canon of St. Michael's Church of Lucca, and was called Messer Antonio as a sign of respect. He had no family other than a sister, whom he married off to Buonaccorso Cennami; but since Buonaccorso died and left her a widow, she decided not to marry again and returned to live with her brother.

Messer Antonio had a vineyard behind the house he lived in which could easily be reached from many directions since it was bordered by many gardens. One morning, just after sunrise, while Madonna Dianora (for that was Messer Antonio's sister's name) was walking through the vineyard while picking certain herbs for seasonings, as is the custom of women, she heard a rustling under a vine in the thicket and, turning her glance there, she heard a weeping sound. She moved toward the noise and uncovered through the foliage the hands and face of a baby boy who seemed to be asking for her help. Half amazed and frightened, but full of compassion and wonder, she took the child in her arms, brought him home, washed him, wrapped him in the usual white swaddling clothes, and presented him to her brother on his return home. When he had heard the story and had seen the child, Antonio was no less filled with pity and wonder than she; the two of them discussed what course of action they should take and decided to raise the boy themselves, since he was a priest and she had no children. They took a nurse into their home, and the brother and sister brought the baby up as if he were their own son; and when they baptized him, they named him Castruccio in memory of their father.

Castruccio's charm grew with his years, for in everything he showed ability and prudence; and he quickly learned everything Antonio taught him to do. Wanting to make him a priest in order to relinquish to him his canonry and other benefices some day, Messer Antonio trained him accordingly. But he had come upon a mind totally alien to priestly pursuits, for as soon as Castruccio reached the age of fourteen and began to fear Antonio less—and Madonna Dianora not at all—he laid his church books aside and began to occupy himself with weapons; nor did he delight in anything save handling them or in running, jumping, wrestling, and other sports wherein he could show the greatest strength of mind and body, for he far surpassed others of his own age. Whenever he read, nothing pleased him except those accounts of wars or of the deeds of the greatest men. Because of this, Messer Antonio suffered immeasurable unhappiness and distress.

There was, in the city of Lucca, a nobleman of the Guinigi family called Francesco, who far outstripped all the other people of Lucca in wealth, looks, and ingenuity. He was a professional soldier and had long fought under the Visconti of Milan; and because he was a Ghibelline, he was admired above all the others of that faction in Lucca. Since he was in Lucca and met with his fellow citizens morning and evening under the loggia of the Podestà, which is at the head of the Piazza di San Michele (the main square of Lucca), he saw Castruccio a number of times in the company of his neighborhood friends playing those games I mentioned above; and since it seemed to Francesco that besides surpassing them all Castruccio had a kingly authority over them, and that they, in certain respects, loved and respected him, he became very anxious to learn who he was. Informed by some bystanders as to Castruccio's identity, he became ever more anxious to have him in his service. And so, one day, after having summoned him, Francesco asked where he would rather be, in the house of a nobleman who would teach him how to ride and bear arms, or in the house of a priest, where he would hear nothing but masses and church services. Messer Francesco realized how happy Castruccio was to hear horses and weapons discussed but observed that the boy was a bit hesitant to speak. When Messer Francesco encouraged him to talk, he replied that if his guardian agreed, nothing could please him more than to leave behind his studies for the priesthood and take up those of a soldier. His reply pleased Francesco very much, and in a few days he arranged things so that Messer Antonio placed Castruccio into his keeping. Messer Antonio was persuaded more by the boy's nature than by anything else, judging that he could not keep him long in his present state.

Castruccio thus passed from the house of Messer Antonio Castracani, the canon, to that of Messer Francesco Guinigi, the condottiere. It is extraordinary to think how in a very short time he acquired all those abilities and habits required of a true gentleman. He first became an excellent horseman, riding even the wildest horse with skill; and in jousts and tournaments, although he was still quite young, he was more outstanding than the others. No matter what the feat of strength or skill was, he found no man to surpass him. To this were added good manners, especially an extremely modest nature; no one ever saw him perform an act or say a word that was displeasing, and he was respectful to his elders, modest to his equals, and polite to his inferiors. All these things made him loved not only by the entire Guinigi family but by the whole city of Lucca.

At about the time when Castruccio was eighteen years old, the Ghibellines were chased out of Pavia by the Guelfs, and Messer Francesco Guinigi was sent by the Visconti of Milan to help them. With him went Castruccio, who was put in charge of the whole company. Throughout this expedition Castruccio gave so many indications of his prudence and his courage that no one who took part in the campaign made as much of a reputation as he did; and his name became great and honored not only in Pavia but in all of Lombardy.

Returning to Lucca much more respected than when he had left, Castruccio never missed the chance to make friends, using every means necessary for gaining the friendship of men. But Messer Francesco Guinigi died, leaving behind him a son of thirteen named Pagolo. Francesco made Castruccio tutor and guardian of his property. Summoning him before his death, he begged him to raise his own son with the same devotion with which Castruccio himself had been raised, and to return to his son whatever gratitude he had not yet been able to render to the father. After Guinigi's death and Castruccio's guardianship of Pagolo, Castruccio grew so much in reputation and in power that the goodwill he enjoyed in Lucca began to turn to envy—so much so that many slandered him and considered him a suspicious man with the heart of a tyrant. Chief among these was the head of the Guelf faction, Messer Giorgio degli Opizi. Hoping to become ruler of Lucca after Francesco's demise, he came to feel that Castruccio, who had gained control because of his merits, had stolen his opportunity; and because of this he spread rumors to put Castruccio in a bad light. At first Castruccio was only put off by this, but soon he became apprehensive, for he believed that Messer Giorgio would not rest until he had brought him into disfavor with the lieutenant of King Robert of Naples, who might have him thrown out of Lucca.

At that time, Uguccione della Faggiuola d'Arezzo was lord of Pisa, first having been elected captain by the people and later having made himself ruler. With Uguccione were some Luccan exiles of the Ghibelline faction with whom Castruccio plotted in order to reinstate them with Uguccione's assistance; he also made his scheme known to his friends inside the city, who could no longer stand the power of the Opizi. Having told them what they should do, Castruccio cautiously fortified the Onesti tower and filled it with munitions and abundant provisions in order to be able, if necessary, to hold out there for several days. During the night that he and Uguccione had decided upon, he gave the signal to Uguccione, who had come down with many men onto the plain between Lucca and the mountains; and when he saw the sign, Uguccione advanced on St. Peter's Gate and set the entrance ablaze. At the same time Castruccio called the people to arms by a prearranged signal and forced the gate from the inside, so that when Uguccione and his troops had entered, they occupied the area, killed Messer Giorgio together with his entire family and many of his friends and supporters, and drove out the governor. Uguccione reorganized the city's government as he pleased, damaging it in the sense that, as the figures show, more than one hundred families were banished from Lucca. Of those who fled, some went to Florence while others went to Pistoia, both cities held by the Guelf faction and consequently eventually to become enemies of Uguccione and the people of Lucca.

Since the Florentines and the other Guelfs felt that the Ghibelline party had seized too much power in Tuscany, they agreed to restore the exiles from Lucca. Organizing a huge army, they entered the Nievole Valley and occupied the city of Montecatini; from there they set up camp at Montecarlo in order to have a clear passage to Lucca. Meanwhile, Uguccione assembled a goodly number of Pisans, Luccans, and, in addition, a large number of German mounted troops that he had brought with him from Lombardy, and he moved toward the Florentine camps. Hearing that the enemy was drawing near, the Florentine troops left Montecarlo and placed themselves between Montecatini and Pescia; Uguccione set up his troops below Montecarlo, two miles away from the enemy. For several days there were only some light skirmishes between the cavalry of both armies, for Uguccione had taken ill and the Pisans and the Luccans were avoiding a pitched battle.

But his illness grew more serious, and Uguccione withdrew to Montecarlo for treatment, leaving Castruccio in charge of the army. This caused the downfall of the Guelfs, for they took heart, thinking that the enemy army was without a leader. Castruccio knew this and waited several days to reinforce their belief, pretending to be afraid and not letting anyone leave the fortifications. The Guelfs, on their side, became more arrogant as they observed this fear, and each day they presented themselves drawn up in battle formation before Castruccio's army. When Castruccio believed that he had fostered in them enough courage and had learned their battle order, he decided to fight. First he made a speech to encourage his own soldiers and showed them that victory was assured if they were willing to follow his commands.

Castruccio had noticed how the enemy had placed its strongest forces in the center ranks and its weaker men on the flanks; he consequently did the opposite, putting his bravest men on his flanks and his weakest men in the middle. He left camp with this plan of battle, and when he came within sight of the enemy army, which had, as it usually did, moved up insolently to offer battle, he ordered that the middle ranks advance slowly while the units on the flanks charge ahead In this manner, when the battle was joined only the flanks of the two armies fought while the center remained stationary, since Castruccio's center had stayed so far behind that those of the enemy's center did not make contact. Thus, Castruccio's best men fought the weakest troops of the enemy, and their best soldiers stood still without being able either to harm the enemy facing them or to give aid to their comrades. Both flanks of the enemy were, without difficulty, put to flight; those in the center, seeing themselves exposed on their flanks, fled without having had the opportunity to show their bravery. The rout and the slaughter were great, for there were more than ten thousand men killed; among them were many leaders and great knights of the Guelf party from all over Tuscany, as well as many princes who had come to help them, including Piero, the brother of King Robert, Carlo, his nephew, and Filippo, ruler of Taranto. Castruccio's losses did not reach three hundred; among these was that of Francesco, Uguccione's son, a valiant young man who was killed during the first charge.

This rout made Castruccio's name truly great—to such an extent that Uguccione became so jealous and suspicious of his position that he could think of nothing but how to eliminate him, believing that he had lost power, and not gained it, by this victory. While he thought in these terms and waited for an honest opportunity to bring it about, it happened that Pier Agnolo Micheli, a man of worth and of great esteem, was killed in Lucca. His murderer sought refuge in Castruccio's home. When the police came to arrest him, they were repulsed by Castruccio; as a result, the murderer saved himself. Hearing this, Uguccione, who was then in Pisa, felt that he now had a good reason to punish him. Calling his son, Neri, to whom he had given the rule of Lucca, he ordered him to arrest and execute Castruccio under the pretense of inviting him to a banquet. Castruccio therefore went to the ruler's palace without fearing any harm; he was first detained for supper by Neri and then arrested. But Neri, fearing that the people might revolt if he executed him without any good reason, kept him alive in order that Uguccione might give him more detailed instructions. The latter, cursing the slowness and cowardice of his son,

left Pisa for Lucca with four hundred horsemen to finish
the matter. He had gone no farther than Bagni when the
Pisans revolted, killed Uguccione's lieutenant and the
other members of his family who had stayed behind in
Pisa, and proclaimed Count Gaddo della Gherardesca as
their ruler. Uguccione heard about what had happened in
Pisa before reaching Lucca, but he thought it unwise to
return since the Luccans might close the gates of the city
on him, following the example of the Pisans. But the people of Lucca, having heard about the news from Pisa,
found the means to liberate Castruccio in spite of the fact
that Uguccione had come to Lucca. They first began to
speak disrespectfully in groups around the public squares,
then to make noise, and finally to take up arms, demanding that Castruccio be released. Uguccione was so afraid
that he released him from prison. Whereupon Castruccio
immediately joined his supporters and, with the aid of the
people, attacked Uguccione. When he saw that he had no
alternative, Uguccione fled with his friends and went to
Lombardy to serve the Della Scala family, where he died
in poverty.

From the status of a prisoner Castruccio became, in all
but name, prince of Lucca, and with the aid of his friends
and the recent favor of the people he managed to be
named captain of their army for a year. Having obtained
this, in order to establish his reputation as a soldier, he
planned to regain for Lucca many of the territories that
had rebelled after Uguccione's departure. So he marched,
with the support of his Pisan allies, against Serezana. In
order to conquer it, he built a fort above it—which has
since been surrounded by a wall by the Florentines, who
today call it Serezanello—and in two months he captured
the town. Then, with this under his belt, he took Massa,
Carrara, and Lavenza, and in a short time he had occupied all of Lunigiana. To block the pass between Lombardy and Lunigiana, he captured Pontremoli and exiled
its ruler, Messer Anastagio Palavisini. Returning to Lucca
after this victory, he was met by the entire population.

Castruccio concluded that he should no longer put off making himself prince; with the aid of Pazzino dal Poggio, Puccinello dal Portico, Francesco Boccansacchi, and Cecco Guinigi—men of great reputation in Lucca who were bribed by him—he became lord and was declared prince by a solemn decree of the people.

At that time, Federigo of Bavaria, king of the Romans, had come into Italy to take the crown of the empire. Castruccio became his friend and went to meet him with five hundred horsemen, leaving Pagolo Guinigi behind in Lucca as his deputy; because of the memory of his father, Castruccio treated him as if he were his own son. Castruccio was received honorably by Federigo, was granted many privileges, and was made his lieutenant in Tuscany. Because the Pisans had driven out Gaddo della Gherardesca, having turned to Federigo for aid out of fear of him, Federigo made Castruccio lord of Pisa. The Pisans accepted his rule because of their fear of the Guelfs, especially the Florentines.

When Federigo returned to Germany, after leaving a governor in Rome, all of the Lombard and Tuscan Ghibellines who belonged to the emperor's camp turned to Castruccio, and each promised him sovereignty over their states if he would assist them to return there. Among these were Matteo Guidi, Nardo Scolari, Lapo Uberti, Gerozzo Nardi, and Piero Buonaccorsi—all Ghibellines and all Florentine exiles. Using their support and his own strength, Castruccio was planning to make himself ruler of all Tuscany. In order to increase his prestige, he made an alliance with Messer Matteo Visconti, Prince of Milan, and called the entire city and the surrounding countryside to arms. Since Lucca had five gates, he divided the territory into five parts and armed each, giving them commanders and banners, so that at short notice he could bring together twenty thousand men, not counting those who could aid him from Pisa. When Castruccio had surrounded himself with these forces and allies, it happened that Messer Matteo Visconti was attacked by the Guelfs of Piacenza, who had exiled the Ghibellines with the support of the Florentines and of King Robert. Matteo therefore asked Castruccio to attack the Florentines so that they might recall their forces from Lombardy. And so Castruccio attacked the Arno Valley and occupied Fucecchio and San Miniato, doing great damage to the countryside; whereupon the Florentines were forced to recall their troops. No sooner had they come back into Tuscany than Castruccio was himself forced to turn back to Lucca.

The Poggio family in that city was powerful, not only because it had supported Castruccio but also because it had made him ruler. Thinking that it had not been rewarded according to its merits, the family conspired with other families of Lucca to foment rebellion and to drive Castruccio out of the city. Taking advantage of an opportunity one morning, they assaulted Castruccio's lieutenant in charge of justice and killed him. They wanted to go on to incite the populace to revolt, but Stefano di Poggio, a peace-loving old man who had taken no part in the conspiracy, came forward and by means of his authority compelled his family to lay down their arms, offering himself as a mediator between them and Castruccio in order to obtain their goals. And so they abandoned their arms with no more caution than when they had taken them up; meanwhile, hearing the news from Lucca, Castruccio left Pagolo Guinigi in charge of the main army and, without losing any time, came to Lucca with part of his forces. Finding the disturbance under control, contrary to his fears, and thinking that he could easily make himself secure there, he placed his armed supporters in all the strategic positions. Stefano di Poggio, believing that Castruccio was under an obligation to him, went to find him and begged him on behalf of his family (but not on his own account, thinking that he needed no such mercy) to make allowances for youth and to remember the old friendship and the obligation owed to their family. To this Castruccio replied graciously and told him

not to worry, saying that he was happier to see the disturbances quelled than he was angry over their beginning;
and he asked Stefano to bring them all to him, saying that
he thanked God for the opportunity to demonstrate his
clemency and goodwill. When they had all come forward,
trusting in the word of both Stefano and Castruccio, they
were imprisoned and, together with Stefano, executed.

The Florentines had meanwhile recovered San Miniato. Castruccio felt that he should put an end to this war,
for until he could be sure of Lucca he could not leave
home. Tempting the Florentines with a truce, he found
them eager to agree, for they were worn out and anxious
to put an end to their expenditures. A two-year truce was
signed, and each side kept what it held. When Castruccio
was rid of the war, in order not to run the risks he had incurred before, he used various pretexts and excuses to
eliminate all those in Lucca who might aspire to his position. Nor did he forgive anyone, stripping them of their
citizenship, their property, and for those whom he could
lay his hands on, of their lives, saying that he had learned
by experience not to trust any of them. Furthermore, to
increase his security he built a fortress in Lucca, using the
materials from the towers of those he had exiled or
murdered.

While Castruccio had halted his war with the Florentines and was fortifying himself in Lucca, he did not cease
doing those things that would increase his greatness without war. Having a great desire to occupy Pistoia, since he
felt he might have a foothold in Florence in holding that
town, in various ways he gained the friendship of the
whole mountain area and conducted himself in such a
manner that all of the Pistoian factions trusted him. The
city was split in those days, as always, between the Whites
and the Blacks. The leader of the Whites was Bastiano di
Possente; that of the Blacks, Iacopo da Gia. Each had secret communications with Castruccio, and each wanted to
exile the other to such an extent that, finally, after much
mutual suspicion, they came to blows. Iacopo fortified the

Florentine gate and Bastiano the Luccan gate. Relying more upon Castruccio than upon the Florentines, since they both judged him quicker in matters of war, each secretly asked him for help. Castruccio promised aid to both, telling Iacopo that he would come in person and Bastiano that he would send his protégé, Pagolo Guinigi. Giving each of them a meeting time, he sent Pagolo by way of Pescia while he came directly to Pistoia; by midnight, as Castruccio and Pagolo had planned, both were in Pistoia, each being received as a friend. Once inside the city, Castruccio gave a signal to Pagolo when he thought the time was right, after which one killed Iacopo da Gia and the other murdered Bastiano di Possente; all their partisans were either captured or executed. Pistoia fell to them without further opposition. Having thrown the Signoria out of the palace, Castruccio forced the people to render obedience to him, cancelling many old debts and making many promises. And he did the same thing in the surrounding countryside, a large part of which had run to see the new prince, so that everyone, filled with hope and moved, in large measure, by Castruccio's abilities, settled down.

At that time the Roman people began to riot because of the high cost of living, blaming this condition on the absence of the Pope, then living in Avignon, and cursing the German authorities. As a result, daily murders and other disorders occurred. Enrico, the emperor's lieutenant, could do nothing about it. This caused Enrico to suspect that the Romans might call in King Robert of Naples, chase him out of Rome, and return the city to the Pope. Having no closer friend to whom he could turn than Castruccio, he sent him a message asking him not only to send help but to come in person to Rome. Castruccio judged that he could not ignore the request if he wanted to render a service to the emperor; furthermore, since the emperor was not in Rome, he could see no other course of action. Leaving Pagolo Guinigi in Lucca, he set out for Rome with six hundred mounted men, where he was re-

ceived by Enrico with the greatest honors. In a very short
time his presence gave the emperor's party so much prestige that, without bloodshed or violence, he restored
order. Castruccio removed the cause of the disturbances,
since he had a great deal of grain brought in by sea from
the Pisan area. Afterward, partly by means of threats and
partly by punishing the Roman leaders, he returned the
people willingly to the rule of Enrico. Castruccio was
named a senator of Rome and was given many other
honors by the Roman people. Castruccio assumed this office with the greatest of ceremony and wore a brocaded
toga bearing an inscription in front that read, "He is the
man God wills," and another in the back that read, "He
shall be what God wills."

Meanwhile, the Florentines, angry that Castruccio used
the truce to take control of Pistoia, were scheming about
how to make the city rebel—something they thought
would be an easy matter because of his absence. Among
the Pistoian exiles in Florence were Baldo Cecchi and Iacopo Baldini, both men of authority and ready to risk
everything. These men had secret contacts with their
friends inside Pistoia. With the aid of the Florentines,
they entered Pistoia by night and drove out Castruccio's
supporters and officials, killing some of them and restor-
ing the city to its former liberty. This greatly annoyed and
displeased Castruccio. Taking leave of Enrico, he returned to Lucca by forced marches with his troops. When
they heard of his return, the Florentines, believing that he
would not stand idle, decided to anticipate him and to
enter the Nievole Valley first with their troops, thinking
that if they occupied the valley they would cut off the
road needed to reoccupy Pistoia. They raised a large army
composed of all the Guelf sympathizers and entered Pistoian territory. At the same time, Castruccio arrived with
his troops at Montecarlo. When he had learned where the
Florentine army was located, he decided neither to meet it
in the plain of Pistoia nor to wait for it in the plain of Pescia, but rather to confront it in the Serravalle Pass if that

were possible. He believed that if this plan worked, his victory would be assured, since he had learned that the Florentines had thirty thousand men while he had chosen twelve thousand of his own. And although he had faith in their ability and industry, he was nevertheless afraid of being surrounded by a superior force in a battle joined in an open space.

Serravalle is a fort between Pescia and Pistoia, set on a hill that closes the Nievole Valley, not exactly on the pass itself but about two bowshots above it. The passage through it is narrow rather than steep, since it slopes up gently on both sides; but it is so narrow that twenty men standing side by side would span it, especially where the waters divide on the hill. This was the spot where Castruccio meant to face the enemy, both because his smaller forces would have an advantage and because his men would only see the enemy the minute the battle started; for Castruccio feared that his troops might be frightened if they saw ahead of time how great the size of the enemy was. Messer Manfredi, of German descent, was the keeper of the castle; he had been placed in charge of the town as a common ground for both Lucca and Pistoia before Castruccio took Pistoia. Neither city had reason to attack him, since he had promised to remain neutral and to have no obligations to anyone; because of this, and because of his strong position, he had remained in power. But in view of these new circumstances, Castruccio grew anxious to occupy the stronghold. Being very friendly with a certain citizen there, he arranged with him to have four hundred of his men let in to kill the ruler the night before the battle was to begin.

Once things were organized in this manner, he did not move the army from Montecarlo in order to encourage the Florentines to enter the pass. Since the latter wished to shift the fighting from Pistoia to the Nievole Valley, they camped below Serravalle, intending to cross the hill the next day. But, having taken the castle that evening without a sound, Castruccio left Montecarlo at midnight and arrived in silence with his troops at the foot of Serravalle in the morning. And so, at the same time, each on his own side, both he and the Florentines began to climb the slope. Castruccio had sent his foot soldiers along the main road and a band of four hundred cavalry toward the castle on the left. The Florentines, on the other side, had sent ahead four hundred horsemen; they had moved their infantry, stationing their men-at-arms behind them. They did not expect to find Castruccio on the hill, since they did not know that he had taken the castle. So the Florentine cavalry, having climbed the slope, came upon Castruccio's foot soldiers unexpectedly, and they found themselves so close to their enemy that they hardly had time to lace their helmets. Since, therefore, the unprepared were assaulted by the prepared and well organized, Castruccio's troops attacked valiantly and their opponents could hardly resist. Nevertheless, some fought back, and by the time the noise reached the rest of the Florentine camp everything was confused: the horsemen were hemmed in by the infantry; the infantry by the horsemen and the wagons; the commanders could neither go forward nor backward because of the narrowness of the place; the result was that no one knew what they could or should do in all this confusion. In the meantime, the Florentine cavalrymen, fighting the enemy infantry, were killed and slaughtered without being able to defend themselves because of the difficulty of the terrain; nevertheless, they resisted more out of tenacity than ability, for they had the mountains on their flanks, their friends behind them, and the enemy in front of them, which left them no means of escape.

Meanwhile, Castruccio, seeing that he did not have enough men to rout the enemy, sent a thousand foot soldiers through the castle; having them descend together with four hundred horsemen that he had sent ahead, they hit the enemy on their flanks with such fury that the Florentine soldiers, unable to withstand the impetus of the charge, fled, defeated more by the terrain than by the enemy. The rout began with those who were in the rear, toward Pistoia; they spread out over the plain, each saving his own neck as best he could.

This was a great and bloody rout. Many leaders were captured, among them Bandino de' Rossi, Francesco Brunelleschi, and Giovanni della Tosa—all Florentine noblemen. Also soldiering with the Florentines were many other Tuscans and Neapolitans who had been sent by King Robert to aid the Guelfs.

As soon as the Pistoians heard about the defeat, they drove out the Guelf party without delay and gave themselves up to Castruccio. Not content with this, Castruccio occupied Prato and all the strongholds of the plain on both sides of the Arno River; he camped with his forces in the Peretola Plain, two miles from Florence. There he stayed for many days, dividing up the booty and celebrating his victory; he had money coined and he organized races to be run by horses, men, and whores in order to insult the Florentines. Nor did he miss the chance to bribe some noble citizens in order to have the gates of Florence opened at night; but the plot was discovered, and Tommaso Lupacci and Lambertuccio Frescobaldi were captured and beheaded.

Terrified by their defeat, the Florentines now saw no way to save their freedom. In order to be more certain of his aid, they sent ambassadors to King Robert of Naples announcing that the city and control over it were his. The king accepted, not so much because of the honor shown him by the Florentines but rather because he knew how important it was for his own state that the Guelfs control Tuscany. Agreeing with the Florentines that they should pay him two hundred thousand ducats annually, he sent his son, Carlo, to Florence with four thousand horsemen.

Meanwhile, the Florentines were relieved somewhat of Castruccio's men, since he was obliged to leave their territory and to go to Pisa to repress a conspiracy organized against him by Benedetto Lanfranchi, one of the city's first citizens. Unable to bear the fact that his city was in servitude to a Luccan, Benedetto plotted against him, planning to occupy the citadel and to kill Castruccio's supporters after driving out the garrison. But since, in these matters, a group small enough to keep the secret is not large enough to execute the design, while Benedetto was searching for more conspirators he found one who revealed the plan to Castruccio. Also incriminated by this disclosure were Bonifacio Cerchi and Giovanni Guidi, two Florentines who were exiled in Pisa. Whereupon Castruccio had Benedetto seized and killed; the rest of his family was banished, and many other noble citizens were beheaded. And since it appeared that Pistoia and Pisa were somewhat disloyal to him, he tried to secure them by means of diligence and force. This gave the Florentines enough time to regroup their troops and to await the arrival of Carlo. When he arrived, they decided not to waste any time and gathered together a vast group, calling to their assistance almost all the Guelfs of Italy; they made up a huge army of more than thirty thousand infantry and ten thousand horse. After discussing where they should attack first, Pistoia or Pisa, they resolved to strike first at Pisa—this seemed the plan most likely to succeed because of the recent conspiracy there, and it seemed more profitable since they thought that Pistoia would surrender automatically once Pisa fell.

The Florentines therefore left the city with this army on the first of May, 1328, immediately occupied La Lastra, Signa, Montelupo, and Empoli, and arrived with their army at San Miniato. Castruccio was not at all afraid when he heard about the huge army the Florentines had fielded against him, for he believed that this was the moment for Fortune to put the rule of Tuscany within his grasp; he felt that the enemy would not make a better showing at Pisa than they had at Serravalle, and that they had no hopes of regrouping themselves as they had done previously. Having gathered together twenty thousand of his foot soldiers and four thousand cavalrymen, he camped at Fucecchio and sent Pagolo Guinigi with five thousand lancers to Pisa. Fucecchio is situated on a stronger site than any other castle in the area of Pisa, being in between the Gusciana Canal and the Arno River and somewhat above the plain. Once there, the enemy could not prevent the arrival of supplies from either Lucca or Pisa unless they divided their forces; nor could they march to meet him or go toward Pisa without a positive disadvantage: in the first case they could be trapped between Castruccio and the men from Pisa, and in the second they would have to cross the Arno; with the enemy on their backs, this would be very dangerous. In order to encourage them to cross the river, Castruccio did not place his troops along the Arno's banks but rather along Fucecchio's walls, leaving plenty of room between the river and himself.

After occupying San Miniato, the Florentines debated their next move: whether to go on to Pisa or meet Castruccio. Having considered the difficulties of each alternative, they decided to engage his forces in battle. The Arno was low enough so that it could be forded, but only in such a way that the infantry would be up to their shoulders in water and the horsemen up to their saddles. On the morning of the tenth of June, the Florentines began to cross, in battle formation, part of their cavalry and a battalion of ten thousand infantry. Castruccio was ready. Intent on finishing what he had in mind, he attacked them with a battalion of five thousand infantry and three thousand cavalry; not allowing them time to leave the water, he fell upon them suddenly. He also dispatched a thousand light infantry downstream and upstream. The Florentine foot soldiers were weighted down by their arms and the water and had not yet climbed up the opposite bank. Although a few made it across, the horsemen made the way more difficult for others to cross, having broken up the river bottom. Thus, finding the passageway so uneven, many horses turned over on their riders and others got so stuck in the mud that they could not retreat. When the Florentine commanders saw the difficulty of crossing in that spot, they made their men withdraw and go higher up the river in order to find a fresh place with a more suitable riverbank. Those troops that Castruccio had sent up the river opposed this move; these soldiers were lightly armed with round shields and spears and struck the enemy in the face and the chest while screaming loudly. So frightened were the horses by these cries and by their wounds that, unwilling to go on, they fell back upon each other. The struggle between Castruccio's men and those who did cross was bitter and terrible; many fell on each side and each tried with all its might to overcome the other. Castruccio's troops wanted to throw their opponents into the river, while the Florentines wanted to push his men back to make room for those who were leaving the water to fight. To this tenacity were added the exhortations of the officers. Castruccio reminded his men that these were the same enemy troops that they had defeated not long ago at Serravalle; the Florentines, on the other hand, reproached their men for allowing themselves to be defeated by so few opponents. Seeing that the battle was wearing on, that both his men and their adversaries were already worn out, and that there were many dead and wounded on each side, Castruccio sent forward another troop of five thousand foot soldiers; after leading them behind those who were fighting, he ordered the ones in front to separate, one part turning to the right, the other to the left, as if they were in retreat. This strategy gave the Florentines room to move ahead and to gain some ground, but when their tired troops came into contact with Castruccio's fresh men, it did not take long for the latter to push the former back into the river. So far, the cavalry on either side had no advantage; knowing his own to be inferior, Castruccio had merely ordered his cavalry officers to hold the enemy. He hoped to beat their foot soldiers; once that was accomplished, he could more easily destroy their horsemen. Everything went according to plan, for when he saw that the enemy foot soldiers had retreated into the river he sent the rest of his infantry against the enemy cavalry; the foot soldiers wounded the enemy with darts and lances, and since his own horsemen were pressing against them with even greater force, they were put to flight. The Florentine commanders, realizing the difficulties their horsemen were having in getting across, tried to cross their infantry downstream in order to attack Castruccio's flanks. But since the banks were steep and were held by Castruccio's men, they tried in vain. Thus the enemy was routed, to Castruccio's great honor and glory, and of the entire force not more than a third survived. Many of their leaders were captured; Carlo, King Robert's son, together with Michelagnolo Falconi and Taddeo degli Albizzi, who were Florentine commissioners, fled to Empoli. The booty was sizable and the slaughter was very heavy, as one might imagine to be the case in such a battle: within the Florentine army, 20,231 perished, while Castruccio's forces lost 1,570.

But Fortune, hostile to his glory, took life away from him instead of giving it to him—it interrupted those plans that Castruccio had intended to carry out for a long time, plans that only death could have prevented him from carrying out. All during that day of battle Castruccio struggled hard; then, when it ended, all tired and drenched with sweat, he stopped at the gate of Fucecchio to review his troops, to thank and receive them personally, as well as to be ready to deal with any enemy force that might pose a threat. He thought it was the duty of a good general to be the first to mount his horse and the last to dismount. Thus, while standing exposed to a wind—an almost always unhealthy one that usually rises up from the Arno at noon—he caught an icy chill; he paid no attention to it, for he was used to such discomforts, but it was the cause of his death. The following night he was struck by a very strong fever and his temperature continued to rise; all the doctors considered the illness fatal, and when Castruccio learned this, he called Pagolo Guinigi and spoke these words to him:

"If I had known, my son, that Fortune had wanted to cut me down in the middle of that journey's path leading to the glory which I, through my many successful deeds, had promised myself to attain, I would have toiled less and left you fewer enemies and less envy, though a smaller state. I would have been happy to rule Lucca and Pisa and I would not have taken the Pistoians and angered the Florentines with so many injuries; rather, making each of these two peoples my allies, I would have led a quieter, if not longer, life and would have left you, without a doubt, a more stable and secure state, although a smaller one. But Fortune, who wishes to be the arbiter of all human affairs, did not grant me sufficient judgment early enough to understand her, nor enough time to be able to overcome her. You have heard—since many have told you and I have never denied it—how I entered your father's service while still young, lacking all those aspirations that should attract every noble mind, and how I was raised and loved by your father more than if I had been of his own blood. As a result, under his guidance, I became valorous and able to obtain that fortune that you yourself have observed. And since, at the point of death, he entrusted you and your property to my care, I have raised you with this same love and have increased your inheritance with the same faith that bound and still binds me. And since not only was what your father left you yours, but also what Fortune and my ability have earned, I decided not to marry so that love for my sons would not prevent me in any way from showing such gratitude toward your father's family as I felt obliged to show. I am leaving you, therefore, a large state, and this pleases me; but because I leave it to you in a weak, unstable condition, I am very unhappy. You control the city of Lucca, which will never be content under your rule; you rule Pisa, where the citizens are by nature treacherous and fickle, and which, however used to being dominated it has been at times, will never tolerate a Luccan as its lord. Pistoia is still yours, but it is somewhat untrustworthy because of internal divisions and it remains angry at our family because of recent injuries. Nearby, you have the offended Florentines, harmed by us in a thousand ways but not destroyed, to whom the news of my death will be more pleasing than the conquest of all Tuscany. You cannot count on the emperor or the princes of Milan because they are far away, lazy, and their aid comes late. Therefore, you should trust only in your own energy, in the memory of my ability, and in the reputation you will gain from this present victory. If you know how to use this reputation with prudence, it will help you reach a truce with the Florentines, who, being terrified by this present rout, should willingly consent. As for them, while I sought to make them my enemies and thought that their enmity would bring me power and glory, you must try to make them your friends at all costs, because their friendship will bring you security and comfort. It is very important in this world to know oneself and to know how to measure the strength of one's mind and one's condition, and anyone who is not suited to deeds of war ought to try to reign with the arts of peace. My advice to you is to turn to these arts and strive, by this means, to enjoy the fruits of my labors and dangers; you should manage easily if you take my maxims to be true. And you will be obligated to me in two ways: first, because I left you this realm, and second, because I taught you how to keep it."

Having summoned those citizens of Lucca, Pisa, and Pistoia who had served under him, and having commended Pagolo Guinigi to them, making them swear obedience to him, he died, leaving happy memories of himself with all those who knew of him and with all those who were his friends, and he left as much regret behind as did any prince who had died at any other time. His funeral was celebrated with the most solemn rites, and he was buried in San Francesco of Lucca. But Fortune and ability were not as kind to Pagolo Guinigi as they had been to Castruccio, for not much later he lost Pistoia and then Pisa; he held Lucca, but only with difficulty, and it remained under his family until the days of Pagolo, his great-grandson.

Castruccio was, therefore, according to all that we have seen, a man unusual not only for his own day but also for past times. He was physically of above-average height, and every limb was in perfect proportion to the other; and he was so gracious in bearing and so human in his dealings with others that never did anyone who spoke with him leave dissatisfied. His hair was almost red, and he wore it cut above his ears; and always, at all times, even when it rained or snowed, he went about bareheaded.

He was gracious to his friends, terrible to his foes, just with his subjects, unfaithful to foreigners; if he could conquer by trickery, he never tried to win by force, for he said that it was the victory, not the method of achieving it, that brought one glory.

No one was ever more bold in risking danger, nor more reluctant to leave it. He used to say that men ought to try everything and fear nothing since God loved strong men and always punished the weak by means of the strong.

He was also amazing in conversation and full of witty remarks, sometimes sharp, sometimes urbane; and as he never minced words with others, he never became angry when others did the same with him. There are records of remarks he made as well as ones that were made to him.

When a friend reproved him for having bought a partridge for a ducat, Castruccio said: "You would not pay more than a penny for it." When his friend admitted that he was right, Castruccio replied: "A ducat is, for me, worth much less."

Once there was a flatterer in his presence. To show his contempt for the person, Castruccio spat upon him, whereupon the man said: "In order to catch a small fish fishermen let themselves get entirely soaked by the sea; to land a whale I can well afford to let myself get wet from a little spit." Castruccio not only tolerated this reply but rewarded it.

Someone spoke ill of him, saying that he lived too well, to which Castruccio replied: "If this were a vice, there would not be such splendid banquets on the feast days of our saints."

Passing through a street and seeing a young man all red from blushing because he had been seen leaving a brothel, Castruccio said: "Don't be ashamed when you leave but when you enter."

When a friend gave him a carefully tied knot to loosen, he said: "Idiot, do you think I want to undo something that gives me so much trouble when it is tied?"

When Castruccio remarked to someone who was a professional philosopher, "You are like dogs that always stay around whoever feeds them best," the other replied: "On the contrary, we are like doctors who go to the houses of those who need us most."

Traveling from Pisa to Livorno by sea and being overtaken by a dangerous storm that frightened him very much, he was reproved for his fear by one of his companions, who claimed that he never feared anything; to this Castruccio answered that he was not surprised, since each man values his life as much as it is worth.

Asked by someone what he had to do to be respected, Castruccio said: "When you go to a banquet, don't be like a bump on a log."

When someone bragged about having read many things, Castruccio remarked: "It would be better to boast of having remembered many of them."

When somebody boasted of drinking a great deal without becoming intoxicated, he said: "An ox does exactly the same thing."

Castruccio once had a young girl with whom he lived; he was criticized for this by a friend, who said that it was especially bad that he had let himself be taken by a woman. To this Castruccio retorted: "You are mistaken. I took her, not she me!"

When another person accused him of eating overly delicate foods, he said: "You would not spend as much as I do for them." And when the man admitted that this was correct, he added: "Therefore, you are a bigger miser than I am a glutton."

Once he was invited to supper at the home of Taddo Bernardi of Lucca, a very rich and extravagant man. When he arrived at the house, Taddo showed him a room completely decorated with tapestries and with a floor made of precious stones of various colors arranged in the shape of flowers, branches, and various plants. After having collected a good deal of saliva in his mouth, Castruccio spat it all into Taddo's face. When the man complained, Castruccio explained: "I wanted to spit in a place that would offend you the least."

Asked how Julius Caesar died, he remarked: "May God grant that I die the same way."

One night, at the house of one of his noblemen, where a number of women had been invited to make merry, he was dancing and enjoying himself more than was fitting to his station; rebuked for this by a friend, he remarked: "Anyone who is thought to be wise by day will never be considered a fool by night."

Once, when a man had come to beg a favor of him, Castruccio pretended not to hear, and the man threw himself at his knees. When Castruccio criticized him for doing so, he retorted: "It is your fault, since your ears are in your feet." Whereupon Castruccio gave him double the favor he requested.

He used to say that the road to Hell was easy since you could get there downhill and with your eyes closed.

When someone once asked him a favor by using many superfluous words, Castruccio exclaimed: "The next time you want something of me, send someone else."

The same kind of man once bored him with a long

speech that finally concluded: "Perhaps I have tired you by too much talking." To this Castruccio replied: "Not at all. I haven't heard a word you said."

He used to say of a man who had been a beautiful boy and was now a handsome man that he had caused too much harm, for at first he used to take the husbands away from their wives and now he took the wives away from their husbands.

He asked an envious man who was laughing: "Are you laughing because you are doing well or because someone else is in trouble?"

While he was still under the guidance of Messer Francesco Guinigi, one of his friends said: "What must I give you for you to let me slap your face?" Castruccio replied: "A helmet."

Having executed a citizen of Lucca who had been one of the reasons for his greatness, and subsequently being told that it was wrong to kill one of his old friends, he replied that this was mistaken, since he had killed a new enemy.

Castruccio praised greatly those men who picked wives and then did not marry them, as well as those who wanted to go to sea but never went.

He said that he was always amazed at how men, when buying a vase of earthenware or of glass, always sounded it out to find out if it were good, yet when choosing a wife were content only to see her.

When a person asked him, as he was about to die, how he wished to be buried, he replied: "With my face downward, since I know that this country will turn upside down when I am gone."

Asked if he had ever considered becoming a monk to save his soul, he replied that he had not, since it seemed strange to him that Brother Lazarus should go to Heaven and Uguccione della Faggiuola to Hell.

Asked when one should eat to stay healthy, he answered: "If you are rich, when you are hungry; if you are poor, when you can."

Seeing one of his gentlemen being buttoned up by his servant, he remarked: "I hope to God he also spoon-feeds you."

Noticing that someone had written over his doorway in Latin letters "May God guard this house from the wicked," he quipped: "That means that the owner cannot go in there himself!"

Passing through a street where there was a small house with a huge door, he said: "That house is going to run away through that door."

When he had been informed that a foreigner had corrupted a young boy, he said: "He must be from Perugia."

Once, when he asked what town had a reputation for cheaters and charlatans, he was answered, "Lucca," since everyone there was naturally that way, except for Bonturo Dati.[1]

When Castruccio was arguing with an ambassador of the King of Naples about the property of exiles, he became rather angry. The ambassador said to him: "So you don't fear the king?" Castruccio replied: "Is he good or evil, this king of yours?" Hearing that he was good, Castruccio replied to the ambassador: "Then why should you want me to be afraid of a good man?"

I could recount many other things, all of which reflect his wit and his seriousness, but let these sayings suffice as proof of his great qualities.

He lived forty-four years, and he was like a prince no matter what Fortune dealt him. And as there were many evidences of his good luck, he also wished there to be some tokens of his bad fortune. Because of this, the handcuffs with which he was chained in prison can still be seen in the tower of his home, where he himself placed them in order that they might always testify to his adversity. And

[1] Here Machiavelli refers to the gibe at Lucca's reputation for barratry he had read about in Dante's *Inferno,* XXI, 41. Bonturo Dati was apparently the most corrupt official in Lucca at the beginning of the fourteenth century.

because he was, when living, inferior neither to Philip of Macedonia, Alexander's father, nor to Scipio of Rome, he died at the same age as both of them; and without a doubt he would have surpassed the one and the other if instead of Lucca he had had Macedonia or Rome for his native land.

From
THE HISTORY OF
FLORENCE

EDITORS' NOTE

Although Machiavelli never obtained a post with the Medici rulers of Florence that matched his own estimation of his political talents, he was finally given a commission from the university (the Studio fiorentino) in 1520 to compose a history of Florence. When he presented the manuscript, totaling eight books, of this history to Pope Clement VII (Giulio de' Medici) in 1525, he joined a tradition of humanist historiography that originated in the Florentine chancery in the fifteenth century and culminated in the masterful History of Italy written by Machiavelli's friend Francesco Guicciardini and published in Florence in 1561. Early Renaissance humanists had revived the art of historical narrative, taking Livy's history of republican Rome as their model for similar treatments of their own cities. Several of Machiavelli's predecessors in the Florentine chancery—Leonardo Bruni (1374–1444), Poggio Bracciolini (1380–1459), and Bartolommeo della Scala (1428–1497)—produced Latin histories which Machiavelli knew and studied along with his favorite classical authors. His own History of Florence, first published in 1532, was widely circulated throughout Renaissance Europe. It received a French translation in 1557 that was reprinted several times, three editions of a Latin version that first appeared in 1564, and an English edition in 1594.

In addition to a dedication and a preface, the history was divided into eight books covering Florentine affairs from the city's earliest days until 1492. Machiavelli apparently intended to continue the narrative, but the task was never completed. Unlike the earlier Latin works, which had stressed Florentine foreign relations and the republic's struggle for survival against the Visconti tyrants of Milan, Machiavelli's history applies a spirit of civic humanism to internal affairs, civil discord, and conspiracies, in keeping with the importance he gives these topics in his theoretical analyses of politics in The Prince *and, especially,* The Discourses. *It is possible to view* The History of Florence *as a casebook illustrating, in the particular instance of a single modern city, the truth of the more abstract concepts derived from the classical example of Rome in* The Discourses. *The comparison between the ancient model of civic excellence and the contemporary model of civic corruption, treated directly in one chapter of the history, is implicit throughout. The original eight books of the work are divided into the following broad subjects: Florence from the decline of the Roman empire to 1434 (I); the origins of Florence and its early history to 1353 (II); Florence from 1353 until 1414 (III); Florentine affairs from 1414 until 1434 (IV); the rule of Cosimo de' Medici until the battle of Anghiari, 1434–1440 (V); Cosimo's hegemony, 1440–1463 (VI); Florentine affairs from Cosimo's death until the early years of the rule of Lorenzo de' Medici, Il Magnifico, 1463–1478 (VII); Florence under Lorenzo, from the Pazzi conspiracy until his death, 1478–1492 (VIII).*

The present translation contains the following selections: the complete dedication and preface to the work, which explains Machiavelli's view of history; chapter one of book three, which compares Rome to Florence; chapter one of book five, which outlines Machiavelli's views on historical cycles (this should be compared to a similar passage in The Discourses, *II, 2); and chapters one through six of the seventh book and the last chapter of the eighth book, which contain the very famous portraits and political evaluations of Cosimo de' Medici and Lorenzo il Magnifico that were to influence generations of future historians.*

To the Most Holy and Blessed Father,
Our Lord Clement VII, from
His Humble Servant Niccolò Machiavelli

Since Your Holiness, Most Blessed and Holy Father, commissioned me while you were still a cardinal to write about the deeds accomplished by the Florentine peoples, I have used all the diligence and skill that has been granted me by nature and experience in order to satisfy you. And since I have reached that point of time in my writing when, as a result of the death of the Magnificent Lorenzo de' Medici, the shape of Italy was changed, and since the affairs which then followed were greater and of more consequence, and must consequently be described with a greater and loftier spirit, I thought it best to bind all that I have written up until those times in one volume and to present it to Your Most Blessed Holiness in order that you may begin to taste the fruits of your seeds and of my labors in some small measure.

As you read, Your Holiness will see, after the Roman empire began to lose strength in the West, how many disasters and how many rulers Italy endured for centuries as she changed her governments; you will observe how the Pope, the Venetians, the Kingdom of Naples, and the Duchy of Milan seized the hegemony and territories of that province; you will see how your native city, withdrawing her allegiance from the emperors as a result of internal division, continued to remain divided until she began to fall under the shadow of your family. And, since Your Blessed Holiness commissioned and commanded me, in particular, to write about the deeds of your ancestors in such a way that I should be far removed from any intent to flatter (for however much it pleases you to hear the true praises of men, so much more do false and obsequious ones displease you), I am very much afraid that I may appear to Your Holiness to be disobeying your orders in describing the kindness of Giovanni, the wisdom of Cosimo, the humanity of Piero, and the magnificence and prudence of Lorenzo. I beg forgiveness from Your Holiness for this if these descriptions or others displease you because they are inaccurate. But, discovering how much praise there was for them in other histories written at various times, I was forced either to describe them as I found them or to be silent. And if beneath their distinguished deeds there lay hidden some ambition contrary to the public welfare, as some men contend, I am not obliged to write about it if I cannot recognize it; for in all of my works I have never allowed a dishonest act to be concealed by an honest cause, nor have I wanted a praiseworthy deed to be obscured and appear as if it had been done for another reason.

But how far removed I am from flattery can be seen in all of the aspects of my history, and most particularly in the public speeches and the private remarks (both those quoted directly and those reported by others), which retain the ideas and the order suitable for a person who speaks without any hesitation. I avoid, nevertheless, offensive words in all places, since they are neither necessary nor do they suit the dignity and the truth of history. No one, therefore, who rightly examines my writings can accuse me of flattery, especially when one notices that I have said little about the accomplishments of Your Holiness's father. This is due to the brevity of his life, during which he had no chance to make a name for himself; as a result, I have not glorified him in my writing. Nonetheless, his accomplishments were most grand and magnificent, for he engendered Your Holiness, an action that counterbalances those of his ancestors, one that will bestow more fame upon him than the years of his life malicious Fortune stole from him. And so, Most Holy and Blessed Father, I have tried in this history of mine to satisfy everybody without staining the truth. Perhaps I have not satisfied anyone. If this be the case, it would not surprise me, for I think it is impossible to describe the affairs of one's own times without offending many people. Nevertheless, I enter the battle with cheer, hoping that just as I am honored and supported by the kindness of Your Holiness, so also shall I be assisted and defended by the armed legions of your most holy judgment. And I shall continue my undertaking with that same spirit and confidence with which I have written up to this time, as long as my life and the favor of Your Holiness do not abandon me.

PREFACE

When I first decided to write about the internal and external affairs of the Florentine peoples, my intention was to begin my narration the year of the Christian Era, 1434, at which time the Medici family, because of the merits of Cosimo and Giovanni, his father, had gained more authority than any other family in Florence. I believed that Messer Leonardo Bruni d'Arezzo and Messer Poggio Bracciolini, two most excellent historians, had narrated, in detail, all the events that occurred until that time. But after I had read their writings with great care, for the purpose of studying their technique of organization and style so that in imitating them I might render my own history more pleasing to readers, I found that they were very diligent historians in describing the wars carried on by the Florentines with foreign princes and peoples; however, concerning civil discord, internal conflicts, and the effects these have had, I find that they are totally silent about one part of them, whereas the other part they describe so briefly that their readers can derive no profit or pleasure therefrom. They did this, I believe, either because they felt that these affairs were so unimportant as to be unworthy of preservation for posterity in writing or because they feared that they might offend the descendants of those whom they would have to treat in their writings. These two reasons, with due respect to them, seem to me unworthy of great men, for if anything delights or instructs in history it is that which is described in detail; if any lesson

is useful to the citizens who govern republics it is that
which demonstrates the causes of the hatreds and the factions of a city in order that these men may preserve their
unity through the wisdom gained from the sufferings of
others. And if the example of any state is moving, that
which treats of a man's own native city is even more
moving and more useful when he reads about it; and if
internal strife was ever worthy of note in a republic, that
of Florence is extremely noteworthy, for most other republics about which we have any record have been satisfied with one single division, which, according to the
circumstances, has either expanded or ruined its government. Not content with one faction, Florence has produced a number of them. In Rome, as everyone knows,
after the kings were exiled a breach occurred between the
nobility and the common people which continued until
the city's downfall. In like manner, the same thing occurred in Athens and in all the other republics that
flourished in those days. But Florence's factions were first
divided among the nobles, then between the nobles and
the middle classes, and finally between the middle classes
and the masses; and it frequently happened that when one
of these factions triumphed it split in two. These factions
resulted in many deaths, exiles, and the destruction of
many families—as many as ever occurred in any city of
which we have a record. And truly, in my judgment, it
seems that no other example demonstrates the vigor of
our native city so well as does the strength of these factions, which would have had enough power to ruin the
greatest and most powerful city. Nevertheless, our city
seemed to become ever greater because of this. The ability
of those citizens and the strength of their intelligence and
spirit, which enabled them to make themselves and their
native city great, was such that those who remained free
of evil influence could achieve more with their ability to
exalt Florence than the evil nature of those circumstances
which might have weakened her could do to destroy her.
And without a doubt, if Florence, after she had liberated

herself from the Holy Roman Empire, had been fortunate enough to have instituted a form of government that might have kept her united, I do not know what republic, modern or ancient, would have been superior to her, for she would have been blessed with much military genius and civilian skill. For it is evident that even after she had expelled as many Ghibellines as could fill all of Tuscany and Lombardy, one year before the battle of Campaldino, the Guelfs and those who remained in the city produced on the field of battle, from among their own citizens, twelve hundred knights and twelve thousand infantrymen in the war against Arezzo. Afterward, in the war against Filippo Visconti, Duke of Milan, Florence was forced to make use of her economic strength and not her own troops (since they had by that time been destroyed); in fact, the Florentines, during the five-year duration of the war, spent 3.5 million florins. Not content with peace, when this war ended, the Florentines attacked Lucca in order further to demonstrate the power of their city.

Therefore, I cannot see any reason why these factions are not worthy of being described in detail. And if those very noble historians were reluctant to offend the memory of those they were to discuss, they were mistaken and showed that they understood very little about human ambition and man's desire to perpetuate his name and that of his ancestors; nor did they remember that many men have tried to acquire fame through unworthy deeds when they did not have the opportunity to do so by means of some praiseworthy deed; nor did they consider how matters of intrinsic importance, such as those of government and affairs of state, no matter how they are carried on or whatever goal they have, are always considered more in terms of honor than of censure by those who carry them out. Having considered these things myself, I changed my plan and decided to begin my history with the foundation of our city. And because it is not my intention to duplicate the work of others, I shall describe in detail only those affairs which occurred inside the city until 1434, and I shall speak of external affairs only insofar as it is necessary to explain internal ones. Then, for events occurring after 1434, I shall describe both in detail. Furthermore, in order that this history be better understood for all times, before I deal with Florence I shall describe how Italy came under the rule of the powers that governed her at that time. All these matters, both Florentine and Italian, will fill four books: the first will briefly describe all the events that took place in Italy from the decline of the Roman Empire until 1434; the second will begin with the foundation of the city of Florence and continue up to the war that Florence waged against the Pope after the expulsion of the Duke of Athens; the third will end in 1414 with the death of King Ladislaus of Naples; and with the fourth book we shall have reached the year 1434. From that time on, affairs, both inside and outside of Florence, will be described in detail up to our present day.

* * *

BOOK III

CHAPTER 1 [ROME AND FLORENCE COMPARED]

The serious and natural enmity that exists between the common people and the nobility, resulting from the desire of the latter to command and the former not to obey, is the cause of all the evils that arise in cities; for from this clash of dispositions everything that disturbs a republic takes its nourishment. This kept Rome disunited; this kept Florence divided as well (if it be permitted to compare lesser things to greater ones); and it happened to have produced different effects in both cities. For the early disputes in Rome between the people and the nobility were settled by argument, while those in Florence were settled by fighting. In Rome they were resolved by laws, in Florence by the exile and the death of many citizens. The Romans continually improved their military skill,

while the Florentines continually lost it. These disputes in
Rome led that city to shift from a state of equality for all
citizens to an extreme inequality, while those in Florence
led her from a state of inequality into a remarkable condition of equality. These different results must have come
from the different goals these two peoples had in mind;
for the Roman people wanted to enjoy the principal
honors together with the nobility, while the Florentine
people fought so that they could govern themselves without the participation of the nobility. And because the desire of the Roman people was more reasonable, their
offenses against the nobility were more bearable, so that
the nobility easily conceded without resorting to force of
arms. As a result, after some arguments the nobles agreed
upon a law that satisfied the common people and preserved the dignity of the nobility. On the other hand, the
desire of the Florentine people was injurious and unjust,
so that the nobility prepared to defend itself more force-
fully; thus, from this came bloodshed and exile for her citizens; those laws which were then instituted were not for
the common good but for the benefit of the victor.

Because of this, it came about that as a result of the
victories of the common people the city of Rome became
more distinguished; for since the common people could
participate in the administration of the magistrates, the
army, and the provinces along with the nobility, they acquired the same skill as the nobility. And the city grew in
power because ability increased there. But in Florence,
when the common people triumphed the nobles were deprived of offices; and if they wished to acquire them
again, it was necessary for them not only to pretend that
they were like the common people but also actually to become like them in their policies, their spirit, and their
manner of living. From this arose the variations in the
family coats of arms and the alterations in the family titles
that the nobles effected in order to appear more like the
people; they did this in such a way that the military skill
and generosity of spirit in them were extinguished; such

qualities could not be rekindled in the common people, since they had never existed. Florence thus became more and more humble and abject. And where Rome had seen the virtue of her citizens reduced to pride, and had come to such a pass that she could not be governed without a prince, Florence reached a condition where she could easily be reformed by some wise lawgiver and could be given any sort of government. This becomes quite clear if one reads the preceding book, which treated the birth of Florence and the origins of her liberty, the causes of her factions, and how the division between noble and commoner ended with the tyranny of the Duke of Athens and the ruin of the nobility. Now there still remains to be described the struggles between the masses and the middle classes and the various circumstances that produced them.

* * *

BOOK V

CHAPTER 1 [MACHIAVELLI'S CYCLE OF HISTORY]

In most instances, in the course of the variations states undergo, they usually move from order to chaos and then back again from chaos to order. Since Nature has not allowed earthly affairs to remain stationary, as soon as they reach their final state of perfection they must go down, possessing no further potential for rising; likewise, when they have descended and have reached the lowest possible level (because of their disorders), they must rise since they cannot possibly go lower. Thus, they always descend from good to bad and rise from bad to good. For ability brings about tranquillity, and tranquillity laziness, and laziness chaos, and chaos ruin; and, in like manner, from ruin is born order, from order ability, and from this quality glory and good fortune. And so, prudent men have observed that literature develops after arms, and that in nations and city-states generals are born before philosophers. For after an effective and well-organized militia has produced victories, and these victories have ensured tranquillity, the strength of such brave minds cannot be corrupted with a more honorable laziness than that of literature, nor can this laziness enter into well-organized cities with a greater and more dangerous deception than with that of literature. Cato was well aware of this when Diogenes and Carneades, both philosophers, came to Rome as ambassadors to the senate; when he saw that the Roman youth began to admire these men, aware of the evil that could enter his native city as a result of this honorable laziness, he made it a law that no philosopher could be received in Rome. Nations have come to ruin because of this; and when this has happened and men have become wiser through their trials, they return to order, as I said before, if they do not remain weakened by some extraordinary force.

These causes sometimes created happiness and sometimes misery in Italy, first through the ancient Tuscans and later through the Romans. And nothing has been built upon the Roman ruins that would in some way revive Italy, so that under the rule of a skillful prince she might be able to advance gloriously. Nevertheless, in some of the new cities and territories of Rome there arose among the ruins such great ability that although one of them could not dominate the others, there was nevertheless such unity and organization among them that they defended Italy and freed her from the barbarians. Among these territories, the Florentines were not the least significant in authority or power, even though they possessed a smaller territory; on the contrary, because of their central position in Italy, their wealth, and their readiness for war, they either successfully sustained any war waged against them or they were victorious together with their allies.

If, therefore, peacetime of long duration did not come about as a result of the vigor of these new principalities, neither were there dangerous times characterized by the harshness of war. For a period during which principalities often attack each other with troops cannot be termed a time of peace; nor can there be wars wherein men do not kill, cities are not sacked, and principalities are not destroyed, for these wars arose from such a weakness that they were begun without fear, carried on without danger, and terminated without damage. As a result, that spirit which is usually extinguished in other provinces because of a lengthy peace was destroyed in Italy by the vileness of these wars, as one can clearly recognize from that which we shall describe as having occurred from 1434 until 1494. There the reader will see how a new road was finally opened to the barbarians and how Italy put herself back into slavery under such peoples. And if the deeds accomplished by our princes at home and abroad will not be read with admiration for these princes' ability and greatness, as is done with those of the ancients, perhaps they will be considered for their other qualities with no less astonishment, when the reader sees how many most noble peoples were held back by such weak and badly administered armies. And if, in describing the events that occurred in this wasted world, the bravery of the soldier, the courage of the captain, or the patriotism of the citizen are not recorded, one will be able to see with what artifice, deceit, and cunning the princes, soldiers, and leaders of republics conducted themselves in order to maintain reputations that they did not deserve. This, perhaps, will not be less useful than an acquaintance with ancient history, for if the latter incites the noble mind to imitation, the former will demonstrate what to avoid or to suppress.

* * *

BOOK VII [COSIMO DE' MEDICI]

CHAPTER 1

... and because, in writing about foreign affairs, I have arrived at the year 1463, it is necessary to go back many

years if I am to narrate the troubles that occurred inside
the city. But first I wish to point out, as is my custom, that
those who hope that republics can be unified are greatly
mistaken in this belief. It is true that some internal divisions harm republics while others benefit them. Those
which harm them involve factions and partisans. Since a
founder of a republic cannot prevent strife from occurring, he can at least see to it that there are no factions.
Thus, he should note that there are two means of acquiring a reputation among the citizens of his city: by practicing public service and by pursuing private goals. Publicly,
citizens gain a reputation by winning a battle, taking a
town, carrying out a diplomatic mission with speed and
prudence, and advising the republic wisely and successfully. Privately, citizens earn fame by helping this or that
citizen, defending them from the magistrates, lending
them money, getting them unmerited offices, and by grati-
fying the masses with games and public gifts. From this
method of behavior arise factions and partisans, and a
reputation gained in such a manner is as offensive as the
other is beneficial, for a reputation gained by public
means is not corrupted by factionalism since it is founded
upon a common, not a private, good. And although one
cannot prevent great hatreds even among citizens who act
for the common good, nevertheless, when they have no
partisans who follow them out of self-interest they cannot
harm the republic; on the contrary, they must benefit it
since it is necessary for them to work for the republic in
order to fulfill their goals; and they must keep close watch
on one another to see that civil liberties are not abused.
The Florentine quarrels always involved factions and
were therefore always harmful. Even a winning faction
remained united only so long as its opponent existed; but
when the defeated faction was destroyed, not being restrained by fear or internal control, the dominant faction
would break up again. In 1434 Cosimo de' Medici's faction was in control, but because the defeated faction was
large and was composed of very powerful men, Cosimo's

party remained united and humble for a time out of fear; since it did not break up or make itself invidious to the populace by corrupt practices, every time that organization had need of the people's support to reassert its authority, it always found the people disposed to grant to its leaders all the authority and power they desired. Thus, from 1434 until 1455, a total of twenty-one years, Cosimo's faction gained the authority of the *balìa*[1] through the councils six times in the normal legal manner.

CHAPTER 2

As we have stated several times, there were in Florence two very powerful citizens, Cosimo de' Medici and Neri Capponi. Of these two men, Neri was one of those individuals who had acquired his reputation by means of public service, so that he had many friends but few partisans. On the other hand, Cosimo had both public and private avenues to political influence, and he had both friends and partisans. While both men were alive they remained united, and they always obtained what they wanted from the people without any difficulty, for they combined benevolence with power. But when the year 1455 arrived, Neri died and the opposing faction was dissolved. The government had trouble in reasserting its authority. Cosimo's own friends, being very powerful in the government, were the cause of this, for they no longer feared their opposition, which was removed, and they now hoped to diminish Cosimo's power. This gave birth to that factional dispute which took place later, in 1466. Those in charge of the government urged in the councils, where the public administration was discussed, that the power of the *balìa* not be reassumed, that the voting bags be closed, and that the magistrates be chosen by lot on the basis of the scrutinies of the past elections. In order to

[1] *Balìa* refers to the extraordinary powers temporarily bestowed upon a commission set up to deal with a crisis. It was not intended to replace normal institutions but rather to supplement them in difficult times.

check this move, Cosimo had two possible alternatives: to forcibly recapture the government together with his partisans, who had remained with him, and throw out his opponents; or to let matters take their course and to allow his friends to see, with the passage of time, that they were not diminishing his reputation but rather their own. Of these two remedies, he chose the second, for he knew very well that with this means of governing he ran no risk, since the voting bags were full of the names of his friends and he could reassert his authority when he pleased. Therefore, when the city had begun to choose its officials by lot, the masses believed that they had regained their liberty and had acquired magistrates who were chosen, not by the powerful, but by themselves, since now one friend of a powerful man was beaten, and now another. Thus, those men who had been used to seeing their homes teeming with guests and full of presents found them empty of goods and people. They realized that they were the equals of those whom they had deemed vastly inferior, and they saw as their superiors those whom they had deemed their equals. They were neither revered nor honored; on the contrary, they were often mocked and criticized, and they and the republic were discussed openly in every street and piazza. They soon realized that they, and not Cosimo, had lost the state. Cosimo acted as if this were not the case, and when any decision which pleased the people was made, he was the first to favor it. But what frightened the wealthy most, and what gave Cosimo the best opportunity to make them draw back, was that the tax system of 1427 might be reinstated, wherein taxes would be apportioned by law rather than according to influence.

CHAPTER 3

When this tax system was reestablished and the magistrate to administer it had already been appointed, the most influential men banded together and begged Cosimo to rescue them and himself from the hands of the masses and to return the government to that esteem which had brought them honors and had given him power. Cosimo replied that he would be happy to do so, but that he wished the law to be passed in a legal manner, as a reflection of the will of the people, and not by force, which he absolutely opposed. An attempt was made to set up a new law for a *balìa* in the councils, but it did not pass. Therefore, the wealthy citizens turned to Cosimo and with the greatest humility begged him to agree to a popular assembly. Cosimo flatly refused this request, for he wished to reduce them to a state of desperation that would make them fully recognize their error. And when Donato Cocchi, then Gonfaloniere of Justice, tried to call an assembly without his consent, Cosimo had him so ridiculed by the Signori, who were seated with him, that he became angry and was sent home like a fool.

Nevertheless, since it is not prudent to let matters run their course to the point where they get out of control, Cosimo decided that it was time to take things in hand when Luca Pitti, a brave, audacious man, became Gonfaloniere of Justice, so that if any blame arose from this undertaking it would be placed upon Luca and not upon himself. At the beginning of his term, Luca several times proposed the establishment of a new *balìa* to the people; not obtaining this, he threatened those who were seated in the councils with arrogant and spiteful words. To these words he later added deeds, for in August of 1458, on the eve of St. Lorenzo, after he had filled the palace with armed soldiers, he called the people into the piazza and with force and arms made them consent to what they had previously refused to accept freely. Thus, the government had been reestablished again and the *balìa* had been created, the most important magistrates being chosen according to the wishes of the few. In order to begin with terror a government that had been created by force, they banished Messer Girolamo Machiavelli, along with some others, and many more were deprived of their positions.

Messer Girolamo was declared a rebel for not observing the rules of his banishment. While traveling about Italy urging the princes to move against his native city, he was arrested in Lunigiana through the treachery of one of the Signori there, and was brought to Florence, where he was put to death.

CHAPTER 4

This type of government lasted for eight years. It was oppressive and violent, since Cosimo was already old, tired, and weakened by poor health; since he could not pay as much attention to public affairs as he used to do, the city was plundered by just a handful of citizens. Luca Pitti was knighted as a reward for all he had done for the benefit of the republic. In order to be equally generous, he decreed that those who had formerly been called the Priors of the Guilds should henceforth be called the Priors of Liberty, so that they would at least retain the name, if not the substance, of what they had lost. He also decreed that where the gonfaloniere had formerly been seated above and to the right of the magistrates, in the future he should sit in their midst. And so that God might appear to participate in this undertaking, public processions and solemn church services were organized to give thanks for the restored privileges. Messer Luca was richly rewarded with gifts from the Signoria and Cosimo, an act that was repeated by the entire city as if in a competition, and it was the opinion of observers that the presents reached the sum of twenty thousand ducats. His reputation reached such heights, therefore, that it was not Cosimo but Messer Luca who governed the city. He became so confident of himself that he began the construction of two buildings, one in Florence[1] and the other at Ruciano,

---

[1] This building, although acquired in 1549 by Eleonora of Toledo, wife of Cosimo I, Grand Duke of Tuscany, is still known as the Pitti Palace, which houses one of the most important art collections in Italy.

about a mile from the city, both magnificent and regal in size. The one in the city was much larger than any other building ever built by a private citizen to that day. He spared no means whatsoever in their completion, for not only did citizens and private individuals give him gifts and supply him with materials needed for their construction, but entire towns and peoples also gave him aid. Besides this, all the exiles and anyone who had committed murder, theft, or anything for which he feared public punishment could find refuge within the buildings, provided that he could make himself useful in their construction. The other citizens, although not engaged in building to the extent he was, were no less violent or greedy, so that if Florence had had no foreign wars to destroy her, she still would have been ruined by her own citizens.

During this time, as we have said, the wars of the Kingdom of Naples took place. The Pope waged war in Romagna against the Malatesta family because he wished to despoil them of Rimini and Cesena. So Pope Pius wasted away his pontificate in these undertakings and preparations for a campaign against the Turks.

CHAPTER 5

But Florence continued with her internal squabbles and her difficulties. The disunity in Cosimo's party began in 1455, for the reasons mentioned above, but because of his prudence, as we have previously explained, this discord was silenced for a time. In 1464 Cosimo became gravely ill and departed from this life. Both his friends and his opponents mourned his death, since the latter, who did not love him for political reasons, saw the rapacity of the citizens while he was alive, when respect for him had rendered these citizens more bearable. They feared that they would be completely ruined now that he was dead, and did not have much faith in his son Piero. In spite of the fact that he was a good man, they nevertheless considered Piero sickly and a novice in politics; they feared that he might be obliged to show respect for the most greedy members of the Medici faction, who, without a bit in their mouths, would be able to increase their extortions. Therefore, everyone deeply mourned Cosimo's passing.

Cosimo was the most renowned and illustrious citizen outside of the military profession who ever lived, not only in Florence but in every other city of which we have a record; for he not only surpassed all of his contemporaries in wealth and authority but also in generosity and prudence; and among those qualities which contributed to make him the prince of his native land, the most important were his generosity and his magnificence. His generosity was even more evident after his death, when his son Piero took stock of his assets, for there was no citizen of any standing in the city who had not borrowed a large sum of money from Cosimo; many times he would assist a nobleman when he heard of his need without even being asked to do so. He showed his magnificence through the many public buildings he constructed. He not only restored but completely rebuilt the monasteries and churches of San Marco and San Lorenzo, the convent of Santa Verdiana in Florence and San Giacomo, the abbey in the hills of Fiesole, and a church of the minor friars in the Mugello. Besides all this, he had altars and splendid chapels built in Santa Croce, in the Servi, in the Angioli, and in San Miniato, and he filled them all with vestments and everything necessary for the adornment of divine services. To these sacred buildings were added his private homes: one in the city (an appropriate place for such a citizen) and four outside it, at Careggi, Fiesole, Cafaggiuolo, and Trebbio—all kingly palaces and not the type for private citizens. And since he was not satisfied with the reputation the magnificence of his buildings had won him in Italy, he had a lodging for sick and poor pilgrims built in Jerusalem. He spent an enormous amount of money on all these buildings. And although his private homes, and all his other works and actions, were of a princely nature—for he alone was prince in Florence—nevertheless everything was tempered by his prudence, so that he never presumed to rise above the status of a public citizen: in his conversation, his servants, his traveling, his mode of life, and in his relations he was always similar to the average citizen; for he knew that a constant display of pomp causes more envy among men than those actions tempered with honesty and lack of ostentation. Obliged to find wives for his sons, he did not seek princes for relatives. He married Giovanni to Cornelia degli Alessandri and Piero to Lucrezia de' Tornabuoni; of the grandchildren born to Piero, he married Bianca to Guglielmo de' Pazzi and Nannina to Bernardo Rucellai. No other man in his time, either in states ruled by princes or in republics, equaled him in intelligence. This is why, during so many changes of Fortune and in such an unstable city with its whimsical populace, he was able to hold control of the government for thirty-one years. For, being very prudent, he recognized problems from a distance and consequently had time either to keep them from growing or to prepare himself so that they might not harm him if they did grow. In this manner, he not only surpassed the ambition of his fellow citizens but also that of many princes; he did so with so much success and prudence that anyone who became his ally or an ally of his native city ended up as either equal or superior to his enemies, whereas anyone who opposed him either lost his time, his money, or his state. The Venetians can testify to this, for they were always superior to Duke Filippo Sforza when they were allied with Cosimo against him, but without his support they were always defeated, first by Duke Filippo and later by Duke Francesco. When they joined forces with King Alfonso of Naples against the Republic of Florence, Cosimo emptied Naples and Venice of money with his credit; they were thus forced to accept a peace agreement that he decided to concede to them. Therefore, the problems that Cosimo experienced both inside and outside the city brought glory to him and injury to his enemies; internal strife always increased his power in Florence, and external struggles always increased his strength and reputation. He added to the domain of his republic Borgo San Sepolcro, Montedoglio, Casentino, and Val di Bagno. And so, his ability and good fortune destroyed all his enemies and exalted his friends.

CHAPTER 6

He was born in 1389 on the feast day of St. Cosimo and St. Damian. His early life was full of trials—as his exile, imprisonment, and near death demonstrate. From the Council of Constance, where he had gone with Pope John, he was forced to flee in disguise, after the Pope's fall, in order to save his life. But after he had passed the age of forty, he lived happily; not only those who supported him in public enterprises but also those who administered his riches throughout Europe participated in his success. From this contact many Florentine families became excessively rich, as happened to the Tornabuoni, the Benci, the Portinari, and the Sassetti. Besides these people, all those who depended upon his advice and his fortune grew rich; and although he constantly spent money on the building of churches and for charitable causes, he used to complain to his friends at times that he was never able to spend so much for the honor of God that he might be able to find Him in his account books as a debtor. He was of middle stature, with an olive complexion and a venerable aspect. He was not learned, but he was very eloquent and gifted, with a natural prudence. He was therefore generous to his friends, compassionate to the poor, sharp in conversation, cautious in advice, quick in his executions, and witty and serious in his sayings and replies. Messer Rinaldo degli Albizzi, in the first days of his exile, sent him a message declaring that the hen was hatching an egg, to which Cosimo replied that it could hardly hatch outside of its nest. And to other rebels who made him understand that they were still awake he quipped that he believed them, since he had robbed them of their sleep. When Pope Pius called forth the princes for an attack on the Turks, Cosimo said of the Pope that he was an old man who was undertaking a young man's task. To the Venetian ambassadors who came with King Alfonso's envoy to complain of the republic he showed his uncovered head, asking them what color it was. When they responded, "White," he replied: "It will not be long before your senators have hair as white as mine." A few hours before his death, his wife asked him why he kept his eyes closed, to which he answered: "In order to get used to it." After his return from exile, some citizens said of him that he was ruining the city and was acting against God by banishing so many men of quality. He replied that it was better to damage a city than to lose it; that a length of rose-colored cloth was sufficient to make a gentleman; and that states were not held with rosary beads in hand. These remarks gave his enemies an opportunity to accuse him of being a man who loved himself more than his native city and this world more than the next. One could cite many other witty remarks of his, but they would be superfluous. Cosimo was also an admirer and a patron of learned men; because of this, he brought to Florence Argyropoulos, a very learned Greek of the time, so that young Florentines could learn the Greek language as well as other subjects from him. He nurtured in his own home Marsilio Ficino, second father of the Platonic philosophy, whom he dearly loved. In order that Ficino might more comfortably pursue his studies and Cosimo might be able to visit him with greater ease, he gave him some property near his own at Careggi. Therefore, his wisdom, his riches, his way of life, and his good fortune made him feared and loved by the citizens of Florence and exceptionally respected by the princes not only of Italy but of all Europe. Because of this, he left such a foundation to his heirs that they were able to equal him in ability and to surpass him in good fortune. That authority which Cosimo had enjoyed in Florence they were able to possess

not only in that city but in all of Christendom. Nevertheless, in the final years of his life he experienced very great
sorrows, for, of his two sons, Piero and Giovanni, the latter, on whom he most relied, died, and the former was
sickly and, as a result of the weakness of his body, poorly
suited for either public affairs or business. After the death
of his son, he had himself carried about the house and
would say with a sigh: "This is too large a house for so
small a family." The greatness of his spirit was also tried
by the fact that he felt he had not increased Florentine
dominions by any honorable acquisition. He was even
more upset because he believed that he had been tricked
by Francesco Sforza, for when he was count he had promised Cosimo that when he had taken control of Milan he
would attack Lucca for the Florentines. This did not happen, for Sforza changed his mind with his change in fortune, and after becoming Duke of Milan he wished to
enjoy that rank with the peace that he had gained in war;
he therefore did not wish to undertake either Cosimo's
campaign or that of anyone else. While he was Duke, he
waged only those wars which were necessary for his own
defense. This was a cause of great annoyance to Cosimo,
since it appeared to him that he had expended effort and
expense to produce an ungrateful, unfaithful man. Besides this, he felt that because of his illness he could not
devote his former energies to public and private affairs.
He saw both going to ruin because the city was being destroyed by its citizens and his possessions were being used
up by his employees and his sons. All these matters made
his last years unsettling ones. Nevertheless, he died with a
great reputation, both within Florence and elsewhere. On
his death, all of the citizens and all of the Christian
princes mourned with Piero, his son. He was accompanied to his grave with the greatest of ceremony by all of
the citizens and was buried in San Lorenzo. Inscribed on
his tomb by public decree were the words: "Father of the
Country." If, in describing the deeds of Cosimo, I have
imitated those who write about the lives of princes rather

than those who write about general history, it need not cause any amazement, for as he was such an extraordinary man in our city's history, I felt compelled to praise him in this unusual way.

* * *

BOOK VIII

CHAPTER 36 [MACHIAVELLI'S ESTIMATION OF LORENZO IL MAGNIFICO]

When the War of Sarzana had ended, the Florentines experienced a period of great prosperity which lasted until 1492, when Lorenzo de' Medici died: for Lorenzo, whose authority and good sense had brought about the end of the wars in Italy, had turned his mind to his own greatness and to that of his city. He married off Piero, his firstborn, to Alfonsina, the daughter of the knight Orsini; then he had his second son, Giovanni, raised to the rank of cardinal. This was most remarkable and without precedent, for he was promoted to such a rank even before he reached the age of fourteen: this was the ladder that would raise his house to the skies, as actually happened in the following years. As for his third son, Giuliano, because of his youth and the short time Lorenzo lived he could not provide him with any extraordinary fortune. Of his daughters, the first he married to Jacopo Salviati, the second to Francesco Cibo, the third to Piero Ridolfi; the fourth, whom he had married to Giovanni de' Medici to keep the family unified, died. In his private business affairs he was extremely unlucky. In large measure, his personal property was lost as a result of the poor management of his administrators, who ran his affairs as if they were princes and not private citizens. As a result, his native city was constrained to grant him a subsidy consisting of a large sum of money. Thus, in order not to tempt Fortune further, he abandoned mercantile investments and

turned to landed property as a sounder and more stable
form of wealth. He purchased property in the regions
around Prato, Pisa, and the Pesa Valley, which was more
fitting for a king than a private citizen in terms of its
financial return and the quality and magnificence of its
buildings.

After this, he turned his attention to beautifying and
enlarging his city. Where there were open areas without
buildings he ordered the construction of new streets filled
with new buildings. As a result, the city became larger
and more beautiful. He fortified the castle of Firenzuola,
in the middle of the mountains toward Bologna, so that
people in his state might live in tranquillity and security
and his enemies could be repulsed or fought off at a distance. Toward Siena he began the foundations of Poggio
Imperiale, which was to be made very strong. Toward
Genoa he blocked off the enemy's approach through the
acquisition of Pietrasanta and Sarzana. Then, by means
of subsidies and supplies he kept his friends, the Baglioni
and the Vitelli, in power in Perugia and Città di Castello;
he himself controlled the government of Faenza. All these
policies provided strong defenses for his city. In these
times of peace he always kept the city in a constant state
of feasting; tournaments and representations of historical
deeds or triumphs were often presented there. His goal
was to keep the city content, the people united, and the
nobility respected. He greatly loved any man who was
outstanding in his profession, and he favored men of letters: Messer Agnolo da Montepulciano, Messer Cristoforo
Landino, and Messer Demetrius the Greek bear witness
to this fact. This was why Count Giovanni della Mirandola, a man who was almost divine, forsook all the other
regions of Europe he had visited and, moved by Lorenzo's
generosity, made his home in Florence. Lorenzo took
great pleasure in architecture, music, and poetry; many
poetic works still exist which were not only written but
also commented upon by him. And in order that the
young people of Florence might be able to train them-

selves in the study of the humanities, he opened a center in the city of Pisa where the most excellent men in all of Italy were brought. He built a monastery near Florence for Friar Mariano da Ghinazzano, of the Order of St. Augustine, since he was such an excellent preacher.

Lorenzo was particularly dear to Fortune and to God; because of this, all his undertakings reached a successful conclusion, while those of his enemies ended unhappily; for, besides the Pazzi conspiracy, Battista Frescobaldi tried to kill him in the Carmine church and Badinotto di Pistoia attempted to do so in his villa at Pistoia. Each of these men, together with their co-conspirators, suffered a most just punishment for their evil plans. Lorenzo's manner of living, his wisdom, and his good fortune were admired and recognized not only by Italian princes but also by those far away from Italy. Matthew, King of Hungary, sent him many indications of the love he bore for him; the Sultan sent his envoys laden with gifts; the Grand Turk placed in his hands the murderer of his brother, Bernardo Bandini. Such things made him very respected in Italy. His prestige increased each day as a result of his prudence, for he was eloquent and witty in discussing matters, wise in resolving problems, and quick and courageous in the execution of his policies. Nor can one point to any vices that might stain such great virtues, although he was extremely given over to affairs of love, delighted in being around men who were quick and witty, and enjoyed childish games which were not appropriate for a man of his station; he was often observed joining in the games of his daughters and his sons. When one considered both his frivolous side and his serious side, one saw in him two different persons, joined in an almost impossible union. The last years of his life were full of difficulties caused by the illness which afflicted him seriously, for he was plagued by intolerable stomach pains; they attacked him with such severity that he died of them in April 1492, at the age of forty-four. Never did a man die, either in Florence or in all of Italy, who had such a reputation for

wisdom or who was so deeply mourned by his native city.
And since his death would bring about great disasters, the
heavens produced many obvious signs, among them a
lightning bolt which struck the highest point of the
Church of Santa Reparata so violently that a large part of
the steeple collapsed, to the great surprise and amazement
of everyone. All the citizens and all the princes of Italy
mourned his passing; this was clearly demonstrated, for
there was no one who did not send envoys to express his
grief. And the events that took place after his death
showed that they had good reason to be sorrowful, for,
with Italy deprived of his advice, those who remained
could find no way to satisfy or check the ambition of Lodovico Sforza, the Duke of Milan. No sooner had
Lorenzo died than Lodovico's ambition caused evil seeds
to grow which no man alive could destroy, and which,
after a short time, began and still continue to grow into
the destruction of Italy.

THE VIKING PORTABLE LIBRARY

The Portable Sherwood
Anderson
Edited by Horace Gregory

The Portable Beat Reader
Edited by Ann Charters

The Portable Blake
Edited by Alfred Kazin

The Portable Cervantes
Edited by Samuel Putnam

The Portable Chaucer
Edited by Theodore Morrison

The Portable Chekhov
Edited by Avrahm Yarmolinsky

The Portable Conrad
Edited by Morton Dauwen Zabel

The Portable Conservative
Reader
Edited by Russell Kirk

The Portable Malcolm Cowley
Edited by Donald W. Faulkner

The Portable Stephen Crane
Edited by Joseph Katz

The Portable Dante
Edited by Paolo Milano

The Portable Emerson
*Edited by Carl Bode and
Malcolm Cowley*

The Portable Faulkner
Edited by Malcolm Cowley

The Portable Greek Historians
Edited by M. I. Finley

The Portable Greek Reader
Edited by W. H. Auden

The Portable Graham Greene
Edited by Philip Stratford

The Portable Hawthorne
Edited by Malcolm Cowley

The Portable Henry James
Edited by Morton Dauwen Zabel

The Portable Thomas Jefferson
Edited by Merrill D. Peterson

The Portable James Joyce
Edited by Harry Levin

The Portable Jung
Edited by Joseph Campbell

The Portable Kipling
Edited by Irving Howe

The Portable D. H. Lawrence
Edited by Diana Trilling

The Portable Abraham Lincoln
Edited by Andrew Delbanco

The Portable Machiavelli
*Edited by Peter Bondanella and
Mark Musa*

The Portable Karl Marx
Edited by Eugene Kamenka

The Portable Medieval Reader
*Edited by James Bruce Ross and
Mary Martin McLaughlin*

The Portable Arthur Miller
Edited by Harold Clurman

The Portable Milton
Edited by Douglas Bush

The Portable Nietzsche
Edited by Walter Kaufmann

The Portable North American
Indian Reader
Edited by Frederick Turner

The Portable Dorothy Parker
Edited by Brendan Gill

The Portable Plato
Edited by Scott Buchanan

The Portable Poe
Edited by Philip Van Doren Stern

The Portable Romantic Poets
*Edited by W. H. Auden and
Norman Holmes Pearson*

The Portable Renaissance
Reader
*Edited by James Bruce Ross and
Mary Martin McLaughlin*

The Portable Roman Reader
Edited by Basil Davenport

The Portable Shakespeare
Edited by Marshall Best

The Portable Bernard Shaw
Edited by Stanley Weintraub

The Portable Steinbeck
Edited by Pascal Covici, Jr.

The Portable Swift
Edited by Carl Van Doren

The Portable Thoreau
Edited by Carl Bode

The Portable Tolstoy
Edited by John Bayley

The Portable Mark Twain
Edited by Bernard De Voto

The Portable Twentieth-
Century Russian Reader
Edited by Clarence Brown

The Portable Victorian Reader
Edited by Gordon S. Haight

The Portable Voltaire
Edited by Ben Ray Redman

The Portable Walt Whitman
Edited by Mark Van Doren

The Portable Oscar Wilde
*Edited by Richard Aldington and
Stanley Weintraub*

The Portable World Bible
Edited by Robert O. Ballou